THE SELF-HELP SOURCEBOOK

Your Guide to Community and Online Support Groups

6th Edition

Compiled and edited by

Barbara J. White and Edward J. Madara

American Self-Help Clearinghouse
Northwest Covenant Medical Center
25 Pocono Road
Denville, New Jersey 07834-2995

Phone: (973)625-3037
TDD/TTY: (973)625-9053
Website: http://www.cmhc.com/selfhelp

Made possible by an initial grant from

*Hoffmann La Roche, Inc.
Department of Community Affairs
Nutley, New Jersey*

THE SELF-HELP SOURCEBOOK:
YOUR GUIDE TO COMMUNITY AND ONLINE SUPPORT GROUPS

Library of Congress Card Catalog Number: 97-075663
ISBN: 0-9634322-7-3
ISSN: 8756.1425

Published by Northwest Covenant Medical Center

The logo on the cover was specifically designed for our Self-Help Clearinghouse in 1981 by Ben Ruiz.

~ DEDICATION ~

To all the self-help group founders who have had the courage to take those first steps, as well as those group members who are ever giving of themselves. Very real heroes...ordinary people who so often do such extraordinary things. Helping to make self-help groups into the truly unique caring communities that they come to be. This work is dedicated to their spirit... those whose efforts may never be fully acknowledged, because in very selfless or often anonymous ways, they placed group needs ahead of personal recognition. May their initiative, dedication, and tireless volunteer efforts be an inspiration to others who follow.

~ IN MEMORY ~

*This edition of the Sourcebook is dedicated to **David Blumenfeld**, who volunteered countless hours at the Clearinghouse. David was a very special person who gave freely of himself to help others. We will truly miss him.*

ACKNOWLEDGMENTS

First, we wish to express our sincerest and continued appreciation to all the **mutual aid self-help group members** who contributed information on their work in order to make this resource guide possible.

We are grateful to those persons who have consistently provided leads on new groups and resources that have been included in this new edition, especially **John Grohol** (Founder, Mental Health Net), **Keith Humphreys** (Stanford University School of Medicine), **Julie Gordon** (Founder, MUMS: A National Parent-to-Parent Network), **Dr. Tom Ferguson, Dr. LeClair Bissel, Dr. Arlette Lefebvre, Patricia Becker** (Rainy Day People Self-Help Clearinghouse) **Betsy Wilson** (Let's Face It), **Joal Fischer** (SupportWorks), and **Patricia Green** (Information Exchange).

We extend our heartfelt appreciation to each of our outstanding volunteers - **Joanne Bessor, Elaine Bloom, Dolores Bruzzi, Pat de la Fuente, Lois Fallat, Esther Foster, Mindy Herman, Marie Lattari, Pete Lodato, Howard Neu, Shirley O'Loughlin, Jeanne Rohach, Terry Salis, Harry Salle, Paul Thormann, Elliot Udenfriend,** and **Helen Weiss.** Without their hard work and consistent efforts, this edition of the Sourcebook truly would not have been published. Through their continued updating, handling of referrals, detective work in tracking down new groups, and related support efforts, they continue to give of themselves to help so many others.

Thanks to the Clearinghouse staff who also worked hard on this effort - **Wendy Rodenbaugh** and **Karen Fehre.** We would also like to acknowledge **Jeffrey Schiller** who has spent countless hours upgrading our software program, MASHnet.

Appreciation is also given to the **New Jersey State Division of Mental Health Services** for their funding of the first statewide self-help clearinghouse in the country and the development of our national database that has helped so many hundreds of New Jersey residents start new self-help groups.

Finally, we wish to thank **Hoffmann La Roche, Inc.** for their support which made the Self-Help Sourcebook a reality and an on-going resource to communities across the country--as well as their initial support over thirteen years ago that resulted in publishing the first Directory of Self-Help Groups in New Jersey. ♦

FOREWORD

- Alfred H. Katz, DSW

The biennial publication of this Sourcebook has been an extremely useful service for many people with diverse interests - individuals who are looking for a group to meet their special needs, professionals seeking an appropriate referral point for a client, or information about a problem, academics and researchers who want local or national self-help group contacts and information, policy-makers at all levels of government, media people seeking personal reactions to recent crises.

But the significance and value of this publication exceeds the simple purpose of providing accurate information on the growth and ever-widening scope of the world of self-help, mutual aid groups. It marks the growing maturity and acceptance of a dynamic social movement that is increasingly seen as an integral part of the American culture, way of life and ethos, and as an important social resource. The values of cooperative self- organization, non-bureaucratic mutual helping methods exemplified by the hundreds of organizations listed in this Sourcebook have penetrated the general culture inescapably and irreversibly. Self-help is seen as a social resource so that people no longer have to suffer in isolation or feel despair that they can find no help in confronting and coping with their problems.

Self-help, mutual aid groups provide an accepting environment of social support that may not be available from other sources - family, neighbors, friends, work-mates and social institutions, such as religious, human service and educational organizations. Their help can have the intimacy and informality of the best family and neighborly assistance to those with short-term or longer needs. There is usually no financial barrier to joining them and using their services--need, and a wish to participate are the only criteria for membership.

They usually bring together accurate, up-to-date information on resources and methods for coping with the problem; they often include people at different stages of dealing with it, so that newcomers can learn from the more experienced.

Both the 12-step groups on the A.A. model and non-12-step groups provide philosophies and methodologies for personal growth and change, role models of people who successfully cope, recognition for personal effort and achievement, and opportunities to contribute to the well-being of others. Many groups also engage in education and actions and advocacy that have furthered and often led to change in government and private institutional policies and programs. A result of these varied activities and interactions in the self-help groups is a growth in self-confidence, self-esteem and psychological well-being for the individual member, and of confidence, cohesion and effectiveness of the group. In these ways, the self-help movement can be viewed as an important contributor to social development - the historic process of growth toward a positive, humane, people-oriented society. Self-help's philosophy is that of working with people in a mutually helping way, that is non-bureaucratic, holistic, open to change, and that recognizes and seeks to optimize the inherent strengths and capacities of individuals, families, community groups and institutions.

This is not to imply that self-help is a panacea for all problems--material, environmental, political, of the society, or that self-help groups are without many difficulties--internal strains of growth, lack of resources, personality and program conflicts, leadership burnout, and so on. Like all human organizations, they are subject to human weaknesses, and do not always overcome them.

But as the vast variety and continuing dynamic growth of groups this Sourcebook illustrates, in last years of the 20th century America (and elsewhere in the modern world), they are an indispensable human resource, a permanent and major social utility. ♦

Dr. Katz has served as Professor (Emeritus) in the U.C.L.A. departments of Medicine, Public Health, and Social Welfare. His twelve books, and more than one hundred professional articles, have included Parents of the Handicapped (1961), wherein he was the very first to describe the phenomena of self-help groups as "self-organized groups," The Strength in Us: Self-Help Groups in the Modern World (1976), Helping One Another: Self-Help Groups in a Changing World (1990), Self-Help: Concepts and Applications (1992), and Self-Help in America: A Social Movement Perspective (1993). In regards to promoting an increased recognition and understanding of self-help group efforts, he has been a consultant to the World Health Organization, the Ford Foundation, and many government and voluntary agencies.

Dr. Katz has also planned and developed the world's first journal focused specifically on self-help groups, The International Journal of Self-Help and Self-Care, being published by Baywood Publishing Company, 26 Austin Ave., Amityville, NY 11701, phone: 800-638-7819.

TABLE OF CONTENTS

HEALTH (Cont'd)

HEALTH (Cont'd)

HEALTH (Cont'd)

HEALTH (Cont'd)

HOW TO USE THE SOURCEBOOK

TO FIND A GROUP

To find a mutual aid self-help group for your concern, you may want to begin by glancing over the section on **Self-Help Clearinghouses** to see if there is a clearinghouse which serves your community. Self-help clearinghouses can provide you with information on existing local self-help groups, especially on many of those local "one-of-a-kind" groups that are not affiliated with any of the national self-help organizations listed in this directory.

If there is no self-help clearinghouse in your area, or a local clearinghouse has no group information, go to the **key word index** at the end of the book to find page references for a specific self-help group issue. The index will refer you to pages in the directory where any groups related to that listing will be found.

While looking for an appropriate group, you may want to check several types or categories of groups to find the various groups that may be helpful to you. As an example, if you are looking for a group for a parent who is raising a child with a rare illness, you may want to first look under the specific disorder (e.g. Aarskog Syndrome, Fragile-X Syndrome, etc), then look under the groups dealing with any traits associated with the disorder (e.g. craniofacial disfigurement, visual impairment, etc). You then might also check the generic groups for parents of disabled children, general parenting groups, and so on. You might also want to look through the Toll-Free Specialty Helplines to find other agencies that may be of assistance (e.g., education, equipment, etc.)

In the self-help group listing section, please note the various types of entries included. Most of the entries are for **national or international self-help organizations**. In italics, we have noted the area served (national or international), the number of affiliated groups, and the year founded. You can then use the information in the group listing to contact these national groups to determine if they have any local meetings or chapters in your area. Even if they have no group in your area, you may want to subscribe to their newsletter or participate in any other mutual support activities they offer (e.g. correspondence or phone network, conferences, etc.). In addition, they may be able to provide you with information on starting a group in your area.

We also refer to **support networks** which are mutual help exchanges that (often because the condition is rare) don't have face-to-face groups, but do have interactive correspondence exchange, phone networks, national or regional conferences, or newsletters. Similarly, when we could not find a group or network, we have sometimes included an **Online Resource** should you have computer access.

We have also included **model** groups which have only one meeting or are limited to one geographic area. **We have included the model groups primarily to help persons who may be interested in starting such a group in their local community,** so they do not have to "reinvent the wheel." We kindly request that you only contact model groups if you are interested in developing a group in your community, since model groups often are very limited in their ability to respond to more general inquiries.

There are some issues for which we have been unable to identify any national, or model self-help groups (e.g. rape). However, there are resources available to help those persons interested in developing support systems around such issues. Entries entitled **Resource** (organizations providing technical support and/or information and referrals), and **How-To Guide** (manual or how-to material) offer assistance that may be of benefit to you.

If you are interested in finding support groups online, look at Chapter 3.

TO FORM A GROUP

If you are indeed interested in starting a new group in your local area, we have included some suggestions in Chapter 2 on **"Starting Groups in the Community."** In that same chapter we have included some separate guidelines for the professional who seeks to help start a self-help group, ideally serving as an "on tap, not on top" consultant to persons interested in developing a group. If you are interested in forming a group, check with the national and/or model groups listed herein, as well as with any local self-help clearinghouses, to learn more about how they might assist you in starting the new group. In most cases, national groups can provide you with assistance and printed guidelines for starting a local affiliated group or chapter.

Thanks to Dr. John Grohol, we have an additional chapter on **"Starting a New Online Support Group"** for those who have internet access and would like to start a needed network there.

IN CONTACTING ANY GROUP BY PHONE OR MAIL

When writing to a group, always include a **self-addressed stamped envelope** to make it easier for them to respond. Consider sending a small donation. Many of the national group headquarters actually operate out of "kitchen table offices" and most run on "shoestring budgets." When phoning a group, keep in mind that many of these phone contacts are home numbers so please be considerate of the hour at which you phone, and keep in mind the different time zones. Please understand that several tries may be necessary.

We have also included in the Addendum a listing of telephone area code changes that are planned should you experience a problem in calling a group.

OTHER SOURCEBOOK SECTIONS

If you would like to read more about self-help groups, there are a number of references in the Bibliography section. For persons who are interested in empirical research on the effectiveness of self-help groups, we have added Chapter 5. This chapter reviews the various research findings on the effectiveness of self-help groups.

Just as self-help groups provide free information on resources and ways that help people deal with a wide variety of human problems, there are an increasing number of national toll-free helplines that help reduce the frustration in finding such information. Although these helplines are not run by self-help groups, we continue to include a listing of **National Toll-Free Helplines** since they can be helpful, cost-free sources of information for individuals and groups alike.

PLEASE NOTE:

The Clearinghouse has made every effort to include as many different self-help groups as possible. However, the Clearinghouse reserves the right to include or exclude any names, groups or telephone contacts at its absolute discretion. Omission of an organization does not signify disapproval. Inclusion of an organization does not signify approval. The use of any of the materials herein is entirely the responsibility of the reader. The Clearinghouse further disclaims any and all liability for any use or non-use of the materials herein. There are no warranties implied or expressed in any of the data provided herein. The information provided herein is based upon data supplied by the groups themselves. The Clearinghouse is not responsible for printing, insertion or deletion errors.

KNOW OF A NATIONAL OR MODEL GROUPS THAT SHOULD BE INCLUDED IN THE NEXT EDITION OF THE SOURCEBOOK?

We would be most grateful if you would let us know about any new or existing groups that you suggest be included in the next edition of the Sourcebook. We also would appreciate your comments and suggestions as to how the Sourcebook may be improved. Simply advise us by writing to us at: American Self-Help Clearinghouse, Attn: Sourcebook Suggestion, Northwest Covenant Medical Center, 25 Pocono Rd., Denville, N.J. 07834. ◆

ABOUT THE AMERICAN AND
NEW JERSEY CLEARINGHOUSES

The Sourcebook is the result of two self-help clearinghouse programs. Work in supporting self-help group efforts first began in 1978, when here at Northwest Covenant Medical Center we started to pull together a listing of "hard to find" self-help groups for a wide variety of stressful life problems. Most hospital and mental health center staff knew of only a few groups. When we advised them of others, they reported back how grateful their patients were to find out that they were not alone and that there was such a support group available. In 1979, we compiled the first directory of self-help groups in New Jersey. Unlike other directories, we added national and model groups that didn't exist in New Jersey, in order to show people what new self-help groups they could develop if they were willing to join with others. At the same time, we had seen how easy it was for us to link interested people together resulting in the development of many new groups.

In 1980, we submitted a proposal to the New Jersey State Division of Mental Health Services to establish the first statewide self-help clearinghouse in order to increase the awareness, utilization, and development of self-help groups. Subsequently, in January of 1981, the New Jersey Self-Help Clearinghouse was started. With additional new state directory editions, our listings of national and model groups grew - as did the number of people who were able to start new groups throughout the state with assistance from a national or model group listed in the directory. Since its start, the New Jersey Self-Help Clearinghouse has assisted in the development of over one thousand new groups in the state. A wide variety of consultation, training, information and referral services are available to those persons in New Jersey who simply dial us at 800-FOR-M.A.S.H. (Mutual Aid Self-Help).

In 1982, we began to share our national listings with other self-help clearinghouses through our MASHnet computer program and database which has been used by 18 other self-help clearinghouses in the U.S. and Canada. Our M.A.S.H. Networking Project service was then started in 1984 to help individuals outside New Jersey start new networks that didn't previously exist anywhere in the country. Names of persons interested in starting new types of groups were listed on that same database alongside existing groups. In that way, interested callers could be referred to help those starting groups. Over a dozen new "first-of-their-kind" self-help groups or networks were started as a result.

The Clearinghouse listing of national and model groups had proved so helpful to others outside New Jersey, that with funding from Hoffmann La Roche, Inc., the first edition of The Self-Help Sourcebook, was published in 1986 to make that information on those groups more widely available and known.

One way that we have sought to help more people learn about self-help groups is through our outreach efforts to the media. Prior mailings of the Sourcebook, with cover letters suggesting coverage of self-help groups, resulted in significant articles in Psychology Today, USA Today, American Health, FIRST for Women, Parade, New Age, New Physician, Better Homes and Gardens, and many other national magazines, books, and professional newsletters.

In 1990, with funding from the Northwest Covenant Medical Center and the St. Clares-Riverside Foundation, and with the help of additional volunteers, the American Self-Help Clearinghouse program was added. In addition to the Sourcebook, it provides the following services:

Information and Referral For information on a group, phone (973)625-3037, or via TDD (973)625-9053, between 9am and 5pm Eastern time. Staff and volunteers can provide callers with information and contacts on any national self-help groups that deal with their particular concern. If no appropriate national group exists and the caller is interested in the possibility of joining with others to start a local group, we can often provide information on model groups operating in other parts of the country, or individuals who are starting networks and seeking others to help develop them. We also provide callers with information on any local self-help clearinghouse that may exist to serve them in their area. We also have a website: http://www.cmhc.com/selfhelp

Consultation - If there is no group or support network that exists anywhere in the country for your problem and you are interested in starting a mutual help group or network, contact the Clearinghouse for help with suggestions, materials, and networking.

We firmly believe the most powerful potential of self-help is in the ability of people who are in need to come together and start needed new groups and networks. Through the work of both self-help clearinghouses, we strive to help more people tap that potential for the benefit of themselves and for so many others. ♦

> "If the life of a river depended only on the rainfall within the confines of its own banks, it would soon be dry. If the life of an individual depended solely on his own resources, he would soon fall. Be grateful for your tributaries."
>
> - Dr. William Arthur Ward

SELF-HELP PHILOSOPHY

The goal of a self-help group is to empower its members with the tools necessary to make adjustments needed to continue a life of dignity and independence.

Self-Help Groups:

..... share a common (health) concern

..... govern themselves and their agenda with success dependent on each member's feeling of ownership

..... may use professionals as resource people but not as leaders

..... provide non-judgmental emotional support

..... gather and share accurate and specialized information

..... have membership that is fluid--newcomers are helped by veterans and become veterans who may outgrow the need for a group

..... have a cause and actively promote that cause

..... increase public awareness and knowledge by sharing their unique and relevant information

..... charge a small or no dues for involvement

..... and typically struggle to survive

Developed by the **International Polio Network**, 5100 Oakland Ave., #206, St. Louis, MO 63110. Reprinted with permission.

Chapter 1

UNDERSTANDING SELF-HELP GROUPS

*"The only way to help people is to give
them a chance to help themselves."*
- Elbert Hubbard

AN INTRODUCTION
TO SELF-HELP GROUPS

- Phyllis Silverman, Ph.D.

Let me begin by describing my own personal experience in a mutual help group. The first group that I became formally involved in was the La Leche League. It was of interest to me because at that time I was having difficulty in nursing my first child. She was nursing frequently and for excessively long periods of time, she slept very little and fussed when left alone in the crib. A mother of ten said to me: Get an infant seat for the table so she can watch the family and lie down in bed with her when you nurse. With those two statements she changed my entire relationship with my newborn and made the first year of her life a very wonderful and exciting period. That experience introduced me to the value of a "mutual help" group and the knowledge it can provide and helped join my personal and professional interests. (It was at this time that I discovered in my work that another widow was the most appropriate helper for newly widowed.)

A mutual help exchange occurs when people, who share a problem or predicament, come together to help one another. This occurs, for example, when parents form a baby-sitting cooperative. In the broadest sense, such exchanges of resources and care are the basis of society, and no social life is possible without mutual aid. Usually this aid is casual and informal, but natural helping networks sometimes develop into voluntary organizations, intentional communities in which members control the resources and make policy decisions. The help they offer is usually based on the experiences of veteran members. Although such groups are called self-help groups, the term "mutual help" is more appropriate.

As you will see in glancing over the pages of this directory, in our heterogeneous, mobile society of the late 20th century, the number and variety of mutual help groups has been increasing. This is partly a reaction to the expansion of professionalism and the accompanying depersonalization of consumers. There are others who believe that the mutual help movement can democratize and "humanize" the human service system by involving consumers more in their own care. But the development of these organizations is mainly due to people's need to find others like themselves who have experienced a similar problem. Mutual help groups are especially attractive to persons undergoing a transition that requires a shift in social roles -- whether they are recovering alcoholics, former mental patients or new parents.

Mutual help groups are more fluid than bureaucracies or professional organizations, but over time they tend to formalize their policies and practices. Some groups, such as Gray Panthers and the Mental Patient Liberation Movement, are governed wholly by consensus. "Liberation" groups usually avoid hierarchical organization, sacrificing efficiency for maximum participation. Other groups, such as Parents Without Partners, follow parliamentary procedures in establishing committees and electing officers. The La Leche League and others are organized as service delivery systems with authority vested in a national office and leadership recruited through an elaborate ascending hierarchy, always from people who have been helped by the group. But when a hierarchy exists, leaders have no way to enforce their authority, and members leave when the group stops meeting their needs. In many groups an informal consensus determines policy and rules are invented as required.

Actually, most local groups are small (10-20 people) and constantly struggling to survive. The simplest type of national organization is a loose network of autonomous groups. The most common is an association supported by dues from affiliated local branches or chapters that are authorized to use its name. Many of these national associations have paid staff who develop program materials for the local groups and provide consultants from regional offices. Examples are: Alcoholics Anonymous, Parents Without Partners, La Leche League and The Compassionate Friends (for parents who have lost a child).

The support provided by mutual help organizations has a special meaning. The helper and the beneficiary are peers and everyone in the group can be both. Not being bound to the role of either helper or recipient may in itself have therapeutic value. Discovering that others have the same problem, members of mutual help groups no longer feel alone. Their feelings and experiences are legitimized, and they are provided with a framework for coping: "The most important thing for me was finding someone like me. When I walked into the room and found 50 other widows, I can't explain the good feeling it gave me."

Each organization develops a body of relevant information and strategies: "When I get nervous now I follow the guidelines I learned at the meeting; it really works." The best known of these is the "Twelve Steps" of Alcoholics Anonymous, which have been adapted to the needs of many other anonymous groups that you will find in the directory dealing with problems such as gambling, overeating and drug abuse.

Groups concerned with disabilities or with such universal problems as bereavement use a more flexible approach. The wisdom of experience amassed in these organizations provides a unique contribution distinct from the professional knowledge learned in schools. One member of such a group commented "When she said she understood, I knew she meant it. I needed to hear how she managed before anything else." Another person said, "I needed to have a name for what was bothering me. I could figure out what to do when someone explained what I needed, given my situation."

Methods of Helping The assistance provided by mutual help groups may include educational seminars, one-to-one exchanges and social gatherings, in addition to the basic sharing of personal experiences and small informal meetings. "When I got up at a meeting to talk and everyone listened, I can't tell you how much confidence it gave me," says a member of a Laryngectomy Club."

Some organizations have hotlines for immediate aid to persons in need. Many have outreach programs in which members make unsolicited offers of help; for example, members of Mended Hearts visit patients in the hospital before and after coronary surgery, and programs for widows and widowers often send a note to the bereaved shortly after the funeral. One widow said "I would never have gotten out, but when she called and said she was a widow I asked her to come right over. I didn't think I would be able to get up in the morning. She told me everyone feels that way; she did too. If she has energy to help me now, I realized I would be all right. She said it takes time. I needed to know that too."

Many organizations have formal orientation or training programs for outreach volunteers, facilitators in small group discussions, and for officers and leaders of other programs. Observing the usefulness of mutual help groups, professional agencies have begun to sponsor groups of their own, choosing the participants and convening the meetings themselves. Since members do not control resources and direct policy, these are technically not mutual help groups and do not accomplish the same ends. The context in which help is offered may critically change its nature and effects. The more professionals are involved, the more likely it is to resemble group therapy or another professional service under a different name. This can be unintentionally deceptive.

Professional human service agencies and mutual help groups sometimes have a tense and competitive relationship. Group members sometimes believe themselves to have been ill-served by professional helping systems, and members may be encouraged to only consult one another. Historically, professionals have sometimes tried to co-opt mutual help organizations, and they are often regarded as intruders. When groups turn to agencies for assistance, a struggle for control may result.

But most mutual help organizations are not anti-professional and collaboration is possible if there is a mutual respect and understanding. For example, La Leche League, the Ostomy society (for people who have undergone ileostomy and related surgery), and Recovery, Inc. (serving former mental patients) have professional advisory committees that provide medical information enabling members to become competent consumers of the services they need. Parents Anonymous (for child abusers) has also brought professionals into its programs.

Self-help clearinghouses, which are also listed in this directory, have been instrumental in promoting the increased identification, awareness and utilization of groups through their information, referral and consultation services. Some, like the NJ Self-Help Clearinghouse, have focused their primary efforts on the development of needed new mutual help groups.

In summary, mutual help groups are a powerful and constructive means for people to help themselves and each other. The basic dignity of each human being is expressed in his or her capacity to be involved in a reciprocal helping exchange. Out of this compassion comes cooperation. From this cooperation comes community. With the increased awareness and understanding of these national groups and models, as this resource directory seeks to promote, the number of mutual help communities will continue to grow -- and continue to provide their members with the direction, values and hope they need. In a sense, they speak for all of us since even those of us who study these groups as professionals are consumers. ♦

Dr. Silverman is a Professor on the faculty of the Institute of Health Professions of Massachusetts General Hospital and is the Co-Director of the Child Bereavement Study Project there. She also holds an appointment in the Dept. of Psychiatry at Harvard Medical School. She has served as consultant to several task forces on bereavement, mutual help and prevention and has worked in community agencies both as a case worker and as a researcher. Within the Lab of Community Psychiatry at Harvard Medical School, she developed the concept of the widow-to- widow program and directed the research that demonstrated its effect. In addition to her social work degree from Smith College of Social Work, she holds an MS in hygiene from Harvard School of Public Health and a Ph.D. from the Florence Heller School for Advanced Studies in Social Welfare at Brandeis University. Her works include Helping Each Other in Widowhood, If You Will Lift It I Will Lift It Too, Mutual Help Groups: A Guide for Mental Health Professionals, Mutual Help Groups: Organization and Development, Helping Women Cope with Grief and Widow to Widow.

TO BETTER UNDERSTAND
THE TERM "SELF-HELP GROUP"

Have you ever noticed when you have a problem, how it helps to talk with someone who has had a similar problem? Simply finding others who have "been there" and then realizing that "you are not alone" can be very comforting and helpful. The Sourcebook has been compiled to help you more easily find and form a self-help group—one that can provide such needed support, as well as practical information, education and sometimes needed advocacy.

The self-help groups listed on the following pages can better be described as Mutual Aid Self-Help groups because they derive their energy from members helping one another, without forms or fees. In examining the hundreds of national organizations, societies and foundations that exist for different illnesses, addictions, parenting and other stressful life situations and transitions, we have sought to identify those organizations that provide these mutual help opportunities. In addition to "mutual support," three other key characteristics of self-help groups that constitute our general criteria are: that the group be composed of "peers," people who share a common experience or situation; that the group or network be primarily run by and for its members, who therefore have a sense of "ownership" for the group or network; and that the group be voluntary, non-profit, i.e., they can "pass the hat," charge dues, or fundraise, but there are no fees for services.

Dr. Silverman, in her introduction to self-help groups, describes some of the characteristics and dynamics of self-help groups, and how these differ from professionally-run groups and services. Self-help groups can provide benefits that professional services cannot. But self-help groups are not meant to replace needed professional services, although they supplement, support and sometimes even develop them, as well as often prevent the very need for them.

We should point out that there are other types of community organizations that are sometimes described as self-help, including civic, housing, fraternal, business, ethnic, church and political groups. However, these groups, by their very numbers and broader focus, would warrant or already have separate directories of their own.

Also, please understand that the quality of individual self-help groups differ, sometimes even among those with the same name. Contact and visit the group to see if it is for you. While initial research reflects the value of self-help groups, the ultimate evaluation and very survival of any self-help group is determined by those who attend it and decide to stay and contribute to it.

UNDERSTANDING WHAT SELF-HELP GROUPS DO AND HOW THEY DO IT

- Ed Madara

Self-help groups help their members cope with a wide variety of illnesses, disabilities, addictions, bereavement, parenting and many other stressful life problems. From groups for parents of children born prematurely to those families caring for an elderly-frail parent, there are hundreds of self-help groups listed within these pages that address different problems but function in very similar ways.

WHAT THEY DO

Mutual help groups, as often reflected in their written mission statements, usually have three or four basic functions or purposes in that they provide:

1. **Social Support** - relief from isolation, experiencing the stress-reducing support of others who truly understand. As one group leader expressed it..."The heart of our message is: 'You Are Not Alone.' Our strength has come from sharing our hardship and giving hope to others." In some groups, this support represents genuine "community." Duke University researchers who studied the value of social support to the life expectancy of cardiac patients (as reported in New York Times of Feb. 5, 1992) concluded that "A support group may be as effective as costly medical treatment. Simply put, having someone to talk to is very powerful medicine."

2. **Practical Information** - on the problem or disorder, how to cope on a 24-hour a day basis (sometimes using a particular "program," e.g. the 12-steps), what professional services and other resources are available, alternatives, self-care techniques, research, etc. These help people to recognize that they are not helpless.

3. **Education** - primarily derived from the pooling of members' experiences and coping skills, as well as information on and familiarity with professional services; referred to as "experiential knowledge" (Dr. Thomasina Borkman, 1975). Secondarily, their ability to attract professionals to share their professional knowledge (e.g., to speak at meetings, workshops and/or contribute to newsletter), often leading to collaboration in joint learning, education, treatment and research development efforts.

4. **Advocacy** (an optional function) - advocating to address problems or deficiencies that the members cannot resolve within in their group, but exist in the larger society. Historically, theses groups are the seeds for the development of many long-standing health foundations, societies, and movements dealing with various illnesses, disabilities, and health concerns.

Not all groups (e.g., 12-step groups) involve themselves in pursuing an advocacy purpose and activities.

HOW GROUPS DO IT

Some of the specific principles and group dynamics to be found at work within mutual-help groups and networks are:

1. **The "Helper Therapy" principle** - wherein those who help others are themselves helped (Dr. Frank Riessman, 1965). As heard in some groups, "if you help someone up the hill, you get closer to the top yourself."

2. **Positive Role Models** - those, who have been through it, demonstrate to new members that success, coping and/or recovery is possible ("do-able"). Their example and actions often provide needed encouragement and hope, not otherwise available.

3. **Accessibility** - there are no fees, so they are financially more accessible. They are also psychologically more accessible in several ways: in that they require no forms be submitted; often, as in the many "anonymous" groups, no names need be given; and one can go to a group simply to learn, and does not have to assume "patienthood" to get help. Many groups also have convenient meeting sites in the community, at times that are more convenient than most professional services.

4. **Pooling of Knowledge and Resources** by members, so that all can take advantage of the experiences of many.

5. **Acceptance** - being accepted and understood, often for the first time.

6. **Empowerment** of members by their taking a more active rather than a traditional passive role.

7. **Normalization** - when they see how their experience is similar to others, they finally feel "normal." For what range of differences do exist, their basic human need for feedback (as to how they are doing) is finally met.

8. **Anonymity** is provided by many groups.

9. **The Prevention Equation** (of psychologist Dr. George Albee, 1982) reflects how groups contribute to the prevention of psychopathology and stress-related illness:

$$\text{Incidence of Dysfunction} = \frac{\text{Stress} + \text{Constitutional Vulnerabilities}}{\text{Social Support} + \text{Coping Skills} + \text{Competence}}$$

Groups provide social support, coping skills, and increase competence, thereby reducing incidence. To varying degrees, self-help groups serve a prevention function by enhancing social ties and connections that can serve as a buffer to stress, and by promoting the competency of people to cope with stress and adversity for a full spectrum of life transitions and crises. Dr. Phyllis Silverman (1985) of Harvard University points out that many stressful life transitions cannot be prevented, but that mutual help groups may be "one of the more powerful modalities" for facilitating the learning of coping skills subsequent to stress.

10. Groups turn what society considers a liability (e.g. one's experience as an addict, widow, etc.) into an asset (their unique ability to provide understanding and help others).

Unfortunately, an understanding of these functions and dynamics traditionally has been missing from most professional training curriculum. In 1987, then Surgeon General C. Everett Koop held a national conference that explored the value and potential of self-help groups to public health. The recommendation given the highest priority of over 60 developed at the two day conference, was the need to educate professionals to self-help groups. Dr. Koop later noted:

> "My years as a medical practitioner, as well as my own first-hand experience, has taught me how important self-help groups are in assisting their members in dealing with problems, stress, hardship and pain... Today, the benefits of mutual aid experienced by millions of people who turn to others with a similar problem to attempt to deal with their isolation, powerlessness, alienation, and the awful feeling that nobody understands... Health and human service providers are learning that they can indeed provide a superior service when they help their patients and clients find appropriate peer support." Former Surgeon General C. Everret Koop (in his 1992 foreword to Self-Help: Concepts and Applications, edited by Dr. A. H. Katz et. al., p. xviii).

References:

Albee, G.W., "Preventing Psychopathology and Promoting Human Potential" in American Psychologist, 37 (9), pp.1043-1050, 1982.

Borkman, Thomasina, "Experiential Knowledge: a New Concept for the Analysis of Self-Help Groups" in the Social Service Review, vol. 50, number 3, pp. 445-456, 1975.

Riessman, Frank, "The Helper Therapy Principle" in Social Work, vol. 10, pp. 26-32, 1965.

Silverman, Phyllis, "Tertiary/Secondary Prevention - Preventive Intervention: the Case for Mutual Help Groups" in The Group Workers' Handbook, R. K. Conyne (Ed), Springfield, Il: Charles C. Thomas, pp. 237-258), 1985.

TEN BENEFICIAL WAYS PROFESSIONALS INTERACT WITH GROUPS

1. **Identify and refer** to local groups in your community. They often will reciprocate.

2. **Communicate/collaborate with local groups**, e.g., find out who is the contact person, request their literature, keep brochures on hand, establish liaison, subscribe to their newsletters.

3. **Involve groups in your training and conferences**, e.g., as speakers at inservice trainings, workshops and conferences; or host group demonstration/presentation at staff meeting or for clients.

4. **Provide speaking engagements and/or training** that local groups desire.

5. **Offer actual agency support**, e.g., meeting space, mailings, copying, secretarial help, etc.

6. **Identify need for new groups** in your community and educate others to the potential for developing a specific group based upon a particular national model.

7. **Identify and encourage potential "group starters,"** possibly from veteran patients.

8. **Provide networking assistance** to meet their needs for speakers, advisors, consultants, referrals, researchers, special services or training, loan of newest equipment, etc.

9. **Educate other professionals** to the availability and value of groups, e.g., report upon what you've learned here at agency meetings or professional conferences.

10. **Advocate for increased awareness** and understanding of groups, e.g., development of a local listing or directory that includes them, presentations before agency coalitions or associations, etc.

"When the wise healer's work is done, the people say 'Amazing. We did it all ourselves."

- Lao Tze

PUBLICATIONS BY PROFESSIONALS
ON SELF-HELP

Most of the books and references that best describe mutual aid self-help groups can be obtained from the self-help group contacts listed in this directory. Their materials can often express the purpose and value of the group better than any textbook can. Here are some references which, for the most part, examine self-help groups in general and are written primarily for a professional audience.

Self-Help and Support Groups, by Linda Farris Kurtz, is an excellent classroom text since it provides discussion questions, classroom exercises and assignments for most of the eleven chapters that provide scholarly overviews of group dynamics, membership professional relationships, and other related issues. Published in 1997 by Sage Publications, 2455 Teller Rd., Thousand Oaks, CA 91320 for $21.95 plus postage.

Redefining Self-Help: Policy and Practice, by Frank Reissman and David Carroll, reflects how people with problems can be viewed as resources through self-help groups. With illustrations from various groups, the authors demonstrate how health and human service agencies can benefit from their tapping into the power of self-help organizations. Concepts such as the helper therapy principle, self-determination, and consumer as producer are updated. Published in 1995 by Jossey-Bass, 350 Sansome St., San Francisco, CA 94104.

Understanding the Self-Help Organization, edited by Thomas J. Powell, includes 17 chapters on research on self-help groups and professionally-run support groups. Published in 1994 by Sage Publications.

Self-Help: Concepts and Applications, edited by Alfred Katz, H.L. Hedrick, D.H. Isenberg, L.M. Thompson, T. Goodrich, and A.H. Kutsche, is an informative collection of over 30 perspectives on self-help group dynamics and professional interface. Several chapters examine the value of groups for conditions like AIDS, hearing loss, cancer, death of a child, lupus, and others. There are several chapters that look at professional and self-help group relationships, including the first chapter on empowerment that provides and extensive and updated review of policy and partnership developments. The book, published in 1992, is available from Charles Press, P.O. Box 15715, Philadelphia, PA 19103 for $24.95 postpaid.

The Self-Help Way: Mutual Help and Health by Jean-Marie Romeder with contributions from Hector Balthazar, Andrew Farquharson, and Francine Lavoie, provides an overview of the growth and development of the self-help groups, while probing the dynamics of "the self-help way." With an introduction by former U.S. Surgeon General Koop, it provides a variety of views and insights that would be of interest to both the general public as well as professionals. This 158 page book, published in 1990, is available from Canadian Council on Social Development, P.O. Box 3505, Station C; Ottawa, Ontario K14 4Gl, Canada.

Helping One Another: Self-Help Groups in a Changing World, by Alfred Katz and Eugene Bender (22 chapters examine specific types and general development of self-help groups in relationship to changing social, economic and political scene), 1990, 266 pages, Third Party Publishing, Oakland, CA 94661.

Working With Self-Help, edited by Thomas Powell, includes 17 chapters written primarily for professionals that vary from a look at 12-step programs to self-help and Latino communities, from bereavement groups to parents of the mentally ill in Israel. Printed in 1990, 338 pages, American Association of Social Workers, 7981 Eastern Ave., Silver Spring, MD 20910.

Rediscovering Self-Help: Its Role in Social Care, edited by Diane Pancoast, P. Parker and C. Froland, 1983, SAGE Publications.

The Surgeon General's Workshop on Self-Help and Public Health, printed by the U.S. Department of Health and Human Services, Public Health Service, (summary of presentations and recommendations), printed 1988, 60 pp. (Check with any local self-help clearinghouse serving your area to determine if they can provide a copy).

Self-Help Organizations and Professional Practice, by Thomas Powell, 1987, 366 pages, National Association of Social Workers, 7981 Eastern Ave., Silver Spring, MD 20910.

Helping People To Help Themselves: Self-Help and Prevention, edited by Leonard Borman, Leslie Borck, Robert Hess and Frank Pasquale, 1982, 129 pages, Haworth Press.

Mutual Help Groups: Organization and Development, by Phyllis R. Silverman (guide to starting groups, with attention of professional relationship and roles), 1980, 143 pages, SAGE Publications, P.O. Box 5024, Beverly Hills, CA 90212.

The Self-Help Revolution, by Alan Gartner and Frank Reissman, (Series of 18 essays that review particular groups, professional interface and evaluation), 1984, 266 pages, Human Sciences Press, 72 Fifth Avenue, New York, N.Y. 10011.

Rediscovering Self-Help: Its Role in Social Care, edited by Diane Pancoast, P. Parker and C. Froland, 1983, SAGE Publications.

Helping People to Help Themselves: Self-Help and Prevention, edited by Leonard Borman, Leslie Borck, Robert Hess and Frank Pasquale, 1982, 129 pages, Haworth Press.

Self-Help Groups for Coping with Crisis, by Morton A. Lieberman and Leonard D. Borman (review of literature and research on groups), 1979, 462 pages, Jossey Bass Publishers, San Francisco, CA.

"Hospitals and Self-Help Groups: Opportunity and Challenge" by E. Madara and W.D. Neigher, Health Progress, Vol. 67, No. 3, April, 1986, pp. 42-45. Mutual Help Groups: Organization and Development, by Phyllis R. Silverman (guide to starting groups, with attention to professional relationships and roles), 1980, 143 pps, SAGE Publications, P.O. Box 5024, Beverly Hills, CA 90212.

Self-Help in the Human Services, by Alan Gartner and Frank Reissman (reviews range, variety and principles of groups), 1977, Jossey Bass Publishers, San Francisco, CA.

Support Systems and Mutual Help: Interdisciplinary Explorations, edited by Gerald Caplan and Marie Killilea, (contains excellent chapter on literature review by Marie Killilea), 1976, 325 pages, Grune and Stratton, Inc.

The Strength in Us: Self-Help Groups in the Modern World, edited by Alfred H. Katz and Eugene I. Bender (history, typology, political aspects), 1976, 258 pages, New York: New Viewpoints Press.

The Recovery Resource Book, by Barbara Yoder (Describes different self-help groups, agencies, books, and other resources dealing with various addictions and dependencies - providing samples of groups' materials), 1990, New York: Simon and Schuster, 314 pages.

"Clergy and Self-Help Groups: Practical and Promising Relationships" by E. Madara, and B.A. Peterson, The Journal of Pastoral Care, Vol. 41, No. 3, September, 1987, pp. 213-220.

"Introducing and Tapping Self-Help Mutual Aid Resources," by C.J. Paskert, and E.J. Madara, Health Education, (written for school personnel), Vol. 16, No. 4, Aug/Sept., 1985, pp. 25-29.

"The Self-Help Clearinghouse Operation: Tapping the Resource Development Potential of I & R Services," by E. Madara. Information and Referral: The Journal of the Alliance of Information and Referral Systems, (written primarily for I & R agencies) Vol. 12, No. 1, Summer, 1985, pp. 42-57.

"Self-Help and How We Teach Tomorrow" What's New in Home Economics, (written primarily for teachers), Vol. 17, No. 4, December, 1983, pp. 1 and 4.

Chapter 2

STARTING GROUPS IN THE COMMUNITY

"Never doubt that a small group of thoughtful, committed citizens can change the world: indeed it's the only thing that ever has." — Margaret Mead

INTRODUCTION TO STARTING A GROUP

The most exciting and powerful capability of self-help groups is that ordinary people can start them in their local communities when none currently exist, and then go on to provide extraordinary help to others. These group founders don't require a government grant, an agency, endowment, or an office - just the inspiration and help of a national or model group, and a few other people who share the concern and interest. The groups listed in the Sourcebook provide such inspiration, helping people to more quickly and readily network, organize, educate, or advocate to meet their needs. In this chapter, we provide you with some of the practical nuts and bolts of starting a **face-to-face community** group.

We have added the section on how to serve as a **group contact person** since that is a role that most group founders initially fill. It is also a position that is often filled by several members, since many groups try to have two or three persons serving at the same time.

The final section in this chapter is written specially for **professionals** who are helping to develop a group--which calls for their serving primarily in the role of a consultant.

If you cannot find enough people in your area to start a group, or the nature of your problem prevents you from attending an existing face-to-face group, you have two options. First, because an ever increasing number of people are using personal computers to start support groups online, we've added a separate chapter kindly contributed by John Grohol on the basics of **starting on online support group** on the Internet (see **Chapter 4**). But before turning to that chapter, follow the suggestions in Chapter 3 to determine if there is an existing online group you can join.

If you to want to start a needed national group for a rare disorder, and you cannot go the computer route, a second option is to start a traditional "support network" that uses a combination of correspondence, phone and other interactive media to help members help one another. Because such an occasion is rare, we have not included suggestions here. But call our Clearinghouse for help if you want to start such a support network that doesn't yet exist in the world.

IDEAS & CONSIDERATIONS FOR STARTING A SELF-HELP MUTUAL AID GROUP

- Edward J. Madara

Self-help groups offer people who face a common problem the opportunity to meet with others and share their experiences, knowledge, strengths and hopes. Run by and for their members, self-help groups can better be described as "mutual help" groups.

Hundreds of these groups are started each week across the nation by ordinary people with a little bit of courage, a fair sense of commitment, and a heavy amount of caring. The following guidelines are based on our experience at the Self-Help Clearinghouse helping hundreds of individuals to start groups. While there is no one recipe for starting a group (different national groups offer different model approaches), we have listed below a few general considerations and strategies that you may find helpful.

1. <u>Don't Re-invent the Wheel.</u> If you are interested in starting a group around a particular concern or problem, find out who is doing it now or has done it before. Check with your local self-help clearinghouse or helplines serving your area to find out about existing local groups. Use the Sourcebook to find any national offices or model groups that address your concern. Contact these existing groups by phone or mail. Ask for any "how-to" starter packet information they may have, or sample materials they have used, e.g. flyers, press releases, etc. If you do have a local self-help clearinghouse in your area, determine how they can help you in starting a group, e.g. materials, workshops, listing your interest in their newsletter, etc. If you're trailblazing and developing a completely new type of self-help group, consider attending a few meetings of other self-help groups to get a feel for how they operate--then borrow or adapt what you consider their best techniques to use in your own group.

2. <u>Think "Mutual-Help" From the Start.</u> Find a few others who share your interest in starting (not simply joining) a self-help group. Put out flyers or letters that specifically cite your interest in hearing from those who would be interested in "joining with others to help start" such a group. Include your first name and phone number. Xerox copies and post them at places you feel most appropriate, e.g., library, community center, or post office. Mail copies to key people whom you think would know others like yourself. You can also have a notice published in your local newspaper or church bulletin. When, hopefully, you receive a response, discuss with the caller what their interests are, share your vision of what you would like to see the group do, and finally ask if they would be willing to share the work with you for a specific period of time (e.g., eight months or so) to try to get the group off the ground. Suggest that the work could be greeting people at the door and introducing new members, bringing refreshments, making coffee, co-chairing or helping to run the meeting, etc. Once a

couple of people have said yes, you have a "core group" or "steering committee" - and you won't have to do it alone. It's much easier to start a group if the work is shared. But most importantly, if several people are involved in the initial work at that first meeting (refreshments, publicity, name tags, greeting new people, etc.), they will model for newcomers what your self-help mutual aid group is all about-- not one person doing it all, but dependent upon the individual volunteer efforts and the active participation of all the other members.

3. <u>Find a Suitable Meeting Place and Time.</u> Try to obtain free meeting space at a local church, synagogue, library, community center, hospital or social service agency. If you anticipate a small group and feel comfortable with the idea, consider initial meetings in members' homes. Would evening or day meetings be better for members? Most prefer weeknights. It is also easier for people to remember the meeting time if it's a fixed day of the week or month, like the second Thursday of the month, etc.

4. <u>Publicize and Run your First Public Meeting.</u> Reaching potential members is never easy. Depending upon the problem area, consider where potential members go. Would they be seen by particular doctors or agencies? Contacting physicians, clergy or other professionals can be one approach to try. Posting flyers in post offices, community centers, hospitals, libraries is another. Free announcements in the community calendar sections of local newspapers can be especially fruitful. Consider simply calling the paper and asking to speak with an editor to suggest an article on the group and the issue. Editors are often grateful for the idea. The first meeting should be arranged so that there will be ample time for you to describe your interest and work, while allowing others the opportunity to share their feelings and concerns. Do those attending agree that such a group is needed? Will they attend another meeting, helping out as needed? What needs do they have in common that the group could address? Based on group consensus, make plans for your next meeting.

5. <u>Identify and Respond to the Felt Needs of Your Members.</u> If your group is new and doesn't follow a set program for helping members help one another, always remember to plan your groups' activities and goals based upon the expressed needs of your members. Share your vision. At the very first meeting, go "round-robin" permitting each member an opportunity to say what they would like to see the group do. Then discuss these needs and come to a consensus as to which ones you will address first. Don't make the same mistake that some professionals make in professionally-run groups--of thinking that you know the members' needs without ever asking them. Remember to regularly ask your new members about their needs, and what they think the group might do to meet those needs. Similarly, be sure to avoid the pitfall of the core group members possible becoming a clique. The welcoming of new people into the group is a process that continues well beyond welcoming them at the door.

6.   <u>Future Meeting.</u> Other considerations for future meetings may be the following:

    A.   <u>Defining the purpose(s) of the group</u>. Are they clear? You may want to add them to any flyer or brochure that you develop for the group. Some groups also include any guidelines that they have for their meetings right on their flyer or brochure.

    B.   <u>Membership</u>. Who can attend meetings and who cannot? Do you want regular membership limited to those with the problem and an associate membership for spouses and family?

    C.   <u>Meeting format</u>. What choice or combination of discussion time, education, business meeting, service planning, socializing, etc. best suits your group? What guidelines might you use to assure that discussions be non-judgmental, confidential and informative? Topics can be selected or guest speakers invited. A good discussion group size may be about 7 to 15. As your meeting grows larger, consider breaking down into smaller groups for discussion.

    D.   <u>Phone network</u>. Self-help groups should provide an atmosphere of caring, sharing and support for their members. Many groups encourage the exchange of telephone numbers or a telephone list to provide members with help over the phone when it is needed between meetings.

    E.   <u>Use of professionals</u>. Consider using professionals as speakers, advisors, consultants to your group, and as sources of continued referrals.

    F.   <u>Projects</u>. Begin with small projects, e.g. developing a flyer, obtaining newspaper coverage by calling editors, issuing a newsletter, etc. Rejoice and pat yourselves on the back when you succeed with these first projects. Then, if the group desires, work your way up to more difficult tasks and projects, e.g. planning a conference, advocating the introduction of specific legislation, etc.

    G.   <u>Sharing responsibilities and nurturing new leaders</u>. You will want to look for all the different, additional roles that people can play in helping other members and making the group work, e.g., group librarian, arranging for speakers, greeter of new members, group liaison with an agency, etc. In asking for volunteers, it's sometimes easier to first ask the group what specific tasks they think would be helpful. You'll come to know the special satisfaction and benefits of helping others. Remember to give all your members that same opportunity to help. By sharing responsibilities you help create opportunities for others to become key members and leaders in the group.

H. Lastly, expect your group to experience regular "ups and downs" in terms of attendance and enthusiasm. It's natural and to be expected. You may want to consider joining or forming a coalition or state association of leaders from the same or similar types of self-help groups, for your own periodic mutual support and for sharing program ideas and successes.

The suggestions above are basic ones you need to know. We've added some additional sections here that can provide you with more ideas on how to handle specific tasks related to starting and running a group.

SUGGESTIONS FOR LOCATING A MEETING SPACE

The most obvious place to have a small meeting, especially a first meeting of your core group, is in someone's home. If you expect more people than such a space can hold, or if you personally prefer not to open your home to people who are (initially) strangers, consider the possibilities listed below:

-   Churches are the most common public meeting place for self-help groups and seem the most cooperative. Contact your pastor, rabbi or priest to request a room for your meeting. A personal connection is the best, and could mean no charge initially. More and more churches have been requiring a minimal donation to go towards heating and utilities.

-   Community organizations or agencies such as Community Mental Health Centers, Red Cross, Salvation Army, Rotary, Lions, Kiwanis, or Senior Citizens centers will sometimes provide space free of charge for self-help group meetings. Again, does anyone in your group personally know a staff member or officer? Your local library or daycare centers and schools, bank, municipal town hall or community college are other facilities where self-help groups hold meetings.

-   Hospitals are another option, especially if your group is health related. Contact the community relations department or the social services department to request a meeting space.

-   Your local YMCA/YWCA also can provide meeting space for your group. Contact their community relations person.

Availability of a kitchen or a sink with running water is desirable for making coffee or other refreshments. It is helpful to place chairs in a circle or around a table. In this way, members may face each other and the atmosphere is friendlier and more supportive. A table can serve to display books, pamphlets, announcements and other printed materials. A small storage space can also be helpful for storing supplies, etc., if it one could be made available.

When inquiring about a meeting place, be sure to communicate the fact that your group is a voluntary, non-profit organization that intends to provide a service to the public free of charge. Be clear on the specific nights that you would like your meetings to take place, how long they will be, and who will be responsible for opening and closing the facility. Such attention to detail will serve you and your group well!

IDEAS FOR STRUCTURING YOUR GROUP MEETING

Meeting formats for self-help groups range from loosely structured discussion groups to more formally structured meetings. If you are not following the specific program of an established national group, the following may be helpful. These activities are common to some self-help group meetings and can be used as an initial guide for structuring your meeting. It is not necessary to incorporate every activity mentioned here in each meeting agenda.

1. Welcoming New Members: It is a practice of many self-help groups that a volunteer member greets and welcomes new members at the door when they arrive, introducing them to other members, especially those who have a similar situation.

2. Formal Opening of Meeting: At the agreed upon time, the meeting should be called to order by the chairperson. Some groups open their meetings with a welcoming statement, a formal statement of the group's purpose, and possibly more, e.g., a serenity prayer.

3. Introduction of Members: Going around the room, each member can introduce himself/herself and may state their reason for coming to the group. This is especially appropriate for new groups forming to help members get to know one another and learn about common concerns.

4. Discussion, Education, and Information Sharing: For new groups, it is helpful to regularly ask members to suggest topics that are of interest to them. Groups can also invite guest speakers to address issues. Tapes, books or articles can be reviewed and discussed. Time is allotted for sharing of personal experiences and helping each other.

5. Business/Planning Section: This time can be set aside for any business the group wishes to do, such as planning projects, arranging future meetings (choosing topics, speakers, etc.), making announcements, collection of dues.

6. Formal Closing: It is important that some signal be given to indicate that the meeting is formally closed, e.g., a closing statement or other ritual at the end of each meeting. Members are reminded of time and place of next meeting.

7. Refreshments are often served after some meetings, providing an important time for informal meeting and conversation.

IDEAS FOR RECRUITING GROUP MEMBERS

Here are some possible techniques for recruiting group members. Simply sit down with several group members to review and discuss these ideas. Select which ones will be tried and those persons who will be in charge of carrying each out.

- Draw-up and distribute a one page flyer on your group.

- Place notices in key posting areas: post offices, churches, community centers, clubs, organizations, shops, hospitals, nursing homes, libraries, or doctors' offices.

- Publicize your group in a local newspaper by asking the editor if they would be interested in doing a story on your group.

- Phone clergymen, doctors, agency directors, social workers, media, nurses, (i.e. anyone who might be sympathetic to your need), and ask them if they would make referrals.

- If you have a local self-help clearinghouse, contact them to make sure that they know about your group so that they can make appropriate referrals.

- Talk to persons from similar self-help groups and ask what methods they found most helpful in recruiting group members.

- Contact local agencies, associations and foundations that address your concern. Ask if they would help.

- Call your local information and referral helpline/hotlines - make sure they have your group in their listings.

- Identify organizations that print community or social service directories, contact them and request your group be included.

- Write a brief notice to be placed in a church bulletin/newsletter. Consider other newsletters, YMCA's, office on aging, etc.

- Write a "letter-to-the-editor" explaining the group's purpose.

- Write two sentences explaining how the group is starting and where to call for information, and send it to local radio stations, requesting they air it as a community service announcement.

- Establish a Speakers Bureau and offer to make presentations before community service organizations, agency staff meetings, church groups, and others.

GUIDELINES FOR GROUP DISCUSSION

Self-help groups can be as formal or informal as their members wish. But some groups find discussion easier if there are some general guidelines to follow. Here are some examples to choose from. Guidelines can be included in the group's brochure, so that new members know from the outset what the ground rules are.

- We know what we share about our personal lives is confidential - what is said in the group stays in the group.

- We encourage members to share their strengths, skills, insights, successes, and their hopes.

- We encourage "I" statements, so that everyone speaks in the first person.
- It is important that we actively listen when someone is talking and avoid having side conversations.

- We try not to discuss persons who are not present.

- Each person has the right to take part in any discussion or not.

- We each share the responsibility for making the group work.

- Each member's right to anonymity is respected.

- The primary responsibility of the leader/facilitator, if there is one, is to ensure that the group is a "safe place" for its members to disclose their personal stories, fears, etc.

- It is recognized that the leader/facilitator, if there is one, is not the "expert".

- We, having benefitted from the help of others, recognize the need for offering our help to others in the group.

"Through a willingness to risk the unknown, to venture forth into unfamiliar territory, you can undertake the search for your own self--the ultimate goal of growth. Through reaching out an committing yourself to dialogue with fellow human beings, you can begin to transcend your individual existence, becoming at one with yourself and others. And through a lifetime of such committment, you can face your final end with peace and joy, knowing that you have lived your life well."
- Author unknown

POSSIBLE DISCUSSION QUESTIONS

While well established groups usually have developed structured exercises to help members share their experiences, strengths, hopes, coping skills, and practical information, other groups simply plan initial group discussions on the basis of their members' common needs and interests. Consider just surveying the members and have them select those discussion topics that interest them the most. Then members can take turns on different days to simply introduce a chosen topic by giving a brief summary of the issue and then introducing discussion questions. If they need to prepare, they can read up on the topic or ask other members about their experiences or perspectives. Topics could range from education to advocacy issues, but the most important point is that the topic be based on the needs of your members.

Discussion can also be based on discussion questions, determined by members beforehand. Here are some suggested questions that can be used for a particular health problem or disability. They would need to be revised for other types of issues. Members may want to review them and select those they would like to schedule for a particular day. On the day or night of the discussion, individuals could go "round-robin." taking turns answering.

Remember that the purpose of asking these questions is to help individuals share, think about, and learn from each others' experiences and insights. There are no right or wrong answers, only answers reflecting the different personal experiences and views that people have in coping with their stresses and challenges. It's important that the group shouldn't be too large, to be sure to allow each person the opportunity to talk. If it is too large, consider breaking into smaller groups.

1. Who has been most supportive to me in helping me deal with this condition? What have they done or said that has helped me the most?

2. Who has been least supportive? What have they done or said that has not helped?

3. What did I used to think about people who had this problem before I knew I had it? What's the most important point that the public should know about this that they don't know now? How can or should they best be taught?

4. How did I feel and react when I was first told that I (or another family member) had _____? How has my attitude changed with time and experience?

5.   What was my family and friend's reaction to the news that I had _____? How did it differ from what I expected? From what I wanted?

6.   How do people react to me when they learn that I have _____? Have I been able to shape people's reactions to me? How?

7.   What would I say in a note or a letter to someone (or their spouse/family) who was facing what I have faced?

8.   What is the worst problem that I must face as a result of this?

9.   Who is the easiest person to talk to about this? Why? Who is the hardest person to talk to about this? Why?

10. If I am seeing a doctor, what could I tell him/her to better help me?

11. Generally, how has my life changed? What new values and priorities do I have now that I did not have before?

12. In what ways does the life event or illness control my life? In what ways have I learned ways to regain control of my life?

13. For what in my life am I most grateful? What do I now like most about my life?

14. What long term goals have I set for my life? What is the major goal and how do I plan to reach it?

15. If I have learned anything special about life or human nature as a result of my situation, what is it?

"Start your own community... It won't be easy. You'll be scared. You will often feel that you don't know what you're doing. You'll have a difficult time persuading people to join you... there will be anger, anxiety, depression, even despair. But keep going into the night. Don't stop halfway. It may seem like dying, but push on. And then suddenly you will find yourself in the clear of the mountaintop, and you'll be laughing and crying and feeling more alive than you have in years - maybe more alive than you've ever been."

- *M. Scott Peck, The Different Drum, 1987.*

SOME HELP FOR THE HELPER:
A GUIDE FOR THE GROUP CONTACT PERSON

- By Barbara White and Pat de la Fuente

As a contact person, you are the essential link between someone in need and your self-help group. When a prospective member finally gets the courage to call, your response can determine whether or not that person will come to your meeting. You will also be a crucial link to the public at large; your name and phone number will appear on your group's media announcements and flyers. Your responsibilities can seem overwhelming unless you have support--that's where this Guide comes in. Designed primarily for the new contact person, we hope this Guide will be useful to experienced contact people as well.

Some contact people with experience in self-help groups have already given us some good advice, which can be summed up as: "Know yourself." One group leader described the ideal contact person as "patient, compassionate, understanding." Another advises contacts to be "sensitive to other people's needs, but not so overly sensitive that you take their problems home with you." Other groups look for a "good listener--willing to listen to a 40-minute phone conversation;" "someone who knows when to share the load with others in the group;" "someone able to give full attention to a person in crisis." Chances are, if you and your group want you to be a contact person, you already have many of these qualities.

Most groups have found that callers are most comfortable talking with a contact person who shares their problems and is involved in the group. This is especially true of groups that deal with very sensitive issues such as incest, AIDS, child abuse, etc. In some instances, it is much more comfortable for the caller to be offered the option of talking with someone of the same gender, age group, or having the same condition or experience, etc. It is advisable that contact people have a good deal of experience dealing with their own situation, which places them in a much better position to be of help to others.

A few groups prefer a professional as the contact person to determine whether the caller can be helped by the group or requires an alternative such as individual therapy. However, a new person often prefers to talk to someone who has "been there." If, after doing some soul-searching, you feel that you know yourself and the needs of your group, this guide may be able to help you.

SETTING UP A TELEPHONE SYSTEM

As always, the best advice is: don't try to do it alone! Is there a way to rotate coverage of the phones? Can your flyers list two or more phone numbers? The phone company has a "call forwarding" service which, although expensive, may make it possible for several members to act as telephone contact people.

Answering Machines: Pros and Cons

Answering machines are great for taking messages when you are away. They can also give you the opportunity to return calls at your convenience, when you are not busy with personal matters and you have the emotional energy to respond to someone who needs support. If you do use an answering machine, the message should include:

-    Your name and the name of your group.
-    Date, time and place of the next meeting (updated regularly)
-    Best time for you to return the call
-    Name and phone number of another contact person, if available.

Try not to crowd the message tape with too much information; it can confuse the caller. When recording your outgoing message, be aware that cute, unusual, loud or outlandish messages can turn potential members away. And make sure you call back promptly.

But answering machines do have their drawbacks. Some callers are not comfortable leaving messages on machines, especially when talking about personal matters. Picking up the phone to make the call may have taken tremendous courage, and callers may become frustrated and discouraged when they hear a recorded message. Nothing can replace a caring human voice and a listening ear.

Answering Service

Some groups, particularly large organizations with many chapters, employ an answering service or local hotline to be used as the main number for callers seeking information about their groups. Although answering services can be efficient, and sometimes offer their services around the clock, they tend to be less personalized than contact people. They lack the firsthand experience with the group and the problem which helps people make the decision of whether or not they want to attend a meeting. Services can, however, offer the names and phone numbers of local members should someone want to talk. Answering services can be costly and have limitations; however, they are an alterative for groups who receive a lot of calls.

RESPONSIBILITIES OF A CONTACT PERSON

One experienced contact person described responsibility as "the ability to respond." Your response to callers can include listening to them, educating them about your group, encouraging them to come to group meetings, and referring them to other resources.

Listening

Being a good listener is probably the most important quality of a contact person. Here are some ways to brush up on your skills.

1. **Compliment the courage of the caller.** As a self-help group contact person you are often the first person the caller has reached out to and asked for help. Many people find it exceedingly difficult to admit they need help with a problem. To go one step further and ask a stranger for help is clearly a courageous act. To support a caller who may be extremely anxious during this initial contact, it is helpful to compliment the person on having the courage to call.

2. **Use the caller's name frequently.** If the caller has given you a first name, remember it and use it frequently during the phone conversation. This helps communicate a sense of caring about the caller and gives the conversation a friendly tone.

3. **Be an active listener.** Most of us need a little time before we feel comfortable enough to talk about sensitive issues. Encourage callers to tell their story and express their concerns and feelings without interrupting or pressuring them to get to the point. Bear in mind that sometimes a caller's true concerns will come up later in the conversation.

4. **Clarify the person's problem or need.** During the course of the conversation, clarify the caller's problems and expectations. If your group is not likely to meet the caller's expectations, let the person know and, if possible, refer them to a more appropriate resource.

5. **Be clear about your limitations.** Rather than present yourself as an "authority" on the issue, be yourself, another person who shares the caller's problem, and focus on sharing what has worked for you.

6. **Share some of your experience.** While sharing experiences is fundamental to self-help, during this initial contact, talk about your own situation only as it relates to the caller's experience. Refrain from overwhelming callers with your problems.

7.   **Follow through on promises.** The credibility of your group is at stake. If you make any promises (e.g. returning the call, sending literature, etc.), try to follow through as soon as possible. If you do not have the time, ask for some back-up from other group members.

Educating Callers About Your Group

You need to tell callers the purpose of your group and what it does and does not offer. Try to be as accurate as possible. Although you may be very enthusiastic about your group, too much enthusiasm during this initial contact, particularly regarding your group's philosophy or beliefs, can turn people away. Beware of overwhelming your caller.

Try to offer "cautious optimism". Often a caller believes that you and your group can "make it all better." You need to remind the person that recovery is an ongoing process which won't happen overnight (or ever), but you can also offer something positive such as "now you know that a support group exists, and we are here for you."

Callers will need factual information, such as the date, time and meeting place of your group. They may also have some basic questions such as:

1.   What is the purpose of your group? (e.g. is the main focus educational, mutual support, social, advocacy)

2.   What are the group members like? (e.g. How many people attend meetings, what is the ratio of males to females at meetings, what is the average age of members; etc.)

3.   Are the members' problems the same or similar to the caller's concerns? (e.g. How broad is the focus; has anyone experienced the same or similar loss, medical treatment, illness, problem, etc.)

4.   How does the group work? (e.g. Does it follow the 12-step program; is it facilitated by a professional; how is it structured, does everyone have to talk, are there guest speakers, etc.).

5.   Are there any fees associated with the group? (e.g. are their membership dues; do you pass the hat; do you need to buy literature; etc.)

Encouraging Callers to Attend Group Meetings

Since people often get nervous at the prospect of attending a meeting with a group of strangers, your job as contact person is to lesson some of that anxiety and make it possible for them to take that next step. Some useful strategies include:

1. **Acknowledge the caller's concerns** Letting a person know that most people feel nervous about coming to a first meeting can be reassuring to a caller. Offer to meet prospective members at the door of the meeting place a few minutes before the meeting begins to help them get acquainted. Just knowing that you will be greeted by a somewhat familiar person can help a person feel more comfortable.

2. **Describe a typical group meeting.** People tend to be more willing to approach new situations if they know what to expect. In describing a typical meeting include general information and a description of how a meeting works. Reassure the caller that the group respects a persons' decision not to participate in group discussion. This is particularly important for people who are anxious about talking in front of groups.

3. **Respect a caller's decision not to attend a meeting.** Let callers decide if and when they are ready to come to a meeting, and respect that decision. People who are initially hesitant sometimes need to give their situation a little more thought before they're ready to take that next step.

4. **Set limits on your availability to listen.** Since a group helps in ways that extend far beyond a phone call, keep in mind that your job is to help people take their next step toward helping themselves...joining a mutual help group.

Handling Difficult Calls and Helping Callers Through Difficult Situations

Experienced self-helpers understand that "difficult people" are actually just "people experiencing difficulty." These difficulties can be expressed in a variety of ways which may try your patience. Below are some suggestions for dealing with some of these other situations.

1. **Unwilling or "unready" to attend a meeting.** People dealing with a difficult situation may need to vent their anger and frustration during a contact call. After you have provided a caller with the opportunity to express feelings, the person may be ready to listen to suggestions and information about your group. But sometimes, after a lengthy talk or several phone calls, a person still may not want to attend a meeting. At that point, you can say they you cannot provide any more help, emphasize that the group can offer more information and support than you can provide over the phone. Don't be surprised if the person calls back later, relieved that someone finally listened, and is now ready to hear about a self-help group.

2. **Long Phone Calls.** If a caller starts to repeat previous statements or begins bringing up new information not relevant to support groups issues, it's time

to end the call. A useful technique for this situation is to let the caller know that you think what they are saying is important; so important in fact, that it should be saved for the whole group to hear. Another approach is to let the caller know that while you cannot stay on the phone, you will be happy to pick up this discussion at the next group meeting.

3. **Phone Calls at Inconvenient Times.** If you do not use an answering machine, you may be plagued by inquiries at times when you are least able to focus attention on the caller. One way of dealing with this situation is to gently say "I only have a few minutes to talk right now. I'd be happy to call you back at a later time." If the caller sounds upset, the value of a backup contact person is that you can refer them to another resource. Acknowledge the caller's feelings and needs and offer them the alternative (e.g. "You sound upset and I understand your need to talk right now. Unfortunately, I was just leaving but let me give you a number of another person that may be able to talk with you now"). Always let a caller know that you are sorry that you cannot talk with them at the moment, but that you would be very happy to talk with them when you have the time to really listen. Be careful not to sound as if you do not care or won't make the time to listen or you may lose a prospective member. On the other hand, don't berate yourself for not being able to be available all the time.

4. **A Person in Crisis.** For most contact people, veterans and newcomers alike, the most difficult caller you may encounter is the person who is suicidal or experiencing an emotional crisis. The call is difficult for a number of reasons, not the least of which is the contact person's concern for "doing the right thing." Keep in mind that as a contact person, it is not your job to provide crisis intervention. Your major goal is to try to calm the caller down so that you can refer them to an appropriate resource or collect enough information (e.g. name and location, to get a local emergency team to the caller).

If faced with a crisis call here are some pointers:

-   **Use a calm, reassuring voice.** A calm voice can help calm a distraught caller. Gently acknowledge their feelings, e.,g. "You sound upset. Just take your time we'll talk when you are ready" or "Why don't you take a couple of deep breaths to make you feel better." Let them know that it's all right that they are upset. Realize that it was probably very hard for them to call a stranger in their time of crisis, and they may even feel a little foolish. Helping the caller to feel more relaxed might enable them to explore with you other support networks they may have, such as family, clergy, mental health center, or friends. You may ask, "Can you talk to a family member about this?" or "Have you considered professional help to get over this rough time?"

- **Be empathetic.** Let the caller know that you understand and care. Make an occasional "Mmm hmm" so that they know you are listening. Let them do most of the talking.

- **Make referrals.** If they are still in crisis, refer them to local emergency resources (i.e. mental health center, hospital emergency room , police department, or hotline.). If a caller is in imminent danger of committing suicide, it is imperative that you try to find them professional help as quickly as possible.

- **Know your local resources.** This is not the time to go hunting for information. Always keep a current listing of local resources near your phone. It might be a good idea to call the local mental health centers, emergency rooms, and helplines beforehand to find out exactly what kind of services they provide, and how you can use them if you are ever faced with a crisis call. Call the phone company to find out if they offer any special codes to use to help the police track down calls.

- **Know your role and accept your limitations.** Many contact people participate in their group because they want to help other people. However, helping people to help themselves is not the same as rescuing. As a contact person, you are probably not trained in crisis intervention. You can listen to the person in crisis, and make referrals, but it is important to acknowledge your limitations.

- **Referring callers to other resources.** It vital to have a list of local resources when dealing with someone in crisis. In addition, you will probably find it helpful to maintain an updated list of community resources such as physicians, social workers, home health aides, etc.

Dealing with the Media

If your group is large enough, you may be able to have someone else handle phone calls from the media (newspapers, radio and television), while you attend to prospective members. Keep in mind that publicity of any kind is likely to generate a large number of phone calls, and you may be overwhelmed. Don't be afraid to ask other group members for help. It is your job to develop rapport with the media so your ability to discuss issues clearly and enthusiastically will be a great asset to your group.

Obscene Phone Calls

The best way to handle an obscene phone call is to hang up. Many times the caller's sole purpose is to get a reaction. If you merely hang up instead of responding or listening, the caller may stop calling. If the caller persists, contact the phone company. Making an obscene call is against the law.

PREVENTING BURNOUT

Burnout is a serious problem with no easy solutions. However, you can work to organize your group so that no one is unduly stressed. Suggested strategies to prevent burnout include:

- Have more than one contact person and rotate the name of the first person listed on any publicity material. This will provide a more even distribution of calls among your contact people with no one serving as the "one and only."

- Use one telephone number to give out names of contact persons to call. (You can even use an answering machine to give out the names and numbers of contact persons.) These names can be changed every month or so. This way, many members share the responsibility throughout the year.

- Limit the contact person's length of service. If your group receives many phone calls, it can help to know that you will be rotated off duty after a certain amount of time. Just anticipating the "foreverness" of the duty can accelerate burnout.

- Develop structured guidelines. Some groups develop specific guidelines on how to handle certain situations or types of calls (e.g. talking with the media, handling inappropriate callers, how long to talk with a caller, etc). This policy can relieve the contact of worrying too much about handling certain situations. Written guidelines also ensure continuity and consistency between contact persons and can serve as a training manual for members new to the group.

- Share with your group. As a final point, please keep in sight the fact that you are a member of a support group...people helping people. If you feel overburdened or it you are concerned about a particular call, share your feelings with the other members of your group. That's what it's all about.

~

THE SERENITY PRAYER

God grant me
the Serenity to accept the things I cannot change,
the courage to change the things I can,
and the wisdom to know the difference.

- Reinhold Niebuhr

DEVELOPING SELF-HELP GROUPS:
TEN STEPS & SUGGESTIONS FOR PROFESSIONALS

- Edward J. Madara

Among the variety of roles that professionals play in support of self-help groups - which range from providing referrals, to being a guest speaker or serving as a group advisor - no role is more challenging and productive over the long term than that of helping to create a new, free, on-going self-help group. It appears that about one out of every three self-help groups is started with some help from a professional. By the very nature of his or her work and specialty, the professional is in a favorable position to identify and link persons who have the potential to start a mutual help group.

For most professionals helping to start a free, on-going self-help group, the task involves their assuming what very well may be a new type of professional role--that of a consultant in a group organization. The following serves as an overview of ten basic steps that the professional can follow in helping self-help groups organize. These are suggested guidelines that have proven helpful to many professionals. It represents one general approach. Actual group development and the sequence of steps may vary slightly, based upon choice of a particular self-help group model or other special circumstances, preferences or opportunities. The ten steps are to:

1. Acquire a Basic Understanding of Self-Help Group Dynamics and Benefits. The professional who contemplates starting a self-help group is probably already aware of the general needs for such a group (e.g., social support, experiential knowledge, normalization, shared coping skills, helper-therapy, positive role models, etc.) and has recognized the way in which the group could supplement professional services. The professional needs to familiarize him/herself with the basic understanding of self-help group dynamics, and how they differ from professionally-run therapy or support groups. For a better understanding as to how self-help groups operate as mutual help organizations, the professional can refer to readings on mutual help (see bibliographical section). An excellent way to learn is simply to attend a local group that has meetings open to professionals.

2. Assess Current Groups and Models. If you have determined that a need exists for a particular type of self-help group, check as to what national or model self-help groups may already exist for that problem. At the same time, you also want to confirm that there is no local chapter or similar group already existing in your immediate area. A variety of these national and model self-help groups print development manuals or helpful "How to Start" guideline materials that you should obtain and review.

3.   <u>Identify Persons Interested in Starting a Group</u>. Identify at least two former/current patients or clients who have experienced the problem, and who express an interest "in starting" a group. Simply having persons interested "in joining" a group is not sufficient. Ideally you will want to include "veterans" who have had greater experience at coping with the problem and are willing to help others. Some opportunities for locating potential group founders include: contacts with other professionals and agencies; announcements at the conclusion of educational programs or conferences on the topic; and registration of your specific group interest in starting a group with your local self-help clearinghouse if there is one.

4.   <u>Form a Core Group</u>. Once several persons have been identified, the next step is to have a preliminary meeting to organize these persons into a "core group." The professional will want to confirm their interest and emphasize that this is a "mutual help" effort to create a mutual help group. All members of the core group should be expected to contribute in some way to the development of the group by sharing in the work. They should make this commitment to one another, possibly for a specific period of time.

5.   <u>Clarify and Negotiate the Relationship</u>. It is important at this preliminary meeting to clarify the professional's role in relationship to the development of the group. The most appropriate role for the professional to assume at this stage is that of a consultant. A common pitfall for professionals is to continue at this time to play the traditional role of leader, which promotes ongoing dependence on the professional, while also stifling the member's own sense of responsibility and ownership that spark the very energy and dynamics of most mutual help groups. The role of the consultant, the types of assistance available, and a time frame for providing consultation, should be explained and agreed upon with members of the core group. The consultation would focus primarily on group organization, but also might include help in resource identification, skills building, program development, and collaboration in problem solving. As in the case of any consultant, the professional provides advice and counsel, but does not assume responsibility for leadership, decision making or group tasks, unless the group requests such assistance. Some groups refer to this as being "on tap, not on top." The importance of the members themselves taking responsibility for the group, and the professional serving in an ancillary role, is key.

6.   <u>Advise on Planning and Publicizing First Public Meeting</u>. With the consultative relationship established, members of the core group should turn their attention to their first project - the first general meeting of the self-help group. Core group members should share responsibilities for the meeting. This they can do by sharing tasks such as serving as co-chairpersons, making arrangements for the meeting space, serving as greeter, making refreshments and coffee, etc. Shared responsibilities reduce

the high risk of "one leader burn-out" that is often faced when only one person assumes the responsibilities. More importantly, at that first meeting core members will "model," by their shared volunteer activities, what mutual help is--not one person doing it all, but shared responsibilities and contributions by members. Core group members can begin work on publicity, letters to the editor, putting notices in church bulletins, printing and distribution of flyers, etc. The professional can assist in promoting referrals to this first meeting by contacts with other key professionals, agencies and associations.

7.   <u>Assist at the First Meeting</u>. A professional's participation in the first meeting may vary from providing moral support to core group members who are chairing the meeting to addressing the group as a speaker, or possibly even being a co-leader if necessary. The role should be minimal in order to allow the group to exercise and develop its own group competencies. Time should be allowed for all members to introduce themselves and describe the needs they feel the group might address. It will take several meetings of trust-building before members take more initiative in contributing to group discussion and work. At the close of the first meeting there should be general consensus on the needs for a group and agreement on a suitable site and time for a second meeting. It is easier for people to remember future meeting times if it is held on a particular day of the week or month, e. g., the second Thursday of the month.

8.   <u>Advise on Plans for Subsequent Meetings and Continued Organizational Development</u>. The format for future meetings should include a portion of time devoted to the "business" of developing the organization, as well as discussion. Many groups include guest speakers, films, or special service projects as part of their educational program for members. For example, one service would be the establishment of an audio tape library of guest speaker presentations. Another would be development of a lending library of books and medical articles on the specific problem the group addresses. Future projects may include community education and visitation programs. The organizational structure for the group may be as formal or informal as members prefer--with or without elected officers and written by-laws. But general guidelines for group meetings and discussion, which the professional can help the group develop, are often helpful. Another helpful resource that the group can begin to develop is that of a professional advisory committee. The group itself may decide to establish several working committees, e.g., program, publicity, or study committees, to examine needs that were prioritized at the first meeting.

9.   <u>Identify and Address Any Special Problems</u>. With any consultation there often is the need to "trouble-shoot" or address new problems as they arise. The professional, as a consultant, can be very helpful in advising the group of solutions to problems that they may encounter, e. g., handling a member

who dominates discussion, or increasing membership through better publicity. Problem solving should usually be a collaborative effort with members. It is also important to note the responsibility for addressing these problems should continue to be focused on group competencies, rather than too quickly providing professional intervention at times critical to group development.

10. <u>Review and Evaluate Role</u>. At the conclusion of the consultation time period, an assessment of the consultation and a reassessment of the professional role should take place jointly between the consultant and consultee. If the group is operating without problems, the consultation may be terminated. At the request of the group, the professional may remain available on an ad hoc basis as a consultant. He or she may also assume a somewhat different role, such as a resource or agency liaison person who may continue to attend meetings to answer questions related more to their expertise rather than group process issues. At other times the professional may be called upon to assume additional temporary roles, such as serving as a trainer in skills-building.

In summary, an important factor in the development of a viable and self-sustaining mutual help group is the need for the professional to assume a consultation role. This permits the group members to assume responsibilities for the operation of the organization, for exercising and developing group competencies, and for addressing the felt and unmet needs of its members. The extent to which members perceive the group as "their own" will directly determine the amount of responsibility they take for it and the amount of investment they make in it. The importance of self-help, as ultimately reflected in the members' ability to take responsibility for the group, is crucial to developing and realizing many of the unique benefits that self-help groups have to offer. ♦

"Today, the benefits of mutual aid are experienced by millions of people who turn to others with a similar problem to attempt to deal with their isolation, powerlessness, alienation, and the awful feeling that nobody understands...The future of health care in these troubled times requires cooperation between organized medicine and self-help groups to achieve the best care for the lowest cost."

Former Surgeon General C. Everett Koop, for the Forward of the book, <u>Self-Help: Concepts and Applications</u>, Charles Press, 1992, p. xviii.

Chapter 3

FINDING AND JOINING
ONLINE MUTUAL HELP GROUPS

"It only takes an outstretched hand."
- Rod McKuen

WHERE IT'S AT - THE INTERNET

The number and variety of online mutual help groups continues to rapidly grow on the Internet. In the group descriptions here in the Sourcebook, you'll find that approximately 70% of the national and international groups already have web sites and/or e-mail addresses. Some of these community groups have web sites with interactive message boards, or they will cite related web sites, "mailing lists" and/or "newsgroups" that deal with their particular issues.

Therefore, to find an existing online support group, you may want to first see if the "real world" group description here in the Sourcebook has an e-mail address and/or a web page address. If the group has an e-mail address, you can send a message asking if they can refer you to any online self-help groups. If they have a web page, you can visit and see if they either have an interactive message board or a chat area there. Since most of the online support groups are not affiliated with an existing national group, they may have neither. Keep in mind that some self-help groups can be expected to change their online addresses. To check on possible updates, visit our American Self-Help Clearinghouse web site, which is kindly hosted within Mental Health Net at http://www.cmhc.com/selfhelp

Another key option is to check the Internet for existing groups. To find an existing online support network or group, visit the following web sites:

For mailing lists dealing with your issue:

    Liszt (http://www.liszt.com)
    List Of Lists (http://catalog.com/vivian)

For newsgroups and web pages:

    Dr. John Grohol's "Pointers Page" (http://www.grohol.com)

    Mental Health Net (founded by, and with helpful web page evaluations by Dr. Grohol and readers) use "Quickfind" (http://www.cmhc.com)

If you're not familiar with the jargon, we should explain that self-help support networks on the Internet take three major forms:

First, a "mailing list" or "listserv" delivers to each member (who has subscribed to that list) every message that is posted to that list by any other member. Every member gets every posting as a separate e-mail message.

To browse examples of mailing list messages from over 200 mailing lists that operate on the St. John's University server (due to the dedicated and wonderful work of Dr. Bob Zenhausern of the Psychology Department there), go to http://MAELSTROM.STJOHNS.EDU   and click on the "List Archives." Included here is the "BORDERPD" Borderline Personality Disorder Support Group (160 subscribers) and the "EC-GROUP" Esophageal Cancers Discussion (233 subscribers).

A second way that people share their experiences, strengths and hopes is through a newsgroup. There are many hundreds of "newsgroups." A newsgroup stores messages on a computer in a central location, which can be read and replied to by users. Examples of newsgroups include:

> Recovery from sexual abuse (alt.sexual.abuse.recovery)
> Moderated version (alt.sexual.abuse.recovery alt.abuse-recovery)
> Partners of sexual abuse survivors (alt.support.abuse-partners)
> Dystonia (abnormal muscle contractions) (alt.support.dystonia)
> For people with personality disorders (alt.support.personality)
> Post polio syndrome (alt.support.post-polio)

The third type of mutual help are the increasing number of **web sites** that are much more interactive than they web sites originally were, since they have added message boards and/or chat conference areas.   Here's a sample of interesting mutual help web sites:

Transformations (http://www.transformations.com) was started on the Internet by group leaders from eWorld when that commercial service ended. A wide variety of recovery and health support groups meet (and new group development is welcomed) here through both the scheduled live chat meetings and the message boards.

Med Help International (http://www.medhelp.org) has one of the most extensive consumer health libraries online, and has developed such innovations as "The Patient Network - putting patients in touch with other patients, for the purpose of sharing information & support," and the Cleveland Clinic Neurology Forum for the discussion of dozens of neurological disorders.

Madness (http://www.madnation.org) is the web site of mental health resources for the MADNESS listserv discussion group, which is one of the main listserv groups for mental health consumers/survivor.

Parents' Place (http://www.parentsplace.com) includes scheduled live chats for parents of teens, grandparents raising grandchildren, as well as At-Home Dads network.

Medsupport (http://medsupport.org) is a member-run mutual help web site with various forums and live chats (e.g., for multiple sclerosis, sarcoidosis, celiac disease, others).

SeniorNet "Round Tables" (http://www.seniornet.org). The "Health Matters" Round Table alone has some 30 discussion topics.

Ability Online (http://www.ablelink.org), first started by Dr. Arlette Lefebvre at Toronto's Sick Children's Hospital, is now run by children with chronic illnesses and disabilities who communicate with both their well and unwell peers.

THE COMMERCIAL COMPUTER SYSTEMS

Many people's first online experience is often with one of the commercial computer networks, like America-On-Line, CompuServe, Prodigy or MicrosoftNet. A drawback is that group meetings there are restricted only to paying members of that particular service--if their members can find the group. Despite their each operating a modern information service, they score poorly in providing centralized and comprehensive information on where a particular issue is discussed.

On the positive side, they all offer users the ability to: read, post and exchange messages within various forums; search various database libraries; conference and chat with others in one-to-one or "online" group meetings. Commercial services provide their own software which is relatively user-friendly. They charge various monthly fees for a minimum hours or unlimited services. All now provide varying access to the Internet and its many networks and resources.

America-On-Line has an extensive number of both message boards and real-time chat meetings. To find most of the live meetings, use the keyword "HEALTHLIVE" to see the weekly AOL live chat groups (which are unfortunately only listed by the day of the week rather than by the issue). While the use of their "keywords" continues to be limited mostly to forum names, the "Search" function that appears on their main page is better, but still limited.

A few examples of unique real-time groups on AOL are:

> Monday: **Thyroid Cancer Mutual Support Group**, 8pm ET; and the **Lymphoma Chat**, 11pm

> Tuesday: **Loved Ones of Cancer Survivors**, 7PM; and the **Avascular Necrosis & Chronic Muscular-Skeletal Diseases Support Group**, 10pm

> Wednesday: **Colon Cancer Mutual Support**, pm; and SISTERS (Survivors of Incest and Sexual Traumas Encouraging Recovery and Support), 9 pm

Thursday: **Kidney Cancer Mutual Support**, 10pm; and a **Friends With Eating Disorders Chat**, 11pm

Friday: **Post Traumatic Stress Disorder Support Group**, 11pm

Saturday: **Young Adults With Cancer**, 2pm

Sunday: **"Healing Hearts" (for Parents Who Lost Children to Heart Defects)**, 7pm; and a **Sinus Mutual Support Group**, 8pm

AOL networks or forums having a good number mutual-help groups include: Better Health & Medical Network, Online Psych, TalkWomen, Addiction & Recovery Forum, Parent Soup, disABILITIES Forum, and SeniorNet. Each forum has a message board, text databases, and software library.

CompuServe is the oldest commercial service, where mutual help takes place within a variety of forums: the Recovery Forum, Health & Fitness Forum, ADD (Attention Deficit Disorder) Forum, Human Sexuality Open Forum (has a shyness section as well as closed conferences requiring pre-registration for survivors of emotional, physical or sexual abuse), Cancer Forum (has message sections that are mostly arranged by specific types of cancer), Diabetes, and Disabilities Forum.

Prodigy has several forums for mutual aid, especially the Medical Support BB, and a variety of scheduled self-help meetings of different groups in its "Chat" section. Like with CompuServe, any individual can add a new subject heading at any time. Other Prodigy forums include the Health Board; the Crohn's and Colitis Forum, and the Veterans BB.

THE VALUE OF ONLINE GROUPS

Online support groups continue to overcome some of the traditional barriers to self-help group participation: the lack of an existing local group to attend, lack of transportation or time available for travel, rarity of the condition, 24-hour a day caregiver responsibility by the bedside, or the mobility limitations of even the most severe physical disability. People share from their hospice bed or their mountain bungalow. In the new information age, the personal computer hooked into a network is a very empowering tool.

While more online self-help groups or conferences are being held in real time, the most prevalent forms of mutual help are the message threads to be found in message sections on every system. These discussion threads take on the form of a self-help group in slow motion. Unlike real-time mutual help, responses are usually carefully and thoughtfully prepared offline before being posted in response.

In real-time conferencing, there is usually a facilitator who keeps track of whose turn it is to speak. Often the procedure is that people request to comment by typing an· "!" or indicate they have a question by typing a "?." Then the facilitator recognizes them in turn.

Currently, online communication is an equalizer. In communicating with other people online, there are no visual distractions. There are no signs of social status, age, dress, weight, race or appearance. People are seen for their words, ideas and emotions when they decide to express them. A partial substitute to aid in expressing emotions are a range of punctuations called "emoticons" used to express, e.g., a smile :-)   surprise : - o   or hugs for a person (((recipient's name))).

Many groups are also finding the online networks to be very helpful to advocacy efforts. According to Fred Fay, Director Emeritus of the National Spinal Cord Injury Association, passage of the Americans With Disabilities Act was made possible, in part, by the ongoing online updates shared among persons with disabilities, that identified key legislators to contact at critical points as the bill made its way through Congress.

As the number of persons online grows, it becomes easier for those who share a less common or a temporary health concern to meet. New types of support networks are developing online that do not exist in the community. For example, the number of people who recently had or were anticipating gall bladder surgery led to a "Gall Bladder Club" discussion section on Prodigy. Mothers with physical disabilities meet on America-On-Line to discuss issues such as how to best transport their child in their wheelchair with them. When no support groups existed in the community for veterans with Persian Gulf Syndrome problems, they discussed the issues online.

Networking has often been the first activity leading to the early identification of new or growing health/social problems, the organization of actual mutual aid self-help groups, and the development of more formal health and social service organizations. The seeds of many long-standing health foundations, societies, and agencies dealing with various health and social problems have historically first taken the form of mutual aid self-help groups or networks. These community support services were often created by individuals and/or families as they networked with one another and became aware of both their common needs and their abilities to help one another through group support and action. These small informal networks are often the first to provide support, information, skills sharing, education of professionals, and needed advocacy. The increased use of such computer networks could therefore help promote the more rapid and increased development of new self-help organizations that provide needed support, education, and advocacy for new or developing health issues or problems. Online support networks, especially for the less common or newer illnesses, serve as "lightning rods" for registries or needed research pools. In collaboration with professionals online, groups can also provide beneficial feedback for improving services and systems. So if you are interested in starting a needed new support network online that doesn't yet exist, in addition to the next chapter by Dr. Grohol on how to start an online support group, please call us at the Clearinghouse for additional suggestions.

OTHER WAYS THE INTERNET MIGHT BE HELPFUL TO YOU

To find **research medical journals and literature,** a number of web sites offer free **Medline** searches, (e.g., Mental Health Net http://www.cmhc.com/medline)

Need to check out the precise location of that group meeting you may want to visit, but aren't sure where it is located?   Use the Lycos **"Roadmap"** (http://www.lycos.com/roadmap.html) which provides instant maps for anywhere in United States based upon the street address you enter. Yahoo has a version too. Try zooming in and out, then print and/or e-mail map to another.

Interested in, or planning to conduct **professional research of self-help groups**? There's the "Discussion of Research into Self-Help and Mutual Support" mailing list.   To   subscribe   to   SLFHLP-L   send   them   an   e-mail   message (listserv@listserv.utoronto.ca). In the message section, type "SUB SLFHLP-L YourFirstName YourLastName."

Want information on **clinical research trials** that are available?   See the CenterWatch web site (http://www.centerwatch.com), Register to receive e-mail information on new trials as they are announced for your disorder.

For   **consumer   health   and   drug   information,**   "HealthTouch" (http://www.healthtouch.com/) is used in many pharmacies across the country.

Self-care information (http://www.healthy.net/selfcare) includes Dr. Ferguson's "DocTom's Self-Care Online Journal" and Medical Self-Care for Common Health Conditions.

Tools for Non-Profit Organizations (http://www.contact.org/tools/tools.htm)

Fundraising   Resources   on   the   Net   (http://www.clark.net/pub/pwalker/ Fundraising_and_Giving/)

In summary, the range of online networks is providing more individuals worldwide with peer support and information they need.   Online systems are overcoming barriers of distance, time, and disability.   Community centers and social agencies will hopefully join public libraries in providing needed access to computers for those who cannot afford them.   Overall, better understanding and use of these empowering tools and networks will expand mutual help networks worldwide to better meet people's needs and improve the quality of our lives.

Chapter 4

STARTING A NEW ONLINE
SUPPORT GROUP

John M. Grohol, Psy.D.

(John Grohol, Ph.D., is founder of Mental Health Net, and has authored The Insider's Guide to Mental Health Resources Online; New York: Guilford Press, 1997, a comprehensive guide evaluating different Internet resources in psychology, psychiatry, self-help and patient education.)

Unlike anything else in this world, the Internet offers people the ability to connect personally with one another through self-help support groups covering a wide variety of medical and mental health concerns. New groups which address concerns not currently covered by an existing online group are easily created. All it takes is a short amount of your time and the desire to create a gathering place for people with a specific disorder. This article pools together all the experience and knowledge about the Internet I've gained over the past few years, and organizes it so that you can create an online self-help support group with minimal effort.

Just three easy steps are needed to create a new self-help support group online.

1. DOES A RESOURCE ALREADY EXIST ONLINE FOR YOUR CONCERN?

Just a note about language used throughout this article. When referring to a "concern" or topic," I'm speaking of topics such as "depression," "panic attacks," "cancer support," etc. These are very much real disorders which cause very real pain in many people's lives.

Before venturing off into the great Internet wilderness and chopping down trees helter skelter to build your log house that will act as a refuge for all abuse survivors, you'd better make sure that:

A) someone else doesn't already own the land; and,
B) another house doesn't already exist for those same individuals.

It's easy to overlook this step in one's haste to find or create new support groups online. Providing a simple way to determine if a support group already exists is precisely the reason I began compiling all the Pointers on my Web site (*http://www.grohol.com/*). The newsgroup and mailing list Pointers are simple indices of online support groups.

The support groups that have been created on the Internet historically have tended toward the more rare conditions. Of course, some old newsgroups, such as alt.support.depression, are the exception to this. Mailing lists especially seem to be more oriented toward rare conditions than are newsgroups, because of the intention and philosophical differences between these two types of communication. I'll explain more about that distinction below.

If you've looked at my Pointer indices and didn't find any newsgroups or mailing lists devoted to your topic, it is a wise idea to look around just a little bit further to make sure nothing else already exists online which addresses this support topic. Doing your "homework" now will benefit your case and argument later if you choose to go the newsgroup route. It really makes little difference if you're creating a mailing list, except that you could be possibly duplicating the work and effort of someone else for little reason.

To ensure your proposed group doesn't already exist somewhere online, I recommend going on the Web and doing a little research on three specific Web sites. These sites are all "keyword" searchable. Therefore, don't waste any time exploring them. Go right to their respective search options and type in your keyword(s). For our example of survivors of people who suffered from a heart attack, these keywords may be things like: *heart attack support group*. (Generally, you should stay away from using plurals when using a search engine.)

These are the three resources you should check:

- Liszt (*http://www.liszt.com*) For mailing list topics. I typed in "heart attack" and found nothing.
- Alta Vista Web Search Engine (*http://www.altavista.digital.com*) I typed in "heart attack support group" and found a lot of articles on heart attacks, but nothing really mentioning support groups for survivors or the like.
- Mental Health Net Subject Guide (*http://www.cmhc.com*) I typed in "heart attack support group" and found nothing of use.

It may also be helpful to check your local list of newsgroups (for instance, through your Web browser, if it supports such an option) to see if any newsgroup name stands out as being perhaps appropriate for your topic. I can't tell you how exactly to do this, because Web browsers and newsgroup software are all very different.

You can also check out any other search engine you may like on the Web (such as Yahoo or Lycos), just to be on the safe side, but it's not necessary. At this point, we looked around pretty thoroughly for this topic and couldn't find it anywhere.

Now what?

2. DO I WANT TO CREATE A MAILING LIST, A NEWSGROUP OR SOMETHING ELSE?

Mailing lists are discussions which are conducted entirely through one's e-mail box. Since most everyone who owns a computer also has e-mail capabilities, you can likely subscribe to an Internet mailing list with little trouble. Discussion takes place when people who are signed up for the list (or "subscribed" to it, like a magazine subscription, but at no charge) write to the "list." This "list" is nothing more than a particular e-mail address; the e-mail address points to a piece of software on a machine somewhere. This special software takes mail written to it and simply sends a copy of it out to everyone else also subscribed to the list. In this simple manner, a discussion can take place electronically. You write to the list, everyone else sees your message as a piece of e-mail in their e-mail box. Then, perhaps someone replies to it and sends their reply to the list too. The next day, you go to read your e-mail and ta-da! The reply is sitting there waiting in your e-mail box. People like mailing lists because they're very easy to use since all you need do is sit back and watch your e-mail box fill up with messages.

I believe that people also like mailing lists because they tend to cater more to smaller groups of people. A "small" group in this context may consist of between 30 and 500 people, and very rarely over 1,000 individuals. In contrast, the average readership of a newsgroup (explained in greater detail below) ranges anywhere from 15,000 to 100,000 individuals daily. While 300 people may seem like a lot for a support group, it's not nearly so bad when you take into account that all the people who subscribe to a particular mailing list don't write (or "post," as they say online) something to it every day. In fact, only 1 out of every 20-30 people on a mailing list post to it on any given day. Ten to fifteen messages per day can be expected from a 300-person mailing list.

Mailing lists are also more private than newsgroups. Whereas anything written on a newsgroup is out there for the whole world to read and reply to, mailing lists exist only in people's e-mail boxes. A person has to specifically go out of their way to find a mailing list, and then send a specific command to be able to subscribe to the list. This means a mailing list can be relatively more intimate and feel more private.

The disadvantage to setting up and running a mailing list is that it can be time-consuming and frustrating. The system you use to access the Internet (whether it's through a university, a local Internet service provider (ISP), America OnLine or Prodigy, a free-net, or some other service) must be able to support the creation of mailing lists with special software. If the system doesn't currently have that software, it is easily obtained. You will, however, have to convince the people who administer your Internet service that it would be beneficial for them to get it. Then you'll have to learn how to use it (it comes with instructions). Each piece of software is different, so again, I cannot offer many specifics here. Some examples of popular mailing list software are Majordomo, listserv and listproc. Mailing lists can be easy to set up and maintain, or they can be the hardest thing you've ever done online; much depends on the helpfulness of your system administrators and your own familiarity and comfort with computers.

Newsgroups, on the other hand, are relatively hassle-free once they've been created. Their creation, however, is their main drawback. Whereas it only takes a willing system administrator and the right software (usually already installed) for a mailing list to be created instantly today, newsgroups go through a strange, archaic process of creation which varies dramatically depending upon the type of newsgroup you'd like to create.

"Newsgroups" is the term for the Internet's public discussion forums or "bulletin boards," and they are collectively known as "Usenet." When people speak of Usenet, they're talking about the newsgroups part of the Internet (just like there's also a Web part, a gopher part, an ftp part, etc.). Newsgroups are arranged into hierarchies. For instance, the newsgroup sci.psychology.misc resides in the meta-hierarchy of sci (for science), and the sub-hierarchy of psychology. The misc. stands for miscellaneous, or a catch-all group for any scientific topic related to psychology. There are two main types of newsgroups: Those that are in the "Big 8" hierarchy and those that are not (for instance, "alt" newsgroups). The Big 8 is a term to describe the original, basic seven hierarchies that evolved (recently an eighth was added) over the years: sci, news, misc, comp, rec, talk, soc, and humanities. Newsgroups that exist in one of these hierarchies are only created after a standard set of guidelines are followed, a vote is taken of anybody who cares to vote online, and the group passes or fails its vote. Since this is a whole culture unto itself, I cannot go into the details of how to do this (or, more interestingly, why it exists at all). If you're really brave and interested in this sort of thing, read the following newsgroups: news.groups and news.answers and anything else in the news. hierarchy. There are many FAQs (Frequently Asked Question files) which exist online that answer any questions you may have about this process.

For this article, we're more concerned with are newsgroups outside of this Big 8 hierarchy, and specifically, those in the "alt" hierarchy. Alt was conceived as an alternative to the rigid creation guidelines of the Big 8, allowing people to virtually create new newsgroups at will. Of course, even this has its own culture and set of informal guidelines.

What are the differences between a newsgroup which resides in one of the "Big 8" hierarchies and one which exists in the "alt" hierarchy? The advantage to a Big 8 newsgroup is that once one of these newsgroups passes its vote, it is created virtually world-wide as a legitimate newsgroup which most people can easily access. The disadvantage to creating a Big 8 group is that it takes at least 2 to 3 months to go through the process, and it helps to know the process intimately (by reading news.groups and becoming familiar with the newsgroup creation guidelines) to ensure passage. The advantage to the "alt" hierarchy is that a newsgroup can usually be created within a week or two after being proposed, but its propagation throughout the world is more limited. This is because many sites don't carry every newly-created "alt" group anymore unless specifically requested by one of the their users, because there are so many new ones created every week.

Many sites, regardless of the worth of certain "alt" groups, reject the entire alt hierarchy outright because of some of the negative things found within it (e.g., the "alt.sex." sub-hierarchy). This means that some users may never be able to see or read your new newsgroup. It's a tricky decision to make, but most people go with the "alt" creation anyway because it's so much easier and quicker.

While newsgroups can also be moderated (where an individual is designated to screen all articles before they get sent to the newsgroup), this is again a complicated process which I cannot go into here. Moderation is a great idea for low volume newsgroups, but it doesn't make much sense in most support groups, since they tend to be of higher volume.

Unlike mailing lists, newsgroups are open to the whole world. While this is good in terms of reaching more people who might need the group's help, it's also bad because it attracts some rather unpleasant people from time to time. These individuals often think people need to "just get over it," whatever "it" is. Others want to sell the readers of the group stuff. Others will offer a miracle cure. Others will suggest turning to a cult. Newsgroups attract all sorts of people, but they can usually be handled with some finesse.

Some of these things also occur on mailing lists, so this reason alone shouldn't deter you from starting a new newsgroup.

There are additional forms of support online you should be familiar with, but won't discuss in detail here. Discussion groups that occur exclusively on Web sites that anyone may access are becoming more popular nowadays, but you need to have a Web site (or know someone who will start such a forum for you) to be able to take advantage of this. An interactive, real-time chat is also popular for some topics, but it usually takes some publicity and a fair amount of planning to achieve "critical mass" (e.g., enough people in the chat to make it feel worthwhile to the participants). These live chats usually come from a mailing list or newsgroup, not the other way around. Mental Health Net (*http://www.cmhc.com*) is a large Web site which hosts both Web-based discussion groups and Web-based chats.

3. CREATE IT!

<u>Mailing Lists</u>: Mailing lists are simple to create because most systems already have the software necessary to run them. All you need to do then is contact someone in charge at your Internet service provider's company (a system administrator, customer service representative, etc.) and explain that you'd

like to create a mailing list for other survivors of people who suffered from a heart attack.

They will assist you in setting up the mailing and will provide you with the necessary instructions to run it. If the service representative does not know how to help you, you can either:

A) nicely harass the people in charge to get the mailing list software and install it on their system so you can set up this list;
b) find a willing service provider online who can set up the mailing list for you (St. John's University is one such place. Contact Dr. Robert Zenhausern on the Web at *http://rdz.stjohns.edu/*); or
c) create a newsgroup instead.

After you've gotten it created, there's a mailing list devoted to disseminating announcements of new mailing lists only. You'll want to place an announcement on this mailing list to get the word out about your new group. Send an e-mail message to: *new-list@listserv.nodak.edu*; the subject should read: Name of list - Short description. Include a fuller description of the list, its purpose, contact information, and subscription information in the body of your e-mail. Many system administrators already know about this list and will take care of posting your announcement to it. Don't forget to choose a name for your mailing list. It can be anything, but something simple yet descriptive is usually best. For our example, we may choose something like "Heart-Attack Survivors" and the subscription name might be shorter than that, such as simply "heartsurvivors." The full name of the list and the subscription name can be different, but the subscription name should be one word and easy to associate with your subject.

<u>ALT News Groups:</u> The following pertains only to the creation of "alt" newsgroups found in the "alt" hierarchy. It doesn't pertain to any other type of newsgroup or hierarchy.

First, make sure you can subscribe to the newsgroup called "alt.config." This newsgroup is where discussion takes place about creating new "alt" newsgroups. You're not going to get very far if you can't read this newsgroup for at least a few days. Read the newsgroup for a few days and look for a FAQ (Frequently Asked Questions file) that has a title of "So You Want To Create an Alt Newsgroup" (also currently available on the Web at: *http://www.cis.ohio- state.edu/~barr/alt-creation-guide.html*). Read it carefully.

You need to choose a name for your proposed newsgroup. Read the "How to Name a Newsgroup" file (*http://www.tezcat.com/~haz1/alt/naming.html*) to find out how to pick an appropriate name for your new group. Our sample topic has been survivors of people who suffered from a heart attack. That's not all going to fit in a newsgroup name, especially when most newsgroup names are nothing fancier than "alt.support.depression" or "alt.support.cancer." The name should not contain any abbreviations or any part longer than 14 characters. The only really accepted punctuation used in a name is a dash. Periods should not be used to spell out a sentence or a term. So alt.support.survivors.of.people. who.suffered.from.a.heart.attack isn't a valid name (and will be laughed out of alt.config if you suggested it!). Neither is alt.support.survivors-of-people- who-suffered-from-a-heart-attack because that last part with all those dashes is definitely more than 14 characters.

Now, post your first message to "alt.config" describing your desire to create a new "alt" newsgroup:

> *Subject: Proposal: alt.support.survivors.illness*
>
> *I would like to propose the creation of a new alt.support group for the discussion and support of family members and individuals who have suffered through any type of illness, such as heart attacks or strokes. I already looked extensively online for a support group which covers this topic and found nothing which was specifically designed to help survivors of general medical and mental health conditions. I think this group, then, would fulfill this need.*
>
> *I'm not sure whether the name should be alt.support. survivors.illness or alt.support.illness.survivors. Suggestions and comments are appreciated.*

I decided to go with a broader category in my final name, because one of the things I learned in alt.config is that broader general categories such as this one are more likely to gain broader general support from the readers of alt.config. In the body of your message, you should again state the name of the proposed group and a rationale for wanting it created. This can include "Because there's nothing else out there for people looking for support as survivors of loved ones who suffered from a heart attack." This is where your previous research really pays off big time, because nobody can contradict this argument. You may also wish to explain why this topic is not better suited for a mailing list. It's usually sufficient to say that you don't have mailing list resources available to you (if that's true), or some other similar reason. Encourage others to voice their support about the topic and/or the proposed group name.

Someone will usually reply to your article in the newsgroup within the next few days. One of these replies is usually from one of the alt.config "regulars" who helps guide the creation of new alt groups. These people change from year to year, as some get tired of doing it and others take their place. I try and read alt.config on a regular basis and reply to any alt.support. or alt.psychology. proposal. Usually such replies are going to be supportive, with suggestions for a slightly different name being the most common reply. Be flexible! Don't get so hooked on a newsgroup name that you let this nitpick sink your proposal. If you find another name you can go with in this discussion, repost your proposal after about a week with the new name specified.

Once discussion has ended (if it's not a particularly controversial newsgroup topic or name, which most support groups aren't), it will take another week or two before control messages, which actually create the newsgroup, are sent out. Again, regulars of alt.config, including myself, regularly do these as well without needing to be asked. It takes another few days for that control message which creates the newsgroup to reach your particular site, and even then, as discussed previously, your site may still not automatically create the new newsgroup. You may then have to send a polite e-mail to your Internet service provider's news administrator or customer service representative (again!?) and ask them to create this new newsgroup at your site. This communication may not be necessary, but if you haven't seen your new support group at your site a week or so after discussion has ended, then you might have to do it. This e-mail might look like:

I recently suggested that alt.support.survivor.illness be created on alt.config. After discussion had ended, it was agreed that this would be a beneficial group to create, and so some people created it two weeks ago. Unfortunately, I haven't seen it show up on our site here yet, so I was wondering if you could create it locally so that I may be able to access it and the support it offers to me and thousands of other people around the world. Thank you very much.

Your support group has been created!

You can now also hopefully access it at your site to read messages and post to it. You should post an introductory message in it and if you wrote a charter for the newsgroup, post it now too. A charter--which is not necessary for alt groups, but might be beneficial nonetheless--is just a short description of what is and is not appropriate for posting to the newsgroup. Introduce yourself and invite others to post something in reply.

The wonders of self-help groups online await you. These guidelines will hopefully make it a little bit easier for you to accomplish what seems at first to be very difficult, but in reality is relatively simple. There are no guarantees here, though, and your support group, whether a mailing list or a newsgroup, still may fail if nobody reads it or posts messages to it. It helps to advertise it around on other newsgroups and mailing lists, let other people know it exists, and encourage people to join in the discussion. Sometimes it just takes one person to make all the difference in the world. You can be that one. Good luck.

Chapter 5

A REVIEW OF RESEARCH ON THE EFFECTIVENESS OF SELF-HELP / MUTUAL AID GROUPS

Elaina M. Kyrouz, Ph.D. and Keith Humphreys, Ph.D.
Veterans Affairs Health Care System
and Stanford University School of Medicine
Palo Alto, California

For the past few decades, researchers have been evaluating the effects of self-help/mutual aid groups on participants. Most research studies of self-help groups have found important benefits of participation. Unfortunately, few of these studies have gotten into the hands of self-help group members, clearinghouse staff and others who wish to advocate for self-help/mutual aid. The purpose of this chapter is to help correct this problem by summarizing the best research supporting the effectiveness of self-help groups in a brief and clear fashion.

As we read over research on the effects of mutual help groups, we noticed a common confusion. Many studies that claim to study self-help groups are actually studies of psychotherapy or support groups solely led by a professional who does not share the condition addressed by the group. We excluded such studies from this review. Instead, we focused on groups where the participants all shared some problem or condition and ran the group on their own. In a very few cases, we included studies where a group was co-led by a professional and by a self-helper. Professional involvement in an advisory or assistance capacity did not rule a study out of consideration, because in the real world, many member-run self-help groups use professional advisors.

We have been selective about the methodological strengths of the studies we chose to summarize. Many studies have demonstrated that if the current members of any self-help group are surveyed at any given time, the members will respond positively about the group and say that it helps them. Such studies (which are sometimes called "single-group cross-sectional surveys") have some value, but they do not tell us much about how members change over time, or whether members change more than non-members. For this reason, we focus here primarily on studies that compared self-help participants to non-participants, and/or gathered information repeatedly over time (that is, "longitudinal" studies). Because we focus on studies with these characteristics, the following is only a subset of research on self-help effectiveness. At the same time, relative to the research literature as a whole, it is a methodologically stronger subset of studies. Hence, this should make the results presented here more convincing to people outside and inside of the self-help movement.

In the brief summaries below, we have tried to use as little jargon as possible. One exception to this rule is to use the scientific convention of using the letter "N" to refer to the number of people participating in each research project. For the sake of space and simplicity, we have generally omitted most details about how the study was conducted and about secondary and non-significant findings. Readers who wish to have further details about any particular study can use the reference information provided to locate the original sources.

RESEARCH REVIEWS

MENTAL HEALTH GROUPS

Edmunson, E.D., J.R. Bedell, et al. (1982). Integrating Skill Building and Peer Support in Mental Health Treatment: The Early Intervention and Community Network Development Projects. Community Mental Health and Behavioral Ecology. A.M. Jeger and R.S. Slotnick. New York: Plenum Press: 127-139.

After ten months of participation in a patient-led, professionally supervised social network enhancement group, one-half as many former psychiatric inpatients (N=40) required rehospitalization as did non-participants (N=40). Participants in the patient-led network also had much shorter average hospital stays (7 days vs. 25 days). Furthermore, a higher percentage of members than non-members could function with no contact with the mental health system (53% vs. 23%).

Raiff, N. R. (1984). "Some Health Related Outcomes of Self-Help Participation." Chapter 14 in The Self-Help Revolution, edited by Alan Gartner and Frank Riessman. New York: Human Sciences Press.

Highly involved members of Recovery, Inc. (N=393, mostly female and married), a self-help group for former mental patients, reported no more anxiety about their health than did the general population. Members who had participated for two years or more had the lowest levels of worry and the highest levels of satisfaction with their health. Members also rated their life satisfaction levels as high or higher than did the general public. Members who had participated less than two years, were still on medication, lived below the poverty level, or lacked social-network involvements also appeared to benefit from group participation, although to a lesser degree.

Kennedy, M. (1990). **Psychiatric Hospitalizations of GROWers. Paper presented at the Second Biennial Conference on Community Research and Action, East Lansing, Michigan.**

This study found that 31 members of GROW, a self-help organization for people with chronic psychiatric problems, spent significantly fewer days in a psychiatric hospital over a 32-month period than did 31 former psychiatric patients of similar age, race, sex, marital status, number of previous hospitalizations and other factors. Members also increased their sense of security and self-esteem, decreased their existential anxiety, broadened their sense of spirituality, and increased their ability to accept problems without blaming self or others for them.

Galanter, M. (1988). **"Zealous Self-Help Groups as Adjuncts to Psychiatric Treatment: A Study of Recovery, Inc." American Journal of Psychiatry 145(10): 1248-1253.**

This study surveyed 356 members of Recovery, Inc., a self-help group for nervous and former mental patients, and compared them to a 195 community residents of similar age and sex. Although about half of the Recovery Inc. members had been hospitalized before joining, only 8% of group leaders and 7% of recent members had been hospitalized since joining. Members used more outpatient non-psychiatric resources than did the community sample.

Kurtz, L. F. (1988). **"Mutual Aid for Affective Disorders: The Manic Depressive and Depressive Association." American Journal of Orthopsychiatry 58(1): 152-155.**

This study found that 82% of 129 members of the Manic Depressive and Depressive Association reported coping better with their illness since joining the self-help group. The longer they were members and the more intensely they were involved with the group, the more their coping had improved. Further, the percentage of members reporting being admitted to a psychiatric hospital before joining the group was 82%, but the percentage reporting hospital admission after joining was only 33%.

Lieberman, M. A., Solow, N. et al. (1979). **"The psychotherapeutic impact of women's consciousness-raising groups." Archives of General Psychiatry 36: 161-168.**

32 participants in women's consciousness-raising groups were studied over a 6 month period. Over the course of the study, participants reported decreased distress about their target problem, increased self-esteem, and greater self-reliance. They also reported greater identification with feminist values and politics.

WEIGHT LOSS GROUPS

Grimsmo, A., G. Helgesen, et al. (1981). "Short-Term and Long-Term Effects of Lay Groups on Weight Reduction." British Medical Journal 283: 1093-1095.

These researchers conducted three studies of mostly female participants in 8-week peer-led weight-loss groups in Norway (Grete Roede Slim-Clubs). The first study gathered information from 33 women before, during, immediately after, and 1 year after participation. Participants lost an average of 14.3 pounds while they were in the group, and had kept almost all of it from coming back by the end of the year (they had an average of 12.1 pounds less weight). The second study surveyed 1000 people who had completed the group from 1 to 5 years previously, and found that average weight loss remained stable for the first couple of years and was still 5 - 6% below starting weight after 5 years. The third study surveyed more than 10,000 participants before and immediately after participation, and found an average weight loss of 15.2 pounds.

Peterson, G., D.B. Abrams, et al. (1985). "Professional Versus Self-Help Weight Loss at the Worksite: The Challenge of Making a Public Health Impact." Behavior Therapy 16: 213-222.

This study compared 30 employees assigned to a professionally-led weight-loss group with 33 employees assigned to a peer-led group. Both groups used "Learn to Be Lean" workbooks based on behavioral therapy principles. Members of both groups lost weight in equal amounts over a six-month period. The peer-led group was only half as costly as the professional-led group.

ADDICTION-RELATED GROUPS

Alemi, F., Mosavel, M. Stephens, R., et al. (1996). "Electronic Self-Help and Support Groups." Medical Care 34(Supplement): OS32-OS44.

This was a study of 53 pregnant women who had a history of drug use. Participants, most of whom were African-American, were assigned either to attend face-to-face biweekly self-help group meetings (N=25) or to participate in self-help meetings operated over a voice bulletin board accessed by phone (N=28). In the bulletin board group, participants could leave voice mail messages for the entire group to hear. Significantly more women participated in the voice mail group (96% of those assigned) than in the face-to-face self-help groups (32% of those assigned). Bulletin board participants made significantly fewer telephone calls and visits to health care clinics than did individuals assigned to participate in the face-to-face group. Both groups had similar health status and drug use at the end of the study.

Christo, G. and S. Sutton (1994). "Anxiety and Self-Esteem as a Function of Abstinence Time Among Recovering Addicts Attending Narcotics Anonymous." British Journal of Clinical Psychology 33: 198-200.

Members of Narcotics Anonymous (NA) self-help groups (N=200) who stayed off drugs for three years or more while they were members showed no more anxiety and no less self-esteem than a comparison group of 60 never-addicted students. The longer people remained members while staying off drugs, the less anxiety and the more self-esteem they experienced.

Emrick, C. D., J. S. Tonigan, et al. (1993). Alcoholics Anonymous: What is Currently Known? In Research on Alcoholics Anonymous: Opportunities and Alternatives, edited by Barbara S. McCrady and William R. Miller. New Brunswick, NJ: Rutgers Center of Alcohol Studies, pp. 41-75.

Using meta-analysis of more than 50 studies, these authors report that AA members stayed sober more if they (1) had an AA sponsor, (2) worked the "twelfth step" of the program, (3) led a meeting, (4) increased their degree of participation over time, or (5) sponsored other AA members. The study also found that professionally treated alcoholic patients who attend AA during or after treatment are somewhat more likely to reduce drinking than are those who do not attend AA. Membership in AA was also found to reduce physical symptoms and to improve psychological adjustment.

Hughes, J. M. (1977). "Adolescent Children of Alcoholic Parents and the Relationship of Alateen to These Children." Journal of Consulting and Clinical Psychology 45(5): 946-947.

This study compared 25 Alateen members with 25 non-members who had an alcoholic parent and 25 non-members with no alcoholic parent. Adolescents with an alcoholic parent who were members of Alateen experienced significantly fewer negative moods, significantly more positive moods and higher self-esteem than those who were not members. In fact, Alateen members had self-esteem and mood scores similar to those of adolescents who did not have an alcoholic parent.

Humphreys, K., B. E. Mavis, and B. E. Stoffelmayr (1994). "Are Twelve Step Programs Appropriate for Disenfranchised Groups? Evidence from a Study of Posttreatment Mutual Help Involvement." Prevention in Human Services 11(1): 165-179.

One year after being admitted to a public substance abuse treatment agency, Caucasian- and African-Americans were attending mutual help (Narcotics Anonymous, Alcoholics Anonymous) groups at the same rate. African-American participants (N=253) in NA and AA self-help groups showed significant improvements over twelve months in six problem areas (employment, alcohol, drug, legal, psychological, and family). African-American self-help group participants had significant more improvement in their medical, alcohol, and drug problems than did African-American patients who did not participate in self-help groups after treatment.

Humphreys, K. and R. H. Moos (1996) "Reduced Substance-Abuse-Related Health Care Costs among Voluntary Participants in Alcoholics Anonymous." Psychiatric Services, 47, 709-713.

Over a period of three years, alcoholics who initially chose to attend AA were compared to those who sought help from a professional outpatient treatment provider (total N=201). Those who chose to attend AA had 45% ($1826) lower average per-person treatment costs than did those who chose outpatient treatment. Despite the lower costs, AA attenders also experienced significant improvements in alcohol consumption, dependence symptoms, adverse consequences, days intoxicated and depression. These outcomes did not differ significantly from those of alcoholics who chose professional treatment. This was true both at one year and at three years after the beginning of the study.

Jason, L. A., C. L. Gruder, et al. (1987). "Work Site Group Meetings and the Effectiveness of a Televised Smoking Cessation Intervention." American Journal of Community Psychology 15: 57-77.

This study compared the effects of two smoking cessation programs at work. One hundred and ninety-two workers viewed a television program and used a self-help manual, while 223 workers had these materials supplemented by 6 self-help group meetings. Group meetings were led by recruited smoking employees who had been given a three-hour training session in how to lead groups. The two programs were implemented at 43 companies. Initial rates of quitting smoking were significantly higher for the 21 companies that used self-help groups (average of 41% vs. 21% of participants). Group participants also smoked significantly fewer cigarettes per day, with lower tar, nicotine and carbon monoxide content. Three months later, an average of 22% of group participants had continued not to smoke, compared to 12% in companies with no self-help groups.

McAuliffe, W. E. (1990). "A Randomized Controlled Trial of Recovery Training and Self-Help for Opiod Addicts in New England and Hong Kong." Journal of Psychoactive Drugs 22(2): 197-209.

This study randomly assigned volunteer graduates from substance abuse treatment programs (N=168) to participate in RTSH (Recovery Training and Self-Help), an aftercare program that combined professionally led recovery-training sessions with peer-led self-help sessions. Participants in the recovery program significantly reduced their likelihood of relapse into opiod addiction compared to those who received only referrals to other programs and crisis-intervention counseling. The RTSH program helped unemployed participants find work and reduced criminal behavior.

McKay, J. R., A. I. Alterman, et al. (1994). "Treatment Goals, Continuity of Care, and Outcome in a Day Hospital Substance Abuse Rehabilitation Program." American Journal of Psychiatry 151(2): 254-259.

Male substance abuse patients (N=180, 82% African American, mostly low income) who participated in self-help groups (Alcoholics Anonymous, Narcotics Anonymous) after treatment significantly reduced their frequency of alcohol and cocaine use by the 7-month follow up. Participants with high self-help attendance rates used alcohol and/or cocaine less than half as much as did those with low self-help attendance. This was true regardless of previous substance use and whether or not they completed a 4-week hospital rehabilitation program. Hence, the effects of self-help groups were not simply due to motivation or other characteristics of the individuals who participated.

Pisani, V. D., J. Fawcett, et al. (1993). "The Relative Contributions of Medication Adherence and AA Meeting Attendance to Abstinent Outcome for Chronic Alcoholics." Journal of Studies on Alcohol 54: 115-119.

A group of 122 mostly male, white alcoholic patients admitted to short-term hospital treatment programs participated in this study. In the 18 months following treatment, the more days the patient attended Alcoholics Anonymous self-help meetings, the longer their abstinence lasted. AA meeting attendance improved abstinence considerably more than did adherence to prescribed medication.

Walsh, D. C., R. W. Hingson, D. M. Merrigan, et al. (1991). "A Randomized Trial of Treatment Options for Alcohol-Abusing Workers." The New England Journal of Medicine 325(11): 775-782.

Workers assigned to participate in Alcoholics Anonymous self-help groups reduced their drinking problems over a two-year period. Furthermore, compulsory AA groups (N=83) did not significantly differ from compulsory inpatient treatment (N=73) in their effects on job-related outcomes of participants. Costs of inpatient treatment averaged 10 percent less for AA participants than for hospital rehabilitation participants.

Tattersall, M. L. and C. Hallstrom (1992). "Self-Help and Benzodiazepine Withdrawal." Journal of Affective Disorders 24(3): 193-198.

This study followed members (N=41) of TRANX (Tranquilizer Recovery and New Existence), a British self-help organization that provided telephone counseling and support groups to its members. Members were mostly white women who had been addicted to tranquilizers for an average of 12 years.

During a 9-month period, members of the group were more likely to stop using tranquilizers than were individuals (N=76) who made an initial telephone contact but did not become a member. Most members (73%) also reported that the symptoms for which they had initially been prescribed tranquilizers improved, and 65% reported that they were at least moderately satisfied with their withdrawal in terms of its effects on their subjective quality of life.

BEREAVEMENT GROUPS

Caserta, M. S. and Lund, D. A. (1993). "Intrapersonal Resources and the Effectiveness of Self-Help Groups for Bereaved Older Adults." Gerontologist 33(5): 619-629.

Widows and widowers over age 50 who participated in bereavement self-help groups (N=197) experienced less depression and grief than nonparticipants (N=98) if their initial levels of interpersonal and coping skills were low. Those with initially high interpersonal skill levels also benefitted from participation if they participated in the groups for longer than eight weeks.

Lieberman, M. A. and L. Videka-Sherman (1986). "The Impact of Self-Help Groups on the Mental Health of Widows and Widowers." American Journal of Orthopsychiatry 56(3): 435-449.

This study followed 36 widowers and 466 widows, 376 of whom were members of the bereavement self-help group THEOS. Over a period of one year, THEOS members who formed social relationships with other group members outside group time experienced less psychological distress (depression, anxiety, somatic symptoms) and improved more in psychological functioning (well-being, mastery, self-esteem) than did non-members and members who did not form such relationships.

Vachon, M.L.S., W.A.L. Lyall, et al. (1980). "A Controlled Study of Self-Help Intervention for Widows." American Journal of Psychiatry 137(11): 1380-1384.

Women (N=162) whose husbands had died within the past month were studied over a two-year period. Half of these women were assigned to participate in a "widow-to-widow" program. After 6 months in the program, participants were more likely than non-participants to feel more healthy and to feel "better," and less likely to anticipate a difficult adjustment to widowhood. After 12 months, participants were more likely than non-participants to feel "much better," to have made new friends, and to have begun new activities, and were less likely to feel constantly anxious or to feel the need to hide their true emotions. Participation facilitated adjustment both inside the person (in their relationship with themselves) and outside the person (in their relationships with others).

Marmar, C. R., M. J. Horowitz, et al. (1988). "A Controlled Trial of Brief Psychotherapy and Mutual-Help Group Treatment of Conjugal Bereavement." American Journal of Psychiatry 145(2): 203-209.

Bereaved women who sought treatment for grief after the death of their husband were randomly assigned to either professional psychotherapy (N=31) or self-help groups (N=30). Self-help groups worked just as well as the therapy. Participants and non-participants in the self-help groups reduced stress-specific and general psychiatric symptoms such as depression equally. They also experienced similar improvements in social adjustment and work functioning.

Videka-Sherman, L. and M. Lieberman (1985). "The Effects of Self-Help and Psychotherapy Intervention on Child Loss: The Limits of Recovery." American Journal of Orthopsychiatry 55(1): 70-82.

This study compared white, mostly female bereaved parents who had received psychotherapy (N=120) to those who attended a Compassionate Friends (CF) bereavement self-help group sporadically (N=81), actively (N=25) or actively with social involvement with group members outside the group (N=97). Active participation in the self-help group accompanied by involvement with group members outside the group increased bereaved parents' comfort in discussing their bereavement with others and reduced parents' self-directed anger. Psychotherapy did not have these effects. CF members reported that group involvement had increased their self-confidence, sense of control, happiness, and freedom to express feelings, and decreased their depression, anxiety, guilt, anger, and isolation.

DIABETES GROUPS

Gilden, J.L., Hendryx, M.S., et al. (1992). "Diabetes Support Groups Improve Health Care of Older Diabetic Patients." Journal of the American Geriatrics Society 40: 147-150.

Male diabetic patients were randomly divided into three groups. The first group (N=8) received no intervention. The second group (N=13) received a six-session education program on diabetes self-care. The third group (N=11) received the education program plus 18 meetings of a patient-led self-help group. The patient-led group focused on coping skills, group discussions, structured social activities, and continuing diabetes education. At the end of the study, those who participated in both the education program and the patient-led group had better diabetes knowledge and quality of life and lower depression than non-participants. The participants in the peer-led group also reported less stress, greater family involvement, and better glycemic control than the patients who received no intervention.

Simmons, D. (1992). "Diabetes Self Help Facilitated by Local Diabetes Research: The Coventry Asian Diabetes Support Group." Diabetic Medicine 9: 866-869.

Researchers assessed members of a self-help group for South Asian diabetics in England (N=53) for levels of glycated hemoglobin and knowledge about diabetes. Those who attended the group twice or more during a year had a significantly greater drop in glycated hemoglobin levels and a significantly greater increase in knowledge about diabetes. Although professionals helped start the group, it continues to operate independently, emphasizing education, mutual support, information sharing, and family social activities.

CAREGIVERS GROUPS

Minde, K., N. Shosenberg, et al. (1980). "Self-Help Groups in a Premature Nursery--a Controlled Evaluation." Behavioral Pediatrics 96(5): 933-940.

Parents of premature infants were randomly assigned to participate in support groups in a hospital. The weekly groups (1.5 to 2 hours long) focused on coping and were co-led by a nurse and by a mother of a premature infant. Speakers were also brought in from outside periodically. Compared to 29 parents who did not participate, the 28 participants visited their infants in the hospital significantly more often, and touched, talked to, and gazed at their infants more often during visits. Participants also rated themselves more competent at infant care. Three months after their babies were discharged, group participants continued to show more involvement with their infants during feedings and were more concerned about their infants' general development.

Toseland, R.W., Rossiter, C.M., and Labrecque, M.S. (1989). "The Effectiveness of Two Kinds of Support Groups for Caregivers." Social Service Review, September: 415-432.

This study divided 103 adult women caring for frail older relatives into three conditions: participation in a peer-led self-help group, participation in a professional-led support group, and no participation in either group. Groups met for eight weekly two-hour sessions. Both groups focused on enhancing coping skills. Compared to non-participants, women who participated in either type of group experienced significantly greater (1) increases in the size of their support network, (2) increases in their knowledge of community resources, (3) improvement in their interpersonal skills and ability to deal with the problems of caregiving, (4) improvement in their relationships with their care receivers, and (5) decreases in pressing psychological problems.

GROUPS FOR ELDERLY PERSONS

Lieberman, M.A. and Bliwise, N.G. (1985). "Comparisons Among Peer and Professionally Directed Groups for the Elderly: Implications for the Development of Self-Help Groups." International Journal of Group Psychotherapy 35(2): 155-175.

This study compared participants (86 women and 22 men) in peer-led and professionally-led SAGE (Senior Actualization and Growth Explorations) self-help groups for the elderly to those who were on a waiting list to join the groups. Members of both types of SAGE groups felt they achieved their desired goals to a greater extent than those in the waiting-list group. Participation in either SAGE group also reduced psychological problems, such as nervousness and depression.

CANCER GROUPS

Maisiak, R., M. Cain, et al. (1981). "Evaluation of TOUCH: An Oncology Self-Help Group." Oncology Nursing Forum 8(3): 20-25.

This study surveyed 139 members of TOUCH, a self-help group for cancer patients in Alabama. TOUCH focuses on teaching its members about cancer and training them to be peer counselors to help other patients. The longer members participated in a group, the more they improved their knowledge of cancer, their ability to talk with others, their friendships, their family life, their coping with the disease, and their following of doctors' orders. The percentage of people indicating their coping was very good after TOUCH was 59%, more than double the percentage indicating it was very good before TOUCH (28%).

Spiegel, D., Bloom, J. R., Kraemer, H.C. and Gottheil, E. (1989). "Effect of psychosocial treatment on survival of patients with metastatic breast cancer." The Lancet October 14: 888-891.

Participants in this study were 86 women undergoing treatment for metastatic breast cancer. A subset of these women (N=50) were randomly assigned to have their oncologic care supplemented with a weekly support group. The support groups were co-facilitated by a therapist who had breast cancer in remission and a psychiatrist or social worker. The sessions focused on living life fully, improving communication with family members and doctors, facing death, expressing emotions such as grief, and controlling pain through self-hypnosis. On average, support group participants lived twice as long as controls (an average of almost 18 months longer).

CHRONIC ILLNESS GROUPS

Becu, M., Becu, N., Manzur, G. and Kochen, S. (1993). "Self-Help Epilepsy Groups: An Evaluation of Effect on Depression and Schizophrenia." Epilepsia 34(5): 841-845.

Argentine researchers conducted a 4-month longitudinal study of 67 epileptic patients who participated in weekly self-help group meetings. Epileptic patients trained by psychologists led the groups. Group participants had decreased depression and other psychological problems over the course of the study.

Hinrichsen, G.A., T.A. Revenson, et al. (1985). "Does Self-Help Help? An Empirical Investigation of Scoliosis Peer Support Groups." Journal of Social Issues 41(1): 65-87.

Adults with scoliosis who had undergone bracing or surgery and participated in a Scoliosis Association self-help group (N=33) were compared to adults with similar treatment who did not participate in the group (N=67). Compared to non-participants, group participants reported (1) a more positive outlook on life, (2) greater satisfaction with the medical care they received, (3) reduced psychosomatic symptoms, (4) increased sense of mastery, (5) increased self-esteem, and (6) reduced feelings of shame and estrangement.

Nash, K.B. and K.D. Kramer (1993). "Self-Help for Sickle Cell Disease in African American Communities." Journal of Applied Behavioral Science 29(2): 202-215.

This study focused on 57 African Americans who had been members of self-help groups for sickle-cell anemia. The members who had been involved the longest reported the fewest psychological symptoms and the fewest psychosocial interferences from the disease, particularly in work and relationship areas.

Sibthorpe, B., D. Fleming, et al. (1994). "Self-Help Groups: A Key to HIV Risk Reduction for High-Risk Injection Drug Users?" Journal of Acquired Immune Deficiency Syndromes 7(6): 592-598.

Injection drug users (N=234) who had shared a dirty needle in the previous 30 days were followed over six months. Those who attended self-help groups (mostly Narcotics Anonymous and Alcoholics Anonymous) during that time were almost twice as likely to report reducing or eliminating their risk of exposure to HIV compared to those who did not attend such groups.

Note: This paper is in the public domain and can be photocopied. Preparation of this paper was supported by the Department of Veterans Affairs Mental Health Strategic Health Group.

Chapter 6
SELF-HELP CLEARINGHOUSES

To find a local self-help group for your concern, review the list of self-help clearinghouses below to see if there is one that serves your area. Self-Help Clearinghouses provide information on local support groups, especially the one-of-a-kind groups that are not affiliated with any national self-help organization. In addition, many of the clearinghouses listed below provide consultation to new and existing groups, training workshops, "how-to" materials for starting and maintaining groups, directories of local groups, and other services of interest to self-help groups.

UNITED STATES

ALABAMA

SHINE *(Birmingham area)* Volunteer-run self-help clearinghouse that provides information on self-help groups in the Birmingham area. Write: SHINE, c/o Bill Russell, P.O. Box 7767, Birmingham, AL 35228. Call (205)251-5912. Leave a message on answering machine and a volunteer will call back.

ARIZONA

Self-Help Umbrella *(Statewide)* Provides information and referrals to support groups statewide. Offers assistance in starting groups. Write: Self-Help Umbrella, P.O. Box 472, Scottsdale, AZ 85252. Call (602)231-0868.

ARKANSAS

Helpline *(Northeast area)* Provides information and referral to self-help groups in the seven northeast counties. Distributes literature on starting groups. Write: Helpline, P.O. Box 9028, Jonesboro, AR 72403-9028. Call (870)932-5555; FAX: (870)931-5056; *E-mail*: janie@inso/wwb.net

CALIFORNIA

Mental Health Association of Yolo County *(Davis)* Provides information and referrals to support groups in Yolo County. Offers assistance in starting local support groups. Provides training workshops, how-to materials, directory of local groups, consultation to existing groups, conferences, and speakers bureau. Write: MHA of Yolo County, P.O. Box 447, Davis, CA 95617. Call (916) 756-8181 (Mon-Fri, 9am-3pm).

SHARE! (The Self-Help And Recovery Exchange) *(Los Angeles)* Provides information and referrals to self-help groups in the Los Angeles area. Offers technical assistance for new and ongoing self-help group meetings. Provides meeting space for groups. Write: SHARE!, 5521 Grosvenor Blvd., Los Angeles, CA 90066. Call (310)305-8878 (Mon-Fri, 10am-4pm PT; 24 hour voice mail with information on the most requested groups).

Friends Network *(Modesto)* Information and referrals to local self-help groups. Helps develop new groups, and provides support, resources, publicity and education to existing groups. Publishes directory of self-help groups. Write: Friends Network, 800 Scenic Dr., Modesto, CA 95350. Call (209)558-7454.

Mental Health Association *(Sacramento)* Provides training and technical assistance to people starting new groups. Collects data on existing groups and identifies the need for new groups. Conducts community education about self-help. Write: MHA, 8912 Volunteer Lane, #210, Sacramento, CA 95826-3221. Call (916)368-3100; FAX: (916)368-3104.

Self-Help Connection *(San Diego County - Mental Health Groups Only)* Provides information and referral to free and low cost mental health support groups in San Diego County. Also provides support in starting and maintaining support groups. Publishes yearly directory of groups. Write: Self-Help Connection, c/o MHA San Diego County, 2047 El Cajon Blvd., San Diego, CA 92104-1091. Call (619)543-0412.

Helpline *(Greater San Francisco area)* Provides information and referrals to support groups in an 11 county area. Offers assistance in starting groups and community education. Also provides information and referrals to local services and agencies. Write: Helpline, N. Calif. Council for the Community, 50 California St., #200, San Francisco, CA 94111. Call 800-273-6222 (from 510, 707 and 916 area codes) or (415)772-4357; FAX: (415)391-8302; TTY: (415)772-4440 (Mon-Fri, 8am-5pm). Accepts collect calls.

CONNECTICUT

Connecticut Self-Help Support Network *(Statewide)* Provides information and referrals to support groups. Provides technical assistance in starting and maintaining groups, group leadership training, educational workshops and conferences. Publishes directory of self-help groups, newsletter, and other publications. Write: Connecticut Self-Help Support Network, c/o Terry Freeman, Consultation Center, 389 Whitney Ave., New Haven, CT 06511. Call (203)624-6982; FAX: (203)562-6355.

HAWAII

United Self-Help *(Statewide -Mental Health Groups Only)* Dedicated to serving consumers of mental health services. Provides information and referrals to a variety of mental health self-help groups throughout Hawaii. Newsletter. Write: United Self-Help, 277 Ohua Ave., Honolulu, HI 96815. Call (808)926-0466.

ILLINOIS

Illinois Self-Help Coalition *(Statewide)* Provides referrals to self-help groups. Also provides assistance in starting groups, training workshops, consultation to existing groups, how-to materials, conferences, speakers bureau, and a directory of support groups. Write: Illinois Self-Help Coalition, Wright College, 3400 North Austin, Chicago Ill 60634. Call (773)481-8837 (Mon., Thur., Fri., 9:30-4); FAX: (773)481-8917; *Website*: http://www.selfhelp-illinois.org *E-mail*: dipeace@aol.com

Self-Help Center *(Statewide)* Provides information and referral to support groups, publishes directory of groups, and offers technical assistance in developing groups. Write: c/o MHA, 188 W. Randolph, #2225, Chicago, Il 60601. Call (312)368-9070 (Mon-Fri, 9am-5pm).

Self-Help Center *(Champaign County)* Provides information and referral to local support groups. Provides assistance in starting support groups, how-to materials, training workshops, directory ($7 postpaid), specialized group listings, newsletter, consultation to existing groups, and maintains a library of self-help literature. Write: Self-Help Center, Family Service, 405 S. State St., Champaign, IL 61820-5196. Call (217)352-0099; FAX: (217)352-9512; TDD: (217)352-0160; *Website*: http://www.prairienet.org/selfhelp/

Macon County Support Group Network *(Macon County)* Provides information and referrals to local support groups. Write: Macon County Support Group Network, c/o Macon County Health Dept., 1221 E. Condit, Decatur, IL 62521. Call (217)429-HELP (Mon-Fri, 9am-5pm).

IOWA

Iowa Compass *(Statewide)* Provides information and referrals to self-help groups. Offers assistance to new and existing groups. Write: Iowa Compass, University Hospital School, 100 Hawkins Dr., Room S277, Iowa City, IA 52242-1011. Call 800-779-2001 (day). *E-mail*: deb-tiemens@uiowa.edu

KANSAS

Self-Help Network of Kansas *(Statewide)* Information and referral to self-help groups. Developmental assistance and consultation to existing groups or persons interested in starting groups. Community education, training workshops and conferences on self-help. Publishes directory of groups and conducts research. Write: Self-Help Network of Kansas, Wichita State University, Box 34, 1845 Fairmount, Wichita, KS 67260-0034. Call 800-445-0116 (in KS) or (316) 978-3843 (day); FAX: (316)978-3593. *E-mail:* shnofks@wsuhub.uc.twsu.edu

MASSACHUSETTS

Massachusetts Clearinghouse of Mutual Help Groups *(Statewide)* Information and referral to support groups. Consultation to persons interested in starting groups, and to groups already in existence. Publishes directory of groups statewide. Write: c/o Massachusetts Cooperative Extension System, Dept. of Consumer Studies, 113 Skinner Hall, Univ. of Mass., Amherst, MA 01003. Call (413)545-2313 or (413)545-5013; FAX: (413)545-4410.

MICHIGAN

Michigan Self-Help Clearinghouse *(Statewide)* Referrals to support groups statewide. Helps persons to start new groups, and provides consultation to existing groups. Maintains a "seeker" list of persons to be connected to others who share same concerns. Research library, newsletter, speakers bureau, training workshops, written materials, and statewide directory. Write: Michigan Self-Help Clearinghouse, 106 W. Allegan, Suite 300, Lansing, MI 48933-1706. Call (517)484-7373 or 800-777-5556 (in MI only); FAX: (517)487-0827 (Group referrals Mon-Fri, 10am-3pm).

Center For Self-Help *(Southwest Michigan/northern Indiana)* Information and referrals to support groups. Networks individuals, groups, professionals and agencies. Community education. Assists new groups, facilitates group meetings, and holds training workshops. Publishes directory, and newsletter.   Write: Center for Help, Riverwood Center, Attn: Pat Friend, P.O. Box 547, Benton Harbor, MI 49023-0547. Call 800-336-0341 (in MI); (616)925-0952. *E-mail*: pfriend95@aol.com

MISSOURI

Mental Health Association of the Heartland *(Kansas City)* Information and referral to local mental health services, including self-help groups. Speakers bureau, conferences, advocacy for mental health consumers, senior programs, and educational workshops for self-help group leaders. Publishes directory of self-help groups. Write: MHA of the Heartland, 7611 State Line Rd., #230,

Kansas City, MO 64114. Call (816)822-7272 (24 hr. helpline); (816)822-7100 (office); FAX: (816)822-2388.

St. Louis Self-Help Clearinghouse *(St. Louis)* Provides information and referrals to all types of support groups in the St. Louis area. Helps interested persons to start support groups. Provides consultation and technical assistance to new and existing groups. Directory available. Write: St. Louis Self-Help Clearinghouse, c/o MHA of Greater St. Louis, 1905 S. Grand, St. Louis, MO 63104. Call (314)773-1399; FAX: (314)773-5930.

NEBRASKA

Nebraska Self-Help Information Services *(Statewide - Founded 1984)* Provides information and referral to support groups. Offers assistance to new and existing groups. Acts as an answering service to groups. Presentations can be arranged for schools and other interested organizations. Publishes State Directory of self-help groups ($5). Write: Nebraska Self-Help Information Services, 1601 Euclid Ave., Lincoln, NE 68502. Call (402)476-9668; FAX: (402)434-3972; *Website:* http://incolor.inetnebr.com/jmfritts/selfhelp/

NEW JERSEY

New Jersey Self-Help Clearinghouse *(Statewide)* Provides information and referrals to local self-help groups. Offers assistance to new and existing groups. Provides workshops, conferences, newsletter, and directory of support groups ($25). Write: NJ Self-Help Clearinghouse, c/o Northwest Covenant Medical Center, 25 Pocono Rd., Denville, NJ 07834. Call 800-367-6274 (in NJ); (973)625-3037; FAX: (973)625-8848; TDD: (973)625-9053; *E-mail:* njshc@cybernex.net

NEW YORK

New York City Self Help Center *(New York City)* Provides information and referrals to support groups in the five boroughs (Manhattan, Bronx, Staten Island, Queens, and Brooklyn). Offers assistance to new and developing groups. Write: NYC Self-Help Center, 120 West 57th St., New York, NY 10019. Call (212)586-5770; FAX: (212)956-1652.

Brooklyn Self-Help Clearinghouse *(Brooklyn)* Provides information and referral to self-help groups in Brooklyn. Also offers consultation services. Support groups for mid-life women are a special focus of the Clearinghouse. Write: Brooklyn Self-Help Clearinghouse, 30 Third Ave., Brooklyn, NY 11217. Call (718)875-1420 and ask for "Brooklyn Self-Help Clearinghouse."

Long Island Self-Help Clearinghouse *(Long Island)* Provides referrals to local support groups. Offers assistance to new and existing groups. Write: Long Island Self-Help Clearinghouse, c/o NY College of Osteopathic Medicine, NY Institute of Technology, P.O. Box 8000, Old Westbury, NY 11568. Call (516)626-1721 (in area) or 888-SELF-HLP (outside area); FAX: (516)626-9290; *E-mail*: egiannetti@acl.nyit.edu

Westchester Self-Help Clearinghouse *(Westchester)* Acts as a central resource for mutual support groups. Provides confidential information and referral to groups. Assists in the formation of new groups. Trains mutual support group leaders, sponsors workshops and conferences, and provides community education. Publishes directory of self-help groups. Offers phone networks for newly widowed men and women, and newly separated women. Write: Westchester Self-Help Clearinghouse, 456 North St., White Plains, NY 10605. Call (914)949-0788 ext. 237 voice mail; FAX: (914)948-3783.

Self-Help Resource Center *(Broome County)* Provides information and referrals to local self-help groups. Maintains an updated database and publishes a directory of local self-help groups. Works with established and prospective self-help group leaders to assist them in creating and/or developing their groups. Collaborates with community organizations and professionals to identify the need for new groups and to assist in organizing them. Write: Self-Help Resource Center, c/o MHA, 82 Oak St., Binghamton, NY 13905. Call (607)771-8888; FAX: (607)771-8892; *E-mail*: mhaofst@spectra.net

Self-Help Clearinghouse of Cattaraugus County *(Cattaraugus County)* Provides information and referral to local support groups in Cattaraugus and Alleghany counties. Offers assistance in starting new groups. Publishes self-help directory. Holds workshops for group leaders, helps groups find meeting places, and provides other technical assistance and referrals. Write: Self-Help Clearinghouse of Cattaraugus County, c/o American Red Cross, Greater Buffalo Chapter, P.O. Box 67, Olean, NY 14760. Call (716)372-5800.

Information Line of United Way *(Dutchess County)* Maintains a database of information on self-help support groups in the community. This information is also available in publication form that is updated on a yearly basis. The Information Line of United Way maintains and refers people to other services in the community. Write: Information Line of United Way, P.O. Box 832, Poughkeepsie, NY 12602. Call (914)473-1500.

Erie County Self-Help Clearinghouse *(Erie)* Provides information and referrals to local self-help groups. Offers assistance to existing groups that meet at the Mental Health Association. Write: Erie County Self-Help Clearinghouse, c/o MHA of Erie County, Inc., 999 Delaware Ave., Buffalo, NY 14209. Call (716)886-1242; FAX: (716)881-6428.

HealthLink *(Fulton County)* Provides information and referral to local self-help resources. Also publishes a directory of area support groups, and provides technical assistance to new and existing groups. Makes referrals to other local services and agencies. Write: HealthLink, Pyramid Mall, 246 N. Comrie Ave., Johnstown, NY 12095. Call (518)736-1120.

Clearinghouse for Self-Help Groups *(Monroe County)* Provides information and referrals to local support groups. Offers assistance in starting new groups and consultation to existing groups through training workshops, and how-to materials. Publishes directory of local groups ($15 and $2.50 postage/handling). Write: Clearinghouse for Self-Help Groups, 339 East Ave., Suite 201, Rochester, NY 14604. Call Cindy LaCotta (716)325-3145 ext. 14; FAX: (716)325-3188.

Wellness Institute *(Montgomery)* Provides information and referrals about health education programs and support groups to persons throughout Montgomery County and surrounding areas. Write: Sr. Rita Jean Du Brey, Wellness Institute, St. Mary's Hospital, 427 Guy Park Ave., Amsterdam, NY 12010. Call (518)842-1900, ext. 286.

Niagara Self-Help Clearinghouse *(Niagara County)* Provides information and referrals to local support groups. Offers technical assistance to new groups, and networks with other community resources. Helps new group development and holds group leader training. Publishes newsletter, directory of self-help groups, and mental health video/book library. Write: Niagara Self-Help Clearinghouse, c/o MHA of Niagara County, 151 East Ave., Lockport, NY 14094. Call (716)433-3780.

The Volunteer Center of the Mohawk Valley *(Oneida County)* Provides information and referrals to local support groups. Offers assistance to new and existing groups. Write: The Volunteer Center of the Mohawk Valley, 401 Columbia St., Utica, NY 13502. Call (315)735-4463.

Helpline/Rapeline *(Orange/Ulster/Sullivan County)* Provides referrals to local support groups, as well as 24-hour crisis intervention, rape hotline, and information and referral to local services and agencies. Published directory of local services. Write: Helpline, MHA in Orange County, 20 John St., Goshen, NY 10924. Call 800-832-1200 (Orange County only) or (914)294-7411.

The Self-Help Clearinghouse *(Rockland County)* Information and referral concerning self-help groups. Provides consultation and technical assistance to on-going groups and to new groups that are forming. Publishes newsletter, self-help calendar, and directory of groups ($3). Write: Self-Help Clearinghouse, c/o MHA of Rockland, 20 Squadron Blvd., New City, NY 10956. Call (914)639-7400 Ext. 22; FAX: (914)639-7419.

Mechanicville Area Community Services Center, Inc. *(Saratoga County)* Provides information and referral to local self-help groups. Offers consultation and technical assistance to existing groups. Write: Mechanicville Area Comm. Svcs. Ctr., Inc., P.O. Box 3, 6 South Main St., Mechanicville, NY 12118. Call (518)664-8322; FAX: (518)664-9457.

Reachout of St. Lawrence County *(St. Lawrence County)* Provides information and referral to local support groups and other services and agencies in St. Lawrence County. Also has information on national organizations. Provides limited consultation to existing and new groups. Acts as Alcoholics Anonymous answering service. Provides crisis intervention. Write: Reachout, P.O. Box 5051, Potsdam, NY 13676-5051. Call (315)265-2422; FAX: (315)265-1752; *E-mail*: reachout@slic.com

Institute for Human Services/HELPLINE *(Steuben County)* Provides information and referrals to local services and agencies, as well as support groups and information and referrals. Offers assistance to new and existing self-help groups. Also acts as 24-hour crisis line. Publishes newsletter. Write: Institute for Human Svcs., 29 Denison Parkway East, Suite B, Corning, NY 14830. Call 800-346-2211 (in NY); (607)936-3725 (IHS); (607)936-4114 (helpline).

HELPLINE Information and Referral Service *(Syracuse/Onondaga Counties)* Provides information on area self-help groups. Also refers callers to other local services and agencies. Publishes a self-help group directory, a directory of resources of Syracuse and Onondaga Counties, and a Human Services Directory. Write: HELPLINE, The Volunteer Center, Inc., 115 E. Jefferson St., Suite #400, Syracuse, NY 13202. Call (315)474-7011.

Mental Health Association in Tompkins County *(Tompkins County)* Provides information and referral, education, advocacy, respite and family support concerning mental health issues and services. Also makes referrals to support groups and therapists. Publishes a support group guide, guide to alternative therapists, and a directory of local psychotherapists and a newsletter. Write: MHA in Tompkins County, 225 S. Fulton St., Suite B, Ithaca, NY 14850. Call (607)273-9250.

Mental Health Association in Ulster County *(Ulster County)* Provides information and referrals to local support groups. Offers assistance in starting mental health support groups, training workshops, how-to materials, consultation to existing groups. Offers directory, speakers bureau, training programs for families of the mentally ill, and provides models for transitional groups. Write: MHA in Ulster County, P. O. Box 2304, Kingston, NY 12401-0227. Call (914)339-9090, ext. 113.

Wyoming County Chapter Amer. Red Cross *(Wyoming County)* Provides information on local support groups and other services or agencies. Write: c/o Dale Palesh, Wyoming County Chapter Amer. Red Cross, 25 W. Buffalo St., Warsaw, NY 14569. Call (716)786-0540 (day).

NORTH CAROLINA

SupportWorks Self-Help Clearinghouse *(Mecklenberg)* Provides information on support groups in Mecklenberg County. Networks persons seeking mutual support. Offers consultation to people developing new groups. Free or low cost telephone conference calls are available to non-profit organizations. Offers outreach to underserved communities. Publishes "Power Tools" handout on starting groups. Write: SupportWorks, 1018 East Blvd., #5, Charlotte, NC 28203-5779. Call (704)331-9500 (group information); (704)377-2055 (director); FAX: (704)332-2127; Website: http://www.supportworks.org

NORTH DAKOTA

Hot Line *(Fargo/Moorhead area)* Provides information and referral to support groups in the Fargo-Moorhead area, as well as other local services and agencies. Publishes directory of local support groups. Limited consultation available to new and existing groups. Write: Hot Line, P.O. Box 447, Fargo, ND 58107-0447. Call (701)235-SEEK.

OHIO

Greater Dayton Self-Help Clearinghouse *(Dayton)* Provides information and referral to self-help groups in the Dayton area. Technical assistance provided to start new self-help groups. Conducts group effectiveness workshops. Provides self-help group newspaper columns. Write: Greater Dayton Self-Help Clearinghouse, c/o Family Service Assn., 184 Salem Ave., Dayton, OH 45406. Call (937)225-3004; FAX: (937)222-3710; TDD: (937)222-7921.

The Greater Toledo Self-Help Network *(Toledo area)* Provides information and referrals to local self-help groups. Assists area professionals in locating groups for their clients. Consultation to new and existing groups, training workshops, and how-to guidelines. Write: c/o Harbor Behavioral Health Care, 4334 Secor Rd., Toledo, OH 43623. Call (419)475-4449; FAX: (419)479-3230.

OREGON

Northwest Regional Self-Help Clearinghouse *(Northern OR/Southern WA)* Maintains an extensive database of resources and self-help groups in Multnomah, Clackamas and Washington Counties in Oregon, and Clark County in Washington. Assistance to new groups. Publishes Resource File, Self-Help

Group Directory, and Human Services Directory. Write: Northwest Regional Self-Help Clearinghouse, Metro Crisis Intervention, P.O. Box 637, Portland, OR 97207. Call (503)222-5555 (group information); (503)499-4301 (FAX); (503)226-3099 (Admin).

PENNSYLVANIA

Valley Wide Help *(Lehigh area)* Provides information on local support groups in the Lehigh Valley area (Allentown, Easton, Bethlehem, Slate Belt). Also provides referrals to other agencies and services. Write: Valley Wide Help, c/o American Red Cross, 2200 Avenue A, Bethlehem, PA 18017-2181. Call (610)865-4400 (general); FAX: (610)865-5871; TDD: (610)866-0131; Spanish Speaking: (610)866-1089; *Website*: http://www.redcrosslv.org   *E-mail*: lvarc@redcrosslv.org

Self Help Group Network of the Pittsburgh Area   *(Pittsburgh area)* Maintains a listing of self help groups in southwestern Pennsylvania. Provides referral services, information to those who would like to start new groups, consultation, seminars and resource materials on self-help. Publishes directory of self-help groups, newsletter. Write: Self Help Group Network of the Pittsburgh Area, 1323 Forbes Ave., Suite #200, Pittsburgh, PA 15219. Call (412)261-5363; FAX: (412)471-2722; *E-mail:* shgn@trfn.clpgh.org

SHINE (Self-Help Information Network Exchange) *(Scranton area)* Provides information and referral to support groups in Lackawanna County and surrounding northeastern Pennsylvania. Sponsors workshops and special events for self-help advocates. Published brochure and Community resource library. Write: SHINE, 538 Spruce St. Suite 420, Scranton, PA 18503. Call (717)961-1234 (I&R); (717)347-5616 (Admin); FAX: (717)341-5816; *E-mail*: selfhelpnepa@juno.com

SOUTH CAROLINA

Midlands Area Support Group Network   *(Richland/Lexington County)* Provides information and referral to self-help groups in Richland/Lexington County. Write: Midlands Area Support Group Network, c/o Lexington Medical Ctr., 2720 Sunset Blvd., W. Columbia, SC 29169. Call (803)791-2800 (I&R).

TENNESSEE

Mental Health Association of Greater Knoxville *(Knoxville area)* Provides information and referral regarding self-help groups in Knox County and surrounding areas. Offers consultation for persons interested in starting new groups, training for self-help group leaders, and a speakers bureau. Publishes directory of local support groups ($12). Write: c/o Mental Health Assn. of

Greater Knoxville, 110 Westfield Rd. #3, Knoxville, TN 37919. Call (423)584-9125 (Voice/FAX); *E-mail*: mha@korrnet.org; *Website:* http://www.korrnet.org/mha

Self-Help Clearinghouse *(Memphis and Shelby County)* Provides information and referrals to local support groups. Conducts public educational information forums on issues of mental health, professional training and seminars. Offers assistance in starting new groups, speakers bureau, training workshops, and consultation to existing groups, facilitator training, how-to guidelines. Publishes directory of local groups ($15). Write: Self-Help Clearinghouse, MHA of the Mid-South, 2400 Poplar Ave., #410, Memphis, TN 38112. Call Dorothy McClure (901)323-8485 (MHA); FAX: (901)323-0858.

TEXAS

Texas Self-Help Clearinghouse *(Statewide)* Provides information and referral to groups and agencies statewide and consultation to persons interested in starting new groups. Publishes technical manual for starting support groups; FAIR Facilitators Manual (mental health consumers groups); and other manuals. Write: Texas Self-Help Clearinghouse, c/o MHA, 8401 Shoal Creek Blvd., Austin, TX 78757. Call (512)454-3706; FAX: (512)454-3725.

Dallas Self-Help Clearinghouse *(Dallas area)* Provides information and referrals to self-help groups. Printed information available for a small fee to those wishing to start groups. Write: Dallas Self-Help Clearinghouse, c/o MHA of Greater Dallas, 2929 Carlisle, #350, Dallas, TX 75204. Call (214)871-2420; FAX: (214)954-0611.

Support Group Clearinghouse *(El Paso area)* Promotes self-help groups by collecting and disseminating information on local groups, educates the public about the benefits of self-help groups, and provides technical assistance to new and existing groups. Write: Support Group Clearinghouse, c/o Women's Resource Center, 1155 Idaho, Suite B, El Paso, TX 79902. Call (915)544-0782 (limited hours); FAX: (915)544-3913; *Website:* http://rgfn.epcc.edu/users/as796 *E-mail*: as796.rgfn.epcc.edu

Houston Area Self-Help Clearinghouse *(Houston area)* Provides information and referral services for self-help groups in Harris County. Consultation provided for persons interested in developing new groups. Listing of local groups available. Workshops offered on self-help support group facilitation. Write: Houston Area Self-Help Clearinghouse, Attn: Cheryl Amoroso, c/o MHA in Houston and Harris County, 2211 Norfolk, #810, Houston, TX 77098. Call (713)523-8963 (administration) or (713)522-5161 (group information); FAX: (713)522-0698.

MHA Association Information and Referral *(San Antonio area/Bi-lingual)* Information and referral to local support groups. Offers newsletter, speakers bureau, advocacy "Phone-A-Fact" program in Spanish and English. Write: MHA Assn. I&R, 901 NE Loop 410, Suite 504, San Antonio, TX 78209. Call (210)826-2288; FAX: (210)826-9587.

Self-Help Clearinghouse for Tarrant County *(Tarrant and Parker Counties)* Promotes the awareness and development of self-help groups. Information and referrals to support groups, consultation to people interested in starting new groups, and training programs for group facilitators. Write: Self-Help Clearinghouse of Tarrant County, c/o MHA of Tarrant County, 3136 W. 4th St., Fort Worth, TX 76107-2113. Call (817)335-5405; FAX: (817)334-0025.

UTAH

Information and Referral Center *(Salt Lake City area)* Provides information and referral to local self-help groups in the Salt Lake City area. Limited consultation to new and existing groups. Also provides information on other local services and agencies. Write: Information and Referral Center, 1025 S. 700 West, Salt Lake City, UT 84104. Call Robyn Walters (801)978-3333.

VIRGINIA

Support Group Network *(Southeastern VA)* Provides information on local support groups in the "Tidewater" area of southeastern Virginia. Helps persons to start new groups, and provides technical assistance to existing groups. Write: Support Group Network, 405 W. Farmington Rd., Virginia Beach, VA 23454-4021. Call (757)340-9380 (Mon-Fri, 9am-5pm).

NATIONAL

American Self-Help Clearinghouse Maintains database of national self-help groups and model one-of-a-kind groups. Referrals to self-help clearinghouses worldwide. Assistance to persons interested in starting new groups. Publishes directory of national support groups; newsletter. Write: Amer. Self-Help Clearinghouse, c/o Northwest Covenant Med. Ctr., 25 Pocono Rd., Denville, NJ 07834. Call (973)625-9565; FAX: (973)625-8848; TTD: (973)625-9053. *E-mail*: ashc@cybernex.net *Website:* http://www.cmhc.com/selfhelp.

National Self-Help Clearinghouse Information and referral to self-help groups. Conducts training for professionals about self-help and research activities. Publishes manuals, training materials and a newsletter. Write: Nat'l Self-Help Clearinghouse, c/o CUNY, Graduate School and Univ. Ctr., 25 W. 43rd St., Rm. 620, New York, NY 10036. Call (212)354-8525; FAX: (212)642-1956.

CANADA

ALBERTA

Family Life Education Council *(Calgary)* Provides referrals to local self-help groups. Write: Life Education Council, 233 12th Avenue S.W., Calgary, Alberta Canada T2R OG9. Call (403)262-1117; FAX: (403)261-2813.

The Support Network *(Edmonton)* Provides referrals to local self-help groups. Publishes directory of local groups. Write: Support Network, 302-11456 Jasper Ave., Edmonton, Alberta T5K 0M1 Canada. Call (403)482-4636 (information and referrals) (Mon-Fri, 8am-4pm MT); FAX: (403)488-1495; *E-mail:* supnet@compusmart.cb.ca

BRITISH COLUMBIA

Self-Help Resource Association of B.C. *(Vancouver)* Provides referrals to local self-help groups. Offers assistance to new and existing groups, training workshops (facilitation, professionals working with groups, open forums). Publishes directory of support groups. Write: Self-Help Resource Assn. of B.C., #303 -1212 West Broadway, Vancouver, BC Canada V6H 3V1. Call (604)733-6186 (Mon-Fri, 9am-5pm); FAX: (604)730-1015.

MANITOBA

Manitoba Self-Help Clearinghouse Inc. *(Winnipeg)* Provides information on local self-help groups. Offers assistance to new and existing groups, and training workshops (fundraising, proposal writing). Publishes directory of self-help groups. Write: Manitoba Self-Help Clearinghouse Inc., 825 Sherbrooke St., Winnipeg, MB R3A 1M5 Canada. Call (204)772-6979 (Mon-Fri, 10am-3pm; summer Mon-Thur, 10am-3pm); FAX: (204)786-0860.

Self-Help Resource Association of B.C. *(Winnipeg)* Provides information on local self-help groups. Write: Self-Help Resource Association of B.C., Winnipeg Self-Help Resource Clearinghouse, NorWest Coop and Health Center, 103-61 Tyndall Ave., Winnipeg, Manitoba Canada R2X 2T4. Call (204)589-5500 or (204)633-5955

NOVA SCOTIA

Clearinghouse - The Self-Help Connection *(Dartmouth)* Provides referrals to local self-help groups. Offers assistance to new and existing groups, training workshops (facilitation, starting groups, professionals working with groups, troubleshooting for groups). Publishes directory of self-help groups. Write: Clearinghouse - The Self-Help Connection, MHA, 63 King St., Dartmouth,

Nova Scotia Canada B2Y 2R7. Call (902)466-2011 (group referrals) (Mon-Fri, 8:30am-4:30pm); (902)466-2011 (Admin); FAX: (902)466-3300l *E-mail*: ak745@chebuckto.ns.ca *Website*: self-help@chebucto.ns.ca

ONTARIO

Self-Help Resource Center *(Greater Toronto area; lists other Ontario clearinghouses)* Provides referrals to local self-help groups. Provides assistance to new and existing groups, conducts training sessions for new and existing groups. Publishes directory of self-help groups. Write: Self-Help Resource Center, 40 Orchard View Blvd., Suite 219, Toronto, ON M4R 1B9 Canada. Call (416)487-4355; FAX: (416)487-0624.

CMHA Barrie-Simcoe Branch *(Barrie)* Provides referrals to local groups. Assistance to new and existing groups. Write: CMHA Barrie-Simcoe Branch, 5 Bell Farm Rd., Barrie, ON Canada L4M 5G1. Call (705)726-5033 or 800-461-4319 (Mon-Fri, 8:30am-4:30pm); FAX: (705)726-0626; *E-mail*: cmhawrb@golden.net

Peel Public Health Department *(Brampton)* Provides referrals to local self-help groups. Offers assistance to new and existing groups. Write: Peel Public Health Dept., Heart Lake Town Centre, 180B Sandalwood Parkway East #200, Brampton, ON Canada L6Z 4N1. Call (905)791-7800 ext. 7401 (Mon-Fri, 8am-4pm); FAX: (905)848-9176; *E-mail*: healthline@region.peel.on.ca

Rotary Club of Hamilton *(Hamilton)* Provides referrals to local self-help groups. Provides assistance with new and existing groups, conducts training sessions to new and existing groups (starting groups, facilitation, etc). Write: Rotary Club of Hamilton, Self-Help Center, 255 West Ave. North, Hamilton, ON Canada L8L 5C8. Call (905)522-7352 (Mon-Fri, 8:30am-4pm); TDD: (905)522-0434; FAX: (905)522-9374.

CMHA Waterloo Regional Branch *(Kitchener)* Provides referrals to local self-help groups. Offers assistance to new and existing groups. Published directory of local groups. Write: CMHA Waterloo Regional Branch, Self-Help Resource Center, 67 King Street East, Kitchener ON Canada N2G 2K4. Call (519)744-7645 ext. 233 (group referrals) (Mon-Fri, 1pm-5pm); (519)744-7645 (Admin); FAX: (519)744-7066

Community Links Program *(London)* Provides referrals to local self-help groups. Offers limited assistance to new and existing groups. Write: Community Links Program, c/o CMHA London-Middlesex Branch, 648 Huron St., London, ON Canada N5Y 5G8. Call (519)434-9191 (Mon-Fri, 9am-4:30pm); FAX: (519)438-1167; *E-mail*: cmha@info.london.on.ca *Website*: http://www.info.london.on.ca/~cmha

CMHA York Region *(Newmarket)* Provides referrals to local self-help groups. Assistance to new and existing groups. Conducts workshops on facilitation. Published directory of local groups. Write: CMHA York Region, 200 Davis Dr., Newmarket, ON Canada L3Y 2N4. Call (905)898-7466 (Mon-Fri, 8:30am-4:30pm); FAX: (905)898-4390; *E-mail*: cmhayr@hesic.com

CMHA Durham Region *(Oshawa)* Provides information and referrals to local self-help groups. OFfers assistance to new and existing groups. Periodic training workshops are conducted. Publishes directory of self-help groups. Write: CMHA Durham Region, 111 Simcoe Street North, Oshawa Ontario L1G 4S4 Canada. Call (905)436-8760 (Mon-Fri, 9am-5pm); FAX: (905)436-1569

Old Forge Community Resource Center *(Ottawa)* Provides referrals to local self-help groups. Offers assistance to new and existing groups. Published bi-annual directory of self-help groups. Write: Old Forge Comm. Resource Ctr., 2730 Carling Ave., Ottawa, ON K2B 7J1 Canada. Call (613)829-9777 (Mon-Fri, 8:30am-4:30pm ET); FAX: (613)829-9318; *E-mail*: michael@freenet.carleton.ca

Haliburton, Kawartha and Pine Ridge District Health Council *(Peterborough area)* Provides referrals to local self-help groups. Offers assistance in staring new groups. Write: Haliburton, Kawartha and Pine Ridge District Health Council, Self-Help Network, 159 King St., Suite 300, P.O. Box 544, Peterborough, ON Canada K9J 6Z6. Call (705)748-2992 (Mon-Fri, 8:30-9:30); FAX: (705)748-9600; *E-mail*: dhc@knet.flemingc.on.ca *Website:* http://knet.fleming.on.ca/~dhc/dhc.htm

CMHA Perth County *(Stratford)* Provides referrals to local self-help groups. Offers assistance to new and existing groups. Published directory of local support groups. Write: CMHA Perth County, 145 Ontario St., Stratford, ON N5A 3H1 Canada. Call (519)273-1391, ext. 241 (Mon-Fri, 8:30am-4:30pm); FAX: (519)273-0505; *E-mail*: cmha@cyg.net *Website*: http://www.chma@cyg.net

Cochrane District Self-Help Network *(Timmins)* Provides referrals to local support groups. Offers assistance to new and existing groups. Publishes directory of local support groups. Write: Cochrane District Self-Help Network, 273 3rd Ave. #402, Timmins, ON Canada P4N 1E2. Call (705)264-5323; FAX: (705)267-5721; *E-mail*: selfhelp@vianet.on.ca

CMHA Windsor-Essex Branch *(Windsor)* Provides information on local groups. Offers assistance to new and existing groups. Write: CMHA Windsor-Essex Branch, 1400 Windsor Ave., Windsor ON N8X 3L9 Canada. Call (519)255-7440 (group information) (Mon-Fri, 8:30am-5pm); FAX: (519)255-7817.

Oxford County Self-Help Network *(Woodstock)* Referrals to local self-help groups. Offers assistance to new and existing groups. Conducts workshops on facilitation, goal setting, decision-making, etc. Directory of local groups. Write: Oxford County Self-Help Network, 592 Adelaide St., Woodstock, ON Canada N4S 4B9. Call (519)421-2980 (Mon-Fri, 10am-4pm); FAX: (519)421-0826;

Manitoulin Self-Help Group Development Network *(Sudbury)* Provides referrals to local self-help groups. Offers assistance to new and existing groups, workshops. Publishes directory of self-help groups. Write: Manitoulin Self-Help Group Development Network, 505 Frood Rd., Sudbury, ON Canada P3C 5A2. Call (705)677-0308 (Mon-Fri, 8:30am-4:30pm); FAX: (705)677-0270 or (705)673-3354; *E-mail*: shgroups@vianet.on.ca

PRINCE EDWARD ISLAND

Family Support and Self-Help Program *(Charlottetown)* Provides referrals to local self-help groups. Offers assistance to new and existing groups. Workshops on starting groups, facilitation, and professionals working with self-help groups. Publishes directory of local groups. Write: Family Support and Self-Help Program, c/o CMHA, P.O. Box 27875, Charlottetown, PEI Canada C1A 7L9. Call (902)628-1648 (Mon-Thur, 8:30am-4:30pm); FAX: (902)566-4643; *E-mail:* faulk@cycor.ca

QUEBEC

Centre de reference du Grand Montreal *(Montreal)* Provides referrals to local self-help groups. Offers assistance to existing groups. Publishes directory of local support groups. Write: Centre de reference du Grand Montreal, Information and Referral Centre of Greater Montreal, 801 Sherbrooke East, Suite 401, Montreal, Quebec Canada H2L 1K7. Call (514)527-1375 (Mon-Fri, 8:15am-4:30pm); FAX: (514)527-9712

West Island Community Resource Centre *(Pointe Claire)* Provides information on local self-help groups. Write: West Island Community Resource Centre, 114 Donegani, Pointe Claire PQ H9R 2W3 Canada Call (514)694-6404 (Mon-Fri, 9am-4pm); Admin: (514)694-3595; FAX: (514)630-1225.

NEW BRUNSWICK

Self-Help Line/Info Line *(St. John)* Provides referrals to local support groups. Publishes Human Services Directory. Write: Self-Help Line/Info Line, Human Development Council, Box 6125 Station A, St. John NB E2L 4R6 Canada. Call (506)633-4636 (group information) (Mon-Fri, 8:30am-4:30pm); (506)634-1673 (Admin); FAX: (506)634-6080; *E-mail*: hdc@nbnet.nb.ca *Website*: http://www.sjfn.nb.ca/community_hall/h/hman_development_council

INTERNATIONAL

ARGENTINA

Fundacion Precavida, Espinosa 1885, 2nd Floor, "B" Capital Federal, Buenos Aires, Argentina; Phone: (011)54-1-582-8680 (group information); (011)54-1-585-5784 (administration); FAX: (011)54-1-334-1230. Luis Kuncewicz and Dora Kapeluschnik, Coordinators

AUSTRALIA

Western Institute of Self-Help, P.O. Box 8140, Perth Business Center, Western Australia 6849. Phone: (011-61)8-9228-4488 (group information); FAX: (011-61)8-9228-4490. Denise Kelly, Executive Director

The Collective of Self-Help Groups, P.O. Box 251, Brunswick East, Victoria 3057 Australia. Phone: (03)9349 2301

AUSTRIA

Servicestelle Fur Selbsthilfegruppen, Schottenring 24, A-1010 Vienna, Austria. Phone: 01/53-114/81223; FAX: 01/53-114/81228. Ilse Forster, Director

BELGIUM

Trefpunt Zelfhulp, E. Van Evenstraat 2 C, 3000 Leuven, Belgium. Phone: 0032-16-23-65-07; FAX: 0032-16-32-30-52. Anne-Marie Dinneweth, Director. *Website*: http://www.kuleuven.ac.be/pacdep/noial/soc/tzh/zelhulp.htm *E-mail*: anne_marie_dinneweth@soc.kuleuven.ac.be

CROATIA

College of Nursing, University of Zagreb, Mlinarska 38, Y-41000 Zagreb, Croatia. Phone: 0036-72/327-622 ext. 5392 or 0036-72/327-622 ext. 5330; FAX: 0036-72/327-622/5350. Contact Person: Arpad Barath. *E-mail*: arpad@bte.jpte.hu

DENMARK

Center for Frivilligt Socialt Arbejde, Pantheonsgade 5,3, 5000 Odense C, Denmark. Phone: 66-14-60-61; FAX: 66-14-20-17. Ulla Habermann, Executive Director, National Volunteer Centre. *E-mail*: drivsocarb@cybernet.dk

Faellesforeningen for Slevhjaelps-OG, Frivillighedsformidlinger, Sekretariat, Toldbodvej 5, 5700 Suendborg, Denmark. Contact Person: Mellem Mennesker. Phone: 45-62-20-1130; FAX: 45-62-20-11-13.

Kolding Selvhjaelp, Slotsgade 22 - 6000 Kolding, Denmark. Phone: (045) 75-50-79-02, Denmark. Phone: (045) 75-50-79-02; FAX: (045) 75-50-93-73 Director: Grete Brink

Sr - Bistand, Social Radgivning og Bistand, Sortedam Dosseringen 5, st. th., 2200 Kobenhavn N, Denmark. Phone: 0045-3139-7197; FAX: 353-66-395. Jeus Wissing, Director; Helene Olsen, Coordinator

ENGLAND

Self-Help Nottingham, 20 Pelham Road, Sherwood Rise, Nottingham NG5 1AP England, United Kingdom; Phone: 44-0115-969-1514 (general); 44-01150969-1212 (group information); FAX: 44-115-960 20 49. Jan Myers, Team Leader. *Website:* http://www.emnet.co.uk/SelfHelp   *E-mail:* selfhelp@globalnet.co.uk

"Contact-A-Family," *(limited to parents of children with illnesses/disabilities)*, 170 Tottenham Court Road, London, England W1P 0HA United Kingdom. Phone: 00 0171 383 3555; FAX: 0171 383 0259. Contact Person: Carol Youngs. *E-mail*: carol@cafamily.org.ok

GERMANY
(has over 100 clearinghouses. Check with national for locals)

Nationale Kontakt-Und Informationsstelle Zur Anregung Und Unterstuzung, Von Selbsthilfegruppen (NAKOS), Albrecht-Achilles-Strasse 65, D-10709 Berlin, Germany. Phone: 0049-30-891-4019; FAX: 0049-30-893-4014. Klaus Balke, Contact Person

Deutsche Arbeitsgemeinschaft Selbsthilfegruppen, c/o Friedrichstrasse 28, 35392 Giessen, Germany. Phone: 0049-641-99 45612; FAX: 0049-641-99 45609. Jurgen Matzat, contact person

HUNGARY

Self-Help Information Centre, Kira'ly 72, 1068 Budapest, Hungary. Phone: 0036-1-14 10 675; FAX: 0036-1-13 16 112. Ms. Zsuzs Csato, Coordinator

ISRAEL

National Self-Help Clearinghouse, 37, King George Street, P.O. Box 23223, Tel-Aviv 61231 Israel. Phone: 00972-3-62 99 389; FAX: 00972-3-52 54 486. Martha Ramon, Director

JAPAN

Osaka Self-Help Support Center, c/o Osaka Volunteer Association, 1-5-27, Doshin, Kita-ku, Osaka 530 Japan. Phone: +81-6-352-0430; FAX: +81-6-358-2892. Takehiro Sadato, Director; Hiroyuki Matsuda, Contact Person. *E-mail:* GHE01500@niftyserve.or.jp

Self-Help Clearinghouse for Children with Serious Diseases, Japan Welfare of Children and Families Association, (Nihon Jido Bunka Kyokai), Bancho Palace Bldg. 2, Gobancho, Chiyoda-ku, Tokyo, 102 Japan. Phone: 3-3261-3696; FAX: 3-3261-9249. Contact Person: Tomofumi Oka; *E-mail:* kgg01217@niftyserve.or.jp

POLAND

Working Group of the Self-Help Movements, Information Centre, TOPOS, Dluga 38/40, 00-238 Warsaw, Poland. Phone: (48-22)831 22 12; FAX: (48-22)831 47 12. Elzbieta Bobiatynska, Coordinator

SPAIN

TORRE JUSSANA, Avinguda Cardenal Vidal i Barraquer 30, 08035 Barcelona, Spain. Phone: 34 3 407 10 22; FAX: 34 3 407 11 97. Francina Roca, Coordinator. *E-mail:* tjussana@lix.intercom es *Website:* http://www.bcn.es/tjussana

SWEDEN

Distriktlakare *(Lapland only),* Villavagan 14, S-9390 Arjeplog, Sweden. Phone: +46-961-14800; FAX: +46-961-14819. Bo Henricson, Contact Person. *Website*: http://hem.passagen.se/snaps *E-mail*: bo.henricson@nll.se

SWITZERLAND

KOSCH, Selbsthilfezentrum Hinterhuus, Feldbergstrasse 55, CH-4057 Basel, Switzerland; Phone: 0041-061-692 80 00 (Group Info); Phone: 0041-061-692 84 88 (Admin); FAX: 0041-061 692 81 77. Contact person: Verena Vogelsanger

A MESSAGE TO SELF-HELP GROUP MEMBERS

"Though you have lost your dearest treasure, a child, a mate, your reputation, riches, position, health, respect, or self-control, you have given a special gift in return. That is the ability to say to another, 'I know just how you feel.' Ideally, a number of group members become quite well and comfortable, and become so committed, that they stay on to be a source of comfort and strength for new people in the same or similar circumstances. So please consider staying a little longer than you meant to--even for a lifetime, to pass along your message of hope: 'That's just how I felt but here is what I did and it is quite a bit better now.'"

Barbara Fox, Founder
Self-Help Information Service of Nebraska, Inc.

Chapter 7

SELF-HELP GROUPS

"There is a great comfort and inspiration in the feeling of close human relationships and its bearing on our mutual fortunes-- a powerful force, to overcome the "tough breaks" which are certain to come to most of us from time to time.

- Walt Disney

A B U S E

CHILD ABUSE

(Also see Sexual Abuse, Toll-Free Specialty Numbers)

Parents Anonymous *Nat'l. 2300 groups. Founded 1970.* Peer-led professionally-facilitated group for parents who are having difficulty and would like to learn more effective ways of raising their children. Publishes group leaders manual, chapter development manual and other materials available to assist in formation of groups. Many chapters also have children's groups. Write: Parents Anonymous, 675 W. Foothill Blvd., #220, Claremont, CA 91711-3416. Call (909)621-6184; FAX: (909)625-6304; *E-mail:* parentsanon@msn.com *Website:* http://www.parentsanonymous-natl.org

VOCAL (Victims Of Child Abuse Laws) *Nat'l. 150 chapters. Founded 1984.* Aim is to protect the rights of persons falsely and wrongly accused of child abuse, and to obtain more protection for children against abusers within the childrens' services system. Provides referrals to psychologists and attorneys. Newsletter, and chapter development guidelines available. Dues $15. Write: VOCAL, 7485 E. Kenyon Ave., Denver, CO 80237. Call (303)233-5321.

(Model) **CAPS (Child Abuse Prevention Services)** *(formerly Parental Stress Services) 25 sites in Chicago. Founded 1974.* Offers parenting education classes and children's support groups for those involved in stressful family environments. Provides assistance in starting new groups. Write: CAPS, 600 S. Federal, #205, Chicago, IL 60605. Call (312)427-1161; FAX: (312)427-3038.

(Interest in starting) **Shaken Baby Syndrome** *No known support network.* At printing, we had heard from one person who is interested in starting a support network for parents and caregivers of children with shaken baby syndrome, If you are interested in helping to start such a group, contact the Clearinghouse.

SEXUAL ABUSE / INCEST
(Also see Child Physical/Emotional Abuse)

False Memory Syndrome Foundation *Int'l. Founded 1992.* Research-oriented group for persons falsely accused of childhood sexual abuse based on recovered repressed memories. Also for those questioning their memories, and the professionals working with them. Information and referrals, phone support, networking, newsletter, conferences, and group meetings. Write: False Memory Syndrome Fdn., 3401 Market St., Suite 130, Philadelphia, PA 19104. Call 800-568-8882 or (215)387-1865; FAX: (215)387-1917; *E-mail:* pam@linc.cis.upenn/edu or psp@saul.cis.upenn.edu

Incest Survivors Anonymous (I.S.A.) *Int'l. Founded 1980.* Opportunity for men, women and teens to share their experience, strength and hope, so that they may recover from their incest experiences and break free to a new peace of mind. Based on the 12-steps and 12 traditions of A.A. Not open to perpetrators or satanists. Assistance in starting I.S.A. groups. Send a self-addressed stamped envelope to: I.S.A., P.O. Box 17245, Long Beach, CA 90807-7245.

Incest Survivors Resource Network Int'l *Int'l network. Founded 1983 at Friends Meeting House in NYC.* Educational resources for incest survivors and professionals working with survivors. Includes information on forming self-help groups and on mother-son incest. Offers survivor-run helpline. Write: ISRNI, P.O. Box 7375, Las Cruces, NM 88006-7375. Call (505)521-4260 (Mon-Sat., 2pm-4pm; 11pm-midnight ET); FAX: (505) 521-3723; *Website:* http://www.zianet.com/ISRNI *E-mail:* isrni@zianet.com

LINKUP *Int'l network of independent groups. Founded 1991.* Mutual support for survivors of clergy abuse. Aim is to educate victims, clergy, professionals and the public. Provides newsletter, advocacy, conferences, assistance in starting independent groups. Dues $35. Write: LINKUP, 1412 W. Argyle St., Suite #2, Chicago, IL 60640. Call (773)334-2296; FAX: (773)334-2297; *E-mail:* ilinkup@aol.com *Website:* http://www.linkup.org

Parents United International, Inc. *Nat'l. 55 chapters. Founded 1972.* Provides treatment for child sexual abuse including individual and group therapy, and guided self-help. Also for adults molested as children. Chapter development guidelines and training for professionals wishing to start groups. Write: Parents United Int'l, 615 15th St., Modesto, CA 95354-2510. Call (209)572-3446; FAX: (209)524-7780.

SARA (Sexual Assault Recovery Anonymous) Society *Nat'l. 30 groups. Founded 1983.* Education and self-help for adults and teens who were sexually abused as children. Group development guidelines. Assistance in starting groups. Literature on behavior modification. Newsletter. Dues $10. Write: SARA, P.O.

Box 16, Surrey, BC V3T 4W4 Canada. Call (604)584-2626; FAX: (604) 584-2888.

SESAME (Survivors of Educator Sexual Abuse/Misconduct Emerge) *Nat'l network. Founded 1993.* Support and information network for families of children (K-12) who have been sexually abused by a school staff member. Aims to raise public awareness. Information and referrals, phone support, literature, advocacy, newsletter. Write: SESAME, 681 Rt. 7A, Copake, NY 12516. Call (518)329-1265 or (516)489-6406; *E-mail:* jaye@earthlink.net *Website:* http://home.earthlink.net/~jaye/index.html

SNAP (Survivors Network of those Abused by Priests) *Int'l. 15 affiliated groups. Founded 1990.* Support for men and women who were sexually abused by any clergy person (priests, brothers, nuns, deacons, teachers, etc). Extensive phone network, newsletter, advocacy, conferences, information and referrals, advocacy, support group meetings. Assistance in starting new groups. Dues $25. Write: SNAP, 8025 S. Honore, Chicago, IL 60620. Call (312)409-2720.

Survivor Connections, Inc. *Nat'l network. Founded 1993.* Grassroots, activist organization for non-offending survivors of sexual assault by family, ritual, youth leaders, counselors, doctors, clergy, etc. Newsletter, peer-to-peer support groups. Referrals. Maintains database of perpetrators. Write: Frank Fitzpatrick, 52 Lyndon Rd., Cranston, RI 02905. Call Frank Fitzpatrick (401)941-2335 (Voice/FAX).

Survivors of Incest Anonymous (S.I.A.) *Int'l. 500 groups. Founded 1982.* Self-help 12-step program for men and women 18 yrs. or older who have been victims of child sexual abuse and want to be survivors. Newsletter ($15/yr), literature ($33.55 for 42 pieces), assistance in starting groups, volunteer information and referral line, speakers bureau. Send self-addressed stamped envelope to: S.I.A., P.O. Box 21817, Baltimore, MD 21222-6817. Call (410)282-3400; FAX: (410)282-3400.

VOICES In Action, Inc. *Nat'l network. Founded 1980.* Assists victims of incest/child sexual abuse in becoming survivors by helping them locate local support services and treatment. Provides public education on effects of incest. Newsletter ($20). Guidelines on starting self-help groups. Offers special interest correspondence groups, conferences, and publications. Dues $35/yr. (includes newsletter, conference discounts). Write: VOICES in Actions, P.O. Box 148309, Chicago, IL 60614. Call (773)327-1500 or 800-7-VOICE-8: FAX: (773)327-4590; *Website:* http://www.voices-action.org

(Model) **MALE (Men Assisting Leading Educating)** *2 chapters in Colorado. Founded 1991.* Forum for male survivors of childhood sexual abuse to discuss issues, share experiences and exchange ideas. Quarterly newsletter. Other support services planned for the future. Write: MALE, P.O. Box 460171,

Aurora, CO 80046-0171. Call (303)693-9930 or 800-949-MALE; FAX: (303) 693-6059; *Website:* http://www.malesurvivor.org *E-mail:* ftolson@ malesurvivor.org

(Model) **Molesters Anonymous** *10 groups in California. Founded 1985.* Provides support with anonymity and confidentiality for men who molest children. Use of "thought stoppage" technique and buddy system. Groups are initiated by a professional but become member-run. Group development manual ($12.95). Write: Dr. Jerry Goffman, 1850 N. Riverside Ave., Suite 220, Rialto, CA 92376. Call Dr. Jerry Goffman (909)355-1100; FAX: (909)421-3092; *E-mail:* jmgoff@genesisnetwork.net

(Model) **Partners and Friends of Incest Survivors Anonymous** *1 group in NY. Founded 1995.* 12-step group for partners, ex-partners, partners who are also survivors, friends and families of incest survivors. Based on the book by Ken Graber, "Ghosts in the Bedroom." Information and referrals, group meeting, literature, advocacy, and conferences. Assistance in starting similar groups. Write: Kerry C., 601 Camelot Court, Canandaigua, NY 14424. Call (716)393-0587; *Website:* http://www.cs.utk.edu/~bartley/other/pfisa.html *E-mail:* kjcater@mailbox.syr.edu

(Model) **TELL (Therapy Exploitation Link Line)** *1 group in Massachusetts. Founded 1989.* Support for women who have experienced sexual abuse by psychotherapists and other health care professionals. Resource network to help women file complaints and lawsuits, share referrals and network with others. Offers group meetings, information, phone support, help in starting similar groups. Write: TELL, P.O. Box 115, Waban, MA 02168. Call (617)964-8355.

(Model) **WINGS Foundation, Inc. (Women/Men Incested Needing Group Support)** *20 groups in Colorado. Founded 1982.* Promotes healing through support groups to reduce the trauma of incest. Newsletter ($12). Information and referrals, conferences, referrals to therapists, peer support groups for men and women. Assistance in starting new groups. Write: WINGS Fdn., 8007 W. Colfax, CS27, Box 129, Lakewood, CO 80215. Call (303)238-8660 (day); FAX: (303)238-8482; *E-mail:* wingspwr@aol.com

(Resource) **Incest Resources, Inc.** *Founded 1980.* Provides educational and resource materials for female and male incest survivors and for professionals working with them. International listing of survivors self-help groups. Manual for starting survivor self-help groups. For complete information send self-addressed stamped envelope with two 1st class stamps. Write: Incest Resources, Inc., 46 Pleasant St., Cambridge, MA 02139. (NO CALLS PLEASE)

(Resource) **National Organization on Male Sexual Victimization** Information and referrals for male survivors of sexual assault and the professionals working with them. Conference every two years. Referrals to local resources. Newsletter.

Write: NOMSV, P.O. Box 40055, St. Paul, MN 55104. Call 800-738-4181; FAX: (614)445-8283; *Website:* http://www.nomsv.org *E-mail:* nomsv@idd.net

(Online) **More Than Conquerors** *Founded 1995.* List servs for survivors of satanic ritual abuse, ritual abuse, and mind control, and for persons with multiple personality disorder or dissociative identity disorders. Support and information, resources, e-mail pal matching, advocacy, speakers bureau, education, IRC chat room, online newsletter. Write: More Than Conquerors, P.O. Box 70, Liberty Lake, WA 99019-0070. *E-mail:* Conquerors@aol.com

(How-To Guide) **All Together: A Guide for Dissociative Identity Disorder Self-Help Groups.** Since there is no current national group for multiple personality/dissociative disorder, we are providing information on this 53-page how-to guide which was edited by Jody Szczech, and is available for $10 postpaid from: Clearinghouse For Self-Help Groups, 339 East Ave., Suite 201, Rochester, NY 14604; phone: (716)325-3145 ext. 14.

(Note) For **Rape Victims Support Groups** that may exist, contact your local helpline, self-help clearinghouse, rape crisis service, or women's center. We know of no national self-help mutual aid group for rape victims at this time. If you can recommend any local member-run self-help group as a model, or a how-to group development guideline for rape victims, please let us know.

SPOUSE ABUSE / DOMESTIC VIOLENCE
(Also see Toll-Free Specialty Numbers)

Batterers Anonymous *Nat'l. 20 chapters. Founded 1980.* Self-help program for men who wish to control their anger and eliminate their abusive behavior toward women. Buddy system. Group development manual $9.95. Write: Dr. Jerry Goffman, 1850 N. Riverside Ave., Suite 220, Rialto, CA 92376. Call Dr. Jerry Goffman (909)355-1100 (leave message and return address); FAX: (909)421-3092; *E-mail:* jmgoff@genesisnetwork.net

(How-To Guide) **Talking it Out: A Guide to Groups for Abused Women** While we know of no national group to help with the development of a group for battered women, this book discusses how to start a group, how to lead it, group issues, group exercises, groups for specific populations, and how to prevent burnout. Authored by Ginny Ni Carthy, Karen Merriam, and Sandra Coffman. Available for $10.95 plus $1.50 postage from Seal Press, 3131 Western Ave., Seattle, WA 98121-1028.

(Note) **Battered Men** is an issue for which we have received a significant number of inquiries. Regrettably, we are unaware of any national or model self-help support group that has yet been formed. If you learn of any existing group that you would recommend, or are interested in starting such a group, please call the Clearinghouse.

ADDICTIONS

"Help thy brother's boat across, and lo! Thine own has reached the shore."
- Hindu Proverb

ADDICTIONS GENERAL
(Also see specific addiction, Toll-Free Specialty Numbers)

16 Steps of Empowerment *Nat'l. 100+ groups. Founded 1992.* Offers support for a wide variety of quality of life issues, such as addiction, codependency, abuse, empowerment, etc. The 16 steps focus on a positive approach to help members celebrate personal strengths, have choices, stand up for themselves, heal physically, express love, and see themselves as part of the entire community, not just the recovery community. Write: 16 Steps of Empowerment, 362 N. Cleveland Ave., Suite 1, St. Paul, MN 55104. Call (612)645-5782; *Website:* empower16@aol.com

Anesthetists in Recovery *Nat'l network. Founded 1984.* Networking of recovering nurse anesthetists. Telephone support, information and referrals to groups and treatment. Write: Rusty, AIR, 2205 22nd Ave. South, Minneapolis, MN 55404. Call (612)724-8238.

ART (Academics Recovering Together) *Nat'l network. Founded 1989.* Multi-purpose, informal support network for academic professionals in recovery from alcohol/drug addiction. Exchange of information on sabbaticals, relocation, issues surrounding promotion, tenure, etc. Newsletter, information and referrals, phone support. Write: Bruce E. Donovan, Brown University, Box 1865, Providençe, RI 02912. Call (401)863-3831 (day); FAX: (401)863-1961. *E-mail:* Bruce_Donovan@brown.edu

Chemically Dependent Anonymous *Nat'l. 65 affiliated groups. Founded 1980.* Purpose is to carry the message of recovery to the chemically dependent person. For those with a desire to abstain from drugs or alcohol. Offers information and referrals, phone support, conferences. Group development guidelines. Assistance in starting groups. Write: Chemically Dependent Anonymous, P.O. Box 423, Severna Park, MD 21146. Call 888-232-4673; *E-mail:* willieeatlantech.net *Website:* http://www.presstar.com/cda

Dual Disorders Anonymous *Nat'l. 28 groups in Illinois; 20 in other states. Founded 1982.* Fellowship of men and women who come together to help those members who still suffer from both mental disorder and alcoholism and/or drug addiction. Uses the 12-step program of A.A. Group development guidelines. Write: Dual Disorders Anonymous, P.O. Box 681264, Schaumburg, IL 60168-1264. Call (847)956-1660.

Intercongregational Alcoholism Program (ICAP) *Int'l. Founded 1979.* Support network for recovering Roman Catholic women who are, or who have been, members of religious orders, who are in need of help due to alcoholism or chemical dependencies. Information and referrals, assistance in meeting other members, phone support, conferences, newsletters. Write: ICAP, 1515 N. Harlem Ave. #202, Oak Park, IL 60302. Call (708)445-1400; FAX: (708) 445-1418; *E-mail:* lclose@waonline

International Doctors in Alcoholics Anonymous *Int'l network. 175 affiliated groups. Founded 1949.* Opportunity for doctoral level health care professionals to discuss common problems and find common solutions to drug and alcohol problems. Annual meetings (1st week in Aug.), phone support, information and referrals, newsletter. Mutual help meetings at conferences of other organizations. Write: Int'l Doctors in A.A., P.O. Box 199, Augusta, MO 63332. Call (314)482-4548 (day); FAX: (314)228-4102; *E-mail:* IDAAdickMc@aol.com

International Lawyers in Alcoholics Anonymous *Int'l. 40+ affiliated groups. Founded 1975.* Serves as a clearinghouse for support groups for lawyers who are recovering alcoholics or have other chemical dependencies. Newsletter, annual conventions. Group development guidelines. Write: I.L.A.A., c/o Ben G., P.O. Box 552212, Las Vegas, NV 89155-2212. Call (702)455-4827 (day).

International Nurses Anonymous *Int'l network. Founded 1988.* Fellowship of RNs, LPNs and nursing students who are in recovery from chemical dependency, co-dependency, or involved in any 12-step program. Write: c/o Pat Green, 1020 Sunset Dr., Lawrence, KS 66044. Call (913)842-3893; *E-mail:* Patlgreen@aol.com

International Pharmacists Anonymous *Nat'l. Founded 1987.* Fellowship of pharmacists and pharmacy students recovering from any type of addiction. Members must belong to a 12-step group. Newsletter, conferences, meetings, networking. Write: IPA, c/o Nan D., 32 Cedar Grove Rd., Annandale, NJ 08801. Call Nan (908)730-9072 (day) or (908)735-2789 (answering machine and FAX); *Website:* http://www.members.aol.com/mitchf0411/ipapage.htm *E-mail:* nan.davis@hcrhs.hunterdon.k12.nj.us

JACS (Jewish Alcoholics, Chemically Dependent Persons and Significant Others) *Nat'l. Founded 1980.* For alcoholic and chemically dependent Jews, families, friends, associates and the community. Networking, community outreach, retreats, newsletter, literature, spiritual events and speakers bureau. Write: JACS, 426 W. 58th St., New York, NY 10019. Call (212)397-4197; FAX: (212)489-6229; *E-mail:* jacsweb.org *Website:* http://www.jacsweb.org

Just Say No International *Int'l. 13,000 clubs. Founded 1985.* Through its youth power empowerment and leadership model, provides youth with skills necessary to form teams that identify problems, assess, plan and implement service activities in their schools and communities. "Just Say No" provides training, materials, on-going consultation and membership. Supports youth to lead healthy, productive, drug-free lives. Write: Just Say No, 2000 Franklin St., #400, Oakland, CA 94612. Call 800-258-2766; FAX: (510)451-9360; *E-mail:* youth@justsayno.org

National Association of Responsible Professional Athletes *Nat'l network. Founded 1993.* Dedicated to carrying the message of the hazards of addictions to the sports-minded youth of America, through the words and presence of responsible professional athletes and entertainers. Advocacy, information and referrals, and phone support. Dues vary. Write: NARPA, 5008 Eastwinds Dr., Orlando, FL 32819. Call (407)351-2811.

Overcomers In Christ *Int'l. Several sponsoring ministries. Founded 1987.* Recovery program that deals with every aspect of addiction and dysfunction (spiritual, physical, mental, emotional and social). Uses Overcomers Goals which are Christ-centered. Newsletter, information and referrals. Assistance in starting new groups. Literature. Write: Overcomers in Christ, P.O. Box 34460 Omaha, NE 68134-04604. Call (402)573-0966; FAX: (402)573-0960.

Overcomers Outreach, Inc. *Int'l. 700 affiliated groups. Founded 1985.* Christ-centered 12-step support group for persons with any compulsive behavior or addiction, their families and friends. Uses the 12-steps of Alcoholics Anonymous and applies them to the Scriptures. Uses Jesus Christ as "higher power." Supplements involvement in other 12-step groups. Newsletter, group development guidelines, conferences. Dues $10/yr. Write: Overcomers Outreach, 520 N. Brookhurst, #121, Anaheim, CA 92801. Call (714)491-3000 or 800-310-3001; FAX: (714)491-3004; *E-mail:* info@oo.sheperd.com *Website:* http://www.tfs.net/~iugml/oo.html

Psychologists Helping Psychologists *Nat'l network. Founded 1980.* For doctoral-level psychologists or students who've had a personal experience with alcohol or drugs. Aim is to support each other in recovery and help others to recover. Tries to educate psychology community. Regional/national get-togethers, newsletter. Write: Psychologists Helping Psychologists, 3484 S. Utah St., Arlington, VA 22206-1921. Call Ann (703)578-1644 or Martha Dugan (914)887-4043; FAX: (703)243-4470; *E-mail:* AnnS@erols.com

Rational Recovery Systems *Int'l. 800 groups. Founded 1986.* Helps persons achieve recovery from substance abuse and weight problems through self-reliance and self-help groups. Planned abstinence based on addictive voice recognition technique. Newsletter, group development guidelines. Lay-led time limited groups. Write: Rational Recovery Systems, P.O. Box 800, Lotus, CA 95651. Call (916)621-4374 or 800-303-2873; FAX: (916)622-4296; *Website:* http://rational.org/recovery/ *E-mail*: rrsn@rational.com

Recoveries Anonymous *Int'l. 20 groups. Founded 1983.* A solution-focused 12-step fellowship, designed especially for those who have yet to be successful in their search for recovery. For those who know the 12-steps work and want to learn how to use them. Open to anyone, including friends and family. Newcomer guide ($2); Group start-up kit ($25). Write: Recoveries Anonymous, P.O. Box 1212, Hewitt Sq. Stn., E. Northport, NY 11731. Call (516)261-1212.

Recovering Couples Anonymous (RCA) *Int'l. 85 groups. Founded 1988.* 12-step group that helps couples restore intimacy, communication, trust and learn healthier tools for maintaining these elements. For couples involved in a committed relationship. Information and referrals, support group meetings. Group development guidelines ($25). Write: RCA, P.O. Box 11872, St. Louis, MO 63105. Call Judy (314)830-2600; FAX: (314)830-2670; *Website:* http://www.recovering-couples.org

SADD (Students Against Destructive Decisions) *Nat'l. 25,000 groups. Founded 1982.* To help eliminate drunk driving, end underage drinking and drug abuse, alert students to dangers alcohol use and its resulting consequences, and to organize peer counseling programs for students concerned about alcohol and drugs. Newsletter, group development guidelines. Special programs include "Student Athletes Detest Drugs." Write: SADD, P.O. Box 800, Marlboro, MA 01752. Call (508)481-3568; FAX: (508)481-5759.

Secular Organizations for Sobriety (Save Ourselves) *Int'l. 1200 groups. Founded 1986.* Mutual help for alcoholics and addicts who want to acknowledge their addiction and maintain sobriety as a separate issue from religion or spirituality. Newsletter. Guidelines and assistance available for starting groups. Write: S.O.S., P.O. Box 5, Buffalo, NY 14215. Call (310)821-8430; FAX: (310)821-2610; *Website:* http://www.unhooked.com

SMART Recovery Self-Help Network (Self-Management And Recovery Training) *Nat'l. 200+ affiliated groups. Founded 1989.* Network of self-help groups for persons wanting to gain their independence from addictive and compulsive behaviors. An abstinence program based on cognitive-behavioral principles, especially rational-emotive-behavior therapy. Newsletter, information and referrals, literature and assistance in starting local chapters. Write: SMART Recovery Self-Help Network, 24000 Mercantile Rd., Suite 11, Beachwood, OH 44122. Call (216)292-0220 (day) or (216)951-0515; FAX: (216)831-3776; *Website:* http://www.cyberpsych.com/SMART *E-mail:* srmail1@aol.com

Social Workers Helping Social Workers *Nat'l network. Founded 1980.* Supports recovery from chemical dependency among social workers or matriculating students. Newsletter, annual retreat, group development guidelines. Write: SWHSW, P.O. Box 486, Nora Springs, IA 50458-8883. Call David C. Miller, ACSW (515)422-7485 (confidential voice mail) or (515)422-7797; FAX: (515)422-7516; *E-mail:* davidcm@netins.net

TARA (Total Aspects of Recovery Anonymous) *Int'l. 17 affiliated groups. Founded 1989.* 12-step recovery program to provide a loving and safe environment where members are free to address the entire spectrum of addictive and dysfunctional behaviors. Guidelines for developing groups. Write: TARA, 3799 Montclair, Cameron Park, CA 95682. Call (916)676-3366.

(Model) **CAIR (Changing Attitudes in Recovery)** *30 groups in CA. Founded 1990.* Self-help "family" sharing a common commitment to gain healthy esteem. Includes persons with relationship problems, addictions, mental illness, etc. Offers new techniques and tools that lead to better self-esteem. Assistance in starting groups. Handbook ($9.95), audio tapes, leader's manual. Write: Psych. Assoc. Press, 706 13th St., Modesto, CA 95354. Call (209)577-1667 (day); FAX: (209)577-3805.

(Model) **Chapter Nine Group of Hollywood, MD** *1 group in MD. Founded 1989.* 12-step program of recovering couples (substance abuse) in which partners work together. Group name comes from Chapter Nine of the A.A. Big Book "The Family Afterward" based on the belief that members of the family or couples should meet upon the common ground of tolerance, understanding and love. Write: Don Justice, 1168 White Sands Dr., Lusby, MD 20657. Call (410)586-1425; *E-mail:* HAQD45A@prodigy.com

(Model) **Clergy Serving Clergy** *1 group in MN. Founded 1987.* Volunteer group of recovering clergy that give help and support to one another. Assists in the identification, early intervention, proper treatment and productive recovery from the abuse of alcohol or other chemicals by clergy and family members. Write: Clergy Serving Clergy, 3509 Dana Dr., Burnsville, MN 55337. Call (612)894-4582; *E-mail:* rjfrog@aol.com

(Model) **Dentists Concerned for Dentists** *1 group in MN. Founded 1978.* Assists dentists with recovery from alcoholism or chemical dependency, or other human problems (family/marital, mental health, financial, etc). Group development guidelines. Write: Dentists Concerned for Dentists, 450 N. Syndicate #117, St. Paul, MN 55104. Call (612)641-0730.

(Model) **Realtors Concerned for Realtors** *Groups in Boston area. Founded 1993.* To assist real estate professionals, their families, associates, affiliates and employees regarding alcohol and drug abuse through education, support, prevention and recovery programs. Information and referrals, phone support, meetings, conferences, and networking. Help in starting similar programs. Write: John M. Peckham III, 4 Longfellow Pl., #2003, Boston, MA 02114. Call 800-854-7505; FAX: (617)523-4736; *E-mail:* BostonJack@earthlink.net *Website:* http://ourworld.compuserve.com/homepages/peckham

(Model) **Therapists In Recovery (T.I.R.)** *1 group in CA. Founded 1987.* Mutual support for licensed therapists in recovery from alcohol or drug

addiction. Members must belong to a 12-step recovery group. Local group meetings in California, phone support, information and referrals. Assistance in starting similar groups. Dues $36/year. Write: T.I.R., c/o Anderson, P.O. Box 230986, Encinitas, CA 92023-0986. Call Dominick (619)263-1086; *E-mail:* DominickDi@aol.com

(How-To Guide) **Double Trouble in Recovery: How To Start a Double Trouble in Recovery Group** Since there are few national groups for people who are recovering from combined problems of mental illness and chemical dependency, we are providing information on this 28-page how-to guide for starting "Double Trouble" groups. It is available to those outside New York State for $10 postpaid from: MHA in New York, 169 Central Ave., Albany, NY 12206.

ALCOHOL ABUSE
(Also see Addictions General, Toll-Free Specialty Numbers)

A.A. (Alcoholics Anonymous) World Services, Inc. *Int'l. 95000 groups. Founded 1935.* Worldwide fellowship of women and men who have found a solution to their drinking problem. The only requirement for membership is a desire to stop drinking. Supported by voluntary contributions of its members and groups, A.A. neither seeks nor accepts outside funding. Members observe personal anonymity at the public level, thus emphasizing A.A. principles rather than personalities. For more information, check your local phone directory or newspaper. Write: General Service Office, P.O. Box 459 Grand Central Station, New York, NY 10163. Call (212)870-3400; FAX: (212)870-3003; TDD: (212)870-3199; *Website:* http://www.alcoholics-anonymous.org   *E-mail:* 102336.451@compuserve.com

Adult Children of Alcoholics World Services Organization *Int'l. 1500+ meetings. Founded 1977.* A 12-step, 12-tradition program of recovery for adults who were raised in a dysfunctional environment where alcohol or other family dysfunctions were present. Group development guidelines. Newsletter, literature. Write: ACA, P.O. Box 3216, Torrance, CA 90510. Call (310)534-1815; *Website:* http://www.lafn.org/community/aca *E-mail:* aca@lafn.org

Al-Anon Family Groups, Inc. World Services Headquarters *Int'l. 32,000+ groups. Founded 1951.* Fellowship of men, women, children and adult children whose lives have been affected by the compulsive drinking of a family member or friend. Opportunity to grow through living by the 12-steps adopted from A.A. Guidelines for starting groups. Literature available in 29 languages. Write: Al-Anon, 1600 Corporate Landing Parkway, Virginia Beach, VA 23454-5617. Call (757)563-1600 or 800-344-2666 (meeting information, M-F, 8am-6pm ET) or 800-356-9996 (introductory literature); FAX: (757)563-1655; *Website:* http://www.al-anon.org

Alateen *Int'l. 4100+ groups. Founded 1957.* Fellowship of young persons whose lives have been affected by someone else's drinking. An active adult member of Al-Anon serves as a sponsor for each group. Based on the 12-steps and 12-traditions adapted from A.A. Group development guidelines, newsletter. Literature available in 30 languages. Write: Alateen, c/o Al-Anon Family Group Headquarters Inc., 1600 Corporate Landing Parkway, Virginia Beach, VA 23454-56127. Call (757)563-1600 or 800-344-2666; FAX: (757)536-1655; *Website:* http://www.al-anon.org or http://www.alateen.org

Alcoholics Victorious *Int'l. 130 affiliated groups.* Christian oriented 12-step support group for recovering alcoholics. Information and referrals, literature, phone support, conferences, support group meetings, newsletter. Assistance in starting similar groups. How-to materials ($6). Write: Alcoholics Victorious, c/o Int'l Union of Gospel Missions, 1045 Swift St., Kansas City, MO 64116-4127. Call (816)471-8020; FAX: (816)471-3718; *Website:* http://www.iugm.org/av *E-mail:* av@iugm.org

Calix Society *Nat'l. 52 chapters. Founded 1947.* Group of Catholic alcoholics maintaining their sobriety through Alcoholics Anonymous. Concerned with total abstinence, spiritual development and sanctification of the whole personality of each member. Bi-monthly newsletter. Assistance in chapter development. Write: Calix Soc., 7601 Wayzata Blvd., Minneapolis, MN 55426. Call (612)546-0544 (mornings only) or 800-398-0524.

Men for Sobriety *Int'l. 3 affiliated groups. Founded 1976.* Purpose is to help all men recover from problem drinking through the discovery of self through the sharing of experiences, hope and encouragement with other men in similar circumstances. Group recognizes men's complex role in today's society. Write: Men for Sobriety, P.O. Box 618, Quakertown, PA 18951-0618. Call (215)536-8026 (voice/FAX); *Website:* http://www.mediapulse.com/wfs *E-mail:* wfsobriety@aol.com

Moderation Management *Nat'l. 50 groups. Founded 1993.* Support for problem drinkers who want to reduce their drinking, or quit, and make other positive lifestyle changes. For those who have experienced mild to moderate levels of alcohol-related problems. Not intended for alcoholics. Literature, support group meetings, on-line group, handbook available. Assistance in starting new groups. Write: Moderation Management, P.O. Box 27558, Golden Valley, MN 55427. Call (612)512-1484; *Website:* http://comnet.org/mm/ *E-mail:* bkishlin@isd.net

National Association for Native American Children of Alcoholics *Nat'l network. Membership organization. Founded 1988.* Support network for Native American children of alcoholics. Provides education and training, newsletter, annual national conferences, regional training, substance abuse prevention materials, video, resources on alcoholism and substance abuse. Write:

NANACOA, 1402 Third Ave., #1110, Seattle, WA 98101-2118. Call 800-322-5601; FAX: (206)467-7689; *Website:* http://www.nanacoa.org *E-mail:* nanacoa@nanacoa.org

Women For Sobriety *Int'l. 350 groups. Founded 1976.* Program designed specifically to help the woman alcoholic achieve sobriety. Addresses need to overcome depression and guilt. Monthly newsletter, information and referrals, phone support, group meetings, pen pals, conferences, and group development guidelines. Write: Women for Sobriety, P.O. Box 618, Quakertown, PA 18951-0618. Call (215)536-8026 or 800-333-1606; FAX: (215)536-8026. *E-mail:* wfsobriety@aol.com *Website:* http://www.mediapulse.com/wfs

COMPUTER

(Note) **Addiction to Computer Use** is an issue for which we have received a significant number of inquiries. Regrettably, we are unaware of any model or national self-help group that has yet been formed. If you learn of any existing group that you would recommend, or are interested in starting such a group, please call the Clearinghouse.

DEBT / OVERSPENDING
(Also see Addictions General)

Debtors Anonymous *Int'l. 400+ groups. Founded 1976.* Fellowship that follows the 12-step program for mutual help in recovering from compulsive indebtedness. Primary purpose of members is to stay solvent and help other compulsive debtors achieve solvency. Newsletter, phone support network. Write: Debtors Anonymous, P.O. Box 400 Grand Central Station, New York, NY 10163-0400. Call (212)642-8220 (recording).

DRUG ABUSE
(Also see Addictions General, Toll-Free Specialty Numbers)

Co-Anon Family Groups *Int'l. 30 groups. Founded 1985.* 12-step program for friends and family of people who have problems with cocaine or other drugs. Phone support, help in starting new groups. Write: Co-Anon, P.O. Box 64742-66, Los Angeles, CA 90064. Call (714)647-6698.

Cocaine Anonymous *Int'l. 2000 chapters. Founded 1982.* 12-step fellowship of men and women who share their experience, strength and hopes that they may solve their common problem and help others to recover from addiction. Quarterly newsletter. Group starter kit available. Write: Cocaine Anonymous, 3740 Overland Ave., Suite C, Los Angeles, CA 90034-6337. For local chapters call 800-347-8998 (24 hrs.) or (310)559-5833 (business office); FAX: (310)559-2554; *E-mail:* cawso@ca.org *Website:* http://www.ca.org

Families Anonymous *Nat'l. 500+ groups. Founded 1971.* Mutual support for relatives and friends concerned about the use of drugs or related behavioral problems. Based upon the 12-step program adopted from A.A. Newsletter. Write: Families Anonymous, P.O. Box 3475, Culver City, CA 90231-3475. Call 800-736-9805 or (310)313-5800; FAX: (310)313-6841; *Website:* http://www.earthlink.net/ ~ famanon.ondex.html*E-mail:*famanon@earthlink.net

Marijuana Anonymous *Int'l. 100+ groups. Founded 1989.* Fellowship of men and women who desire to stay clean of marijuana. Follows the 12-step program. Literature, starter packets. Meetings on AOL. Write: M.A., P.O. Box 2912, Van Nuys, CA 91404. Call 800-766-6779 (recorded message). *Website:* http://www.marijuana-anonymous.org *E-mail:* info@marijuana-anonymous.org

Methadone Anonymous, U.S.A. *Int'l. 458 affiliated groups. Founded 1991.* Self-help group for, and led by, current and former methadone maintenance treatment patients. Open to anyone interested in recovery from chemical dependency. Literature, conferences, support group meetings. Newsletter. Assistance in starting new groups. Write: Methadone Anonymous, c/o Man Alive Research, Inc., 2100 N. Charles St., Baltimore, MD 21218. Call (410)837-4292; FAX: (410)837-0639; *E-mail:* maworld91@aol.com

Nar-Anon World Service Organization *Int'l. Founded 1967.* Worldwide organization offering self-help recovery to families and friends of addicts. Follows the 12-step program. Provides group packet for starting new groups. Write: Nar-Anon Family Group Headquarters, P.O. Box 2562, Palos Verdes, CA 90274-0119. Call (310)547-5800.

Narcotics Anonymous *Int'l. 21,000+ groups. Founded 1953.* Fellowship of men and women who come together for the purpose of sharing their recovery. There are no dues, fees, or registration requirements. The only requirement for membership is the desire to stop using drugs. Information is available in several languages, on audio tapes and in Braille. Write: N.A., P.O. Box 9999, Van Nuys, CA 91409. Call (818)773-9999; FAX: (818)700-0700; *Website:* http://www.wsoinc.com *E-mail:* info@wso.com

National Family Partnership *(formerly Parents for Drug-Free Youth) Nat'l. 100+ affiliates. Founded 1980.* Drug prevention and education, information, networking, and guidelines for parents forming community groups to address drug prevention. Two-day drug prevention education workshops for junior and high school students. Legislative advocacy on federal level and information resource for state and local efforts. Newsletter. Write: Nat'l Family Partnership, 11159 B S. Towne Square, St. Louis, MO 63123. Call (314)845-1933; FAX: (314)845-2117; *Website:* http://www.cybercity.piedmont.net/NFP/ *E-mail:* www.NFP.org or redribbon.org

Pill Addicts Anonymous *Int'l. 6 groups. Founded 1979.* Fellowship for all who seek freedom from addiction to prescribed and over-the-counter mood-changing pills and drugs. Sharing of experience, strength and hope to stay clean and help others achieve sobriety. Follows the 12-steps of A.A. Group development guidelines. Write: Pill Addicts Anon., P.O. Box 13738, Reading, PA 19612-3738.

(Model) **Benzodiazepine Anonymous** *1 group in Los Angeles, CA.* Mutual support for persons in recovery from an addiction to benzodiazepines (Xanax, Halcion, Valium, Ativan, Dalmane, Librium, etc) or other addicting prescription drug. Supportive, concerned group for all with a desire to stop using prescription drugs. Uses B.A. 12-steps and 12-goals. Open to families. Assistance in starting new groups. Write: B.A., 11633 San Vicente Blvd., Suite 314, Los Angeles, CA 90049. Call Caroline Kearney-Hirshfeld (310)652-4100.

(Model) **Pills Anonymous** *2 groups in NY City area.* Self-help, self-supporting, anonymous 12-step program, based on A.A., for those who want to help themselves and others recover from chemical addiction. Groups meets in New York City. Call (212)874-0700 (answering machine).

GAMBLING
(Also see Addictions General)

Gam-Anon Family Groups *Int'l. 500 groups. Founded 1960.* 12-step fellowship for men and women who are husbands, wives, relatives or close friends of compulsive gamblers who have been affected by the gambling problem. Purpose is to learn acceptance and understanding of the gambling illness, to use the program to rebuild lives, and give assistance to those who suffer. Write: Gam-Anon, P.O. Box 157, Whitestone, NY 11357. Call (718)352-1671 (Tues. and Thurs., 9am-5pm).

Gamblers Anonymous *Int'l. 1200 chapters. Founded 1957.* Fellowship of men and women who share experiences, strength and hope with each other to recover from compulsive gambling, following the 12-step program. Chapter development kit. Monthly bulletin for members. Write: G.A., P.O. Box 17173, Los Angeles, CA 90017. Call (213)386-8789; FAX: (213)386-0030; *Website:* http://www.gamblersanonymous.org *E-mail:* isomain@gamblersanonymous.org

OVEREATING
(Also see Addictions General)

Food Addicts Anonymous *Int'l. 141 affiliated groups worldwide. Founded 1987.* Fellowship of men and women who are willing to recover from the disease of food addiction. Primary purpose is to maintain abstinence from sugar, flour and wheat. Follows 12-step program. Information and referral, pen pals, conferences. Assistance in starting groups. Write: F.A.A., 4623 Forest Hill Blvd. #109-4, W. Palm Beach, FL 33415. Call (516)967-3871.

O-Anon *Int'l. 9 affiliated groups. Founded 1979.* Fellowship of friends and relatives of compulsive overeaters. Follows the 12-step program adapted from A.A. Newsletter. Group development guidelines. Write: O-Anon, P.O. Box 748, San Pedro, CA 90733. Call (310)547-1570.

Overeaters Anonymous *Int'l. 9,000 groups. Founded 1960.* A 12-step fellowship which meets to help one another understand and overcome compulsive eating disorders. Also groups and literature for young persons and teens. Magazine, group development guidelines. Write: O.A., P.O. Box 44020, Rio Rancho, NM 87174-4020. Call (505)891-2664 or look in white pages for local number. *Website:* http://www.overeatersanonymous.org   *E-mail:* overeater@technet.nm.org

SEX / LOVE ADDICTION
(Also see Addictions General)

Augustine Fellowship, Sex & Love Addicts Anonymous (S.L.A.A.) *Int'l. 1300 affiliated groups. Founded 1976.* 12-step fellowship based on A.A. for those who desire to stop living out a pattern of sex and love addiction, obsessive/compulsive sexual behavior or emotional attachment. Newsletter, journal, information and referrals, conferences, phone support. Group development guidelines ($10). Write: Augustine Fellowship, P.O. Box 650010, West Newton, MA 02165-0010. Call (617)332-1845; *E-mail:* slaafws@aol.com

COSA (Codependents of Sex Addicts) *National. 50+ affiliated groups. Founded 1980.* A self-help program of recovery using the 12-steps adapted from A.A., for those involved in relationships with people who have compulsive sexual behavior. Assistance in starting new groups. Newsletter ($12). Write: NSO COSA, Inc., 9337-B Katy Freeway, #142, Houston, TX 77024. Call (612)537-6904.

S-Anon *Int'l. 100 affiliated groups. Founded 1984.* 12-step group for persons who have a friend or family member with a problem of sexual addiction. Assistance for starting groups. Conferences. Quarterly newsletter ($10). Write: S-Anon, P.O. Box 111242, Nashville, TN 37222. Call (615)833-3152; FAX: (615)331-6901; *Website:* http://www.sanon.org *E-mail:* saif@sanon.org

Sex Addicts Anonymous *Int'l. 500 groups. Founded 1977.* Fellowship of men and women who share their experience, strength, and hope with one another that they may overcome their sexual addiction and help others recover from sexual addiction or dependency. Guidelines available for starting new groups. Educational booklet. Monthly newsletter. Write: S.A.A., P.O. Box 70949, Houston, TX 77270. Call (713)869-4902.

Sexaholics Anonymous *Int'l. 700 chapters. Founded 1979.* Program of recovery for those who want to stop their sexually self-destructive thinking and behavior. Mutual support to achieve and maintain sexual sobriety. Telephone network, quarterly newsletter, literature and books. Write: S.A., P.O. Box 111910, Nashville, TN 37222-1910. Call (615)331-6230; FAX: (615)331-6901; *Website:* http://www.sa.org *E-mail:* saico@sa.org

Sexual Compulsives Anonymous *Int'l. 150+ groups. Founded 1982.* Fellowship of men and women who share their experience, strength and hope that they may solve their common problem and help others to recover from sexual compulsion. Newsletter, information and referrals, phone support, conferences. Write: Sexual Compulsives Anonymous, P.O. Box 1585, New York, NY 10011. Call 800-977-4325; *E-mail:* info@sca-recovery.org *Website:* http://www.sca-recovery.org

Sexual Recovery Anonymous *Int'l. 19 affiliated groups. Founded 1990.* 12-step fellowship of men and women who share their experience, strength and hope with each other that they may solve their common problem and help others to recover. For those with a desire to stop compulsive sexual behavior. Write: S.R.A., P.O. Box 73, New York, NY 10024. Call (212)340-4650 (recorded information) or (604)290-9382 (British Columbia, Canada); *Website:* http://www.ourworld.compuserve.com/homepages/sra/

SMOKING
(Also see Addictions General)

Nicotine Anonymous World Services *Int'l. 500+ groups. Founded 1985.* 12-step program for people who want to recover from nicotine addiction and live free of nicotine in all forms. Newsletter ($7/yr). Guidelines and assistance available for starting groups. Some meetings on America Online. Write: NAWS, P.O. Box 591777, San Francisco, CA 94159-1777. Call (415)750-0328; FAX: (972)492-0832; *Website:* http://rampages.onramp.net/~nica *E-mail:* nica@onramp.net

WORKAHOLICS

Workaholics Anonymous World Service Organization, Inc. *Int'l. 80 groups. Founded 1983.* 12-step group for men and women who feel their work lives have gotten out of control. Also for family members and friends. Support in solving problems of compulsive overworking. Weekly meetings. Group development guidelines. Include self-addressed stamped envelope. Write: Workaholics Anonymous, P.O. Box 289, Menlo Park, CA 94026-0289. Call (510)273-9253.

BEREAVEMENT

"He that conceals his grief finds no remedy for it."
- Turkish Proverb

BEREAVEMENT (GENERAL)
(Also see Death of Child, Suicide Survivors, Widowhood)

COPS (Concerns of Police Survivors, Inc.) *Nat'l. 25 chapters. Founded 1984.* Peer support for spouses and families of law enforcement officers who died in the line of duty. Quarterly newsletter, departmental guidelines, peer support, conferences. Also COPS Kids program for children that offers peer support, counseling, and grief seminars. Write: COPS, c/o Suzie Sawyer, P.O. Box 3199, S. Highway 5, Camdenton, MO 65020. Call (573)346-4911; FAX: (573)346-1414; *E-mail:* cops@iland.net *Website:* http://www.iland.net/cops

National Donor Family Council *Nat'l. 52 affiliated groups. Founded 1991.* Mutual support for families who donated the organs/tissues of a loved one who died. Provides literature, programs and local resources. Newsletter, pen pals, conferences, advocacy. Write: Nat'l Donor Family Council, c/o Nat'l Kidney Fdn., 30 E. 33rd St., New York, NY 10016. Call 800-622-9010; FAX: (212)689-9261; *Website:* http://www.kidney.com

RAINBOWS *Int'l. 7000 affiliated groups. Founded 1983.* Establishes peer support groups in churches, schools or social agencies for children and adults who are grieving a death, divorce or other painful transition in their family. Groups are led by trained adults. Newsletter, information and referrals. Write: RAINBOWS, 1111 Tower Rd., Schaumburg, IL 60173. Call 800-266-3206 or (847)310-1880; FAX: (847)310-0120; *Website:* http://www.rainbows.org *E-mail:* rainbowshdqtrs@worldnet.att.net

Twinless Twin Support Group *Int'l network. Founded 1985.* Mutual support for twins who have lost their twin or multiple(s). Information and referrals, phone support, conferences. Parents of young survivor twins welcome. "Twinless Times" and "Twinsworld" newsletters ($25/yr.) Group development guidelines. Assistance in starting local groups. Several videos. Write: Twinless Twin Support Group, c/o Dr. Brandt, 11220 St. Joe Rd., Fort Wayne, IN 46835-9737. Call Dr. Raymond Brandt (219)627-5414; *E-mail:* brandt@mail.fwi.com *Website:* http://www.fwi.com/twinless

Wings of Light, Inc. *Nat'l. 3 support networks. Founded 1995.* Support and information network for individuals whose lives have been touched by aircraft accidents. Separate networks for: airplane accident survivors; families and friends of persons killed in airplane accidents; and persons involved in the rescue, recovery and investigation of crashes. Information and referrals, phone support. Write: Wings of Light, 16845 N. 29th Ave., Suite 1-448, Phoenix, AZ 85023. Call 800-613-8531 or (602)516-1115; FAX: (602)572-2511; *Website:* http://www.flightdata.comwol *E-mail:* awaaswings@aol.com

(Resource) **Pet Bereavement** For those who are having difficulty coping with the death of a pet, there are some pet bereavement support groups around the country. The Delta Society maintains a national listing of pet loss resource persons, a few of whom have support groups. For a local referral send a self-addressed stamped envelope to: Delta Soc., P.O. Box 1080, Renton, VA 98057-1080. Call (206)226-7357 (day).

(Note) **Accidental Deaths, People Who Feel Responsible for**, is an issue for which we have received a significant number of inquiries. Regrettable, we are unaware of any model or national self-help support group that has yet been formed. If you learn of any existing group that you would recommend, or are interested in starting such a group, please call the Clearinghouse.

DEATH OF A CHILD / FETAL LOSS

Alive Alone, Inc. *Nat'l network. Founded 1988.* Self-help network of parents who have lost an only child or all of their children. Provides education and publications to promote communication and healing, to assist in resolving grief, and to develop means to reinvest lives for a positive future. Write: Alive Alone, c/o Kay Bevington, 11115 Dull Robinson Rd., Van Wert, OH 45891.

AMEND (Aiding Mothers and Fathers Experiencing Neonatal Death) *Nat'l network. Founded 1974.* Offers support and encouragement to parents having a normal grief reaction to the loss of their baby. One-to-one peer counseling with trained volunteers. Write: AMEND, 4324 Berrywick Terrace, St. Louis, MO 63128. Call (314)487-7582.

Bereaved Parents of the USA *Nat'l. 31 affiliated groups. Founded 1995.* Designed to aid and support bereaved parents and their families who are struggling to survive their grief after the death of a child. Information and referrals, newsletter, phone support, conferences, support group meetings. Assistance in starting groups. Write: Bereaved Parents of the USA, P.O. Box 95, Park Forest, IL 60466. Call (708)748-7672; FAX: (708)748-9184.

CHUCK (Committee to Halt Useless College Killings) *Nat'l network. Founded 1979.* Support for families who have lost a child to hazing or alcohol in fraternity, sorority or other college group. Advocacy to change hazing laws. Education on the dangers of such practices. Information and referrals, phone support, speakers bureau. Write: CHUCK, P.O. Box 188, Sayville, NY 11782. Call Eileen Stevens (516)567-1130.

CLIMB, Inc. (Center for Loss In Multiple Birth) *Int'l network. Founded 1987.* Support by and for parents who have experienced the death of one or more of their twins or higher multiples during pregnancy, birth, in infancy, or childhood. Newsletter, information on specialized topics, pen pals, phone support. Materials for twins clubs, helping professionals, and loss support groups. Write: CLIMB, P.O. Box 1064, Palmer, AK 99645. Call (907)746-6123 (after 10am); *E-mail:* climb@pobox.alaska.net

Compassionate Friends, The *Nat'l. 600 chapters. Founded 1969.* Offers support, friendship and understanding to parents and siblings grieving the death of a child. Telephone support, information on the grieving process, monthly chapter meetings. National newsletter ($20/yr.) and sibling newsletter ($10/yr.) Resource guide. Write: The Compassionate Friends, P.O. Box 3696, Oak Brook, IL 60522-3696. Call (630)990-0010; FAX: (630)990-0246. *E-mail:* tzht72a@prodigy.com

Open ARMS (Abortion Related Ministries) *Nat'l. Affiliated groups. Founded 1986.* Christian post-abortion support group open to anyone suffering from abortion's emotional aftermath. Provides newsletters, phone support, conferences, information and referrals. Group development guidelines ($12). Write: Open ARMS, c/o Patti Goodoien-Slauson, P.O. Box 9292, Colorado Springs, CO 80932. Call (719)573-5790.

Parents of Murdered Children *Nat'l. 300 chapters and contact persons throughout US and Australia. Founded 1978.* Provides self-help groups to support persons who survive the violent death of someone close, as they seek to recover. Newsletter; court accompaniment also provided in many areas. Write: Parents of Murdered Children, 100 E. 8th St., 8-41, Cincinnati, OH 45202. Call (513)721-5683; FAX: (513)345-4489; *E-mail:* NatlPOMC@aol.com *Website:* http://www.metroguide.com/pomc

SHARE: Pregnancy and Infant Loss Support, Inc. *Nat'l. 110 chapters. Founded 1977.* Mutual support for bereaved parents and families who have suffered a loss due to miscarriage, stillbirth or neonatal death. Newsletter, pen pals, information for professionals, caregivers and pastoral care. Chapter development guidelines. Write: SHARE, c/o St. Joseph's Health Ctr., 300 First Capital Dr., St. Charles, MO 63301-2893. Call 800-821-6819 or (314) 947-6164; FAX: (314)947-7486; *Website:* http://www.nationalshareoffice.com

SIDS Alliance *Nat'l. 50 chapters. Founded 1962.* Emotional support for families of sudden infant death syndrome victims. Supports research, educates the public. Newsletter, telephone support network, chapter development guidelines. Write: SIDS Alliance, 1314 Bedford Ave., #210, Baltimore, MD 21208. Call 800-221-7437; (410)653-8226 (within MD); FAX: (410)653-8709.

Tender Hearts *Int'l network. Sponsored by Triplet Connection. Founded 1983.* Network of parents who have lost one or more children in multiple births. Information on selection reduction. Newsletter information and referrals, phone support and pen pals. Write: Tender Hearts, c/o Triplet Connection, P.O. Box 99571, Stockton, CA 95209. Call (209)474-0885; FAX: (209)474-2233; *Website:* http:/www.inreach.com/triplets *E-mail:* triplets@inreach.com

Unite, Inc. *Nat'l. 14 groups. Founded 1975.* Support for parents grieving miscarriage, stillbirth and infant death. Support for parents through subsequent pregnancies. Group meetings, phone help, newsletter, annual conference. Group facilitator and grief counselor training programs. Professionals in advisory roles. Write: Unite, Inc., c/o Janis Heil, Jeanes Hospital, 7600 Central Ave., Philadelphia, PA 19111-2499. Call (215)728-3777 (tape) or (215)728-4286.

(Model) **Abortion Survivors Anonymous** *1 group in Colorado. Founded 1989.* 12-step support for persons affected by an abortion loss. For those seeking to recover from the impact of abortion in their lives and relationships. 12-step workbook ($15). Write: Abortion Survivors Anonymous, P.O. Box 1533, Alpine, CA 91903. Call Sarah (619)445-1247 or Mary (619)578-9079.

SURVIVORS OF SUICIDE

American Foundation for Suicide Prevention *Nat'l. 12 chapters. Founded 1987.* Provides state directories of survivor support groups for families and friends of a suicide. Information regarding suicide statistics, prevention and surviving. Write: Amer. Suicide Fdn., 120 Wall St., 22nd fl., NY, NY 10005. Call 888-333-2377 or (212)363-3500; FAX: (212)363-6237; *E-mail:* 76433.1676 @compuserve.com or mingenth@ccsny.com *Website:* http://www.afsp.org

Ray of Hope, Inc. *Nat'l. 13 affiliated groups. Founded 1977.* Mutual support groups for after-suicide bereavement. Educational materials on suicide postvention. Offers books on suicide and grief (call for price list). Also provides telephone counseling. Assistance in starting survivor support groups. Write: Ray of Hope, P.O. Box 2323, Iowa City, IA 52244. Call (319)337-9890.

(Model) **Heartbeat** *21 groups in Colorado. Founded 1980.* Mutual support for those who have lost a loved one through suicide. Information and referrals, phone support, chapter development guidelines ($15). Speakers on suicide bereavement. Write: Heartbeat, 2015 Devon St., Colorado Springs, CO 80909. Call (719)596-2575.

(Resource) **American Association of Suicidology** Provides referrals to 350 self-help groups for survivors of suicide nationwide. Directory of groups ($9). Newsletter, pamphlets, etc. available for a fee. Manual on starting self-help groups ($18). Write: American Assn. of Suicidology, 4201 Connecticut Ave., NW, #310, Washington, DC 20008. Call (202)237-2280.

WIDOWS / WIDOWERS

Beginning Experience, The *Int'l. 140 teams. Founded 1974.* Support programs for divorced, widowed and separated adults and their children enabling them to work through the grief of a lost marriage. Write: The Beginning Experience, 1209 Washington Blvd., Detroit, MI 48226. Call (313)965-5110; FAX: (313)965-5557.

COPS (Concerns of Police Survivors, Inc.) *Nat'l. 22 chapters. Founded 1984.* Peer support for spouses and families of law enforcement officers who died in the line of duty. Quarterly newsletter, departmental guidelines, peer support, conferences. Also COPS Kids program for children that offers peer support, counseling, and grief seminars. Write: COPS, c/o Suzie Sawyer, P.O. Box 3199, S. Highway 5, Camdenton, MO 65020. Call (573)346-4911; FAX: (573)346-1414; *E-mail:* cops@iland.net *Website:* http://www.iland.net/cope

Society of Military Widows *Nat'l. 27 chapters. Founded 1968.* Support and assistance for widows/widowers of members of all U.S. uniformed services. Help in coping with adjustment to life on their own. Promotes public awareness. Newsletter. Dues $12/yr. Chapter development guidelines. Write: Soc. of Military Widows, 5535 Hempstead Way, Springfield, VA 22151. Call (703)750-1342; *Website:* http://www.penfed.org/naus/home.htm

THEOS (They Help Each Other Spiritually) *Int'l. 70 chapters. Founded 1962.* To assist widowed persons of all ages and their families to rebuild their lives through mutual self-help. Network of local groups. Write: THEOS, 322 Boulevard of the Allies, #105, Pittsburgh, PA 15222-1919. Call (412)471-7779; FAX: (412)471-7782.

Widowed Persons Service *Nat'l. 240 groups. Founded 1973.* A program run in cooperation with AARP and local community groups, providing one-to-one peer support for widows and widowers of all ages. Provides manuals on starting support groups, quarterly newsletter, referral services and public education. Facilitates an on-line bereavement support group on America Online, Mon., 8:30pm ET. Write: WPS, 601 E Street NW, Washington, DC 20049. Call (202)434-2260; FAX: (202)434-6474; *E-mail:* astudner@aarp.org *Website:* http://www.aarp.org

(Model) **TLA (To Live Again)** *24 chapters in Delaware Valley. Founded 1974.* Mutual help organization covering the greater Delaware Valley, for widowed women and men supporting one another through the grief cycle. Monthly meetings, social programs, chapter development assistance, Reach-Out program for newly bereaved, conferences, newsletter. Dues $12/yr. Write: TLA, P.O. Box 415, Springfield, PA 19064-0415. Call (610)353-7740; FAX: (215)634-2633.

DISABILITIES

"When one is helping another, both are strong."
- German Proverb

AMPUTATION / LIMB DEFICIENCY
(Also see Disabilities General; Parents of Disabled, specific disorder)

American Amputee Foundation, Inc. *Nat'l. 11 chapters. Founded 1975.* Information, referrals and peer support for amputees. Hospital visitation and counseling. Magazine, group development guidelines, national resource directory for patients, families and caregivers. "Give A Limb" program. Write: Amer. Amputee Fdn., P.O. Box 250218, Little Rock, AR 72225-0218. Call (501)666-2523; FAX: (501)666-8367.

National Amputation Foundation, Inc. *Nat'l. Founded 1919.* Self-help group for amputees of all ages. "Amp to Amp" program links individuals with others with similar amputations. Dues $25. Newsletter, library of information, advocacy, vocational guidance, information and referrals. Write: Nat'l Amputation Fdn., 38-40 Church St., Malverne, NY 11565. Call (516)887-3600; FAX: (516)887-3667.

(Resource) **Amputee Coalition of America** *120+ groups. Founded 1989.* Coalition of amputees, support groups, professionals and disability-related organizations established to provide outreach, education and empowerment for persons with limb loss. Referrals to support groups. Write: Amputee Coalition of America, P.O. Box 2528, Knoxville, TN 37901-2528. Call 800-355-8772; FAX: (423)525-7917; *E-mail:* acaone@aol.com

AUTISM / ASPERGER SYNDROME
(Also see Parents of Disabled, Disabilities General, Speech)

Autism Network International (ANI) *Int'l. Founded 1992.* Organization run by and for autistic people. Provides peer support and tips for coping and problem-solving. Information and referrals. Advocacy, education. Newsletter ($15). Retreats and conferences. Write: ANI, P.O. Box 448, Syracuse, NY 13210-0448. Call (315)476-2462 (long-distance calls returned collect); *E-mail:* ani-l-request@listserv.syr.edu *listserv discussion forum:* jisincla@ mailbox.syr.edu *Website:* http://www.students.uninc.edu/ ~ bordner/ani/html

Autism Society of America *Nat'l. 200+ chapters. Founded 1965.* Organization of parents, professionals and citizens working together through education, advocacy and research for children and adults with autism. Newsletter, mail order bookstore, annual conference. Write: Autism Society of

125

America, 7910 Woodmont Ave., Suite 650, Bethesda, MD 20814. Call (301)657-0881, 800-3-AUTISM (information and referral only); FAX: (301)657-0869.

(Model) **Advocates for Individuals with Higher Functioning Autism** *Founded 1996.* Support and education for parents of children with higher functioning autism, Asperger syndrome, and other pervasive developmental disorders. Designs activities, educates professionals, provides information and referrals, and distributes literature. Newsletter. Assistance in starting groups. Write: c/o Nina Spooner, 2400 Garth Rd., #4E2, Scarsdale, NY 10583. Call (914)723-5195.

(On-Line) **Asperger Syndrome Support Group** An online support network for parents of children with Asperger. Maintains website and has regular online meetings on America-On-Line. *Website:* http://www.udel.edu/bkirby/asperger *E-mail:* bkirby914@aol.com

BLIND / VISUALLY IMPAIRED
(Also see Disabilities General; Parents of Disabled; specific disability)

Achromatopsia Network   *Nat'l network.*   Information and support for individuals and families concerned with the rare inherited vision disorder achromatopsia, including both rod monochromacy and blue cone monochromacy. Open to persons with similar vision disorders such as hypersensitivity to light and color vision deficiency. Write: Achromatopsia Network, P.O. Box 214, Berkeley, CA 94701-0214. *Website:* http://www.achromat.org/

American Council of The Blind *Nat'l. 70 affiliates. Founded 1961.* Aims to improve the well-being of all blind and visually impaired people and their families through education, support, and advocacy. National conference, information and referrals, phone support, support groups, monthly magazine. Chapter development guidelines. Write: American Council of the Blind, 1155 15th St. NW, #720, Washington, DC 20005. Call 800-424-8666 or (202)467-5081; FAX: (202)467-5085; *Website:* http://www.acb.org *E-mail:* ncrabb@access.digex.net

Association for Macular Diseases, Inc. *Nat'l. Local support groups. Founded 1978.* Support groups for persons suffering from macular diseases and their families. Distributes information on vision aids and research. Provides an eye bank devoted solely to macular disease research. Quarterly newsletter, telephone support network, group development guidelines. Write: Assn. for Macular Diseases, 210 E. 64th St., New York, NY 10021. Call (212)605-3719; FAX: (212)605-3795; *Website:* http://www.macular.org

Blinded Veterans Association *Nat'l. 50 regional groups. Founded 1945.* Information, support and outreach to blinded veterans. Help in finding jobs, information on benefits and rehabilitation programs. Bimonthly newsletter. Chapter development guidelines. Regional meetings. Write: BVA, 477 H St., NW, Washington, DC 20001. Call (202)371-8880 or 800-669-7079; FAX: (202)371-8258; *E-mail:* bva@bva.org

Council of Citizens with Low Vision International *Int'l. (a special interest affiliate of the American Council of the Blind) Founded 1978.* Encourages low vision people to make full use of vision through use of aids, technology and services. Education and advocacy. Newsletter, information and referrals, group development guidelines, scholarships, and conferences. Dues $10/yr. Write: CCLVI, 33 Orange St., Woburn, MA 01801-4605. Call 800-733-2258 or Christine Nason (617)933-6079.

Foundation Fighting Blindness, The *Nat'l. 43 groups.* Supports research into causes, prevention and treatment of retinitis pigmentosa and allied retinal degeneration. Information and referral, conferences. Retina donor program. Confidential registry. Write: Fdn. Fighting Blindness, Executive Plaza 1, Suite 800, 11350 McCormick Rd., Hunt Valley, MD 21031-1014. Call 888-394-3937 or (410)785-1414; TDD: 800-683-5551 or (410)785-9687; FAX: (410) 771-9470; *Website:* http://www.blindness.org

Macular Degeneration International *Nat'l network. Founded 1991.* Mutual support for persons with juvenile and age-related macular dystrophies, their families and friends. Provides information on eye diseases. Conferences, phone support, information and referrals. Also has Stargardt self-help support network. Write: MDI, 2968 W. Ina Rd., #106, Tucson, AZ 85741. Call 800-393-7634 or (520)797-2525; FAX: (520)797-8018; *E-mail:* TPerski@aol.com

National Association For Parents of The Visually Impaired, Inc. *Nat'l. 16 groups. Founded 1980.* Outreach and support for parents of visually impaired children. Promotes formation of local parent support groups. Increases public awareness. Quarterly newsletter. Dues $20/family. Group development guidelines. Write: Nat'l Assn. for Parents of the Visually Impaired, P.O. Box 317, Watertown, MA 02272-0317. Call 800-562-6265 or (617)972-7441; FAX: (617)972-7444.

National Association for Visually Handicapped *Nat'l. 7 affiliated groups in NY and CA. Founded 1954.* Support groups for partially-seeing persons. Some groups are professionally-run. Newsletter, phone support, information and referrals. Guide to starting groups for elders losing sight. Write: NAVH, attn: E. Cohen, 22 W. 21st St., New York, NY 10010. Call (212)889-3141; FAX: (212)727-2931; *E-mail:* staff@navh.org *Website:* http://www.navh.org

National Federation of the Blind *Nat'l. 52 affiliates. Founded 1940.* Serves as both an advocacy and a public information vehicle. Contacts newly blind persons to help with adjustment. Provides information on services and applicable laws. Student scholarships. Assists blind persons who are victims of discrimination. Literature, monthly meetings and magazine. Write: Nat'l Federation of Blind, 1800 Johnson St., Baltimore, MD 21230 Call (410)659-9314. Service for blind seeking employment: 800-638-7518; *E-mail:* nfb@access.digex.net *Website:* http://www.nfb.org

National Organization for Parents of Blind Children *Nat'l. 23 divisions. Founded 1983.* Support for parents of blind children. Serves as both an advocacy and public information vehicle. Provides information on services available. Offers positive philosophy and insights into blindness and practical guidance in raising a blind child. Newsletter, parent seminars, free parents information packet, meetings, conventions. Dues $8/yr. Write: NOPBC, Attn: Barbara Cheadle, Nat'l Org. for Parents of Blind Children, 1800 Johnson St., Baltimore, MD 21230. Call (410)659-9314; FAX: (410)685-5653; *Website:* http://www.nfb.org (display only) or http://www.ftp.nfb.org

Usher's Syndrome Self-Help Network *Nat'l network. 50 affiliated groups. Founded 1983.* A listing of individuals with Usher's Syndrome and their families who are available to others who want to share their experiences. Write: c/o The Fdn. Fighting Blindness, Usher's Syndrome Self-Help Network, Executive Plaza 1, #800, 11350 McCormick Rd., Hunt Valley, MD 21031-1014. Call 800-683-5555 or (410)785-1414; TDD: 800-683-5551 or (410)785-9687; FAX: (410)771-9470; *Website:* http://www.blindness.org

Vision Foundation, Inc. *Nat'l. 30 groups. Founded 1970.* Information and support network for persons coping with sight loss. Sponsors support groups for elders and "mixed" ages. Outreach services, phone support, large print literature and cassettes, newsletter. Dues $15-30/yr. Write: Vision Fdn., Inc., 818 Mt. Auburn St., Watertown, MA 02172. Call (617)926-4232 or 800-852-3029 (in Mass. only); FAX: (617)926-1412.

(Model) **Vision Northwest** *40+ groups in Oregon. Founded 1983.* Mission is to reach out with compassion, encouragement and understanding to those coping with vision loss, their families and friends. Helps persons with vision loss to become more independent through a network of peer support groups. Information and referral, quarterly newsletter. Write: Vision Northwest, 621 SW Alder St., #500, Portland, OR 97205. Call (503)221-0705; FAX: (503)243-2537. *E-mail:* vnw@teleport.com

(Resource) **Lighthouse, Inc., The** Information and directory on over 700 member-run self-help groups and professionally-run support groups across the country for older adults with impaired vision. Information on low vision clinics, vision rehabilitation agencies, products and assistive technology. Newsletter. Write: The Lighthouse, Inc., 111 E. 59th St., New York, NY 10022. Call 800-334-5497 (Voice); (212)821-9713 (TTY); (212)821-9200 (general); *Website:* http://www.lighthouse.org *E-mail:* info@lighthouse.org

BURN SURVIVORS
(Also see Disabilities General, Accident/Trauma)

Burns United Support Group *Nat'l. 3 affiliated groups. Founded 1986.* Support for children and adults who have survived being burned, no matter how major or minor the burn, their families and friends. Outreach visitation, newsletter, pen pals, phone support, assistance in starting groups. Write: Burns United Support Group, c/o Donna Schneck-Smorol, P.O. Box 36416, Grosse-Pointe, MI 48236. Call (313)881-5577; FAX: (313)417-8702.

National Burn Victim Foundation *Int'l. Founded 1974.* Advocacy and services for burn victims and their families. Provides burn-related information and referrals, support system for disaster response, evaluation services for burned children suspected of being abused, community education and burn prevention, and research into new treatments. Forensic burn unit. Newsletter, brochures. Write: Nat'l Burn Victim Fdn., 246A Madisonville Rd., P.O. Box 409, Basking Ridge, NJ 07920. Call Harry Gaynor (908)953-9091; FAX: (908)953-9099; *E-mail:* NBVF@intac.com *Website:* http://www.nbvf.org

Phoenix Society for Burn Survivors, Inc., The *Int'l. 350 area coordinators. Founded 1977.* Recovered burn survivors work with severely burned people and their families during and after hospitalization. Pen pal network, chapter starter kit, quarterly newsletter, phone network, national and international conferences, books, and audio-visual materials. Camps for burned children. Write: Phoenix Soc., 11 Rust Hill Rd., Levittown, PA 19056. Call 800-888-BURN or (215)946-BURN; FAX: (215)946-4788; *Website:* http://www.extension. valberta.ca/frw or http://www.lewisville.com/nporgs/phoenix.html or http://tallahassee.net/~tbr/phoenix.html

DEAF / HEARING IMPAIRED / TINNITUS / MENIERE'S
(Also see specific disorder)

American Society for Deaf Children *Nat'l. 120 affiliates. Founded 1967.* Information and support for parents and families with children who are deaf or hard of hearing. Quarterly newsletter, telephone support network, conferences. Group development guidelines. Dues $30/yr. Write: Amer. Soc for Deaf Children, 1820 Tribute Rd., Suite A, Sacramento, CA 95825-1373. Call 800-942-ASDC (voice and TDD); *E-mail:* asdc1@aol.com

American Tinnitus Association *Nat'l. 102 groups. Founded 1971.* Educational information for patients and professionals. Provides network of services through clinics and self-help groups. Supports research. Quarterly magazine. Self-help group development guidelines. Write: American Tinnitus

Assn., P.O. Box 5, Portland, OR 97207. Call (503)248-9985; FAX: (503) 248-0024; *Website:* http://www.teleport.com/~ata *E-mail:* Tinnitus@ata.org

Cochlear Implant Club International, Inc. *Int'l. 30 affiliated groups. Founded 1985.* Support through fellowship for implant recipients and their families. Pre- and post-op counseling, information on new technology. $18/yr. Speakers bureau. Quarterly newsletter. Chapter development guidelines. Write: Cochlear Implant Club Int'l, P.O. Box 464, Buffalo, NY 14223-0464. Call (716)838-4662 (voice/FAX/TDD); *E-mail:* 76207.3114@compuserve.com

Meniere's Network *Nat'l. 42 groups. Founded 1987.* Education for persons with Meniere's disease about the condition, treatment alternatives and coping strategies. Education for the public and professionals. Newsletter twice per year. Group development guidelines, phone buddies, pen pals. Dues $25/yr. Write: Meniere's Network, 1817 Patterson St., Nashville, TN 37203. Call 800-545-4327; FAX: (615)329-7935; *Website:* http://www.theearfound.com *E-mail:* EARFYI@aol.com

National Association of The Deaf *Nat'l. 51 chapters. Founded 1880.* Nation's largest constituency organization safeguarding the accessibility and civil rights for 28 million deaf and hard of hearing Americans in education, employment, health care, and telecommunications. Primary area of focus include grassroots advocacy and empowerment, captioned media, deafness-related information and publications, legal assistance, policy development and research, public awareness, and youth leadership programs. Write: Nat'l Assn. of the Deaf, 814 Thayer Ave., Silver Spring, MD 20910-4500. Call (301)587-1789 (TTY); (301)587-1788 (Voice), FAX: (301)587-1791; *E-mail:* nhdhq@juno.com *Website:* http://www.nad.org

National Fraternal Society of The Deaf *Nat'l. 80 divisions. Founded 1901.* Self-help organization for deaf and hard of hearing persons, their families and concerned professionals that provide low-cost life insurance, scholarships for students, information and referrals. Fellowship and advocacy. Bi-monthly newsletter. Membership dues vary. Write: Nat'l Fraternal Soc. of the Deaf, 1118 S. 6th St., Springfield, IL 62703. Call (217)789-7438 (TDD); FAX: (217)789-7489; *E-mail:* 104656.272@compuserve.com

Parents Section, A.G. Bell Association for the Deaf *Int'l. 28 affiliated groups. Founded 1958.* Enables parents of hearing impaired children to speak with unified strength on issues which concern them. Serves as clearinghouse to exchange ideas. Magazine, phone support, and conferences. Group development guidelines. Write: Parents Section, 3417 Volta Pl., NW, Washington, DC 20007. Call (202)337-5220 (voice/TTY); *E-mail:* agbell2@aol.com *Website:* http://www.agbell.org

Rainbow Alliance of the Deaf *Nat'l. 23 affiliated groups. Founded 1977.* Promotes the educational, economical and social welfare of deaf and hard of hearing gay and lesbian persons. Discussions of practical problems and solutions. Advocacy, conferences, newsletter, assistance in starting groups. Write: Rainbow Alliance of the Deaf, P.O. Box 66136, Houston, TX 77266-6136. Call (713)521-1104 (TTY); (713)520-2079 (FAX); *E-mail:* pjancott@aol.com *Website:* http://www.deafqueer.org

SHHH (Self Help for Hard of Hearing People, Inc.) *Int'l. 250+ chapters and groups. Founded 1979.* A volunteer, educational organization devoted to the welfare, interests and membership of hard of hearing people, their families and friends. Bi-monthly journal, local group and chapters, referrals. Write: SHHH, 7910 Woodmont Ave., Suite 1200, Bethesda, MD 20814. Call Voice: (301)657-2248 or TTY: (301)657-2249; *Website:* http://www.shhh.org; *E-mail:* national@shhh.org

Usher's Syndrome Self-Help Network *Nat'l network. 50 affiliated groups. Founded 1983.* A network of individuals with Usher's Syndrome and their families who are available to others who want to share their experiences. Write: c/o The Fdn. Fighting Blindness, Usher's Syndrome Self-Help Network, Executive Plaza 1, #800, 11350 McCormick Rd., Hunt Valley, MD 21031-1014. Call 800-683-5555 or (410)785-1414; TDD: 800-683-5551; FAX: (410)771-9470; *Website:* http://www.blindness.org

(Model) **ALDA (Association of Late-Deafened Adults)** *2 affiliated groups. Founded 1987.* To serve the needs of people who become deaf during adulthood. Chapters encourage late deafened adults to meet weekly or monthly to share coping strategies, and conflicts to gain support and encouragement with others. Newsletter, social activities, information and referrals, assistance in starting groups. Write: c/o Diane Takarz, P.O. Box 31871, Chicago, IL 60631-0871. Call Diane (847)294-7787 (TTY); FAX: (847)294-7691; E-mail: aldadiane@aol.com; or write: c/o Kathy Herring, 941 E. 194th St., Glenwood, IL 60425. Call Kathy (708)758-5810 (TTY/FAX); *E-mail:* KSHOT@aol.com

DISABILITIES (GENERAL)
(Also see specific disorder)

American Society of Handicapped Physicians *Nat'l. Founded 1981.* Support and advocacy for handicapped persons who have chosen a career in medicine or health. Promotes unity, continuing education and increased employment opportunities. Encourages and enables networking. Phone support system. Quarterly newsletter. Write: c/o Will Lambert, 105 Morris Dr., Bastrop, LA 71220. Call (318)281-4436.

Barn Builders Peer Support Group *Nat'l network. Founded 1979.* Network that provides peer support for farmers and ranchers with disabilities. Connects recently injured individuals with persons with similar disability. Support through talking, correspondence and visitation. Write: c/o Breaking New Ground, 1146 ABE Bldg., Purdue Univ., West Lafayette, IN 47907-1146. Call (765)494-5088 (Voice/TTY) or 800-825-4264; FAX: (765)496-1356. *Website:* http://abe.www.ecn.purdue.edu/abe/extension/bng/i.html

Coalition for Disabled Musicians, Inc. *Nat'l. Founded 1986.* Introduces disabled musicians to each other who have an understanding of disability-related problems. Assistance, education and workshops for disabled children and adults, whether beginners, amateurs or professional musicians, for in-studio and stage bands. Newsletter, group development guidelines. Specializes in adaptive equipment and techniques. Write: CDM, P.O. Box 1002M, Bay Shore, NY 11706. Call (516)586-0366; *E-mail:* cdmnews@aol.com *Website:* http://www.disabled-musicians.org

C.U.S.A. (Catholics United for Spiritual Action) *Nat'l. 120 correspondence groups. Founded 1947.* Correspondence support groups for persons of all faiths with any type of handicap or chronic illness. Catholic in founding, but open to all. Emphasis on spiritual values and mutual support. Through group letters members find close relationships, understanding and courage. Dues $10/yr. (can be waived). Write: C.U.S.A., 176 W. 8th St., Bayonne, NJ 07002. Call Ann Marie (201)437-0412 (day); *E-mail:* ams4@juno.com

Disabled Artists' Network *Nat'l network. Founded 1985.* Mutual support and exchanging of information for professional visual artists with physical or mental disabilities. Provides information and referrals, pen pal program and reports to active members only. Write: Disabled Artists' Network, P.O. Box 20781, New York, NY 10025. Include self-addressed stamped envelope.

Friends' Health Connection *Nat'l network.* A communication support network that connects people of all ages with any disorder, illness or handicap. Also networks caretakers, families and friends. Members are networked with each other based on health problem, symptoms, hobbies, lifestyle, interests, occupation, location and other criteria, and communicate via letters, phone, tapes, e-mail, and face-to-face. It is intended for emotional support, not for romantic purposes. Fee $30 first year; $15 subsequent years. Write: Friend's Health Connection, P.O. Box 114, New Brunswick, NJ 08903. Call 800-483-7436; FAX: (732)249-9897; *E-mail:* fhc@pilot.njin.net *Website:* http://www.48friend.com

National Council on Independent Living *Nat'l. 181 independent living centers. Founded 1982.* Advocates for the independent living movement and aims to strengthen independent living centers through technical assistance and other membership services. Information and referrals, conferences. Write: Nat'l Council on Ind. Living, 2111 Wilson Blvd., Suite 405, Arlington, VA 22201.

Call (703)525-3406; FAX: (703)525-3409; TTY: (703)525-4153; *E-mail:* ncil@tsbbs02.tnet.com

Siblings for Significant Change *Nat'l network. Founded 1981.* For siblings of handicapped persons. Trains siblings to be advocates for themselves and their families. Networking for support and socializing. Quarterly meetings. Newsletter, phone network, speakers bureau, audio-visual material, chapter development guidelines. Write: Siblings for Significant Change, 105 East 22nd St., Room 710, New York, NY 10010. Call (212)420-0776 or 800-841-8251; FAX: (212)677-0696; *E-mail:* gerri@ix.net.com.com *Website:* http://www.pva.org

Sibling Information Network *Nat'l network. Founded 1981.* Clearinghouse of information related to siblings and families of individuals with developmental disabilities. Quarterly newsletter, pen pal program. Information, referrals, guidelines and resources on sibling support groups. Write: Sibling Info. Network, c/o A.J. Pappanikou Center, 249 Glenbrook Rd., U-64, Storrs, CT 06269-2064. Call (860)486-4985; FAX: (860)486-5087; *E-mail:* speadmo1@ucennvm.ucenn.edu

(Model) **DisAbilities Anonymous** *1 Group in New York City area. Founded 1988.* 12-step program that aims to help members live with more serenity, dignity and comfort with whatever disability, chronic illness, or dysfunction they may have. Provides assistance in starting new chapters. Literature. Call Victor (718)597-6502 or Dianne W. (212)989-3416.

(Model) **Project on Women and Disability** *1 group in Boston. Founded 1987.* Mutual support for women with disabilities. Aims to eliminate sexism and disability bias and to empower women with disabilities as equal and active members of the community. Think tank, phone support, literature, conferences. Dues $40/yr. Write: Project on Women and Disability, 43 Waban Hill Rd. North, Chestnut Hill, MA 02167. Call (617)969-4974.

(Model) **Speaking for Ourselves** *7 groups in PA. Founded 1982.* Self-help advocacy group for people with developmental disabilities. Monthly chapter meetings. Members help each other resolve problems, gain self-confidence, learn leadership skills. Chapter development guidelines. Newsletter. Write: Speaking for Ourselves, 1 Plymouth Meeting, #630, Plymouth Meeting, PA 19462. Call (610)825-4592; FAX: (610)825-4595; *E-mail:* speakingfo@aol.com *Website:* http://www.libertynet.org/~speaking

(Model) **People First** *33 groups in WA. Founded 1977.* Self-help advocacy organization created by and for people with developmental disabilities. Provides help in starting new chapters. Quarterly newsletter. Write: People First, P.O. Box 648, Clarkston, WA 99403. Call (509)758-1123; FAX: (509)758-1289; TDD: (509)758-1123; *E-mail:* pfow@clarkston.com

(On-Line) **Ability OnLine Support Network** An electronic mail system that enables children and adolescents with disabilities or chronic illness to share experiences, information, encouragement and hope through e-mail messages. Primarily operates on BBS, based in Toronto, Canada at (416)650-5422. Also available through telnet at: bbs.ablelink.org. *Website:* http://www.ablelink.org

HEAD INJURY / COMA
(Also see Disabilities General, Brain Tumors,
Parents of Disabled)

Brain Injury Association, Inc *(formerly Nat'l Head Injury Fdn.) Nat'l. 800 affiliated groups. Founded 1980.* Advocacy organization providing services to persons with brain injuries, their families and professionals. Increases public awareness through state associations, support groups, information and resource network, seminars, conferences, literature, and prevention programs. Write: Brain Injury Assn., 1776 Massachusetts Ave., #100, Washington, DC 20036. Call 800-444-NHIF (family helpline) or (202)296-6443; FAX: (202)296-8850; *Website:* http://www.biausa.org

Coma Recovery Association *Nat'l. 2 chapters. Founded 1980.* Support and advocacy for families of coma and traumatic brain injury survivors. Provides information and referrals. Survivor support group meetings for recovering coma victims. Case management. Quarterly newsletter. Write: Coma Recovery Assn., Inc., 100 E. Old Country Rd., #9, Mineola, NY 11501. Call (516)746-7714 or (516)746-7706.

Perspectives Network, The *Int'l network. Founded 1990.* Emotional and informational support and networking for survivors of brain injury, their families and professionals through coordination of non-location dependent peer support groups. Quarterly magazine, peer communication network, workshops, phone support, exchange of information from professionals and survivors. Write: The Perspectives Network, P.O. Box 1859, Cumming, GA 30128-1859. Call 800-685-6302 (voice mail) or (770)844-6898 (Voice/FAX); *E-mail:* dktaylor@tbi.org *Website:* http://www.tbi.org

LEARNING DISABILITY /
ATTENTION DEFICIT DISORDER

ADD Anonymous *Nat'l. 10 affiliated groups. Founded 1996.* Mission is to carry the message of the twelve steps to adults with attention deficit disorder. For those with a desire to learn about and cope with the effects of ADD. Literature, phone support, information and referrals, support group meetings. Assistance in starting groups. Write: ADD Anonymous, P.O. Box 421227, San Diego, CA 92142-1227. Call Valerie or Ron (619)560-6190 (voice/FAX); *E-mail:* addanon@aol.com

AD-IN (Attention Deficit Information Network), Inc. *Nat'l. 25 chapters. Founded 1984.* Volunteer organization with a network of support groups that provide information and support to individuals whose lives have been affected by attention deficit disorder. Education, information and sharing of ideas for parents, adults, educators and medical personnel. Referrals to support groups. Group starter kit ($50). Write: AD-IN, 475 Hillside Ave., Needham, MA 02194-1207. Call (617)455-9895 (Tues. and Thurs., 10am - noon); FAX: (617)444-5466; *Website:* http://www.capecod.net/~awelles *E-mail:* adin@qis.net

CHADD (Children and Adults with Attention Deficit Disorder) *Int'l. 500+ affiliated groups. Founded 1987.* Support for parents with children with attention deficit disorder. Provides information for parents, adults, teachers and professionals. Newsletter, quarterly magazine, annual conference. Guidelines and assistance in starting self-help groups. Dues $35/year. Write: CHADD, 499 N.W. 70th Ave., #101, Plantation, FL 33317. Call (954)587-3700; FAX: (954)587-4599; *Website:* http://www.chadd.org/

Feingold Associations of the U.S. *Nat'l. 12 chapters. Founded 1976.* Help for families of children with learning or behavior problems, including attention deficit disorder. Supports members in implementing the Feingold program. Generates public awareness re: food and synthetic additives. Newsletter. Telephone support network. Write: Feingold Assn. of the U.S., Box 6550, Alexandria, VA 22306. Call (703)768-3287 or 800-321-FAUS; *Website:* http://www.feingold.org

Learning Disabilities Association of America *Nat'l. 600 chapters. Founded 1963.* Organization formed by concerned parents, devoted to defining and finding solutions for the broad spectrum of learning problems. Information and referrals, advocacy. Newsletter, bi-annual journal. Chapter development guidelines. Write: Attn: Jean Peterson, L.D.A. of America, 4156 Library Rd., Pittsburgh, PA 15234. Call (412)341-1515; FAX: (412)344-0224; *E-mail:* ldanatl@usaor.net *Website:* http://www.ldanatl.org

National ADDA (Attention Deficit Disorder Assn.) *Nat'l network.* Dedicated to advocating for adults and children with attention deficit disorders through education to increase awareness and understanding of ADD. Newsletter, information and referrals, national conference, speakers bureau. Sets standards for treatments. Assistance in starting groups. Dues $35/yr. Write: Nat'l ADDA, 9930 Johnnycake Ridge Rd., #3E, Mentor, OH 44060. Call 800-487-2282; (216)350-9595 (Admin); FAX: (216)350-0223; FAX on demand: (313)769-6729 (group information, order forms, etc.) *Website:* http://www.add.org *E-mail:* natladda@aol.com

"The best way to cheer yourself up is to try to cheer someone else up."
- Mark Twain

MENTAL RETARDATION / DOWN SYNDROME
(Also see specific disorder; Parents of Disabled)

Arc, The *Nat'l. 1100 chapters. Founded 1950.* Provides support for people with mental retardation and their families. Advocacy groups and direct services. Bi-monthly newsletter, and quarterly newspaper. Chapter development guidelines. Write: The Arc, 500 E. Border St. #300, Arlington, TX 76010-7444. Call (817)261-6003; FAX: (817)277-3491; TDD: (817)277-0553; *Website:* http://thearc@org.welcome.html *E-mail:* thearc@metronet.com

Down Syndrome with Growth Failure Support Network *Nat'l network. Founded 1989.* Network and exchange of information for parents of children with Down Syndrome with growth failure. Information and referrals, phone support, pen pals, conferences, literature. Newsletter ($20/year). Write: c/o MAGIC Foundation, 1327 N. Harlen, Oak Park, IL 60303. Call 800-3-MAGIC-3. *Website:* http://www.nettap.com/ ~ magic *E-mail:* magic@nettap.com

NADD: An Association for Persons With Developmental Disabilities and Mental Health Needs *Nat'l. 4 affiliated groups. Founded 1983.* Promotes the development of resources for persons with mental retardation and mental illness through education, advocacy, research and exchange of information. Conferences, audio tapes, books, and directory of members. Write: NADD, 132 Fair St., Kingston, NY 12401. Call (914)331-4336; FAX: (914)331-4569.

National Down Syndrome Congress *Nat'l. 600+ parent group networks. Founded 1974.* Support, information and advocacy for families affected by Down syndrome. Promotes research and public awareness. Serves as clearinghouse and network for parent groups. Newsletter ($20/yr). Annual convention, phone support, chapter development guidelines. Write: Nat'l Down Syndrome Congress, 605 Chantilly Dr., #250, Atlanta, GA 30324-3269. Call 800-232-NDSC or (404)633-1555 (day); FAX: (404)633-2817; *Website:* http://www.coral.net/ ~ ndsc/ *E-mail:* ndsc@charitiesusa.com

Sibling Information Network *Nat'l network. Founded 1981.* Clearinghouse of information related to siblings and families of individuals with developmental disabilities. Quarterly newsletter, pen pal program. Information, referrals, guidelines and resources on sibling support groups. Write: Sibling Info. Network, c/o A.J. Pappanikou Center, 249 Glenbrook Rd., U-64, Storrs, CT 06269-2064. Call (860)486-4985; FAX: (860)486-5087; *E-mail:* speadmo1@ucennvm.ucenn.edu

(Model) **Speaking for Ourselves** *7 groups in PA. Founded 1982.* Self-help advocacy group for people with developmental disabilities. Monthly chapter meetings. Members help each other resolve problems, gain self-confidence, learn leadership skills. Chapter development guidelines. Newsletter. Write: Speaking

for Ourselves, 1 Plymouth Meeting, #630, Plymouth Meeting, PA 19462. Call (610)825-4592; FAX: (610)825-4595; *E-mail:* speakingfo@aol.com *Website:* http://www.libertynet.org/~speaking

(Model) **People First** *33 groups in WA. Founded 1977.* Self-help advocacy organization created by and for people with developmental disabilities. Provides help in starting new chapters. Quarterly newsletter. Write: People First, P.O. Box 648, Clarkston, WA 99403. Call (509)758-1123; FAX: (509)758-1289; TDD: (509)758-1123; *E-mail:* pfow@clarkston.com

SPINAL CORD INJURY
(Also see Disabilities General)

National Spinal Cord Injury Association *Nat'l. 55 chapters and support groups. Founded 1948.* Provides information and referrals on many topics to persons with spinal cord injuries and diseases, their families and interested professionals. Group development guidelines, quarterly newsletter, support groups, peer counseling. Write: Nat'l Spinal Cord Injury Assn., 8300 Colesville Rd., Silver Spring, MD 20910-3243. Call 800-962-9629 (helpline); *E-mail:* nscia2@aol.com

Paralyzed Veterans of America *Nat'l. 34 chapters. Founded 1947.* Mission is to take those actions necessary to ensure that spinal cord injured or diseased veterans achieve the highest quality of life possible. Membership is available solely to individuals who are American citizens who suffer from spinal cord dysfunction as a result of trauma or disease. Must have served on active duty and had an honorable discharge. Information and referrals, magazine. Assistance in starting groups. Write: PVA, 801 18th St. NW, Washington, DC 20006. Call (202)872-1300.

Spinal Cord Injury Correspondence Club *Nat'l network. Founded 1997.* Group correspondence club for spinal cord injured quadriplegics to share their experiences, thoughts and ideas. Write: Spinal Cord Injury Correspondence Club, 28225 Waltz Rd., New Boston, MI 48164.

Spinal Cord Society *Int'l. 200+ chapters. Founded 1978.* Citizen advocacy organization of the spinal-injured, families and friends, dedicated scientists and physicians. Ultimate goal is to find a cure through improved treatment and research. Promotes public awareness. Monthly newsletter. Write: c/o Charles Carson, Wendell Rd., Fergus Falls, MN 56537. Call (218)739-5252; FAX: (218)739-5262.

"Success is to be measured, not so much by the position one has reached in life, as by the obstacles which he has overcome while trying to succeed."
- Booker T. Washington

FAMILY / PARENTING

"There is no hope of joy except in human relations."
- *St. Exupery*

ADOPTION

Adoptive Families of America, Inc. *Nat'l. 275+ groups. Founded 1967.* Provides problem-solving assistance and information for adoptive and prospective adoptive families. Creates opportunities for successful adoptive placement. Offers bimonthly magazine, pen pals, phone network, and group development guidelines. Dues $25/yr. Write: Adoptive Families of America, 2309 Como Ave., St. Paul, MN 55113. Call 800-372-3300 or (612)645-9955; FAX: (612)645-0055; *Website:* http://www.adoptivefam.org

Adoptees In Search *Nat'l network. Founded 1975.* For adoptees, adoptive parents and birth parents. Professional help in finding birth relatives. Legislative activities to end closed adoption records. Post-adoption education and counseling services. Search registry. Quarterly newsletter. Tax-deductible donation $75. Send self-addressed stamped long envelope when corresponding. Write: A.I.S., P.O. Box 41016, Bethesda, MD 20824. Call (301)656-8555; FAX: (301) 652-2106; *E-mail:* AIS20824@aol.com

ALMA Society (Adoptees' Liberty Movement Association) *Int'l. 65 chapters. Founded 1971.* Search and support for all persons separated from their original families by adoption. International reunion registry. Newsletter. $65 to register, $45 to renew membership. Write: ALMA Society, P.O. Box 727 Radio City Station, New York, NY 10101-0727. Call (212)581-1568.

Council for Equal Rights in Adoption *Int'l. 354 affiliated groups. Founded 1990.* Mutual support for persons separated by adoption. Referrals to adoption searches and support groups. Newsletter, phone support, conferences, information and referrals, support group meetings. Assistance in starting groups. Meets on America Online. Dues $35/year. Write: Council for Equal Rights in Adoption, c/o Joe Soll, 356 E. 74th St., New York, NY 10021. Call (212)988-0110 (day/eve); FAX: (212)988-0291; *E-mail:* cera@idt.net *Website:* http://idt.net/~cera

CUB (Concerned United Birthparents), Inc. *Nat'l. 14 branches. Founded 1976.* Support for adoption-affected people in coping with adoption. Search assistance for locating family members. Prevention of unnecessary separations. Monthly newsletter. Dues $50/new members, $35/renewals. Pen pals, telephone network. Write: CUB, 2000 Walker St., Des Moines, IA 50317. Call 800-822-2777 or (515)263-9558; FAX: (516)263-9541; *E-mail:* cub@webnations.com *Website:* http://www.webnations.com/cub

National Council for Single Adoptive Parents *Nat'l network. Founded 1973.* Provides information to assist unmarried people to adopt children from the United States and abroad, and to manage as single adoptive parents. Publishes handbook for single adoptive parents ($20). Referrals to local support groups. Write: Nat'l Council for Single Adoptive Parents, P.O. Box 15084, Chevy Chase, MD 20825. Call (202)966-6367 (Voice/FAX).

NOBAR (National Organization for Birthfathers and Adoption Reform) *Nat'l. Founded 1987.* Support and advocacy for fathers who have surrendered children for adoption or who are in jeopardy of being separated from their children by adoption. Newsletter, information and referrals, phone support. Write: NOBAR, c/o Jon R. Ryan, Pres., P.O. Box 50, Punta Gorda, FL 33951. Call (941)637-9035.

North American Council on Adoptable Children *Int'l US/Canada. Umbrella Organization. Founded 1974.* Focuses on special needs adoption. Provides referrals and maintains current listing of adoptive parent support groups which conduct a wide range of activities. Helps new groups get started, and sponsors an annual adoption conference which features workshops for adoptive parents, prospective parents, foster parents, child welfare, professional, and other child advocates. Quarterly newsletter. Membership $40/U.S. and $50/Canada. Parent group manual: Parts I III ($7 each). Write: No. American Council on Adoptable Children, 970 Raymond Ave., #106, St. Paul, MN 55114-1149. Call (612)644-3036 (day); FAX: (612)644-9848; *E-mail:* nacac@aol.com *Website:* http://www.cyfr.umn.edu/adoptinfo/nacac.html

Stars of David, Inc. *Int'l. 35 chapters.* Support and advocacy group for Jewish or interfaith adoptive families, extended families, interested clergy, social service agencies and adoption professionals. Socials, phone help, literature and education. Newsletter. Dues $18/family; $25/agency or professional. Write: Stars of David, 3175 Commercial Ave., #100, Northbrook, IL 60062-1915. Call 800-STAR-349; *E-Mail:* starsdavid@aol.com *Website:* http://www.starsofdavid.org

CHILDLESSNESS
(See also Infertility)

Childfree Network, The *Nat'l. 30+ affiliated chapters. Founded 1992.* Provides support, information and advocacy to childless men, women and couples (whether childless by choice or chance). To create positive climate for singles/couples to choose to remain childless. Bi-annul newsletter, assistance in starting new groups. Dues $28 for newsletter and database inclusion. Write: CFN, 6966 Sunrise Blvd., Suite 111, Citrus Heights, CA 95610. Call (916)773-7178 (recording); *E-mail:* cnetork@aol.com

No Kidding! *Int'l. 250+ chapters. Founded 1984.* Mutual support and social activities for married and single people who either have decided not to have children, are postponing parenthood, are undecided, or are unable to have children. Newsletter. Group development guidelines. Write: No Kidding!, Box 27001, Vancouver, BC, Canada V5R6A8. Call (604)538-7736 (24 hr); FAX: (604)538-7736. *E-mail:* jerry-s@uniserve.com *Website:* http://mypage.direct.ca/d/dsimmer/nokids.html

FOSTER PARENTS / CHILDREN

National Association of Former Foster Children *Nat'l network. Founded 1984.* Mutual support and advocacy for current and former foster children. Support group meetings, newsletter, and phone support. Dues $25. Write: Nat'l Assn. for Former Foster Children, P.O. Box 874 Wall Street Station, New York, NY 10268-0874. Call (212)332-0078; FAX: (212)794-4569. *E-mail:* NAFFC@aol.com

National Foster Parent Association, Inc. *Nat'l. 100+ affiliated groups. Founded 1972.* Support, education and advocacy for foster parents and their children. Resource center for foster care information. Bi-monthly newsletter. Annual national conference. Chapter development guidelines. Write: Nat'l Foster Parent Assn., 9 Dartmoor Dr., Crystal Lake, IL 60014. Call 800-557-5238 or (815)455-2527; FAX: (815)455-1527.

GRANDPARENTING
(Also see Separation/Divorce)

Creative Grandparenting *Nat'l. 2 affiliated chapters. Founded 1990.* Provides education to enable and empower grandparents and older adults to value and encourage the natural development of children as unique individuals. To help persons become better grandparents. Newsletter, conferences, help in starting new groups. Write: Creative Grandparenting, 1003 Delaware Ave.,Suite 16, Wilmington, DE 19606-4711. Call (302)656-2122; FAX: (302)656-3123.

GAP (Grandparents As Parents) *Nat'l. 4 groups. Founded 1987.* Support network and sharing of experiences and feelings between grandparents who are raising their grandchildren for various reasons. Information and referrals, phone support network, group member listings. Assistance in starting groups. Write: GAP, P.O. Box 964, Lakewood, CA 90714. Call (310)924-3996; FAX: (310)714-828-1375.

Grandparents Rights Organization *Nat'l. Founded 1984.* Advocates and educates on behalf of grandparent-grandchild relationships primarily with respect to grandparent visits. Assists in the formation of local support groups dealing with the denial of grandparent visitation by custodial parent or guardian.

Newsletter, information and referrals, conferences. Donations $35/yr. Write: Grandparents Rights Org., 555 S. Woodward #600, Birmingham, MI 48009. Call (248)646-7191 (day); FAX: (248)646-9722.

GRAM (Grandparent's Rights Advocacy Movement), Inc. *Nat'l network Founded 1989.* Assists grandparents whose grandchildren are forced to live in problematic situations because of chemical dependency, death of parents, divorce, abuse or neglect. Information and referrals, groups meetings, literature. Brochure on information for grandparents of children at risk for abuse and neglect. Help in starting groups (for a small fee). Free packet and other literature. Write: GRAM, Box 523, Tarpon Springs, FL 34688-0523. Call (813)937-2317(9am-9pm ET); FAX: (813)938-7115 (call first); *E-mail:* gramps@cftnet.com

GRINS (Grandparent Rights In New Strength) *Nat'l. Founded 1992.* To reunite family bonding and heritage, allowing the ancestry of children, grandparents and relatives to continue after divorce and extraction from parents by Family Social Services. Works with religious, local, state and federal officials to adopt uniform laws allowing visitation. Court and mediation support, phone help. Assistance in starting new groups. Write: GRINS, 0689 CR5, Corunna, IN 46730. Call Ray and Kay Berryhill (219)281-2384.

Young Grandparents' Club *Nat'l. Founded 1989.* Promotes the understanding and education of grandparents to develop close relations between generations. Referrals to local groups, advocacy on grandparents' rights, information and referrals. Offers workshops, classes, seminars, conferences, and networking. Assistance in starting informal neighborhood groups. Write: Young Grandparents' Club, 5217 Somerset Dr., Prairie Village, KS 66207. Call (913)642-8296. *E-mail:* sunielevin@worldnet.atp.net

(Resource) **Grandparents Information Center** *Nat'l.* Provides information and referrals for grandparents raising their grandchildren. Referrals to support groups nationwide. Free publications on a variety of issues related to raising grandchildren, financial assistance, advocacy. Sponsored by AARP. Write: Grandparents Info. Ctr., 601 E St., SW, Washington, DC 20049. Call (202)434-2296.

MARRIAGE

ACME (Association of Couples for Marriage Enrichment) *Nat'l network. Founded 1973.* Network of couples who want to enhance their own relationship as well as help strengthen marriages of other couples. Local chapters sponsor support groups, retreats, workshops. Bimonthly newsletter. Leadership training, conferences. Write: ACME, P.O. Box 10596, Winston-Salem, NC 27108. Call (910)724-1526; FAX: (910)721-4746. *E-mail:* wsacme@aol.com

WESOM (We Saved Our Marriage) *Nat'l. 3 affiliated groups. Founded 1986.* Self-help for spouses whose marriage is affected by infidelity. Helps couples deal with adultery and save their marriage. Assistance available for starting groups. Write: WESOM, P.O. Box 46312, Chicago, IL 60646. Call (312)792-7034.

WOOM (Wives of Older Men) *Int'l network. Founded 1988.* Mutual support to give members the opportunity to feel comfortable socially and familially with their decision to marry someone 8 or more years their senior. Help with step-children, generation gap, rejection, his retirement/her career, etc. Book "Younger Women - Older Men," newsletter, group development guidelines. Dues $20/yr. Write: WOOM, c/o Beliza Ann Furman, 1029 Sycamore Ave., Tinton Falls, NJ 07724. Call (908)747-5586; FAX: (908)389-0304.

(Model) **Interace** *1 group in NY/NJ area. Founded 1983.* Support and advocacy for interracial couples, their children, bi-racial adults, and inter-racial adoptive families. Sharing of concerns such as raising interracial children, family rejection, and housing discrimination. Phone and mail network. Newsletter. Regional meetings in NY and NJ. Write: Interace. P.O. Box 582, Forest Hills, NY 11375-9998. Call Holly and Floyd Sheeger (516)867-5041 (eve).

PARENTING (GENERAL)
(Also see Adoption, Foster Parents, Pregnancy, Grandparents, Multiples, Parents of Disabled, Parents of Abusive Children, Single Parenting)

DAD-to-DAD *Nat'l. 25 chapters. Founded 1995.* Brings at-home fathers together through children's play groups, field trips, dad's night-out dinners and a monthly newsletter. Information and referrals, phone support, literature. Assistance in starting local chapters. Write: DAD-to-DAD, c/o Curtis Cooper, 13925 Duluth Dr., Apple Valley, MN 55124. Call (612)423-3795. *E-mail:* dadtodad@aol.com

FEMALE (Formerly Employed Mothers At the Leading Edge) *Nat'l. 140 groups. Founded 1987.* Support for women who have left the full-time work force to raise their children at home. For all women dealing with transitions between paid employment and at-home mothering. It is not about opposing mother's who work outside the home; rather it is about respecting, supporting and advocating for choice in how one combines working and parenting. Newsletter, chapter development guidelines. Write: FEMALE, P.O. Box 31, Elmhurst, IL 60126. Call (630)941-3553; FAX: (630)941-3551; *Website:* http://www.members.aol.com/femaleofc/home.htm;*E-mail:*femaleofc@aol.com

Full-Time Dads *Nat'l. Founded 1991.* Provides networking and support for fathers (married or single). Provides a forum for sharing information, resources and experiences through bi-monthly journal. Encourages development of local support groups. Newsletter. Write: Full Time Dads, c/o James McLoughlin, 379 Clifton Ave., Clifton, NJ 07011. Call (973)772-9444. *E-mail:* ftdmag@aol.com *Website:* http://www.slowlane.com

MAD DADS, Inc. (Men Against Destruction Defending Against Drugs and Social-disorder) *Nat'l. 49 affiliated groups. Founded 1989.* Grass-roots organization of fathers aimed at fighting gang- and drug-related violence. Provides family activities, community education, speaking engagements, and "surrogate fathers" who listen to and care about street teens. Assistance in starting groups. Also groups for kids, mothers, grandparents. Write: MAD DADS, c/o Eddie Staton, 3030 Sprague St., Omaha, NE 68111. Call (402)451-3500; FAX: (402)451-3477; *Website:* http://maddadsnational.com *E-mail:* maddadsnational@infinity.com

MELD (Minnesota Early Learning Design) *Nat'l. 65+ affiliated programs. Founded 1975.* Discussion groups for parents of pre-school children. Parenting education and support programs for adolescent mothers and fathers, parents who are deaf, Hispanic families, parents of chronically ill or handicapped children, Southeast Asian parents, and first-time adult parents. Write: MELD, 123 N. Third St., Suite #507, Minneapolis, MN 55401. Call (612)332-7563 (Voice/TTY); FAX: (612)344-1959; *E-mail:* meldctrl@aol.com

MOMS Club *Nat'l. 375+ affiliated groups. Founded 1983.* Mutual support for mothers-at-home. Groups provide at-home mothers of children of all ages emotional and moral support, as well as a wide variety of activities. Annual dues vary. Assistance in starting groups. Write: MOMS Club, 814 Moffatt Circle, Simi Valley, CA 93065. Call (805)526-2725; *E-mail:* momsclub@aol.com

MOPS, Int'l (Mothers Of Pre-Schoolers) *Int'l. 1047 affiliated groups. Founded 1973.* Fellowship of mothers of preschoolers (birth to first grade) offering a nurturing, caring environment with a spiritual focus. Activities available for the children. MOPS groups are sponsored by local churches. Newsletter, area conferences, networking, help in starting local chapters. Write: MOPS, 1311 S. Clarkson St., Denver, CO 80210. Call (303)733-5353; FAX: (303)733-5770; *E-mail:* info@mops.org *Website:* http://www.mops.org

National Association of Mothers' Centers *Nat'l. 50 sites. Founded 1981.* Helps women to start mother centers. Research, advocacy, support system for those involved in parenting, pregnancy, childbirth and child-rearing. Non-hierarchal and non-judgmental. Literature, starter's manual ($15). Newsletter. Annual conference. Write: Nat'l Assn. of Mothers' Ctrs., 64 Division Ave., Levittown, NY 11756. Call 800-645-3828 or (516)520-2929 (from NY): FAX: (516)520-1639.

National Parent Center, The *Nat'l. 10 regions. Founded 1976.* Helps parents become actively involved in all aspects of their children's education. Provides training and technical assistance on a local or regional basis. Newsletter. Write: Nat'l Parent Center, 1352 Q St., NW, Washington, DC 20005. Call (202)547-9286; FAX: (202)544-2813.

(Model) **Fathers' Network, The** *1 group in California. Founded 1979.* Aims to increase involvement of fathers in parenting; to encourage mutually fulfilling relationships between fathers and their children; and to challenge traditional"provider" role regardless of marital/custodial status. National men's resource quarterly publication ($10).Resource for information and groups. NOT A DIVORCE RESOURCE. Write: The Father's Network, P.O. Box 800-SH, San Anselmo, CA 94979-0800. Call (415)453-2839; *E-mail:* menstuff@aol.com *Website:* http://www.menstuff.org

(Model) **PEP (Post Partum Education for Parents)** *1 group in California. Founded 1977.* Non-profit, volunteer-run. Emotional support for parents by parent volunteers. Helps parents adjust to changes in their lives that a baby brings. Telephone help. Education on basic infant care and parental adjustment. "Guide for Establishing a Parent Support Program in Your Community" ($10). Monthly newsletter. Group development guidelines. Write: PEP, P.O. Box 6154, Santa Barbara, CA 93160. Call (805)564-3888; *Website:* http://www.marketmedia.com/pep/

(Note) **Parents of Gifted Children** is an issue for which we have received a significant number of inquiries. Regrettably, we are unaware of any national or model self-help support group that has yet been formed. If you learn of any existing group that you would recommend, or are interested in starting such a group, please call the Clearinghouse.

PARENTS OF ABUSIVE / OUT-OF CONTROL ADOLESCENTS / ADULT CHILDREN
(Also see Addictions, Parenting General, Youth, Families of Mentally Ill)

ToughLove International *Int'l. 700+ groups. Founded 1979.* Self-help program for parents, kids and communities in dealing with the out-of-control behavior of a family member. Parent support groups help parents take a firm stand to help kids take responsibility for their behavior. Quarterly newsletter. Group development guidelines. Write: ToughLove Int'l, P.O. Box 1069, Doylestown, PA 18901. Call 800-333-1069 or (215)348-7090 (day); FAX: (215)348-9874.

(Model) **Abused Parents of America** *1 group in Michigan. Founded 1990.* Mutual support and comfort for parents who are abused by their adult children.

Provides technical assistance and advice for starting similar groups. Write: c/o Beulah Warner, 2873 Roosevelt Ave., Kalamazoo, MI 49004. Call Beulah Warner (616)349-6920.

(Model) **Because I Love You: The Parent Support Group** *17 groups in California. Founded 1982.* Self-help groups for parents who have children of all ages with behavioral problems such as truancy, substance abuse, or other forms of defiance of authority. Focus is on parents getting back their self-esteem and control of their home. Write: Because I Love You, P.O. Box 473, Santa Monica, CA 90406-0473. Call (310)659-5289; FAX: (213)585-4762; *E-mail:* BILY1982@aol.com *Website:* http://www.bily.org

PARENTS OF DISABLED / ILL CHILDREN
(Also see specific disorder, Toll-Free Specialty Numbers)

Association for the Care of Children's Health *(formerly Parent Care) Nat'l. Founded 1982.* Partnership of parents and professionals dedicated to improving the quality of care for children and their families through education, dissemination of resources, research and advocacy. Referrals to support groups. Newsletter, journal, magazine, conferences, information and referral. Dues $40-125. Write: ACCH, 7910 Woodmont Ave., #300, Bethesda, MA 20814-3015. Call 800-808-2224, ext. 327 or (301)654-6549; FAX: (301)986-4553; *E-mail:* acch@clark.net *Website:* http://www.acch.org

Association of Birth Defect Children *Nat'l network.* Information and support for families of children with birth defects and developmental disabilities believed to be caused by exposures to drugs, radiation, chemicals, pesticides or other environmental agents. Newsletter. Parent-to-parent networking. National birth defect registry. Write: Assn. of Birth Defect Children, 827 Irma Ave., Orlando, FL 32803. Call (407)245-7035 or 800-313-2232 (message line); FAX: (407)245-7087; *Website:* http://www.birthdefects.org

Family Voices *Nat'l. 50 affiliated groups. Founded 1995.* Grassroots organization that speaks on behalf of children with special health care needs at the national, state and local levels. Encourages and supports families who want to play a role in their child's health care. Advocacy. Literature (Spanish and English). Write: Family Voices, P.O. Box 769, Algodones, NM 87001. Call (505)867-2368; FAX: (505)867-6517; *E-mail:* kidshealth@familyvoices.org *Website:* http://www.familyvoices.org

MELD (Minnesota Early Learning Design) *Nat'l. 65+ affiliated programs. Founded 1975.* Discussion groups for parents of pre-school children. Parenting education and support programs for adolescent mothers and fathers, parents who are deaf, Hispanic families, parents of chronically ill or handicapped children, Southeast Asian parents, and first-time adult parents. Write: MELD, 123 N.

Third St., Suite #507, Minneapolis, MN 55401. Call (612)332-7563 (Voice/TTY); FAX: (612)344-1959. *E-mail:* meldctrl@aol.com

MUMS National Parent-to-Parent Network) *Nat'l. 61 affiliated groups. Founded 1979.* MUMS is a national parent-to-parent organization using one of the largest database in the world (11,000 families in 36 countries). Provides mutual support and networking for families dealing with children with rare birth defects, chromosomal abnormalities or medical or undiagnosed conditions. Also matches families with extremely rare disorders. Newsletter, referrals to support groups, phone support. Assistance in starting groups for rare disorders. Write: MUMS, 150 Custer Crt., Green Bay, WI 54301. Call (920)336-5333(day); FAX: (920)339-0995; *E-mail:* mums@netnet.net   *Website:* http://www. waisman.wisc.edu/ ~ rowley/mums/home.html

NATHHAN (National Challenged Homeschoolers) *Nat'l network. Founded 1990.* Christian, non-profit organization encouraging families with special needs, particularly those who home educate. Newsletter, phone support, information and referrals. Write: NATHHAN, 5383 Alpine Rd., S.E., Olalla, WA 98359. Call (253)857-4257; FAX: (253)857-7764; *E-mail:* nathanews@aol.com

National Father's Network *Int'l. 80+ affiliated groups in U.S., Canada and New Zealand. Founded 1986.* Mutual support and networking for men committed to ensuring the optimum health, well-being and education for their children with chronic illness and or developmental disabilities. Tri-yearly newsletter, curricula, training for providers and family members, regularly scheduled support programs. Assistance in starting groups. Write: Nat'l Father's Network, c/o Kindering Center, 16120 N.E. Eighth St., Bellevue, WA 98008-3937. Call James May (425)747-4004 ext. 218 or (206)284-2859; FAX: (425)747-1069 or (206)284-9664; *E-mail:* jmay@fathersnetwork.org *Website:* http://www.fathersnetwork.org

National Parent Network on Disabilities *Nat'l. 175 affiliated groups. Founded 1987.* Coalition of parent organizations and parents to advocate for parents of persons with disabilities. Provides referrals, newsletter, and networking of organizations to share expertise. Dues vary. Write: Nat'l Parent Network on Disabilities, 1725 King St., Suite 305, Alexandria, VA 22314. Call (703)684-6763 (voice/TDD); FAX: (703)836-1232; *E-mail:* npnd@cs.com *Website:* http://www.npnd.org

SKIP National (Sick Kids Need Involved People) *Nat'l. 22 affiliated groups. Founded 1983.* Purpose is to assist families to procure services necessary for their child with complex health care needs to return and/or stay at home. Information and referrals, phone support. Write: SKIP, 545 Madison Ave., 13th Fl., New York, NY 10022. Call (212)421-9160; FAX: (212)759-5736.

(Model) **Parents Helping Parents** *3 groups in California. Founded 1976.* A resource center for families with children with a need for special services. Education and support for families of children with special needs, and professionals who serve them. Education, specialty programs, family rap groups, peer counseling, training, neighborhood outreach, hospital visitation, online resources, national resource database, sibling program. Newsletter, group development guidelines, and annual symposium. Write: PHP, 3041 Olcott St., Santa Clara, CA 95054-3222. Call (408)727-5775; FAX: (408)727-0812; PHP Online: (408)727-7227; *E-mail:* info@php.com *Website:* http://www.php.com

(Model) **Pilot Parents Program** *1 group in Nebraska. Founded 1971.* Emotional support, factual information, and updated community resources for parents of newly diagnosed handicapped children. Newsletter. Assistance in starting a support program. Write: Pilot Parents Program, 3610 Dodge St., Omaha, NE 68131. Call(402)346-5220; FAX: (402)346-5253; *E-mail:* aadamson@nncf.unl.edu.

(Model) **Washington PAVE** *Statewide Washington. Founded 1979.* Parent-directed organization to increase independence, empowerment and opportunities for special needs children and their families through training, information, referrals and support. Newsletter, phone support, conferences on special education issues. Write: Washington PAVE, 6316 S. 12th, Tacoma, WA 98465, Call (206)565-2266(Voice/TTY) or 800-5-PARENT; FAX: (206) 566-8052; *E-mail:* wapave@aol.com

PARENTS OF MULTIPLES

MOST (Mothers Of SuperTwins) *Nat'l. Founded 1987.* Mutual support for families who have, or are expecting, triplets, quadruplets or more. Provides information, support, resources and empathy during pregnancy, infancy, toddlerhood and school age. Newsletter, networking, phone support. Specific resource persons for individual challenges. Help in starting groups. Write: MOST, P.O. Box 951, Brentwood, NY 11717-0627. Call Maureen Boyle (516)434-6678; FAX: (516)436-5653; *E-mail:* mostmom@nyc.pipeline.com

National Organization of Mothers of Twins Clubs *Nat'l. 460 clubs. Founded 1960.* Mothers of multiple births share information, concerns, and advice on dealing with their unique problems. Literature, quarterly newspaper $15/yr., group development guidelines, bereavement support department, pen pal program. Membership through local clubs. Write: Nat'l Org. of Mothers of Twins Clubs, P.O. Box 23188, Albuquerque, NM 87192-1188.Call 800-243-2276 (referrals only) or (505)275-0955; *E-mail:* nomotc@aol.com *Website:* http://www.nomotc.org/

Triplet Connection *Int'l network. Founded 1982.* Support for families with triplets (or more). Information re: pregnancy and delivery, networking with other families, support for expectant parents as well as parents of older triplets. Pre-term birth prevention information, newsletter. Write: Triplet Connection, P.O. Box 99571, Stockton, CA 95209. Call (209)474-0885; FAX: (209) 474-2233; *Website:* http://www.inreach.com/triplets *E-mail:* triplets@inreach.com

PREGNANCY / CHILDBIRTH / BREASTFEEDING
(Also see Parenting General)

A.S.P.O./Lamaze (American Society for Psychoprophylaxis in Obstetrics). *Nat'l. 22 chapters. Founded 1960.* Dedicated to Lamaze childbirth and prepared parenthood. Includes three categories: professional, provider and family members. Newsletter, publications. Write: ASPO/Lamaze, 1200 19th St., N.W., #300, Washington, DC 20036. Call 800-368-4404 (national referral service) or (202)857-1128; FAX: (202)223-4579; *Website:* http://www.lamaze-childbirth.com *E-mail:* ASPO@sba.com

Cesarean Support Education and Concern *Nat'l. Founded 1972.* Support, information and referral regarding cesarean birth, cesarean prevention, and vaginal delivery after cesarean. Listing of cesarean support groups nationwide. Back issues of newsletter available. Guidelines for starting groups ($2.25). Write: Cesarean Support Education and Concern, 22 Forest Rd., Framingham, MA 01701. Call (508)877-8266 (recorded message).

International Cesarean Awareness Network, Inc. *Int'l. 75 chapters. Founded 1982.* Support for women healing from cesarean birth. Encouragement and information for those wanting vaginal birth after previous cesarean. Education toward goal of lowering the high cesarean rate. Newsletter. Chapter development guidebook. Book and video catalogue. Write: ICAN, 1304 Kingsdale Ave., Redondo Beach, CA 90278. Call (310)542-6400; FAX: (310) 542-5368; *Website:* http://www.childbirth.org/section/ICAN.html *E-mail:* ICANinc@aol.com

La Leche League *Int'l. 3000 chapters. Founded 1956.* Support and education for breastfeeding mothers. Group discussions, personal help, classes and conferences. Publishes literature on breastfeeding and parenting. Bi-monthly newsletter, quarterly abstracts. Telephone support network. Write: La Leche League, 1400 N. Meacham Rd., P.O. Box 4079, Schaumburg, Il 60168-4079. Call 800-LA-LECHE (day) or (847)519-7730; FAX: (847)519-0035; *Website:* http://www.lalecheleague.org

NAPSAC (National Association of Parents and Professionals for Safe Alternatives in Childbirth) *Nat'l. 35 affiliated groups. Founded 1975.* Information and support re: homebirth, family centered maternity care and midwifery. Directory of alternative birth practitioners. Childbirth activist handbook. How-to's for organizing groups. Newsletter. Write: NAPSAC, Rt.

1, Box 646, Marble Hill, MO 63764. Call (314)238-2010; FAX: (573) 238-2010.

National Association of Mothers' Centers *Nat'l. 50 sites. Founded 1981.* Helps women to start mother centers. Research, advocacy, support system for those involved in parenting, pregnancy, childbirth and child-rearing. Non-hierarchal and non-judgmental. Literature, starters manual ($15). Newsletter. Annual conference. Write: Nat'l Assn. of Mothers' Ctrs., 64 Division Ave., Levittown, NY 11756. Call 800-645-3828 or (516)520-2929 (from NY); FAX: (516)520-1639.

Postpartum Support International *Int'l. 250 affiliated groups. Founded 1987.* To increase the awareness of the emotional changes women can experience during pregnancy and after the birth of a baby. Information on diagnosis and treatment of postpartum depression. Education, advocacy, annual conference. Encourages formation of support groups, and helps strengthen existing groups. Phone support, referrals, literature, newsletter. Write: Postpartum Support Int'l, 927 N. Kellogg Ave., Santa Barbara, CA 93111. Call (805)967-7636 (day); FAX: (805)967-0608; *E-mail:* thonikman@compuserve.com

Sidelines National Support Network *Nat'l network. 35 groups. Founded 1991.* Trained former high risk moms provide support to current high risk patients and their families with both community information and emotional support. Information and referrals, phone support, annual magazine. Write: Sidelines Nat'l Support Network, P.O. Box 1808, Laguna Beach, CA 92652. Call (714)497-2265 (7:30-5pm PST); FAX: (714)497-5598; NY/NJ: (914)736-1828. *E-mail:* sidelines@earthlink.net *Website:* http://www.earthlink.net/~sidelines

(Model) **Confinement Line, The** *1 group in Washington, DC area. Founded 1984.* Telephone support network in Greater Washington, DC area for women confined to bed for high risk pregnancy. Newsletter, information and referrals, guidelines and assistance available for starting networks. Write: Confinement Line, P.O. Box 1609, Springfield, VA 22151. Call (703)941-7183 (Mon-Fri, 9am-4pm).

(Model) **High Risk Moms, Inc.** *1 group in Chicago, IL. Founded 1980.* Provides peer support for women experiencing a high risk or problem pregnancy. Offers telephone contacts for bed rest mothers or hospitalized mothers. Also offers newsletter, networking with other groups nationally. Write: High Risk Moms, P.O. Box 389165, Chicago, IL 60638-9165. Call (630)515-5453.

"It is one of the beautiful compensations of this life that no one can sincerely try to help another without helping himself."   *Charles Dudley Warner*

SEPARATION / DIVORCE
(Also see Men, Women, Single Parents, Grandparenting)

ACES (Association for Children for Enforcement of Support) *Nat'l. 350 affiliated groups. Founded 1984.* Information and support for parents who have custody of their children and have difficulty collecting child support payments. Location service on non-payers. Newsletter, information and referrals, assistance in starting local support groups. Write: ACES, c/o Geraldine Jensen, 2260 Upton Ave., Toledo, OH 43606. Call 800-537-7072 or (419)472-6609; FAX: (419)472-6295; *E-mail:* nataces@aol.com *Website:* http://www. childsupport-aces.org

Beginning Experience, The *Int'l. 140 teams. Founded 1974.* Support programs for divorced, widowed and separated adults and their children enabling them to work through the grief of a lost marriage. Write: The Beginning Experience, 1209 Washington Blvd., Detroit, MI 48226. Call (313)965-5110; FAX: (313)965-5557.

Children's Rights Council *Nat'l. 31 groups in 29 states. Founded 1985.* Education and advocacy for reform of the legal system regarding child custody. Newsletter, information and referrals, directory of parenting organizations, catalog of resources, conferences, group development guidelines. Write: Nat'l Rights Council, c/o David L. Levy, Pres., 220 I St.; NE, #140, Washington, DC 20002. Call (202)547-6227; FAX: (202)546-4227.

CODAS (Children of Divorce And Separation) *Nat'l. 50 states in service area. Founded 1980.* Purpose is to provide consultation in areas of child custody, visitation, and child support. Initial custody, joint custody, modification, interstate custody and guardian ad litem services. Write: Dr. Ken Lewis, CODAS, P.O. Box 202, Glenside, PA 19038. Call (215)576-0177; FAX: (215)576-9411; *E-mail:* drkenlewis@juno.com *Website:* http://www.inc.com/users/codas.html

Committee for Mother and Child Rights, Inc. *Nat'l. 50+ affiliated groups. Founded 1980.* Provides emotional support, information and networking for mothers with custody problems related to divorce. (Child support issues NOT included.) Write: Committee for Mother and Child Rights, 210 Ole Orchard Dr., Clear Brook, VA 22624. Call (540)722-3652 (Mon-Fri, 9-5 ET); FAX: (540)722-5677.

Divorce Care *Int'l. 2900 affiliated groups. Founded 1993.* Network of support groups to help people recover from separation or divorce. Information and referrals, support group meetings, literature. Assistance in starting new groups. Write: Divorce Care, 223 S. White, P.O. Box 1739, Wake Forest, NC 27587. Call (919)562-2112; FAX: (919)562-2114; *E-mail:* 72603.1341@ compuserve.com *Website:* http://www.divorcecare.com

Ex-Pose (Ex-Partners Of Servicemen/women for Equality) *Nat'l. Chapters and contact people nationwide. Founded 1981.* Lobbies for more changes in military divorce laws. Dissemination of information on rights. Lawyer referrals. Bi-monthly newsletter. Publishes "Guide for Military Wives Facing Separation and Divorce." Write: Ex-Pose, P.O. Box 11191, Alexandria, VA 22312. Call (703)941-5844 (day) or (703)255-2917 (eve/weekends); FAX: (703)212-6951; *Website:* http://www.geocities.com/pentagon/1352/

Grandparents Rights Organization *Nat'l. Founded 1984.* Advocates and educates on behalf of grandparent-grandchild relationships primarily with respect to grandparent visits. Assists in the formation of local support groups dealing with the denial of grandparent visitation by custodial parent or guardian. Newsletter, information and referrals, conferences. Donations $35/yr. Write: Grandparents Rights Org., 555 S. Woodward #600, Birmingham, MI 48009. Call (248)646-7191 (day); FAX: (248)646-9722.

GRINS (Grandparent Rights In New Strength) *Nat'l. Founded 1992.* To reunite family bonding and heritage, allowing the ancestry of children, grandparents and relatives to continue after divorce and extraction from parents by Family Social Services. Works with religious, local, state and federal officials to adopt uniform laws allowing visitation. Court and mediation support, phone help. Assistance in starting new groups. Write: GRINS, 0689 CR5, Corunna, IN 46730. Call Ray and Kay Berryhill (219)281-2384.

Joint Custody Association *Int'l. 250 affiliated groups. Founded 1979.* Assists divorcing parents and their families to achieve joint custody. Disseminates information concerning family law research and judicial decisions. Advocates for legislative improvement of family law in state capitols. Write: Joint Custody Assn., c/o James A. Cook, 10606 Wilkins Ave., Los Angeles, CA 90024. Call (310)475-5352.

National Organization For Men *Nat'l. 15 chapters. Founded 1983.* Seeks equal rights for men, uniform national divorce, custody, property and visitation law. Offers educational seminars, lawyer referral, and a quarterly newsletter. Write: Nat'l Org. for Men, 11 Park Pl., New York, NY 10007-2801. Call (212)686-MALE or (212)766-4030; *Website:* http://www.tnom.com

North American Conference of Separated and Divorced Catholics *Int'l. 3000+ groups. Founded 1972.* Religious, educational and emotional aspects of separation, divorce, remarriage and widowhood are addressed through self-help groups, conferences and training programs. Families of all faiths are welcome. Group development guidelines. Membership dues $25 (includes newsletter, discounts and resources). Write: NACSDC, P.O. Box 1301, La Grande, OR 97850. Call (541)893-6089 (FAX: dial #51 access code); *E-mail:* nacsdc@eoni.com *Website:* http://www.eoni.com/~nacsdc

RAINBOWS *Int'l. 7000 affiliated groups. Founded 1983.* Establishes peer support groups in churches, schools or social agencies for children and adults who are grieving a death, divorce or other painful transition in their family. Groups are led by trained adults. Offers newsletter, information and referrals. Write: RAINBOWS, 1111 Tower Rd., Schaumburg, IL 60173. Call 800-266-3206 or (847)310-1880; FAX: (847)310-0120; *Website:* http://www.rainbows.org *E-mail:* rainbowshdqtrs@worldnet.att.net

(Model) **New Beginnings, Inc.** *1 Group in Washington, DC area. Founded 1979.* Self-help group for separated and divorced men and women in the DC Metro area. Group discussion meetings, speakers, social events, workshops, and newsletter. Assistance in starting groups. Dues $45/yr; $40/renewal. Write: New Beginnings, Inc., 13129 Clifton Rd., Silver Spring, MD 20904. Call (301)384-0111 (Voice/FAX); *E-mail:* crand20904@aol.com

SINGLE PARENTING
(Also see Parenting General, Widowhood, Separation)

International Youth Council *Int'l. 30 chapters. Founded 1972.* Brings teens from single parent homes together to share ideas and problems, develop leadership skills, and plan fun activities. Networking and guidelines available for starting groups. Sponsored by local chapters of Parents Without Partners. Write: Int'l Youth Council, c/o PWP, 401 N. Michigan Ave., Chicago, IL 60611-4267. Call 800-637-7974 or (312)644-6610; FAX: (312)321-6869.

National Organization of Single Mothers *Nat'l. 3+ affiliated groups with 90 groups in process of formation. Founded 1991.* Networking system serving single mothers. Provides information and referrals for single mothers. Dues $15. Assistance in starting new groups. Write: Nat'l Org. of Single Mothers, P.O. Box 68, Midland, NC 28107. Call (704)888-MOMS; FAX: (704)888-1752; *Website:* http://www.parentsplace.com/readroom/nosm *E-mail:* solomother@aol.com

Parents Without Partners (PWP) *Nat'l. 500+ chapters. Founded 1957.* Educational non-profit organization of single parents (either divorced, separated, widowed or never married). Provides single parent magazine, and chapter development guidelines. Membership dues vary. Write: PWP, 401 N. Michigan Ave., Chicago, IL 60611-4267. Call 800-637-7974 or (312)644-6610; FAX: (312)321-5144; *Website:* http://www.parentsplace.com/readroom/pwp/

Single Mothers By Choice *Nat'l. 20 chapters. Founded 1981.* Non-profit organization that provides support and information to mature, single women who have chosen, or who are considering, single motherhood. Services include "Thinkers" workshops, quarterly newsletter, and membership. List of back issues of newsletter available. Write: SMC, P.O. Box 1642 Gracie Sq. St., New York, NY 10028. Call (212)988-0993.

Single Parent Resource Center *Int'l. 7 affiliated groups. Founded 1975.* Network of single parent self-help groups. Provides information and referral, seminars, consultation, resource library, and newsletter. Working on groups for homeless single parents and mothers coming out of prison. Guidelines and materials for starting parenting and teen groups available. Write: Single Parent Resource Ctr., 31 E. 28th St., New York, NY 10016. Call (212)951-7030; FAX: (212)951-7037; *E-mail:* SJones532@aol.com

(Model) **Single Fathers of Niagara (S.F.O.N.)** *1 group in Ontario. Founded 1992.* Dedicated to helping and supporting all single fathers and their children. Sharing of information and parenting skills to enable single fathers to better guide their children. Provides telephone counseling, networking, referrals and information for custodial and non-custodial parents (Canadian/American). Assistance in starting groups. Write: SFON, Attn: Allen Roth, Pres., 5 Welstead Dr., Unit 15, St. Catharines, Ontario, Canada L2S 3Y1. Call (905)684-3069.

(Model) **Solo Parenting Alliance** *1 group in Seattle, WA. Founded 1990.* Opportunity for solo parents to come together to problem solve and celebrate specific issues facing their families (including parenting, affordable housing, financial independence, etc.) Mutual support groups, parenting classes, and special events available. Provides newsletter, information and referrals, group meetings, and socials. Assistance in starting new groups. Write: Solo Parenting Alliance, 139 23rd Ave. S., Seattle, WA 98144. Call (206)720-1655; FAX: (206)328-8658; *E-mail:* solo@accessone.com *Website:* http://www.accessone.com/~solo

(Model) **Unwed Parents Anonymous** *1 group in Phoenix, AZ. Founded 1979.* 12-step program that offers support to persons affected by an out-of-wedlock pregnancy, including mothers, fathers and grandparents. Encourages pre-marital sexual abstinence and provides parenting guidance. Offers weekly meetings, newsletter, and group development guidelines ($30). Write: Unwed Parents Anonymous, P.O. Box 15466, Phoenix, AZ 85060-5466. Call (602)952-1463; FAX: (602)952-1463 (phone first).

STEP FAMILIES

Stepfamily Association of America, Inc. *Nat'l. 50 chapters. Founded 1979.* Provides information and advocacy for stepfamilies. Offers self-help programs through local chapters, educational resources, quarterly bulletin, and annual national conference. Educational resources catalog available ($1.95). Write: Stepfamily Assn. of Amer., 650 J St., #205, Lincoln, NE 68508. Call 800-735-0329; FAX: (402)477-8317; *E-mail:* stepfam@aol.com

"The deepest need of many is the need to overcome his separateness, to leave the prison of his aloneness."   *- Erich Fromm*

HEALTH

*"The quality of caring for others is healing in the deepest
and most accurate sense."   - M.C. Richards*

8-P DUPLICATION
(Also see Chromosome Disorders)

(Model) **8P Duplication Support Group** *1 group in Dayton, OH. Founded
1994.* Networks parents of children with 8p duplication for mutual support.
Provides information and referrals, phone support, pen pals, and local support
group meetings. Write: 8P Duplication Support Group, c/o Children's Medical
Center, Dept. of Medical Genetics, 1 Childrens Plaza, Dayton, OH 45404. Call
(937)226-8408; FAX: (937)463-5325.

9P-
(Also see Chromosome Disorders)

Support Group for Monosomy 9P *Int'l network. Founded 1983.* Provides
information, parent-to-parent networking and technical support to parents of
children with 9P-. Facilitates research to further understand monosomy 9P.
Provides information, referrals, phone support. Write: Support Group for
Monosomy 9P, c/o Jonathan Storr, 43304 Kipton Nickel Plate Rd., LaGrange,
OH 44050. Call (440)775-4255.

11;22 TRANSLOCATION
(Also see Chromosome Disorders)

International 11;22 Translocation Network *Int'l network. Founded 1996.*
Provides information, support and networking for parents who have a child
affected by 11;22 translocation, a genetic disorder. Supports research. Offers
newsletter, literature, phone support and pen pals. Write: Int'l 11;22
Translocation Network, 232 Kent Ave., Timmins, Ontario, Canada P4N 3C3.
Call (705)268-3099 (Voice/FAX); *E-mail:* stpierre@ntl.sympatico.ca *Website:*
http://www.nt.net/~stpierre/index.html

11Q
(Also see Chromosome Disorders)

European Chromosome 11q Network *Int'l network. Founded 1996.* Mutual
support network of European parents with children with disorders on the long
arm of chromosome 11 (11q). Provides information sharing, conferences, and
a newsletter. Write: Stichting Europees Chromosoom 111 Netwerk, c/o Annet
Van Betuw, Else Mauhsstraat 7, 6708 NJ Wageningen, The Netherlands. Call

+31 317 423345; *Website:* http://www.worldaccess.nl? ~ avbetuw *E-mail:* avbetuw@worldaccess.nl

18Q- CHROMOSOME DEFICIENCY
(Also see Chromosome Disorders)

Chromosome 18 Registry and Research Society *Int'l network. Founded 1990.* Education for families, physicians and the public about the disorders of chromosome 18. Encourages and conducts research into areas that impact families. Links affected families and their physicians to the research community. Newsletter, phone support, information and referrals, pen pals. Dues $20/US; Int'l/$25. Write: Chromosome 18 Registry and Research Soc., c/o Jannine Cody, 6302 Fox Head, San Antonio, TX 78247. Call (210)657-4968; FAX: (201)657-4968; *E-mail:* cody@uthscsa.edu *Website:* http://uthscsa.edu/society/

49XXXXY SYNDROME
(Also see Chromosome Disorders)

49XXXXY *Nat'l network. Founded 1990.* Mutual support and networking for families affected by 49XXXXY disorder. Information and referrals, pen pals, phone support, newsletter. Write: 49XXXXY, c/o Kimberly Jungel, 10001 N.E. 74th St., Vancouver, WA 98662-3801. Call (360)892-7547.

AARSKOG SYNDROME

Aarskog Syndrome Family Support Unit *Int'l network. Founded 1992.* Mutual support and sharing of ideas for families of children and adults affected with Aarskog Syndrome. Offers pen pals, telephone support, information and referrals, newsletter. Write: Aarskog Syndrome Family Support Unit, 62 Robin Hill Lane, Levittown, PA 19055-1411. Call Shannon Caranci (215)943-7131.

ACHROMATOPSIA / MONOCHROMACY

Achromatopsia Network *Nat'l network.* Information and support for individuals and families concerned with the rare inherited vision disorder achromatopsia, including both rod monochromacy and blue cone monochromacy. Open to persons with similar vision disorders such as hypersensitivity to light and color vision deficiency. Write: Achromatopsia Network, P.O. Box 214, Berkeley, CA 94701-0214; *Website:* http://www.achromat.org/

ACID MALTASE DEFICIENCY (POMPE DISEASE)

Acid Maltase Deficiency Association (AMDA) *Int'l network. Founded 1995.* Support and information for persons affected by Pompe Disease (acid maltase deficiency). Newsletter, literature, information and referrals, and phone support.

Supports research into the cause and cure. Write: AMDA, P.O. Box 700248, San Antonio, TX 78270. Call (210)490-7161 (Voice/FAX) or (210)494-6144; FAX: (210)497-3810; *Website:* http://members.aol.com/amdapage/index.htm *E-mail:* tianrama@aol.com

ACIDEMIA

International Organization of Glutaric Acidemia *Int'l network. Founded 1996.* Mutual support for families with children affected by glutaric acidemia. Provides education to aid in the prevention of neurological damage and encourages newborn screening. Offers phone support, information and referrals, newsletter, literature and conferences. Write: IOGA, RR3 Box 167, Jersey Shore, PA 17740. Call (717)321-6487.

Organic Acidemia Association, Inc. *Int'l. Founded 1982.* Support, information and networking for families affected by organic acidemia and related disorders. Yearly membership ($18/yr). Telephone network. Newsletter. Write: Organic Acidemia Assn., c/o Carol Barton, 2287 Cypress Ave., San Pablo, CA 94806. Call (510)724-0297 (eve/weekends).

ADRENAL / ADDISON'S DISEASE

National Adrenal Diseases Foundation *Nat'l. 13 affiliated groups. Founded 1984.* Dedicated to serving the needs of those with adrenal diseases and their families, especially through education, support groups where possible, and "buddy" arrangements. Research is a planned goal. Newsletter, group development guidelines. Write: NADF, 505 Northern Blvd., Great Neck, NY 11021. Call (516)487-4992; *Website:* http://medhelp.netusa.net/www/nadf.htm *E-mail:* nadf@aol.com.

(Resource) **Addison News** *Nat'l network. Founded 1993.* Through newsletter, networks, educates and supports persons with Addison's disease. Newsletter contains information, educational material, personal stories, and lists support groups nationwide. 55pp booklet for parents that shares experiences on coping with Addisonian children. Voluntary donations. Write: Addison News, 6142 Territorial, Pleasant Lake, MI 49272. Call Joan Hoffman (517)769-6891; *E-mail:* hoffmanrj@dmci.net *Website:* http://www2.dmci.net/users/hoffmanrj

AGENESIS OF THE CORPUS CALLOSUM

The ACC Network *Nat'l network. Founded 1990.* Helps individuals with agenesis (or other anomaly) of the corpus callosum, their families and professionals. Helps identify others who are experiencing similar issues to share information and support. Phone support, information, newsletter and referrals. Write: ACC Network, University of Maine, 5749 Merrill Hall, Rm. 18, Orono,

ME 04469-5749. Call (207)581-3119; FAX: (207)581-3120; *E-mail:* UM-ACC@maine.maine.edu

AGNOSIA, VISUAL

International Agnosia Foundation *Nat'l network. 2 affiliated groups. Founded 1987.* Support, information and referrals for persons with primary visual agnosia. Provides phone support, pen pals, conferences and advocacy. Newsletter. Dues $10. Meets on AOL. Write: Michael Herman, 4774 Park Granada, Suite 2, Calabasas, CA 91302-1550. Call (818)996-6464; FAX: (818)222-9124; *E-mail:* tauntra@aol.com

AICARDI SYNDROME

Aicardi Syndrome Newsletter, Inc. *Int'l network. Founded 1983.* Support for families with daughters with Aicardi Syndrome (a rare, congenital disorder in which the corpus callosum has failed to develop). Information and referrals, resources, research projects. Phone support network, research group, newsletters. Dues $25/year. Write: Denise M. Park, P.O. Box 398, Fletcher, OH 45326. Call (937)368-2137 (Voice/FAX).

AIDS / HIV+
(Also see Toll-Free Specialty Numbers)

National Association of People With AIDS *Nat'l. Founded 1986.* Network of persons with AIDS. Sharing of information, and acts as a collective voice for health, social and political concerns. Phone, mail and electronics network, speakers bureau. Bi-monthly medical alert, quarterly newsletter, free publications. Write: NAPWA, 1413 K St., NW, #7, Washington, DC 20005-3405. Call (202)898-0414 (day); FAX: (202)898-0435; *Website:* http://www.thecure.org

(Model) **BEBASHI (Blacks Educating Blacks About Sexual Health Issues)** *1 group in Philadelphia, PA. Founded 1985.* Information and education among the African American and Latino communities about sexual health issues, especially HIV/AIDS. Peer-counseling, guest speakers, testing, social services, support groups, workshops, phone help. Write: BEBASHI, 1233 Locust St., #401, Philadelphia, PA 19107-5414. Call (215)546-4140; FAX: (215)546-4140; *E-mail:* bebashi@critpath.org

(Model) **Body Positive of New York** *1 group in New York City. Founded 1987.* Support and education for people affected by HIV. Information and referrals, public forums, support groups, social activities. Publishes "Body Positive" monthly magazine, "El Cuerjo Positivo" quarterly Spanish magazine. Write: Body Positive of NY, 19 Fulton St., #308B, New York, NY 10038. Call

(212)566-7333; FAX: (212)566-4539; *Website:* http://www.thebody.com
E-mail: bodypos800@aol.com

(Model) **We the People Living with AIDS/HIV of the Delaware Valley** *10
affiliated groups in Delaware Valley area. Founded 1987.* Mission is to help
people with HIV infection become aware of, and make use of, services provided.
To encourage self-empowerment by providing a source of support given by other
HIV+ people. Newsletter, group development assistance. Write: Joe Cronauer,
We The People, 425 S. Broad St., Philadelphia, PA 19147. Call (215)545-6868;
FAX: (215)545-8437; *Website:* http://www.critpath.org/wtp   *E-mail:*
cronauer@critpath.org

ALAGILLE SYNDROME

Alagille Syndrome Alliance *Nat'l network. Founded 1993.* Support network
for anyone who cares about people with Alagille Syndrome, a genetic liver
disorder. Disseminates information. Aims to increase awareness in health
professionals. Newsletter, phone support, information and referrals, scientific
advisory board. Write: Alagille Syndrome Alliance, c/o Cindy L. Hahn, 10630
S.W. Garden Park Pl., Tigard, OR 97223. Call (503)639-6217 (day/eve);
Website: http://www.athenet.net/~luxhoj/alagillesyndrome.html   *E-mail:*
cchahn@worldnet.att.net

ALBINISM / HYPOPIGMENTATION

NOAH (National Organization for Albinism and Hypopigmentation) *Nat'l.
17 chapters. Founded 1982.* Support and information for individuals, families,
and professionals about albinism (a lack of melanin pigment). Encourages
research leading to improved diagnosis and treatment. Newsletter, chapter
development guidelines, national conference. Dues $15-20. Write: NOAH, 1530
Locust St., #29, Philadelphia, PA 19102-4316. Call (215)545-2322 or
800-473-2310; *E-mail:* noah@albinism.org *Website:* http://www.albinism.org/

ALLERGY
*(See also Asthma, Lung Disorders,
Celiac Sprue, specific disorders)*

Asthma and Allergy Foundation of America *Nat'l. 164 affiliated groups and
11 chapters. Founded 1953.* Serves persons with asthma and allergic diseases
through the support of research, patient and public education, and advocacy.
Newsletter, support/education groups, assistance in starting and maintaining
groups. How-to manual and videotape. Write: AAFA, 1125 15th St., N.W.,
#502, Washington, DC 20005. Call (202)466-7643; FAX: (202)466-8940.
Consumers can receive a free packet of information by calling 800-7-ASTHMA;
Website: http://www.aafa.org

ELASTIC (Education for Latex Allergy Support Team Information Coalition) *Nat'l. 47 chapters. Founded 1995.* Information and resource material for those living with and treating latex allergy. Phone support, conferences, literature. Affiliated newsletter "Latex Allergy News" ($40/yr). Dues $15/yr. Assistance in starting similar groups. Regularly exchanges messages on AOL and Netcom. Write: ELASTIC, 196 Pheasant Run Rd., W. Chester, PA 19380. Call (610)436-4801; FAX: (610)436-1198; *E-mail:* ecbdmd@a.ix.netcom.com *Website:* http://www.netcom.com/~nam1/latex_allergy.html or http://www.netcom.com/~ecbdmd/elastic.html

Food Allergy Network, The *Nat'l network. Founded 1991.* Support, coping strategies and information for persons affected by food allergies and anaphylaxis. Aims to increase public awareness. Provides educational materials. Information and referrals, conferences, literature, phone support and newsletter. Write: Food Allergy Network, 10400 Eaton Pl., #107, Fairfax, VA 22030. Call (703)691-3179; FAX: (703)691-2713; *E-mail:* fan@worldweb.net

ALOPECIA AREATA

National Alopecia Areata Foundation *Nat'l. 69 support groups. Founded 1981.* Support network for people with alopecia areata, totalis, and universalis. Goals: set up support groups around country, educate public, fund-raising for research. Bimonthly newsletter, support group guidelines. Write: Nat'l Alopecia Areata Fdn., P.O. Box 150760, San Rafael, CA 94915-0760. Call (415) 456-4644; FAX: (415)456-4274; *E-mail:* 74301.1642@compuserve.com

ALPHA 1 ANTITRYPSIN
(See also Lung Disorders)

Alpha 1 National Association *Nat'l. 60 affiliated groups. Founded 1988.* Emotional support and information for persons with alpha 1 antitrypsin and their families. Networking of members through newsletter. Sharing of current information on treatments and research. Pen pals. Newsletter, group development guidelines. Write: c/o Sandy Brandley, 4220 Old Shakopee Rd., Minneapolis, MN 55437. Call (612)703-9979 or 800-521-3025; *E-mail:* Brandley@winternet.org *Website:* http://www.alpha1.org

ALSTROM'S SYNDROME

International Alstrom's Syndrome *Int'l network. Founded 1992.* Mutual support and networking for families affected by Alstrom's Syndrome. Support and encouragement through newsletter. Write: c/o Janet Seeger, 1006 Howard Rd., Warminster, PA 18974. Call (215)674-1936; *E-mail:* sasf@voicenet.com

ALZHEIMER'S DISEASE
(Also see Caregivers)

Alzheimer's Disease and Related Disorders Assoc., Inc. *Nat'l. 220 chapters, 1,600 support groups. Founded 1980.* Information and assistance for caregivers of Alzheimer's patients. Quarterly newsletter, literature, chapter development kit. Write: ADRDA, 919 N. Michigan Ave., #1000, Chicago, IL 60611-1676. Call 800-272-3900 or (312)335-8700; TDD: (312)335-8882; *Website:* http://www.alz.org

AMBIGUOUS GENITALIA

Intersex Society of North America *Int'l. 2 affiliated chapters. Founded 1993.* Peer support for intersexuals to overcome the stigma of the condition. Education for parents and professionals to provide better care. Newsletter, information and referrals, phone support, literature, advocacy, support group meetings. Internet mailing list to network members. Write: Intersex Soc. of N. Amer., P.O. Box 31791, San Francisco, CA 94131. Call (415)436-0585; *Website:* http://www.isna.org *E-mail:* info@isna.org

AMYOTROPHIC LATERAL SCLEROSIS (ALS) / LOU GEHRIG'S DISEASE

A.L.S. Association *Nat'l. 75+ chapters and support groups. Founded 1972.* Dedicated to finding the cause, prevention and cure of amyotrophic lateral sclerosis, and to enhance quality of life for ALS patients and their families. Quarterly newspaper, chapter development guidelines. Write: A.L.S. Assn., 21021 Ventura Blvd., #321, Woodland Hills, CA 91364. Call (818)340-7500 or 800-782-4747; FAX: (818)340-2060; *Website:* http://www.alsa.org *E-mail:* eajc27b@prodigy.com

ANDROGEN INSENSITIVITY

Androgen Insensitivity Syndrome Support Group *Int'l. 3 affiliated groups. Founded 1988.* Provides information and support to people affected by androgen insensitivity syndrome (AIS) including adults with the condition, parents of AIS children, and professionals working with AIS. Information and referrals, phone support, support group meetings, literature, advocacy, conferences and newsletter. Write: Androgen Insensitivity Syndrome Support Group, 4203 Genesee Ave., #103-436, San Diego, CA 92117-4950. Call (619)569-5254; *E-mail:* aissg@aol.com

"Life only demands from you the strength you possess."
                                                    - Dag Hammarskjold

ANEMIA

Aplastic Anemia Foundation of America *Nat'l. 25 chapters. Founded 1983.* Emotional support and information for persons with aplastic anemia and myelodysplastic syndromes. Financially supports research. Provides free educational materials and updated medical information. Write: Aplastic Anemia Fdn. of America, P.O. Box 613, Annapolis, MD 21404. Call 800-747-2820 or (410)867-0242; FAX: (410)867-0240; *E-mail:* aafacenter@aol.com *Website:* http://www. teleport.com/nonprofit/aafa

Cooley's Anemia Foundation *Nat'l. 16 chapters. Founded 1954.* Education and networking for families affected by Cooley's anemia (thalassemia). Fund-raising for research. Newsletter, annual seminars, research grants, young adult group, patient services, chapter development guidelines. Write: Cooley's Anemia Fdn., 129-09 26th Ave., Flushing, NY 11354. Call (718)321-2873 or 800-522-7222 (in NY); FAX (718)321-3340; *E-mail:* ncaf@aol.com *Website:* http://www.thalassemia.org

Fanconi Anemia Research Fund, Inc. *Int'l network. Founded 1989.* Provides support and exchange of information re: medical advances. Fundraising for research. Newsletter, phone support, semi-annual newsletter, annual family meetings, news bulletins, family directory handbook, annual scientific meetings, grants for scientific research and networking. Write: Fanconi Anemia Research Fund, 1902 Jefferson St., Suite 2, Eugene, OR 97405. Call 800-828-4891 or (541)687-4658; FAX: (541)687-0548; *Website:* http://www.rio.com/ ~ fafund *E-mail:* fafund@rio.com

ANENCEPHALY

Anencephaly Support Foundation *Int'l network. Founded 1992.* Provides support for parents who are continuing a pregnancy after being diagnosed with an anencephalic infant. Information and resources for parents and professionals. Phone support, pen pals, literature. Write: Anencephaly Support Fdn., 30827 Sifton Dr., Spring, TX 77386-2237. Call 888-206-7526; FAX: (281)364-9222 (call first); *Website:* http://www.asfhelp.com *E-mail:* asfaasfhelp.com

ANGELMAN SYNDROME

Angelman Syndrome Foundation, Inc. *Nat'l. 18 affiliated chapters. Founded 1992.* Support and advocacy for persons with Angelman Syndrome, a neurological disorder, their families and interested others. Provides education, information, referrals, literature, newsletter, conferences. Fundraising activities. Promotes research. Dues $25. Write: Angleman Syndrome Fdn., P.O. Box 12437, Gainesville, FL 32604. Call (800)432-6435 (800-IF-ANGEL) or (212)353-0989 (NY); *E-mail:* julhyman@idt.net

ANOPHTHALMIA / MICROPHTHALMIA

ican (Int'l Children's Anophthalmia Network) *Nat'l network. Founded 1994.* Mutual support and networking for families affected by anophthalmia or microphthalmia. Sharing of information. Provides education, gathers medical, legal and governmental information. Supports research. Dues $25. Write: ICAN, Albert Einstein Medical Center, c/o Ctr. for Developmental Medicine and Genetics, 5501 Old York Rd., Philadelphia, PA 19141. Call 800-580-4226 or (215)456-8722; FAX: (215)456-2356; *Website*: http://www.ioi:com/ican

ANORCHIDISM

Anorchidism Support Group - USA *Int'l network. Founded 1995.* Information and support for families and persons affected by anorchidism (absence of the testes) whether congenital or acquired. Newsletter, information and referrals, phone support, pen pals, and literature. USA Contact: c/o Marianne Bittle, 125 Hollyoke Rd., Somerdale, NJ 08083-2619; phone: (609)783-8783; Int'l Contact: Lorraine Bookless, 164, Chatteris Ave., Harold Hill, Romford, Essex, RM3 8EU England; phone: (#44)01708 372597; *E-mail*: MDBittle@aol.com;

APERT SYNDROME

Apert Support and Information Network *Int'l network. Founded 1995.* Provides support to families and individuals facing the challenge of Apert Syndrome, a rare, genetic craniofacial disorder. Information and referrals, newsletter, phone support network, pen pals, and annual family get-togethers. Write: Apert Support & Info. Network, P.O. Box 1184, Fair Oaks, CA 95628. Call (916)961-1092 (Voice/FAX); *E-mail:* apertnet@ix.netcom.com *Listserv*: Apert@listserv.aol.com

Apert Syndrome Pen Pals *Nat'l network.* Group correspondence program for persons with Apert Syndrome to share experiences. Information and referrals, pen pals, phone help. Write: Apert Syndrome Pen Pals, P.O. Box 115, Providence, RI 02901. Call (401)421-9076 (after 4:30pm EST).

APNEA, SLEEP

American Sleep Apnea Association *Nat'l. 200+ affiliated groups. Founded 1990.* AWAKE network groups provide education, support and social interaction for persons with sleep apnea and their families and friends. Publishes newsletter for members ($25/yr). AWAKE meetings are free. Assistance and guidelines for starting groups ($10). Write: ASAA, 2025 Pennsylvania Ave., Suite 905, Washington, DC 20006. Call (202)293-3650; FAX: (202)293-3656; *E-mail*: asaa@nicom.com *Website*: http://www.uasaa.nicom.com

ARACHNOIDITIS

Arachnoiditis Information and Support Network *Nat'l network. 26 affiliated groups. Founded 1990.* Information and mutual support for persons suffering from arachnoiditis. Newsletter and membership ($20). Write: AISN, P.O. Box 1166, Ballwin, MO 63022. Call Cheryl Ahearn (314)394-5741.

ARNOLD CHIARI MALFORMATION

(Online) **World Arnold Chiari Malformation Association** *300 members. Founded 1995.* Provides information and support to persons concerned with Arnold Chiari Malformation via e-mail and the web. *Website:* http://www.geocities.com/hotsprings/2830

ARTHRITIS

Arthritis Foundation *Nat'l. 65 chapters. Founded 1948.* Offers education, support and activities for people with arthritis and their families and friends. Self-help instruction programs. Bimonthly magazine. Special group for children and parents: Amer. Juvenile Arthritis Organization. Write: Arthritis Fdn., P.O. Box 7669, Atlanta, GA 30357-0669. Call 800-283-7800; FAX: (404)872-8694; *Website*: http://www.arthritis.org

Fibromyalgia Network *Nat'l. Founded 1988.* Provides information on fibromyalgia syndrome, chronic fatigue, osteoarthritis, and rheumatoid arthritis. Referrals to self-help groups, patients contacts and health care professionals, and other services. Newsletter, phone support, information and referrals, conferences, and guidelines and assistance in helping new groups. Write: Fibromyalgia Network, P.O. Box 31750, Tucson, AZ 85751-1750. Call 800-853-2929.

(Model) **Young Et Heart** *33 affiliated groups in Calif. Founded 1984.* Education and support for young adults with arthritis and other related diseases, their families and friends. Newsletter, group development assistance, bi-annual symposium, phone peer-counseling, and the Victoria Principal Achievement Award. Write: c/o Amye Leong, 2205 W. 25th St., #12, San Pedro Peninsula, CA 90732. Call (310)831-2212 or local chapter of Arthritis Foundation; FAX: (310)831-2266; *E-mail*: toobionic@aol.com

ARTHROGRYPOSIS

Avenues: A National Support Group for Arthrogryposis *Nat'l network. Founded 1980.* Connects families affected by arthrogryposis with each other for mutual support and sharing of information. Educates medical and social service professionals. Semi-annual newsletter $10/year. Write: Avenues, P.O. Box

5192, Sonora, CA 95370. Call (209)928-3688; *E-mail*: avenues@sonnet.com
Website: http://www.sonnet.com/avenues

ASBESTOS / WHITE LUNG DISEASE
(See also Lung Disease)

Asbestos Victims of America *Nat'l. Founded 1980.* Provides public education regarding asbestos issues, informal counseling, medical, social and legal resources. Links with hospices, disease treatment centers, and other helping professionals. Information re: asbestos in the home, disaster emergency repair, abatement. Brochures, publications, newsletter. Asbestos disease research. Write: Asbestos Victims of America, P.O. Box 66594, Scotts Valley, CA 95067. Call (408)438-LUNG.

White Lung Association *Nat'l. 100+ chapters. Founded 1979.* Educational support and advocacy for asbestos victims and their families. Public education on health hazards of asbestos. Education of workers on safe work practices. Chapter development guidelines. Quarterly newsletter. Films and videotapes available. Dues $25/yr. Write: White Lung Assn., P.O. Box 1483, Baltimore, MD 21203. Call (410)243-5864; FAX: (410)243-5234; *E-mail*: whitelung@aol.com

ASTHMA
(See also Allergies, Lung Disorders)

Asthma and Allergy Foundation of America *Nat'l. 164 affiliated groups and 11 chapters. Founded 1953.* Serves persons with asthma and allergic diseases through the support of research, patient and public education, and advocacy. Newsletter, support/education groups, assistance in starting and maintaining groups. How-to manual and videotape. Write: AAFA, 1125 15th St., N.W., #502, Washington, DC 20005. Call (202)466-7643; FAX: (202)466-8940. Consumers can receive a free packet of information by calling 800-7-ASTHMA; *Website:* http://www.aafa.org

SAY (Support for Asthmatic Youth) *Nat'l. 30 affiliated groups. Founded 1989.* Provides an atmosphere of support, reassurance and fun for children (9-17) with asthma and allergies. Exchanging of personal experiences and concerns. Education, information and referrals, phone support, conferences, pen pals, newsletter, advocacy, literature. How-to on starting groups ($3). Write: SAY, c/o Asthma and Allergy Fdn. of America, Attn: Renee Theodorakis, 1080 Glen Cove Ave., Glen Head, NY 11545. Call (516)625-5735 (day): FAX: (516)625-2976; *Website*: http://www.aafa.org *E-mail*: ReneeThead@aol.com

"We all have the strength to bear the misfortunes of others."
- La Rochefoucauld

ATAXIA

National Ataxia Foundation *Nat'l. 47 groups. Founded 1957.* Assists families with ataxia. Provides education for professionals and the public. Encourages prevention through genetic counseling. Promotes research into causes and treatment. Newsletter, information and referral, assistance in starting support groups. Group development guidelines. Exchanges messages on Prodigy Medical Support/Disabilities BBS. Write: Nat'l Ataxia Fdn., c/o Donna Gruetzmacher, 15500 Wayzata Blvd., Wayzata, MN 55391. Call (612)473-7666; FAX: (612)473-9289; *E-mail*: naf@mr.net   *Website*: http://www.ataxia.org

BATTEN DISEASE

Batten Disease Support and Research Association *Int'l. 18 affiliated groups. Founded 1987.* Emotional support for persons with Batten Disease. Information and referrals, support group meetings, phone support, conferences, newsletter. Assistance provided for starting new groups. Write: Batten Disease Support and Research Assn., 2600 Parsons Ave., Columbus, OH 43207. Call 800-448-4570; *E-mail*: bdsra1@bdsra.com *Website*: http://bdsra.org.

BECKWITH-WIEDEMANN/SIMPSON-GOLABI-BEHMEL ISOLATED HEMIHYPERTROPHY

Beckwith-Wiedemann Support Network *Int'l network. Founded 1989.* Support and information for parents of children with Beckwith-Wiedemann, Simpson-Golabi-Behmel Syndrome, or Isolated Hemihypertrophy, and interested medical professionals. Newsletter, parent directory, information and referrals, phone support. Aims to increase public awareness and encourages research. Write: c/o Susan Fettes, President, 3206 Braeburn Circle, Ann Arbor, MI 48108. Call (313)973-0263; Parents Toll-Free Number 800-837-2976; FAX: (313)973-9721; *E-mail*: a800bwsn@aol.com

BEHCET'S SYNDROME

American Behcet's Association *Nat'l. 30 affiliated groups. Founded 1978.* Mutual support and information for Behcet's patients, their families, and professionals. Newsletter, information and referrals, phone support, pen pals, conferences. Pamphlets, literature, press kit. Meets on Prodigy. Write: ABDA, P.O. Box 6663, Minneapolis, MN 55406-0663. Call 800-7-BEHCET or (612)722-9554; FAX: (612)722-2218; *E-mail*: nyyy49c@prodigy.com *Website*: http://www.netcom.com/ ~ mharting/behcet.html

"Those of us who walk in light must help the ones in darkness up."
                                                                    - Rod McKueen

165

BELL'S PALSY

Bell's Palsy Research Foundation *Nat'l network. Founded 1995.* Provides information and support to persons diagnosed with Bell's Palsy (facial paralysis). Referrals, phone support, advocacy, pen pals, and literature. Donations accepted. Write: Bell's Palsy Research Fdn., 9121 E. Tanque Verde, Suite 105-286, Tuscon, AZ 85749. Call (520)749-4614; *E-mail:* BellsPalsy@aol.com

(Online) **National Bell's Palsy Online Support Group** Support for persons with Bell's Palsy (aka facial paralysis), their families and friends. Newsletter. Meets Sat., 10am-12 noon, and Wed., 8-10pm ET (http://members.aol.com/seabee88/chatabout.html). Write: Nat'l Bell's Palsy Online Support Group, c/o Annette Lemke, 65 Calle El Avion, Camarillo, CA 93010. Call (805)987-3014; FAX: (805)987-3075; *E-mail:* BPSupport@aol.com or Seabee86@aol.com

BENIGN ESSENTIAL BLEPHAROSPASM

Benign Essential Blepharospasm Research Fdn., Inc. *Nat'l. 170 groups. Founded 1981.* Organization of support groups nationwide. Education and research. Networking people with similar symptoms. Doctor referrals. Bimonthly newsletter. Local group development guidelines. Voluntary contributions. Write: B.E.B. Fdn., P.O. Box 12468, Beaumont, TX 77726-2468. Call (409)832-0788 or Mrs. Mattie-Lou Koster, Chairman of the Board (409)832-0788; FAX: (409)832-0890; *E-mail:* bebsf@ih2000.net *Website:* http://www.ziplink.net/~dystonia/blephar1/html

BILE DUCT INJURY

Support Network, The *Nat'l. 3 affiliated groups. Founded 1993.* Support, information, and research for persons who have a bile duct injury after having a laparoscopic cholecystectomy. Information, referrals, literature, advocacy, and pen pals. Occasional newsletter. Write: c/o Elizabeth LaBozetta, 1562 Picard Rd., Columbus, OH 43227-3296. Call (614)235-0421; *E-mail:* labozetta@earthlink.net

BLEPHAROPHIMOSIS PTOSIS EPICANTHUS INVERSUS

BPES Family Network *Nat'l network. Founded 1994.* Information and support to families affected by blepharophimosis, ptosis, epicanthus inversus. A clearinghouse for information, phone support. Write: BPES Family Network, SE 820 Meadow Vale Dr., Pullman, WA 99163-2423. Call (509)332-6628; *Website:* http://www.wsu.edu/8080/~0144069 *E-mail:* ischauble@wsu.edu

BONE MARROW / STEM CELL TRANSPLANT

(Resource) **Blood and Marrow Transplant Newsletter** Quarterly newsletter for bone marrow, peripheral stem cell, and cord blood transplant patients. "Patient to survivor" telephone link available. Free 157-page book on the physical and emotional aspects of these transplants available. Other literature available. Attorney referrals. Write: BMT Newsletter, 1985 Spruce Ave., Highland Park, IL 60035. Call (847)831-1913; FAX: (847)831-1943; *E-mail*: help@bmtnews.org *Website*: http://www.BMTNews.org

BRACHIAL PLEXUS INJURY/ERB'S PALSY

National Brachial Plexus/Erb's Palsy Assn., Inc. *Nat'l network. Founded 1995.* Support and networking for families and health care professionals dealing with brachial plexus injury (Erb's Palsy) which is an injury to the nerves that control arm and hand muscles. Supports research, distributes information. Pen pals, literature, phone support, information and referrals. Write: Nat'l Brachial Plexus/Erb Palsy Assn., Inc., P.O. Box 533, Menasha, WI 54952. Call (920)836-3843; *Website*: http://www.msu.edu/user/castanic

BRAIN TUMOR

Acoustic Neuroma Association *Nat'l. 48 chapters. Founded 1981.* Support and information for patients who have been diagnosed with, or experienced acoustic neuromas or other benign tumors affecting the cranial nerves. Newsletter ($30/yr.), annual national symposium, telephone network, chapter development guidelines. Write: ANA, P.O. Box 12402, Atlanta, GA 30355. Call (404)237-8023; *Website*: http://132.183.175.10/ana/ *E-mail*: ANAUSA@aol.com

American Brain Tumor Association (ABTA) *Nat'l. Founded 1973.* Dedicated to eliminating brain tumors by funding and encouraging research and providing free patient education, materials and resource information. Pen pal program, newsletter, publications, resource listings. Write: ABTA, 2720 River Rd., Suite 146, Des Plaines, IL 60018. Call (847)827-9910; or 800-886-2282 (patient services); FAX: (847)827-9918; *E-mail*: info@abta.org or abta@aol.com *Website*: http://www.abta.org

Brain Tumor Society, The *Nat'l. 5 affiliated groups. Founded 1989.* Non-profit organization committed to finding a cure for brain tumors through fundraising, professional education and patient/family support programs. Sponsors medical seminars, and disseminates educational materials. Newsletter, resource guide. Write: Brain Tumor Society, 84 Seattle St., Boston, MA 02134. Call 800-770-8287 or (617)783-0340; FAX: (617)783-9712; *E-mail:* info@tbts.org *Website:* http://www.tbts.org

Children's Brain Tumor Foundation, Inc. *Nat'l network. Founded 1988.* Provides support services and educational materials for parents of children with, and young survivors of, brain tumors. Conferences, literature, advocacy, phone support, referrals to support groups. Assistance in starting similar support groups. Write: CBTF, 274 Madison Ave., Suite 1031, New York, NY 10016. Call (212)448-9494; FAX: (212)448-1022; *E-mail:* childrensneuronet.org

National Brain Tumor Foundation *Nat'l. 150+ affiliated groups. Founded 1981.* Support and information for persons with brain tumors. Provides funding for research as well as client services for brain tumor patients. Newsletter, information and referrals, conferences, literature, support line. Assistance in starting and maintaining support groups. Write: NBTF, 785 Market St., #1600, San Francisco, CA 94131. Call 800-934-CURE; FAX: (415)284-0209; *E-mail:* NBTF@braintumor.org *Website:* http://www.braintumor.org

CANCER
(Also see specific disorder)

Candlelighters Childhood Cancer Foundation *Int'l. 400+ groups. Founded 1970.* Support for parents of children and adolescents with cancer. Links parents, families and groups to share feelings, exchange information, identify patient and family needs. Health and education professionals also welcomed as members. Newsletter, youth newsletter. Educational materials. Write: Candlelighters Childhood Cancer Fdn., 7910 Woodmont Ave., #460, Bethesda, MD 20814. Call (800)366-2223 or (301)657-8401; *Website*: http://www.candlelighters.org *E-mail*: info@candlelighters.org

DES Cancer Network *Nat'l. Founded 1983.* For DES-exposed women, with a special focus on DES cancer issues. Provides patient support, research advocacy and medical/legal resources. Newsletter ($25). Annual conferences. Write: DES Cancer Network, 514 10th St., NW, #400, Washington, DC 20004. Call 800-DES-NET-4; FAX: (202)628-6217; *E-mail*: desnetwrk@aol.com.

IMPACC (Intestinal Multiple Polyposis and Colorectal Cancer) *Nat'l network. Founded 1986.* Support network to help patients and families dealing with familial polyposis and hereditary colon cancer. Information and referrals, encourages research, and educates professionals and public. Phone support network, correspondence, and literature. Write: IMPACC, P.O. Box 11, Conyngham, PA 18219. Call Ann Fagan (717)788-3712 (eve) or (717)788-1818 (day); FAX: (717)788-4046; *E-mail*: impacc@epix.net

Leukemia Society of America Family Support Group Program *Nat'l. 58 affiliated professionally-run groups. Founded 1949.* Mutual support for patients, family members and friends coping with leukemia, lymphoma, multiple myeloma and Hodgkin's Disease. Monthly meetings. Write: LSA, 600 Third Ave., 4th fl., New York, NY 10016. Call Donna Moss (212)450-8834; FAX:

(212)856-9686; *E-mail*: MossD@leukemia.org *Website*: http://www.leukemia.org

Man To Man Program *Nat'l. 250 affiliated groups. Founded 1990.* Support and education for men with prostate cancer to enable them better understand their options and to make informed decisions. Phone support, information and referrals, support group meetings, education and support visitation program. newsletter. Help in starting new groups. Contact the American Cancer Society at 800-ACS-2345; *Website*: http://www.cancer.org

National Carcinoid Support Group *Nat'l network. Founded 1994.* Peer-to-peer support through networking with others who have carcinoid, a rare form of cancer. Literature, quarterly newsletter. Monthly conference call between interested members. Weekly chats on America Online. Write: Nat'l Carcinoid Support Group, P.O. Box 44233, Madison, WI 53744-4233; *E-mail*: jean@mick.com *Website*: http://members.aol.com/thencsg

National Coalition for Cancer Survivorship *Nat'l. 400 member organizations. Founded 1986.* Clearinghouse for information on cancer survivorship, including support groups nationwide, insurance and employment issues, and advocacy. Assistance in starting cancer support and networking systems. Newsletter. Write: Nat'l Coalition for Cancer Survivorship, 1010 Wayne Ave., #505, Silver Spring, MD 20910. Call (301)650-8868; FAX: (301)565-9670; *Website*: http://www.access.digex.net/~mkragen/cansearch.html

National Kidney Cancer Association *Nat'l. 9 affiliated groups. Founded 1990.* Provides information about kidney cancer to patients and doctors. Conducts research, and advocates on behalf of patients with government and insurance companies. Newsletter, information and referrals, literature, conferences. Write: Nat'l Kidney Cancer Assn., 1234 Sherman, #203, Evanston, IL 60202. Call (847)332-1051; FAX: (847)332-2978; *E-mail*: office@nkca.org *Website*: http://www.nkca.org

National Ovarian Cancer Coalition *Nat'l. 25 affiliated groups. Founded 1995.* Promotes education and awareness re: ovarian cancer for patients, families, and medical community. Information and referrals, conferences, literature, conferences, phone support. Networking. Write: Nat'l Ovarian Cancer Coalition, P.O. Box 4472, Boca Raton, FL 33429. Call (561)393-3220; FAX: (561)361-8804; *E-mail*: ovca@aol.com *Website*: http://www.ovarian.org

Nevoid Basal Cell Carcinoma Syndrome Support Network *Nat'l network. Founded 1994.* Emotional support for persons with nevoid basal cell carcinoma, a very rare condition. Support groups, information and referrals, pen pals, conferences, phone support and a bi-monthly newsletter. Write: c/o Susan Charron, 162 Clover Hill St., Marlboro, MA 01752. Call 800-815-4447 or (508)485-4873; *E-mail*: souldansur@aol.com

Patient Advocates for Advanced Cancer Treatment (PAACT) *Int'l. 600 affiliated groups. Founded 1984.* PAACT provides support and advocacy for prostate cancer patients, their families and general public at risk. Information relative to the advancements in the detection, diagnosis, evaluation and treatments of prostate cancer. Information, referrals, phone help, conferences, newsletters. Group development guidelines. Write: PAACT, P.O. Box 141695, Grand Rapids, MI 49514-1695. Call (616)453-1477; FAX: (616)453-1846.

Reach to Recovery Discussion Groups Local outgrowth of Reach to Recovery Program which in most areas is a one-to-one visitation program for women with breast cancer but in some areas is a support group. For information, call the American Cancer Society 800-227-2345.

Sisters Network *Nat'l. 10 affiliated chapters in NY, AL, TX, LA, MD. Founded 1994.* African-American breast cancer survivors support group that offers support, education, advocacy, training and research. Newsletter, information and referrals, phone support, conferences. Assistance in starting new groups. Write: SN, 8787 Woodway Dr., #4207, Houston, TX 77063. Call (713)781-0255; FAX: (713)780-8998; *Website*: http://users.aol.com/sisternet/sis.html

Us Too, Int'l *Int'l. 400+ affiliated groups. Founded 1990.* Mutual support, information and education for prostate cancer patients, their families and friends. Provides newsletter, information and referrals, phone support, assistance in starting new groups. Write: Us Too Int'l,, 930 N. York Rd., Suite 50, Hinsdale, IL 60521-2993. Call 800-80-US-TOO (800-808-7866) or (630)323-1002; FAX: (630)323-1003; *Website*: http://www.ustoo.com *E-mail*: ustoo@ustoo.com

Y-ME National Breast Cancer Organization *Nat'l. 19 affiliated groups. Founded 1978.* Information and peer support for breast cancer patients and their families during all stages of the disease. Community outreach to educate people on early detection. Hotline, newsletter, group development guidelines, conferences. Write: Y-Me, 212 W. Van Buren St., Chicago, IL 60607-3908. Call 800-221-2141 (24 hrs); FAX: (312)986-0020;. *Website*: http://www.y-me.org/

(Model) **AABCA (African American Breast Cancer Alliance)** *1 group in Minneapolis, MN. Founded 1990.* Support and advocacy for Black women in the Minneapolis area with breast cancer, and their families. Provides information and referrals, education, newsletter, and a forum for women to discuss issues and concerns. Open to anyone interested in supporting and working with this grass-roots organization. Write: AABCA, P.O. Box 8981, Minneapolis, MN 55408. Call (612)825-3675 or (612)731-3792.

(Model) **Bay Area Multiple Myeloma Support Group** *1 group in Oakland, CA. Founded 1990.* Sharing of information and support for persons with multiple myeloma. Exchange of current treatment and techniques. Provides information and referrals, phone support, hospital visits, assistance in starting local groups. Write: c/o Evelyn Hall, P.O. Box 16040, Oakland, CA 94610. Call (510)839-5554.

(Model) **People Living Through Cancer** *2 affiliated groups in Albuquerque, NM area. Founded 1983.* Helps cancer survivors and their loved ones make informed choices and improve the quality of life by sharing in a community of people who have "been there." Newsletter, information and referrals, advocacy. Dues $25/year. Conducts national training for American Indians and Alaskan natives who are interested in developing cancer survivorship programs based on a grassroots program serving pueblo Indians. Write: People Living Through Cancer, 323 Eighth St. SW, Albuquerque, NM 87102. Call (505)242-3263; FAX: (505)242-6756.

(Model) **SHARE: Self-Help for Women with Breast or Ovarian Cancer** *1 group in New York City. Founded 1976. (Bi-lingual)* Support for women faced with the emotional, social and non-medical problems of breast or ovarian cancer. Also groups for family and friends. Groups led by trained leaders who have had breast or ovarian cancer. Educational programs, newsletter, walkathon, and phone support. Write: SHARE, 1501 Broadway #1720, NY, NY 10036. Call (212)382-2111 (breast hotline); (212)719-1204 (ovarian hotline); (212)719-4454 (Spanish hotline), (212)719-0364 (office); FAX: (212)869-3431.

(Model) **SPOHNC (Support for People with Oral and Head and Neck Cancer)** *1 group in New York. Founded 1991.* Patient-directed self-help program offering encouragement, support, acceptance and self-expression for persons with oral and head and neck cancer. Offers small group meetings, phone support, educational programs, newsletter, one-on-one support, and information and referrals. Assistance in starting groups. Write: SPOHNC, P.O. Box 53, Locust Valley, NY 11560-0053. Call Nancy Leupold (516)759-5333; *E-mail*: spohnc@ix.netcon.com *Website*: http://www.cybermedical.com/spohnc

CARBOHYDRATE DEFICIENT GLYCOPROTEIN SYNDROME

CDGS Parent to Parent Forum *Int'l network. Founded 1996.* Support for parents of children with CDGS (carbohydrate deficient glycoprotein syndrome, an inherited metabolic disease affecting all body parts, especially the central and peripheral nervous systems). Support is primarily online, but also provides information and referrals, phone support, advocacy. Bulletin board for families to interact with questions, comments and updates. Call Donna Yunes, 4 Wryan Rd., Derry, NH 03038; phone (603)434-3064; or Debbie Leary, 10238 N.

Bellview Rd., Orangeville, IL 61060; phone (815)789-4744; *Website*: http://www.cdgs.com or http://www.saturn.net/~scottd/cdg1.htm

CARDIO-FACIO-CUTANEOUS SYNDROME

CFC Support Network *Int'l network. Founded 1991.* Mutual support for parents of children with CFC Syndrome. Strives to find and disseminate information on Cardio-Facio-Cutaneous syndrome. Offers newsletter, information and referrals, phone support and a pen pal program. Write: c/o Nancy Carlson, 157 Alder Ave., Egg Harbor Twp., NJ 08234-9304. Call (609)646-5606; *E-mail*: Redsifer@aol.com

CARNITINE DEFICIENCY

ABCD, Inc. (Assisting Babies/Children with Carnitine Disorders) *Nat'l network. Founded 1991.* Parent and professional support groups for those who have suffered with, and are being treated for, carnitine deficiency and related metabolic disorders. Organizes and supports educational and advocacy activities. Newsletter, information and referrals, phone support. Write: ABCD, Inc., 1010 Jorie Blvd., Suite 234, Oak Brook, IL 60523. Call (630)571-9608; FAX: (773)325-9933; *E-mail*: agimbel@mcs.net; *Website*: http://www.abcdnet.org

CARPAL TUNNEL SYNDROME / REPETITIVE MOTION INJURY

Association for Repetitive Motion Syndromes *Nat'l network. Founded 1990.* To support, educate, and protect persons with CTS and related repetitive motion injuries. To work on prevention of CTS for persons at risk. Newsletter, information. Dues $20/ind.; $75/prof.; $150/Corp. Write: Assn. for Repetitive Motion Syndrome, P.O. Box 514, Santa Rosa, CA 95402-0514. Call (707)571-0397 (10-4 PST).

CELIAC SPRUE / DERMATITIS HERPETIFORMIS
(See also Allergies, Gastrointestinal Disorders)

American Celiac Society / Dietary Support Coalition *Nat'l. 66 affiliated chapters. Founded 1976.* Mutual support and information for celiac-sprue patients, families and health care professionals. Buddy system, visitation, phone help system, participation in educational efforts. Also supports dermatitis herpetiformis and Crohn's disease. Newsletter. Write: c/o Annette Bentley, 58 Musano Ct., W. Orange, NJ 07052-4114. Call Annette (973)325-8837 (after 5pm); FAX: (973)669-8808; *E-mail*: bentleac@umdnj.edu

Celiac Sprue Association/United States of America, Inc. *Nat'l. 76 chapters. Founded 1969.* Provides educational materials on celiac sprue and dermatitis herpetiformis to patients, parents of children, and professionals. Provides opportunities for support groups and networking with patients and professionals. Newsletter, annual conference. Group development guidelines. Write: Celiac Sprue Assn. USA, P.O. Box 31700, Omaha, NE 68131-0700. Call (402)558-0600; FAX: (402)558-1347; *E-mail:* 76131.2257@compuserve.com

Gluten Intolerance Group of North America *Nat'l network. Founded 1974.* Provides information and support to persons with celiac sprue or dermatitis herpetiformis, their families and health care professionals. Newsletter ($30), information and referral, conferences, group development guidelines, cookbooks. Write: Gluten Intolerance Group of No. Amer., P.O. Box 23053, Seattle, WA 98102-0353. Call (206)325-6980; FAX: (206)320-1172; *E-mail:* gig@accessone.com

CEREBRAL PALSY
(Also see Disabilities General; Parents of Disabled)

United Cerebral Palsy Association, Inc. *Nat'l. 155 affiliates. Founded 1949.* Supports local affiliates that run programs for individuals with cerebral palsy and other disabilities. Local programs include support groups for parents and adults with cerebral palsy. Quarterly magazine, bi-monthly newsletter, research reports. UCPA Forum on America On-Line. Write: UCP, 1660 L St., NW, #700, Washington, DC 20036-5603. Call 800-872-5827; TTY: (202)542-1266; FAX: (202)842-3519; *Website:* http://www.ucpa.org *E-mail:* ucpnatl@ucpa.org

CHARCOT-MARIE-TOOTH /
PERONEAL MUSCULAR ATROPHY /
HEREDITARY MOTOR SENSORY NEUROPATHY

Charcot Marie Tooth Association *Nat'l. 25 affiliated groups. Founded 1983.* Information and support for patients and families affected by Charcot-Marie-Tooth disorders (also known as peroneal muscular atrophy or hereditary motor sensory neuropathy). Referrals, newsletter, phone help, VCR tapes, support groups, conferences. Write: CMT Assn., 601 Upland Ave., Upland, PA 19015. Call Pat Dreibelbis (610)499-7486 or 800-606-CMTA; FAX: (610)499-7487; *Website:* http://www.charcot-marie-tooth.org *E-mail:* cmtassoc@aol.c9om

C.M.T. International *Int'l network. 2000+ members. Founded 1984.* Sharing and caring for those with Charcot-Marie-Tooth, (also known as peroneal muscular atrophy or hereditary motor and sensory neuropathy). Information for patients and professionals. Newsletter, list of publications on various aspects of CMT available. Write: CMT Int'l, One Springbank Dr., St. Catharines, Ontario, Canada L2S 2K1. Call (905)687-3630 (Mon-Thu, 10-4); FAX: (905)687-8753; *E-mail:* cmtint@vaxxine.com *Website:* http://www.cmtint.org

CHARGE SYNDROME

CHARGE Syndrome Foundation, Inc. *Nat'l network. Founded 1993.*
Networking of families affected by CHARGE Syndrome (Coloboma of the eye;
Heart malformations; Atresia of the nasal passages; Retardation of growth and/or
development; Genital hypoplasia; Ear malformations). Offers booklets,
newsletter, information, referrals, and parent-to-parent support. Bi-annual int'l
conference. Newsletter. Dues $15-$30. Write: c/o Marion A. Norbury, 2004
Parkade, Columbia, MO 65202. Call (573)499-4694. Families only call
800-442-7604; FAX: (573)499-4694 (day/eve); *E-mail:* mnorbury@coin.
missouri.edu   *Website:* http://www.kumc.edu/instructions/medicine/
genetics/support/charge.html

CHEMICAL HYPERSENSITIVITY/ ENVIRONMENTAL ILLNESS

H.E.A.L. (Human Ecology Action League, Inc.) *Nat'l. 60+ chapters.
Founded 1977.* Support, information for persons affected by multiple chemical
sensitivities. Education to increase awareness of toxic substances. Resource list,
bibliographies. Helps local chapters to achieve mutual objectives. Newsletter.
Chapter development guidelines. Directory of HEAL members in healthcare
professions. Write: HEAL, P.O. Box 29629, Atlanta, GA 30359-1126. Call
(404)248-1898; FAX: (404)248-0162; *E-mail*: HEALNatnl@aol.com *Website*:
http://members.aol.com/HEALNatnl/index.com

National Center for Environmental Health Strategies *Nat'l network. Founded
1986.* Clearinghouse services, educational materials, technical support and
policy development for chemically, environmentally or occupationally caused
illnesses and anyone interested in indoor pollution and chemical sensitivity.
Speakers bureau and workshops. Phone help, referrals, publications, newsletter.
Dues: $20/ind.; $25/prof. Call Mary Lamielle (609)429-5358, Write: Nat'l Ctr.
for Env. Health Strategies, 1100 Rural Ave., Voorhees, NJ 08043; *E-mail*:
wjrd37a@prodigy.com

National Foundation for the Chemically Hypersensitive *Nat'l. 40+ chapters.
Founded 1986.* Information and networking for people who have a chemically
induced immune system disorder. Devoted to research, education, and
development of local chapters. Information and referrals. Write: NFCH, 1158
N. Huron Rd., Linwood, MI 48634. Call (517)697-3989.

CHOLESTEROL

(Note) **High Cholesterol** is a condition for which we have received a significant
number of inquiries. Regrettable, we are unaware of any self-help support group
or network that has yet been formed. (There is, however, a toll-free specialty

number to receive literature on cholesterol under the helpline listings.) If you learn of any existing group that you would recommend, or are interested in starting such a group, please call the Clearinghouse.

CHROMOSOME DISORDERS
(Also see specific disorder)

Chromosome Deletion Outreach *Int'l network. Founded 1992.* Support and networking for families having a child diagnosed with any type of chromosome disorder, including deletions, partial duplications, duplications, chromosome rings, inversions, and translocations. Provides phone support, library of information. Dues $10/year (includes quarterly newsletter). Write: C.D.O., P.O. Box 724, Boca Raton, FL 33429-0724. Call Linda Sorg (561)391-5098; FAX: (561)395-4252; *Website*: http://members.aol.com/cdousa/support/htm *E-mail:* CDO@worldnet.att.net

National Center for Chromosome Inversions *Nat'l network.* Mutual support for families affected by chromosome inversions. Information and referrals, phone support, pen pal program. Write: Nat'l Ctr. for Chromosome Inversions, 1029 Johnson St., Des Moines, IA 50315. Call (515)287-6798 (day); *E-mail:* ncfci@msn.com

(Interest in starting) **Chromosome 3 Disorders** *No known support network.* At time of printing, we have heard from one person who is seeking the assistance of others to help start an information-sharing network for parents of children with any type of chromosome 3 disorder. If you are interested, please contact the Clearinghouse for more information.

CHRONIC FATIGUE SYNDROME

CFIDS Association, Inc. *Nat'l. Founded 1987.* For people interested in chronic fatigue and immune dysfunction syndrome. Education, advocacy, funding of research. CFIDS Chronicle newsletter ($35-60). Write: CFIDS Assn., P.O. Box 220398, Charlotte, NC 28222-0398. Call 800-442-3437; FAX: (704)365-9755; *E-mail*: info@cfids.org; *Website*: http://www.cfids.org

CFS Survival Association *Nat'l network. Founded 1993.* To guide, educate and network people with chronic fatigue syndrome on how to survive and win emotionally, physically and financially. Education, advocacy, information and referrals, phone hotline, group support, seminars. CFS Survival Guide Newsletter. Write: CFS Survival Assn., P.O. Box 1889, Davis, CA 95617-1889. Call (916)756-9242 (day).

Fibromyalgia Network *Nat'l. Founded 1988.* Provides information on fibromyalgia and chronic fatigue syndrome. Referrals to self-help groups, patient contacts and health care professionals, and other services. Newsletter, information and referrals, conferences, and guidelines and assistance in starting new groups. Write: Fibromyalgia Network, P.O. Box 31750, Tucson, AZ 85751-1750. Call 800-853-2929; *E-mail*: fmnetter@msn.com

National Chronic Fatigue Syndrome and Fibromyalgia Assn, Inc. *Int'l. 500 affiliated groups and contacts worldwide. Founded 1985.* To educate patients, the public, and the medical profession about chronic fatigue syndrome and fibromyalgia. Support groups, quarterly newsletter, funds research, conducts seminars. Literature available for patients and physicians. Guidelines and assistance available for starting support groups. Write: Nat'l CFS and Fibromyalgia Assn., P.O. Box 18426, Kansas City, MO 64133. Call (816)313-2000 (24 hr. hotline); FAX: (816)524-6782; *E-mail:* keal55a@prodigy.com

CLEFT PALATE

Cleft Palate Foundation *Nat'l. 50 groups. Founded 1973.* Provides information and referrals to individuals with cleft lip and palate or other craniofacial anomalies. Referrals are made to local cleft palate/craniofacial teams for treatment and to parent support groups. Free information on various aspects of clefting is available. Write: Cleft Palate Fdn., 1829 E. Franklin St., #1022, Chapel Hill, NC 27514. Call 800-24-CLEFT or (919)933-9044; FAX: (919)933-9604; *Website*: http://www.cleft.com

(Model) **Prescription Parents, Inc.** *1 group in MA. Founded 1973.* Support group for families of children with cleft lip and palate. Education for parents of newborns, presentations by professionals. Family social events, phone support network, group development guidelines. Write: Prescription Parents, Inc., 22 Ingersoll Rd., Wellesley, MA 02181. Call Amy Kapinos (617)431-1398.

CLOACA / CAVDAL SYNDROME
(Also see Syringomyelia)

Cloaca Syndrome Support Network *Nat'l network. Founded 1990.* Information, support and education for families affected by Cloaca Syndrome (also known as Cavdal Syndrome, Syringomyelia or VATER). Advocacy, literature, phone support. Write: Laurie Schall, 6530 Highway 78, Mazomamie, WI 53560. Call (608)795-2665.

COBALAMIN

The Cobalamin Network *Int'l network. Founded 1985.* Informational and emotional support for families of children affected by inborn errors of cobalamin metabolism. Pen pal programs, phone support. Write: Cobalamin Network, P.O.

Box 174, Thetford Center, VT 05075-0174. Call (802)785-4029 (eve/weekends);
E-mail: SueBee18@valley.net

COCKAYNE SYNDROME / CACHECTIC DWARFISM

Share and Care Cockayne Syndrome Network *(Bi-lingual) Int'l network.*
Founded 1981. Mutual support and networking for families affected by
Cockayne Syndrome (cachectic dwarfism). Sharing of information between
families and professionals. Maintains registry of families. Information and
referrals, newsletter, phone support. Pamphlet available in English, Spanish
and Japanese. Write: Share and Care Cockayne Syndrome Network, P.O. Box
552, Stanleytown, VA 24168. Call (540)629-2369; FAX: (540)647-3739;
E-mail: cockayne@kimbanet.com

COFFIN-LOWRY SYNDROME

The Coffin-Lowry Syndrome Foundation *Int'l network. Founded 1991.*
Provides support through a database of real-life experiences and information on
achievements that can be accomplished through love and early intervention for
families affected by Coffin-Lowry Syndrome. Newsletter, pen pal program,
phone support, information and referrals. Write: Mary Hoffman, 13827 196th
Ave. S.E., Renton, WA 98059. Call (425)204-9176; *E-mail*:
m_c_hoffman@msn.com

COGAN'S SYNDROME

Cogan's Contact Network *Nat'l network. Founded 1989.* Mutual support and
sharing of experiences and strategies for persons with Cogan's Syndrome. Aims
to help people understand Cogan's, a rare disorder that affects hearing, eyes,
balance, etc. Networking, pen pals, literature. Dues $25. Write: Anthony
Yuppa, Cogan's Contact Network, P.O. Box 713, Garfield, NJ 07026-0713.
Call Anthony Yuppa (201)471-3690 (TDD/FAX) or (201)648-2725; *E-mail*:
uscogans@aol.com

COHEN SYNDROME

Cohen Syndrome Support Group *Int'l network. Founded 1996.* Information
and support for families of children with Cohen Syndrome (aka Pepper
Syndrome), a rare, genetic disorder. Parent-to-parent networking, information
and newsletter. Write: Cohen Syndrome Support Group, 7, Woods Court,
Brackley, Northants, England NN13 GHP. Call (01280)704515.

*"The firmest friendships have been formed in mutual adversity, as iron is most
strongly united by the fiercest flame."*   *- Charles Caleb Colton*

CONGENITAL ADRENAL HYPERPLASIA

Congenital Adrenal Hyperplasia *Nat'l network. Founded 1993.* Offers educational and emotional support to families of children with congenital adrenal hyperplasia. Provides information and referrals, pen pal program, phone support, networking. Quarterly newsletter. Assistance in starting new groups. Write: Mary Andrews, CAH Div. of MAGIC Fdn., 1327 N. Harlem Ave., Oak Park, IL 60302. Call 800-3MAGIC3; FAX: (708)383-0899; *Website*: http://www.nettap.com/ ~ magic *E-mail:* magic@nettap.com

CONGENITAL CENTRAL HYPOVENTILATION

CCHS Family Support Network *Int'l network. Founded 1990.* Mutual support to help parents cope with having a child with congenital Central hypoventilation syndrome (aka Ondine's Curse). Provides family newsletter, physician directory, phone support, equipment information, and information and referrals. Aids in research. Write: c/o Mary Vanderlaan, 71 Maple St., Oneonta, NY 13820. Call (607)432-8872; *E-mail:* vanderlaanm@hartwick.edu

CONJOINED TWINS

Conjoined Twins International *Int'l network.* Support for families of conjoined twins, or families who have lost one or more conjoined twin. Phone and pen pal network. Quarterly newsletter. Planning a future mountain camp for families. Write: Conjoined Twins Int'l, P.O. Box 10895, Prescott, AZ 86304-0895.

CORNELIA DE LANGE

Cornelia de Lange Syndrome Foundation, Inc. *Int'l. 2500+ member families. Founded 1981.* To provide parent and family support and education, support research, and create public awareness. Newsletter. Family album available for networking and mutual support. Annual convention. Professional network. Assistance in starting groups. Write: Cornelia de Lange Syndrome Fdn., 302 West Main St., Avon, CT 06001. Call 800-223-8355; FAX: (860)676-8337; *Website*: http://cdlsoutreach.org *E-mail:* CDLSintl@iconn.net

CORTICO-BASAL GANGLIONIC DEGENERATION

(Interest in starting) **Cortico-Basal Ganglionic Degeneration** *No known support network.* CBGD is a rare neurological disorder characterized by cell loss in the brain, for which we do not know of any existing support networks. At the time of printing, we have heard from two persons who are seeking the help of others to start a support network. If interested in helping, please call the Clearinghouse for information.

COSTELLO SYNDROME

International Costello Syndrome Support Group *Int'l network. Founded 1996.* Mutual support for parents of children with Costello Syndrome, a very rare disorder. Information and referrals, literature, phone support, pen pals, online chat room, newsletter. Write: Colin and Cath Stone, 90 Parkfield Rd. North, New Moston, Manchester, M40 3RQ, England. Call 44(0)161-682-2479; *E-mail*: c.a.stone@mmu.ac.uk *Website*: http://sargon.mmu.ac.uk

CRI DU CHAT (5P) SYNDROME

5P- Society *Nat'l network.* Support organization for families having a child with 5P- Syndrome, genetic disorder characterized by a high-pitched cry. Dedicated to facilitating flow of information among affected families and medical professionals. Listing of families in U.S and Canada. Newsletter. Annual meeting. Write: 5P- Society, 7108 Katella Ave., #502, Stanton, CA 90680. Call 888-970-0777; *E-mail*: fivepminus@aol.com *Website*: http://www.fivepminus.org

CROHN'S DISEASE / COLITIS
(See also Allergies, Gastrointestinal Disorders)

CROHNS (Crohns Research Organization Hoping for Needed Support) *Nat'l network. Founded 1983.* Support and information for people who want to know more about Crohns Disease. Information, phone support, support group meetings, conferences, newsletter. Fundraising events. Write: c/o Penny Graham, Box 25, Kennard, NE 68034. Call Flora (402)339-3254 (day/eve) or Penny (402)427-7274 (day/eve).

Crohn's and Colitis Foundation of America (CCFA) *Nat'l. 71 chapters. Founded 1967.* Offers educational programs and supportive services for people with Crohn's disease or ulcerative colitis, as well as their family and friends. Funds research that seeks the cure for these illnesses. Membership benefits include a national magazine, and discounts on books. Free brochures. Dues $25/year. Write: CCFA, 386 Park Ave. South, 17th Fl., New York, NY 10016. Call 800-932-2423; FAX: (212)779-4098; *Website*: http://www.ccfa.org *E-mail*: info@ccfa.org

CYSTIC HYGROMA

CALM (Children Anguished with Lymphatic Malformations) *Nat'l network. Founded 1993.* Networking of families of children with cystic hygroma and lymphangioma for support, sharing of experiences and coping skills, and research. Education, literature, phone support, pen pals, information and referrals, and phone support. Write: CALM, 16 River Bend Rd., Montgomery, IL 60538. Call Tina Baalman (630)906-9028.

CYSTINOSIS

Cystinosis Foundation *Nat'l network. Founded 1983.* All-volunteer, non-profit organization dedicated to providing services for those suffering from cystinosis. Provides information and referrals. Parents directory and national medical registry. Conferences, newsletters, public education, literature. Write: Cystinosis Fdn., 2516 Stockbridge Dr., Oakland, CA 94611. Call 800-392-8458.

CYSTINURIA

Cystinuria Support Network *Int'l network. Founded 1994.* Provides support and an opportunity for sharing information for persons with cystinuria, a kidney disorder that causes kidney stones. Information and referrals, newsletter. Write: Cystinuria Support Network, 21001 NE 36th St., Redmond, WA 98053. Call (206)868-2996 (eve); *E-mail:* cystinuria@aol.com

CYTOMEGALOVIRUS DISEASE, CONGENITAL

Nat'l Congenital Cytomegalovirus Disease Registry *Nat'l network. Founded 1990.* Parent support network that provides support to families of children with CMV. Information and referrals, newsletter, literature. Write: c/o Texas Children's Hospital, 6621 Fannin St., MC3-2371, Houston, TX 77030-2399. Call Allison Istas (713)770-4387; FAX: (713)770-4347; *E-mail:* cmv@bcm.tmc.edu

DANCING EYE SYNDROME/KINSBOURNE SYNDROME OPSOCLONUS MYOCLONUS / MYOCLONIC ENCEPHALOPATHY OF INFANTS

Opsoclonus-Myoclonus Syndrome Parent Talk *Nat'l network. Founded 1994.* Networking for parents of children with opsoclonus-myoclonus syndrome through "Parent Talk" newsletter and phone support. Write: Opsoclonus-Myoclonus Syndrome Parent Talk, 725 North St., Jim Thorpe, PA 18229. Call (717)325-3302.

Dancing Eye Syndrome *Nat'l network. Founded 1992.* Support and information for families of children with Dancing Eye Syndrome (aka Kinsbourne Syndrome, Opsoclonus Myoclonus, or Myoclonic Encephalopathy of Infants), a disorder consisting of loss of balance, irregular eye movements and muscle jerking. Newsletter, phone support. Write: CJ Crick, 78, Quantock Rd., W. Sussex BN13 2HQ, England. Call 01903-532383 (Voice/FAX); *E-mail:* rasr@mistral.co.uk

Moving Forward *Int'l network. Founded 1995.* Disseminates information on myoclonus, a movement disorder of the sensory nervous system. Resource letter and brochures available. Write: Moving Forward, 2934 Glenmore Ave., Kettering, OH 45409. Call (513)293-0409.

DANDY-WALKER SYNDROME

Dandy-Walker Syndrome Network *Int'l network. Founded 1993.* Provides mutual support, information and networking for families affected by Dandy-Walker Syndrome. Phone support. Write: Desiree Fleming, 5030 142nd Path, Apple Valley, MN 55124. Call (612)423-4008.

DeBARSY SYNDROME

DeBarsy Syndrome National Network *Nat'l network. Founded 1997.* Mutual support and sharing of information for families of children with DeBarsy Syndrome, a rare disorder. Write: DeBarsy Syndrome Nat'l Network, Univ. of Nevada, Reno, COE, REPC/285, Reno, NV 89557. Call (702)784-4921; FAX: (702)784-4997; *E-mail:* cdinnel@scs.unr.edu

DELAYED SLEEP PHASE SYNDROME

(Interest in starting) **Delayed Sleep Phase Syndrome** *No support known network.* At time of printing, we have heard from one person who is looking for others who are interested in helping to start a support network for persons with, and parents of children with, delayed sleep phase syndrome. If you are interested in helping, please contact the Clearinghouse for more information.

DES AFFECTED
(Also see Cancer)

DES-Action U.S.A. *Nat'l. 22 groups. Founded 1977.* Informational and emotional support for women who took DES during pregnancy and their children. Support groups, physician referrals, education for the public and health workers. Quarterly newsletter. Group development guidelines. Write: DES-Action USA, 1615 Broadway, #510, Oakland, CA 94612. Call (510)465-4011; FAX: (510)465-4815; *E-mail:* desact@well.com *Website*: http://www.desaction.org

DESMOID TUMORS

(Interest in starting) **Desmoid Tumors** *No known support network.* At time of printing, we have heard from one person who is seeking the assistance of others to help start a national information-sharing support network for persons

affected by Desmoid tumors, a rare, aggressive form of fibromatosis. If you are interested, please contact the Clearinghouse for information.

DIABETES

American Diabetes Association *Nat'l. 51 affiliates. Founded 1940.* Seeks to improve the well-being of people with diabetes and their families. Fundraising for research. Affiliates and chapters provide many support services. $24 dues includes magazine. Write: Amer. Diabetes Assn., 1660 Duke St., Alexandria, VA 22314. Call 800-DIABETES (342-2383) (M-F, 8:30am-8pm); FAX: (703)549-6995; *Website*: http://www.diabetes.org

JDF International, The Diabetes Research Foundation *Int'l. 100 chapters in No. America; 11 int'l affiliates. Founded 1970.* Fundraising for research to find the cause, cure, treatment and prevention of diabetes and its complications. Peer support groups through local chapters. Quarterly magazine. Chapter development guidelines. Write: JDF Int'l, 120 Wall St., New York, NY 10005. Call (212)785-9500, 800-223-1138 or 800-JDF-CURE; FAX: (212)785-9595; *E-mail:* info@jdfcure.com *Website*: http://www.jdfcure/com

(Model) **Diabetics Anonymous** *1 group in Sunnyvale, CA. Founded 1990.* Fellowship of men and women who share their experience, strength, hope and recovery with each other. Primary purpose is the management of diabetes. Meets in the Sunnyvale, CA area. Phone support, assistance in starting new groups. Write: Diabetics Anonymous, P.O. Box 60905, Sunnyvale, CA 94088-0905. Call Jim S. (408)746-2022.

DIABETES INSIPIDUS
(Also see Pituitary Disorders)

Diabetes Insipidus and Related Disorders Network (DIARD) *Nat'l network. Founded 1988.* Emotional and informational support network for persons dealing with any form of diabetes insipidus (nephrogenic or central). Provides education and promotes research. Quarterly newsletter, phone support. Write: DIARD, Anne-Lynne Samole, 235 N. Hibiscus Dr., Miami Beach, FL 33139. Call (305)538-3904; FAX: (305)532-7399; *E-mail:* alkeplar@aol.com *Website*: http://members@aol.com/ruudh/dipage1.htm

Diabetes Insipidus Foundation, Inc. *Int'l network. Founded 1996.* Support for families coping with neurogenic/central, nephrogenic, gestagenic and dipsogenic/polydipsic diabetes insipidus. Provides information and referrals, phone support, and advocacy. Newsletter. Write: Diabetes Insipidus Fdn., 4533 Ridge Dr., Baltimore, MD 21229. Call (410)247-3953.

DYSAUTONOMIA

The Dysautonomia Foundation, Inc. *Int'l. 16 chapters. Founded 1951.*
Information, referrals and fundraising for research and clinic maintenance for
persons affected by dysautonomia. Peer support for families affected by familial
dysautonomia. Newsletter. Write: Dysautonomia Fdn., 20 E. 46th St., #302,
New York, NY 10017. Call (212)949-6644; FAX: (212)682-7625; *Website*:
http://www.med.nyu.edu/fd/fdcenter/html

DYSTONIA

Dystonia Medical Research Foundation *Int'l. 200 chapters. Founded 1976.*
Education, support groups and fund-raising for research. Newsletter, information
and referrals, conferences. Write: Dystonia Med. Research Fdn, 1 E. Wacker
Dr., #2430, Chicago, IL 60601. Call (312)755-0198; FAX: (312)803-0138;
E-mail: dystfndt@aol.com *Website:* http://www.zipnet/users/dystonia

DYSTROPHIC EPIDERMOLYSIS BULLOSA

DEBRA of America (Dystrophic Epidermolysis Bullosa Research Assn.)
Nat'l network. 6 chapters. Founded 1980. Support and information for families
affected by dystrophic epidermolysis bullosa. Promotes research, provides
education for professionals, pen pals, phone network, information and referrals,
newsletter, regional conferences. Write: DEBRA of America, 40 Rector St.,
New York, NY 10006. Call (212)513-4090; FAX: (212)513-4099; *Website*:
http://www.debra.org

EAGLE-BARRETT SYNDROME / PRUNE BELLY SYNDROME

GUMS (Guardians/Grandparents United for Moral Support) *Nat'l network.
Founded 1991.* Support and education for families and professionals concerned
about Eagle-Barrett Syndrome (aka Prune Belly Syndrome). Information and
referrals, networking, pen pals, phone support, literature, advocacy, and
newsletter. Sibling groups. Open to other anomalies. Networking of families.
Write: c/o Joyce Henderson, 4512 Wilcox Pl., Jamesville, NY 13078. Call
(315)492-0090.

EAR ANOMALIES

Ear Anomalies Reconstructed: Atresia/Microtia Support Group *Int'l
network. Founded 1986.* Networking for families whose members have
microtia, atresia, or craniofacial microsomia. Sharing of experiences and medical
information. Phone support, visitation, conferences. Support group meets
periodically in New York City. Write: c/o Betsy Old, 72 Durand Rd.,

183

Maplewood, NJ 07040. Call Betsy Old (973)761-5438 or Jack Gross (212)947-0770.

EATING DISORDERS
(Also see Overeating)

FED (Freedom from Eating Disorders) *Int'l. Founded 1990.* Group of compulsive overeaters, bulimics, and anorexics who share a common goal--to allow Jesus Christ to free them from the bondage of an eating disorder. Information, phone support, literature. Assistance in starting new groups. Write: FED, 14707 SW Parmele Rd., Gaston, OR 97119. Call (503)628-8027.

National Association of Anorexia Nervosa and Associated Disorders, Inc. *Int'l. 300+ affiliated groups. Founded 1976.* Provides information on eating disorder self-help groups, therapy, and referrals to professionals. Meetings led by members with professionals as sponsors. Newsletter. Group development guidelines. Write: ANAD, P.O. Box 7, Highland Park, IL 60035. Call (847)831-3438; FAX: (847)433-4632.

National Eating Disorders Organization *Nat'l. Founded 1977.* Support, referral and education for people suffering from anorexia, bulimia and related eating disorders, their families and friends. Support groups, newsletter, information and referrals, audiotapes. Dues vary. Group development guidelines ($5); information packets ($10). Write: NEDO, 6655 S. Yale Ave., Tulsa, OK 74136-3329. Call (918)481-4044; FAX: (918)481-4076. *Website*: http://laureate.com

ECTODERMAL DYSPLASIAS

National Foundation for Ectodermal Dysplasias *Nat'l network. Founded 1981.* Distributes information on ectodermal dysplasias symptoms and treatments. Provides support programs for families and cooperates with research projects. Monthly newsletter. Annual family conference and regional conferences, dental implant program and scholarship opportunities. Directory of members for informal contacts among families. Write: Nat'l Fdn. for Ectodermal Dysplasias. 219 E. Main St., Box 114, Mascoutah, IL 62258. Call (618)566-2020; FAX: (618)566-4718; *E-mail:* nfed1@aol.com *Website*: http://www.nfed.org

ECZEMA / ATOPIC DERMATITIS

National Eczema Association for Science and Education *Nat'l network. Founded 1988.* Support for persons with atopic dermatitis (a common, chronic, inflammatory skin condition), as well as other forms of constitutional eczema. Promotes education and research. Information & referrals, networking and newsletter. $10 donation. Write: Nat'l Eczema Assn. for Science and Education, 1221 SW Yamhill, Suite 303, Portland, OR 97205. Call (503)228-4430 or (800)818-7546; FAX: (503)273-8778.

EHLERS-DANLOS SYNDROME

Ehlers-Danlos National Foundation   *Nat'l. 18 chapters Founded 1985.* Emotional support and updated information to persons with Ehlers-Danlos Syndrome. Serves as a vital informational link to and from the medical community. Provides physician referral assistance, computerized database to link interested members to communicate with each other, and conducts periodic learning conferences. Write: Ehlers-Danlos Nat'l Fdn., 6399 Wilshire Blvd., Suite 510, Los Angeles, CA 90048. Call (213)651-3038; FAX: (213)651-1366; *E-mail*: Loosejoint@aol.com *Website*: http://www.phoenix.net/~leigh/eds/

ENCEPHALITIS

Encephalitis Support Group *Int'l network. Founded 1994.* Provides support and information for persons with encephalitis (inflammation of the brain) and their families. Links individuals together for mutual support. Aims to educate public and professionals about the condition. Information and referrals, newsletter, computer networking. Encourages local networks. Write: Encephalitis Support Group, c/o Elaine Dowell, Pasture House, Normanby, Sinnington, York Y06 6RH, UK. Call (01)751-433318 (Voice/FAX); *Website*: http://www.connect.org.UK/merseyworld/glaxo   *E-mail*: 101750.730@compuserve.com

(Interest in starting) **Encephalitis/Meningoencephalitis**   At time of printing, we have heard from a parent of a child with meningoencephalitis who would like to find other parents of children with encephalitis to help start a support network in the United States. If interested, please contact the Clearinghouse for more information.

ENDOMETRIOSIS

International Endometriosis Association   *Int'l. 150 support groups and chapters. Founded 1980.* Information exchange, mutual support, educational materials and newsletter. Conducts and promotes research. Phone support network. Wide variety of literature available. Newsletter. Dues $35/year. Chapter development guidelines. Write: Int'l Endometriosis Assn., 8585 N. 76th Pl., Milwaukee, WI 53223. Call 800-992-3636 or (414)355-2200; FAX: (414)355-6065.

"He has not learned the lesson of life who does not every day surmount a fear."
- Ralph Waldo Emerson

EOSINOPHILIA MYALGIA SYNDROME

National Eosinophilia Myalgia Syndrome Network *Nat'l. 8 regional/state groups. Founded 1990.* Mutual support for EMS (eosinophilia myalgia syndrome) survivors and their families. Information and support through group meetings, and online support groups, phone contacts and newsletter. Medical and legal information, advocacy, literature, and conferences. Assistance in starting groups. Write: Nat'l EMS Network, P.O. Box 515, Dumfries, VA 22026-0515. Call (818)362-2299; *E-mail:* Faith@NEMSN.ORG; *Website*: http://www.nemsn.org

EPILEPSY / CONVULSIVE DISORDERS

Epilepsy Foundation of America *Nat'l. 67 affiliates. Founded 1967.* Information and support for people with epilepsy, their families and friends. Pharmaceutical program, newsletter for members. Affiliates' development kit. Referrals to local affiliates (many of which have employment related programs). Information and referrals. Write: Epilepsy Fdn. of Amer., 4351 Garden City Dr., Landover, MD 20785. Call (301)459-3700; Professional Library: 800-332-4050; Consumer Infoline: 800-332-1000; FAX: (301)577-4941; *E-mail:* postmaster@efa.org *Website*: http://www@efa.org

EXTRACORPOREAL MEMBRANE OXYGENATION

ECMO Moms and Dads *Int'l network. Many regional groups. Founded 1987.* Mutual support for parents who have agreed to extracorporeal membrane oxygenation procedure on their infant as a last resort to attempt to save the life. Telephone support, newsletter, pen pal, conferences, information and referrals, help in starting groups. Write: c/o Gayle Willson, Route 1, Box 176AA, Idalou, TX 79329. Call (806)892-3348; FAX: (806)792-1289.

FABRY DISEASE

Fabry Support and Information Group (FSIG) *Nat'l network. Founded 1996.* Dedicated to dispensing information and encouraging mutual self help as a means of emotional support to Fabry patients and family members. Information and referrals, newsletter, networking of members. Write: FSIG, P.O. Box 569, Concordia, MO 64020. Call (816)463-1382; FAX: (816)463-1356; *Website*: http://www.cpgnet.com/fsig.nsf *E-mail:* JJohnson@CPGnet.com

FACIAL DISFIGUREMENT
(Also see specific disorders)

AboutFace *Int'l. 50 chapters. Founded 1985.* Provides information and support to those who have facial differences and their families. Networks families who have similar concerns. Programs of public education and awareness. Newsletter, information and referrals, assistance in starting local groups. Write: AboutFace, Box 93, Limekiln, PA 19535. Call 800-225-FACE; FAX: (610)689-4479; *E-mail:* abtface@aol.com; or (Int'l) 99 Crowns Lane, 3rd Fl., Toronto, Canada M5R 3P4. Call 800-665-3223; FAX: (416)944-FACE.

Let's Face It *Nat'l. US Branch of Int'l. Founded 1987.* Network for people with facial disfigurement. Phone help, pen and phone pals. Referrals to resources. Annual 50-page resource list with over 190 resources available by sending 9" x 12" $3 stamped self-addressed envelope with interest (child or adult). Write: Let's Face It, P.O. 29972, Bellingham, WA 98228-1972. Call Betsy Wilson (360)676-7325; *E-mail:* letsfaceit@faceit.org *Website:* http://www.faceit.org/~letsfaceit/

(Model) **Forward Face** *1 group in New York City. Founded 1978.* Mutual support for people with craniofacial disfigurement and their families. Strongly advocates educating members and the public in the quest for understanding and acceptance. Liaison with medical personnel. Newsletter. Videotapes. Dues $20. Teen/young adult support group. Write: Forward Face, 317 E. 34th St., 9th Fl., Room 901A, New York, NY 10016. Call Kristin Ronelli or Barbara Robinson 800-FWD-FACE (800-393-3223) or (212)684-5860; FAX: (212)684-5864.

FACIOSCAPULOHUMERAL MUSCULAR DYSTROPHY/ LANDOUZY-MUSCULAR DYSTROPHY

FSH Society, Inc. *Nat'l network. Founded 1992.* Support, information, education, networking and advocacy for individuals with facioscapulohumeral disease (aka Landouzy-Dejerine Muscular Dystrophy). Newsletter, support group meetings, conferences, literature. Assistance in starting chapters. Write: FSH Society, 3 Westwood Rd., Lexington, MA 02173. Call Carol Perez (617) 860-0501 (day); FAX: (617)860-0599; *Website:* http://disability.ucdavis.edu

FAMILIAL ERYTHROPHAGOTIC LYMPHOHISTIOCYTOSIS

FEL Network *Int'l network. Founded 1990.* Network for parents of children with familial erythrophagocytic lymphohistiocytosis. Provides information, referral, networking, phone support and current resources. Write: c/o Kay Wojtek, 1807 N. Liano, Fredericksburg, TX 76824. Call (210)997-2483.

FATTY OXIDATION DISORDER
(Also see Metabolic Disorders)

FOD Communication Network - Family Support Group *Nat'l network. Founded 1991.* Opportunity for families dealing with fatty oxidation disorders (i.e. MCAD, LCHAD, LCAD, SCAD) to network with others dealing with these rare, genetic metabolic disorders. Newsletter, information and referrals, phone support, pen pals. Write: Deb and Dan Gould, 805 Montrose Dr., Greensboro, NC 27410. Call (910)547-8682; *E-mail:* GouldDan@aol.com *Website:* http://www.cinternet.net/FOD

FETAL ALCOHOL SYNDROME

Family Empowerment Network (FEN)   *Nat'l network. Founded 1992.* Support, education and training for families and caregivers of children with fetal alcohol syndrome or fetal alcohol effects, and interested professionals. Monthly sharing teleconferences, annual family retreats, conferences, newsletter. Networks families together for support. Dues $5/family; $10/prof. Assistance in starting support groups. Write: FEN, 610 Langdon St., Room 521, Madison, WI 53703. Call 800-462-5254 or (608)262-6590; FAX: (608)265-2329; *E-mail:* Fen@mail.dcs.wisc.edu

Fetal Alcohol Network   *Int'l. Founded 1990.*   Mutual support for parents of persons with fetal alcohol syndrome. Interested in advocacy, educational issues, behavioral problems and accessing community services. Newsletter, conferences. Group development guidelines. Write: Fetal Alcohol Network, 158 Rosemont Ave., Coatesville, PA 19320. Call (610)384-1133; *E-mail:* 72157.564@compuserve.com

Fetal Alcohol Syndrome Family Resource Institute   *Int'l. Founded 1990.* Grass-roots coalition of families and professionals concerned with fetal alcohol syndrome/effects. Educational programs, brochures, information packets. Regional representatives being identified. Support group meetings. Advocacy, information and referrals, phone support, conferences. Write: FAS Family Resource Inst., P.O. Box 2525, Lynnwood, WA 98070. Call 800-999-3429 (in WA); (206)531-2878 (outside WA); FAX: (206)640-9155.

FIBRODYSPLASIA OSSIFICANS PROGRESSIVA

Int'l Fibrodysplasia Ossificans Progressiva Association   *Int'l network. Founded 1988.*   Information and support for people affected by F.O.P. Provides newsletter, pen pals, phone support, conferences, current research information, group development guidelines. Write: Int'l FOP Assn., 1434 Howard St., Petoskey, MI 49770, phone (616)347-1833; FAX: (616)347-7879; or Box 3578 Winter Springs, FL 32708; phone (407)365-4194; *E-mail:* asand@freeway.net

FIBROMYALGIA

Fibromyalgia Alliance of America   *Nat'l. 1800 groups. Founded 1986.* Education and support for persons with fibromyalgia. Provides information and referrals to, and works with, support groups nationwide. Distributes materials to patients, the public, and professionals. Newsletter, phone support, conferences. Assistance in starting new groups. Write: Fibromyalgia Alliance of America, P.O. Box 21990, Columbus, OH 43221-0990. Call (614)457-4222; FAX: (614)457-2729; *E-mail:* Masaathoff@AOL.com.

Fibromyalgia Network   *Nat'l. Founded 1988.*   Provides information on fibromyalgia syndrome and chronic fatigue. Referrals to self-help groups, patients contacts, health care professionals, and other services. Newsletter, information and referrals, conferences, and guidelines and assistance for new groups. Write: Fibromyalgia Network, P.O. Box 31750, Tucson, AZ 85751-1750. Call 800-853-2929; *E-mail:* fmnetter@msn.com

Nat'l Chronic Fatigue Syndrome and Fibromyalgia Association, Inc.   *Int'l. 500 affiliated groups and contacts worldwide. Founded 1985.*   To educate patients, the public, and the medical profession about chronic fatigue syndrome and fibromyalgia. Support groups, quarterly newsletter, funds research, conducts seminars. Literature available for patients and physicians. Guidelines and assistance available for starting support groups. Write: Nat'l CFS and Fibromyalgia Assn., P.O. Box 18426, Kansas City, MO 64133. Call (816) 313-2000 (24 hr. hotline); FAX: (816)524-6782. *E-mail:* keal55a@prodigy.com

FRAGILE X SYNDROME
(Also see Mental Retardation)

FRAXA Research Foundation   *Int'l. 19 affiliated groups. Founded 1994.* Information and support on fragile X syndrome. Funds medical research into the treatment of this disorder. Newsletter, literature. Some chapters have support group meetings. Write: FRAXA Research Fdn., P.O. Box 935, West Newbury, MA 01985-0935. Call (508)462-1990; FAX: (508)463-9985; *E-mail:* fraxa@seacoast.com *Website*: http://www.fraxa.org.

National Fragile X Foundation, The   *Int'l. 81 groups. Founded 1984.* Provides information to promote education and research regarding fragile X syndrome, a hereditary condition which can cause learning problems in both males and females. It is the most common familial cause of mental impairment. Phone support, newsletter, information and referrals. Write: Nat'l Fragile X Fdn., 1441 York St., #303, Denver, CO 80206-2127. Call 800-688-8765 or (303)333-6155; FAX: (303)333-4369; *E-mail:* natlfx@aol.com

FREEMAN-SHELDON

Freeman-Sheldon Parent Support Group   *Int'l network. Founded 1981.* Emotional support for parents of children with Freeman-Sheldon. Also for adults with this syndrome. Sharing of helpful medical literature library. Information on growth and development of individuals affected. Participates in research projects. Members network by phone and mail. Newsletter. Write: Freeman-Sheldon Parent Support Group, 509 E. Northmont Way, Salt Lake City, UT 84103. Call (801)364-7060; *Website*: http://members.aol.com/fspsg *E-mail*: fspsg@aol.com

GASTROINTESTINAL DISORDERS, FUNCTIONAL
(See also Allergies, Celiac Sprue, Crohn's, Irritable Bowel)

American Celiac Society / Dietary Support Coalition *Nat'l. 20 affiliated chapters. Founded 1976.* Mutual support and information for celiac-sprue patients, families and health care professionals. Buddy system, visitation, phone help system, participation in educational efforts. Also supports dermatitis herpetiformis, Crohn's disease, lactose intolerance and other food allergies. Newsletter. Write: c/o Annette Bentley, 58 Musano Ct., W. Orange, NJ 07052-4114. Call Annette Bentley (201)325-8837 (after 5pm).

International Foundation for Functional Gastrointestinal Disorders *Int'l network. Founded 1990.* Non-profit educational foundation that publishes a newsletter and other fact sheets dealing with all types of gastrointestinal dysfunction. Information and referrals, phone support, conferences. Some groups are professionally-run, but others are member-run. Meets on America On-Line. Write: IFFGD, P.O. Box 17864, Milwaukee, WI 53217. Call (414)964-1799; FAX: (414)964-7176; *Website*: http://www.execpc.com/iffgd *E-mail:* iffgd@execpc.com

GASTROINTESTINAL MOTILITY DISORDER
(Also see Pseudo-Obstruction, specific disorder)

American Pseudo-Obstruction and Hirschsprung's Disease Society *Int'l network. Founded 1988.* Answers the needs of families, patients and professionals dealing with gastrointestinal motility disorders in infants and children (including intestinal pseudo-obstruction, Hirschsprung's disease, and gastroesophageal reflux.) Promotes research. Publications, newsletter, video, annual educational symposiums. Adult patients welcomed. Dues vary. Write: APHS, 158 Pleasant St., North Andover, MA 01845. Call (508)685-4477; FAX: (508)685-4488; *Website*: http://www.tiac.net/users/aphs *E-mail*: aphs@mail/tiac.net/users.aphs.

(Model) **PAGER (Pediatric/Adolescent Gastroesophageal Reflux Assn.)** *2 affiliated groups in MD. Founded 1992.* Offers support and information for parents whose children suffer from gastroesophageal reflux, an inappropriate backwash of stomach contents into the esophagus. Educates the public on this disorders. Newsletter, literature, telephone support network. Support group

meetings in Maryland and San Diego. Dues $25/yr. Write: PAGER, P.O. Box 1153, Germantown, MD 20875-1153; *Website:* http://www.reflux.org

GASTROPLASTY

(Model) **Gastroplasty Support Group** *1 group in New Jersey. Founded 1985.* Group of volunteer patients and professionals who educate and provide support for persons contemplating, or who have had silicone gastric banding. Deals with problems associated with weight loss. Monthly update letter, phone network, videotapes. Write: Joyce Dixon, Irvington General Hospital, 832 Chancellor Ave., Irvington, NJ 07111. Call Joyce Dixon (973)399-6080 or Dr. Lubomyr Kuzmak (973)374-1717 (Mon/Thurs/Fri).

GAUCHER DISEASE

National Gaucher Foundation *Nat'l. 10 chapters. Founded 1984.* Information and assistance for those affected by Gaucher Disease. Provides education and outreach to increase public awareness. Operates the Gaucher Disease Family Support Network. Bimonthly newsletter, telephone support, medical board. Write: Nat'l Gaucher Fdn., 11140 Rockville Pike, #350, Rockville, MD 20852-3106. Call 800-925-8885; FAX: (301)816-1516; *E-mail:* Sadamsngf@aol.com *Website:* http://www.gaucherdisease.org

GENETIC DISORDERS
(Also see specific disorders)

Alliance of Genetic Support Groups *Nat'l network.* Consortium of support groups dedicated to helping individuals and families affected by genetic disorders. Information and referrals to support groups and genetic services. Write: Alliance of Genetic Support Groups, 35 Wisconsin Circle, Suite 440, Chevy Chase, MD 20815. Call 800-336-4363 or (301)652-5553; FAX: (301)654-0171; *Website:* http://medhelp.org/www.agsf.htm *E-mail:* alliance@capaccess.org

GLAUCOMA, CONGENITAL

(Interest in starting) **Congenital Glaucoma** *No known support network.* At time of printing, we have heard from one person who is interested in hearing from others who would be interested in starting a support and information-sharing network for persons with congenital glaucoma. If interested, contact the Clearinghouse for information.

"Honor begets honor; trust begets trust; faith begets faith; and hope is the mainspring of life."
                                                                    - Henry L. Stimson

GLYCOGEN STORAGE DISEASE

Association For Glycogen Storage Disease *U.S and Canadian network. 2 affiliated groups. Founded 1979.* Mutual support and information sharing among parents of children with glycogen storage disease. Fosters communication between parents and professionals, creates public awareness, encourages research. Newsletter, phone support, conference. Write: Assn. for Glycogen Storage Disease, P.O. Box 896, Durant, IA 52747. Call (319)785-6038; FAX: (319)785-6038.

GRANULOMATOUS DISEASE, CHRONIC

Chronic Granulomatous Disease Assn.. Inc. *Int'l network. Founded 1982.* Support and information for persons with CGD, their families and physicians. Networking of patients with similar CGD-related illnesses. Support through correspondence and telephone. Newsletter publishes CGD medical and research articles. International registry of patients. All services free of charge to those involved with CGD. Referrals to physicians. Write: CDG Assn., 2616 Monterey Rd., San Marino, CA 91108. Call (818)441-4118 (9am-3pm, or anytime with special concerns); *Website:* http://www.pacificnet.net/~amhurley/ *E-mail:* amhurley@pacificnet.net

GRAVES'/ THYROID DISEASE

National Graves' Disease Foundation *Int'l. 25 affiliated groups in 18 states. Founded 1990.* To establish patient based Graves'/thyroid support groups, support research, provide better treatment, and to increase public awareness. Newsletter, information and referrals, phone support, one-on-one programs, conferences, internet bulletin board, and weekly online chat room. Each group has medical back-up/resource. Write: c/o Dr. Nancy Patterson, 2 Tsitsi Court, Brevard, NC 28712. Call (704)877-5251; *E-mail:* ngdf@citcom.net *Website:* http://www.hgdf.org

GUILLAIN-BARRE SYNDROME

Guillain-Barre Syndrome Foundation International *Int'l. 130 chapters. Founded 1981.* Emotional support, visitation, and education for people affected by Guillain-Barre Syndrome. Promotes support, education and research. Newsletter, pen pals, phone network, group development guidelines, international symposium. Write: Guillain-Barre Synd. Fdn. Int'l, P.O. Box 262, Wynnewood, PA 19096. Call (610)667-0131; FAX: (610)667-7036; *E-mail:* gbint@ix.netcom/gbs *Website:* http://www.webmast.com/gbs

"Nothing lasts forever--not even your troubles."   *Arnold H. Glasow*

HEADACHES

ACHE (American Council for Headache Education) Support Group *Nat'l. 40 affiliated groups. Founded 1990.* An opportunity for headache sufferers to decrease their feeling of isolation, to help them learn more about headaches, and enhance their coping skills. Newsletter, information and referrals, group meetings. Assistance in starting groups. Dues $15. Write: ACHE, 875 Kings Highway #200, Woodbury, NJ 08096. Call 800-255-2243; *Website:* http://achenet.org

National Headache Foundation *Nat'l. 32 affiliated groups. Founded 1994.* Mutual support for chronic headache sufferers and their families. Education on how to deal with chronic head pain. Group meetings, phone support. Public awareness seminars, funds research. Newsletter. Information on diets, and brochures. Write: Nat'l Headache Fdn., 428 W. St. James Pl., 2nd fl., Chicago, IL 60614-2750. Call 800-843-2256 (day); FAX: (810)647-3169; *E-mail:* efbnhf@aol.com

HEART DISEASE
(See also Transplants, specific disorder)

CHASER (Congenital Heart Anomalies - Support, Education, Resource) *Int'l network. Founded 1992.* Opportunity for parents of children born with heart defects to network with other parents with similar needs and concerns. Education on hospitalization, surgeries, medical treatments, etc. Newsletter, heart surgeons and facilities directory. pen pals, information and referral, phone support. Write: CHASER, 2112 N. Wilkins Rd., Swanton, OH 43558. Call Jim and Anita Myers (419)825-5575 (day); (419)825-2880; *CompuServe*: 7505.2742   *E-mail:* myer106w@wonder.em.cdc.gov   *Website:* http://www.csun.edu/~hfmth006/sheri/heart.html

Coronary Club, Inc. *Nat'l. 5 affiliated groups. Founded 1968.* Offers support to heart patients, and provides education on proper heart care and rehabilitation. Literature. Monthly bulletin "Heartline." Dues $29/year. Networking and referrals. Group development guidelines. Write: Coronary Club, Inc., 9500 Euclid Ave., Mail Code E37, Cleveland, OH 44195. Call (216)444-3690 or 800-478-4255; FAX: (216)444-9385.

International Bundle Branch Block Association *Int'l. Organized 1979.* Provides support and information to help bundle branch block persons and families cope. Educates public. Occasional newsletter. Pen pal program, informal phone support system. Guidelines and assistance for starting groups. Voluntary dues $10 (more for professionals). Write: c/o R. K. Lewis, 6631 W. 83rd St., Los Angeles, CA 90045-2875. Call (310)670-9132.

Mended Hearts *Nat'l. 250 chapters. Founded 1951.* Support groups for persons who have heart disease, their families, friends, and other interested persons. Quarterly magazine. Chapter development kit. Write: Mended Hearts, 7272 Greenville Ave., Dallas, TX 75231. Call (214)706-1442; FAX: (214)987-4334; *Website*: http://www.mendedhearts.org

National Society for MVP and Dysautonomia *Nat'l. 59 affiliated groups. Founded 1987.* Assists individuals suffering from mitral valve prolapse syndrome and dysautonomia to find support and understanding. Education on symptoms and treatment. Newsletter, literature. Write: Nat'l Soc. for MVP and Dysautonomia, 880 Montclaire Rd., #370, Birmingham, AL 35213. Call (205)592-5765 (day) or 800-541-8602 (day); FAX: (205)592-5707; *Website*: http://www.mvprolapse.com

Society for Mitral Valve Prolapse Syndrome *Int'l. 12 affiliated groups. Founded 1991.* Provides support and education to patients, families and friends about mitral valve prolapse syndrome. Newsletter, phone support, literature, conferences, support group meetings. Write: Soc. for Mitral Valve Prolapse Syndrome, P.O. Box 431, Itasca, IL 60143-0431. Call (630)250-9327; FAX: (630)773-0478;*Website:*http://www.swiftsite.com/mitralvalveprolapsesyndrome *E-mail:* bonnie0107@aol.com

(Model) **Mitral Valve Prolapse Program of Cincinnati Support Group** *1 group in OH. Founded 1988.* Brings together persons frightened by their symptoms in order to learn to better cope with MVP. Fosters use of non-drug therapies. Supervised exercise sessions, diagnostic evaluations and specialized testing. Information and referrals, conferences, literature, newsletter ($20/yr), group meetings in Cincinnati. MVP hotline. Assistance in starting groups. Write: MVP Prog. of Cincinnati, 10525 Montgomery Rd., Cincinnati, OH 45242. Call (513)745-9911; *E-mail*: kscordo@wright.edu *Website*: http://www.nursing.wright.edu/anp/mvp.htm

(Model) **Young At Heart** *1 group in New York. Founded 1991.* Provides emotional support, information and encouragement to persons with heart conditions, and their families. Focus is on cardiac patients under the age of 50 but all are welcome. Support is offered both on a one-on-one and group basis. Provides information and referrals, phone support, literature. Assistance in starting groups. Newsletter. Write: Young At Heart, P.O. Box 366, Mattydale, NY 13211. Call (315)454-2059 or 800-377-8044 (from 315 area code only); *Website*: http://www.dreamscape.com/young@heart *E-mail:* BarbaraTracy@DEC.com

HELLP SYNDROME

The HELLP Syndrome Society *Int'l network. Founded 1996.* Mutual support, networking, and information for persons affected by HELLP Syndrome

(Hemolysis, Elevated Liver enzymes and Low Platelet count). This syndrome can affect pregnant mothers, and is usually in tandem with pre-eclampsia. Brochure, newsletter. Write: The HELLP Syndrome Society, P.O. Box 44, Bethany, WV 26032. Call Judy Pyle (304)829-4658 or Jennifer and Steve Bohach (614)676-8428; *E-mail:* j.pyle@mail.bethany.wvnet.edu *Website:* http://www.member.aol.com/lindapax/private/hellp.html

HEMANGIOMA
(Also see Vascular Malformations)

Hemangioma Support System *Nat'l network. Founded 1990.* Provides parent-to-parent support for families affected by hemangiomas. Phone support. Write: c/o Cynthia Schumerth, 1218 Monterey Tr., DePere, WI 54115. Call (920)336-9399 (after 5pm CT).

HEMIFACIAL SPASM

Hemifacial Spasm Support Group *Nat'l network. Founded 1991.* Provides information and referrals regarding treatments and doctors for people suffering with hemifacial spasms. Phone support, pen pal program. Write: Hemifacial Spasm Support Group, 9928 Clearfield Ave., Vienna, VA 22181. Call (703)242-2330.

HEMIMEGALENCEPHALY

HME Contact Group *Int'l network. Founded 1991.* Network provides mutual support for parents of children with hemimegalencephaly through shared experiences, phone support and newsletter. Offers literature and information and referrals. Write: HME Contact Group, c/o Dagmar and David Kerr, 3 Linn Dr., Netherlee, Glasgow, G44 3PT Scotland.

HEMOCHROMATOSIS / IRON OVERLOAD DISEASE

Hemochromatosis Foundation, Inc. *Nat'l. 12 chapters. Founded 1982.* Support and information for hemochromatosis families and interested professionals. Promotes general awareness, encourages screenings to identify families; fundraising, videotape, educational materials, genetic counseling, referrals, quarterly newsletter, videotape of Cleveland Clinic Conference, conferences and periodic teleconferences. Send self-addressed stamped envelope with $0.55 postage to: Hemochromatosis Fdn., P.O. Box 8569, Albany, NY 12208. Call (518)489-0972; *Website:* http://branch.com/hemo/hemo.html *E-mail:* skleiner@shiva.hunter.cuny.edu

Iron Overload Diseases Association, Inc. *Int'l network. Founded 1981.* For hemochromatosis (excess iron) patients and their families. Encourages research and public awareness. Organizes self-help groups, acts as clearinghouse for patients and doctors. Bi-monthly newsletter "Ironic Blood." Membership dues $50/yr. Write: Iron Overload Diseases Assn., 433 Westwind Dr., N. Palm Beach, FL 33408. Call (561)840-8512 or (561)840-8513; FAX: (561)842-9881; *Website*: http://www.ironoverload.org *E-mail:* iod@emi.net

HEMOPHILIA

National Hemophilia Foundation *Nat'l. 46 chapters. Founded 1948.* Service to persons with hemophilia and their families. Promotes research. Seeks to increase public awareness and knowledge. Peer-run MANN program for men with hemophilia and HIV. Also program (WONN) for women who have bleeding disorders or are in a relationship with someone who does. Semi-annual newsletter, group development guidelines, annual meeting for patients and professionals. Dues vary. Write: Nat'l Hemophilia Fdn., The Soho Bldg., 110 Greene St. #303, New York, NY 10012. Call 800-42-HANDI or (212)219-8180; FAX: (212)966-9247; *E-mail:* nhfofnyc@aol.com *Website*: http://www.infonhf.org

HEPATITIS
(Also see Liver Disease)

Hepatitis B Foundation *Int'l network. Founded 1991.* Support and information for persons affected by hepatitis B. Supports research for a cure. Advocacy, information and referrals, literature, conferences, phone support, telephone chains, newsletter. Suggested donation $35. Write: Hepatitis B Fdn., 101 Greenwood Ave., Suite 570, Jenkintown, PA 19046. Call (215)884-8786; FAX: (215)887-1931; *E-mail:* info@hepb.org *Website*: http://www.hepb.org

Hepatitis C Foundation *Nat'l. 23 affiliated groups. Founded 1995.* Mutual support for persons with hepatitis C, and their loved ones. Rap sessions, guest speakers, phone help, buddy system. Newsletter. Write: Nat'l Hdqrts. Hepatitis C Fdn., 1502 Russett Dr., Warminster, PA 18974. Call Steve Longello (215)672-2221; FAX: (215)672-1518; *E-mail:* hepatitis_c_foundation@msn.com *Website*: http://www.hepcfoundation.org

Hepatitis Foundation International *Int'l network. Founded 1995.* Grassroots communication/support network for persons with viral hepatitis. Provides education to patients, professionals and the public about the prevention, diagnosis and treatment of viral hepatitis. Phone support network, speaker's bureau, literature. Referrals to local support groups. Quarterly newsletter. Some materials available in Spanish, Mandarin and Vietnamese. Write: Hepatitis Fdn. Int'l, 30 Sunrise Terr., Cedar Grove, NJ 07009. Call Thelma King Thiel (201)239-1035 or 800-891-0707; FAX: (201)857-5044; *Website*: http://www.hepfi.com *E-mail:* hfi@intac.com

HEREDITARY HEMORRHAGIC TELANGIECTASIA/ RENDU–OSLER–WEBER SYNDROME

HHT Foundation International, Inc *Int'l. Founded 1991.* Support for those interested in hereditary hemorrhagic telangiectasia (aka Rendu-Osler-Weber Syndrome) by exchanging information, and research. Aims to protect privacy. Newsletter, conferences, pen pals, scholarships, activities and brochures. Assistance in starting support groups. Dues $35. Write: HHT Fdn. Int'l, P.O. Box 8087, New Haven, CT 06530. Call 800-448-6389 or Rita Van Bergeijk (313)561-2537 (Michigan); FAX: (313)561-4585; *E-mail:* hhtinfo@hht.org *Website:* http://www.hht.org

HERMANSKY-PUDLOCK SYNDROME

Hermansky-Pudlock Syndrome Network *Int'l network. Founded 1992.* Mutual support and education for families affected by Hermansky-Pudlock Syndrome. Networks families together for support. Newsletter, annual conference. Support research. Write: c/o Donna Jean Appell, RN, 1 South Rd., Oyster Bay, NY 11771-1905. Call 800-789-9HPS (voice/FAX) or (516) 922-3440; FAX: (516)922-4022; *E-mail:* appell@theonramp.net *Website:* http://www.medhelp.org/web/htfn.htm

HERNIA, CONGENITAL DIAPHRAGMATIC

CHERUBS Association for Congenital Diaphragmatic Hernia *Int'l network. Founded 1995.* Support and information for families of children born with congenital diaphragmatic hernias. Phone support, pen pals, information and referrals, newsletter. Write: CHERUBS Assn., P.O. Box 1150, Creedmoor, NC 27565. Call Dawn Torrence (919)693-8158; *E-mail:* cherubs@gloryroad.net

HERPES

Herpes Resource Center *Nat'l network. 100 groups. Founded 1979.* Emotional support and education for persons with herpes. Referrals to HELP support groups, which provide a safe, confidential environment in which to obtain accurate information, and share experiences with others concerning herpes. Support group development guidelines. Free pamphlets (send self-addressed stamped envelope with 0.32 stamps). Quarterly journal ($25). Other materials available. Write: Herpes Resource Center, P.O. Box 13827, Research Triangle Park, NC 27709. Call (919)361-8488 (hotline - 9am-7pm) or (919)361-8486 (for starting groups); *Website:* http://sunsite.unc.edu/ASHA

"There is no exercise better for the heart than reaching down and lifting up people.   *- Author unknown*

(Model) **Herpes Anonymous** *1 group in New York. Founded 1984.* Educational and social support for persons with herpes and others interested about herpes. Dedicated to helping others like themselves overcome the social stigmas and embarrassing hardships brought on by this chronic disease. Dues $20/year. Free newsletters, socials. Write: H.A., P.O. Box 278, Westbury, NY 11590. Call Lenny (516)334-5718.

HIDRADENITIS

(Online) **Hidradenitis Support Group** *Founded 1997.* Provides support, information and understanding to persons who suffer from hidradenitis, a rare skin disease affecting the apocrine glands. Sharing of research information. *E-mail:* hidradenitis-request@UserHome.com *Newsgroup:* hidradenitis @UserHome.com *Website:* http://www.cyberhighway.net/ ~ stesia

HISTIOCYTOSIS-X

Histiocytosis Association of America *Int'l. network. Founded 1985.* Mutual support and information for parents and patients with this group of rare disorders. (Includes hemophagocytic lymphohistiocytosis, familial HLH, and familial erythrophagocytic lymphohistiocytosis). Provides parent-patient directory to facilitate networking and communication. Funds research. Literature and pamphlets (bi-lingual), newsletter. Write: Histiocytosis Assn. of America, 302 N. Broadway, Pitman, NJ 08071. Call Jeff and Sally Toughill (609) 589-6606; FAX: (609)589-6614; *E-mail:* histiocyte@aol.com *Website*: http://www.histio.org

HOLOPROSENCEPHALY

(Online) **The Independent Holoprosencephaly Support Site** Sharing of information and support for families of children with holoprosencephaly (a condition that affects the size, number and location of lobes in the brain, and organs such as the heart, eyes and kidneys). Members share messages online. Write: Tim Smith, 13a High St., Twerton, Bath BA2 1BZ England. Call +44 01225 428 434; FAX: +44 01225 428 434; *Listserv:* HPE-request@tream17.com *Website:* http://www.team17.com/ ~ tsmith/HPE *E-mail:* Tim.Smith@gashead.demon.co.uk

HUMAN PAPILLOMA VIRUS / GENITAL WARTS

HPV Support Program *Nat'l. 11 affiliated groups. Founded 1991.* Provides a safe, confidential environment in which to share support and experiences with others who also have the human papillomavirus (also known as genital warts). Information and referrals, pamphlets, quarterly news journal ($25). Assistance in starting new groups. How-to materials. Write: ASHA/HPV Program Coord., Attn: Tracy, HPV Group, P.O. Box 13827, Research Triangle Park, NC 27709-3827. Call 800-227-8922 (Mon-Fri, 8am-11pm) or (919)361-8485 (Admin.); FAX: (919)361-8425; *Website*: http://sunsite.unc.edu/ASHA

HUNTINGTON'S DISEASE

Huntington's Disease Society of America *Nat'l. 32 chapters. Founded 1967.* Provides information and referral to local support groups, chapter social workers, physicians, nursing homes and a variety of other resources via local representatives. Support research into cause, treatment and cure. Provides written and audiovisual materials. Quarterly newsletter. Chapter development guidelines. Write: Huntington's Disease Soc. of America, 140 West 22nd St., 6th Fl., New York, NY 10011. Call (212)242-1968 or 800-345-4372; FAX: (212)243-2443; *Website*: http://hdsa.mgh.harvard.edu   *E-mail*: schoenberga@hdsa.ttisms.com

HYDROCEPHALUS

Guardians of Hydrocephalus Research Foundation *Nat'l network. Founded 1977.* Information and referral service to persons affected by hydrocephalus. Phone networking for parents of children with hydrocephalus. Referrals to doctors, newsletter, literature (in English and Spanish), video. Write: Guardians of Hydrocephalus Research Fdn., 2618 Ave. Z, Brooklyn, NY 11235. Call Kathy Soriano (718)743-4473 or 800-458-8655; FAX: (718)743-1171.

Hydrocephalus Association *Nat'l network. Founded 1984.* Offers mutual support, education and advocacy for parents of children and individuals with hydrocephalus. Provides newsletter, phone support, conferences, information and referrals. Write: Hydrocephalus Assn., 870 Market St. #955, San Francisco, CA 94102. Call (415)732-7040; FAX: (415)732-7044.

National Hydrocephalus Foundation *Nat'l network. Founded 1979.* Support and information for adults with hydrocephalus and for parents of children with hydrocephalus. Support also for persons pregnant with a fetus with hydrocephalus. Quarterly newsletter, reference library, VCR for parents and professionals. Dues $30. Write: Nat'l Hydrocephalus Fdn., 1670 Green Oak Circle, Lawrenceville, GA 30243. Call 800-431-8093: FAX: (770)995-8982; *E-mail:* Ann_Liakos@atlmug.org

HYPERACUSIS / RECRUITMENT

The Hyperacusis Network *Int'l network. Founded 1991.* Mutual support and sharing of information, and education for individuals and their families with hyperacusis and recruitment (hypersensitive hearing). Promotes research into cause and cure. Newsletter, information and referrals, phone support, pen pals. Write: Hyperacusis Network, 444 Edgewood Dr., Green Bay, WI 54302. Call (414)468-4663 (eve); FAX: (414)432-3321; *E-mail:* dmalcore@mail.wisnet.net *Website*: www.sconcept/com/hacusis.html

HYPEREXPLEXIA

Hyperexplexia Contact Group   *Int'l network. Founded 1997.*   Provides understanding and support to families dealing with hyperexplexia (a rare neurological disorder characterized by an excessive startle reaction including muscle stiffness and apnea in response to sudden noise, movement or touch). Aims to educate professionals. Information and referrals, phone support and literature. Write: Steph Samson, 216 Westcott Crescent, Hanwell, London W7 INV England.

HYPERLEXIA

American Hyperlexia Association   *Nat'l network. 20 contacts nationwide.* Provides information and support re: hyperlexia, a disorder characterized by a precocious reading ability, difficulty in understanding verbal language, and abnormal social skills. Newsletter, conferences, literature, phone support, information and referrals. National membership directory. Write: Amer. Hyperlexia Assn., 479 Spring Rd., Elmhurst, IL 60126. Call (630)415-2212; FAX: (630)530-5909; *Website*: http://www.hyperlexia.org/   *E-mail*: info@hyperlexia.org

HYPOGLYCEMIA

HELP, The Institute for Body Chemistry   *Nat'l network. Founded 1979.* Support and information for persons interested in body chemistry, especially hypoglycemia (but includes PMS, low blood sugar, cholesterol management). Promotes research between food and body chemistry. Phone support, referrals to support groups. Assistance in starting groups. Write: HELP, P.O. Box 1338, Bryn Mawr, PA 19010. Call (610)525-1225 (10am-3pm; 8pm-10pm); *Website*: http://www.dynanet.com/ ~ bodychem

Hypoglycemia Association, Inc.   *Int'l network. Founded 1967.*   Education for persons with hypoglycemia and their families. Newsletter. Information on many aspects of low blood sugar. Write: Dorothy Schultz, Pres., Box 165, Ashton, MD 20861-0165. Call (202)544-4044 (recorded message); *E-mail*: bubbha@hooked.net   or   slowup@bigdog.fred.net   *Website*:   http://www.hooked.net/ ~ bubbha/whatsama.htm or http://www.fred.net/slowup/hypo.net

HYPOPARATHYROIDISM

(Resource) **Hypoparathyroidism Newsletter** Support and networking for persons with hypoparathyroidism through newsletter, pen pals and phone contact. Support, information and referrals. Write: James E. Sanders, 2835 Salmon, Idaho Falls, ID 83406. Call (208)524-3857; *E-mail*: jesanders@sisna.com

HYPOPHOSPHATASIA

(Resource) **Hypophosphatasia** The MAGIC Foundation is seeking persons who are interested in becoming involved in a national support network for parents, families and persons with hypophosphatasia, a rare metabolic bone disease. For information, write: MAGIC Fdn., 1327 N. Harlen, Oak Park, IL 60303. Call 800-3-MAGIC-3.

HYPOTHYROIDISM, CONGENITAL

Congenital Hypothyroidism Support Network *Nat'l network. Founded 1989.* Network and exchange of information for parents of children with congenital hypothyroidism, a thyroid deficiency. Information and referrals, phone support, pen pals, conferences, literature. Newsletter ($20/year). Write: c/o MAGIC Foundation, 1327 N. Harlen, Oak Park, IL 60303. Call 800-3-MAGIC-3. *Website*: http://www.nettap.com/ ~ magic   *E-mail*: magic@nettap.com

HYPOTONIA

(Interest in starting) **Hypotonia** *No known network.* At time of printing, we have heard from two persons who are interested in starting an information and support network for parents of children with hypotonia (low muscle tone). If interested in helping, please contact the Clearinghouse for information.

HYSTERECTOMY

Sans Uteri *Nat'l network. Founded 1996.* Support for women facing a hysterectomy, as well as for women who have undergone the procedure. Support for spouses and significant others of women struggling with life after a hysterectomy. Referrals to specialists, support groups. Literature. advocacy. Write: c/o Beth Tiner, 6447 W. 86th Pl., Los Angeles, CA 90045-3746. Call (310)410-9886; *Website*: http://www.2cowherd.net/findings   *E-mail*: findings@2cowherd.net

(Model) **HERS Foundation (Hysterectomy Educational Resources and Services)** *1 group in Pennsylvania. Founded 1982.* An anti-hysterectomy advocacy group that provides information about alternatives to, and

consequences of, hysterectomy. Quarterly newsletter $20/year. Group development guidelines. Write: HERS Fdn., 422 Bryn Mawr Ave., Bala Cynwyd, PA 19004. Call (610)667-7757: FAX: (610)667-8096; *E-mail*: hersfdn@aol.com *Website*: http://www.dca.net/hers

(On-Line) **Hysterectomy Support** *America On Line.* Supportive message exchange section with posts from women who have had hysterectomies. Access: Use keyword "health" to get to "Better Health and Medical Forum." Click on Support Groups.

ICHTHYOSIS

FIRST (Foundation for Ichthyosis and Related Skin Types) *Nat'l network.* *Founded 1981.* Provides support for people with ichthyosis through networking with others. Public and professional education. Supports research on treatment and cure and advocacy issues. Quarterly newsletter, publications, bi-annual conference. Dues $25. Write: FIRST, P.O. Box 669, Ardmore, PA 19003. Call (610)789-3995 or 800-545-3286; FAX: (610)789-4366; *E-mail*: ichthyosis@aol.com

IDIOPATHIC THROMBOCYTOSIS

(Interest in starting) **Idiopathic thrombocytosis** *No known network.* At time of printing, we have heard from one person who would like to develop a support and information network for persons with idiopathic thrombocytosis. If you are interested in helping, call the Clearinghouse for more information.

IDIOPATHIC THROMBOCYTOPENIA PURPURA (ITP)

(Note) **Idiopathic Thrombocytopenia Purpura (ITP)** is a disorder for which we have received a significant number of inquiries. Regrettable, we are unaware of any support group or network that has yet been formed. If you learn of any existing group that you would recommend, or are interested in starting such a group, please call the Clearinghouse.

IMMUNE/AUTOIMMUNE DISORDERS
(See also specific disorder)

American Autoimmune Related Diseases Assn., Inc. *Int'l. 2 affiliated groups.* *Founded 1991.* Mutual support and education for patients with any type of autoimmune disease. Advocacy, referrals to support groups, literature, conferences. Newsletter. Assistance in starting groups. Dues $24. Write: Amer. Autoimmune Related Diseases Assn., 15475 Gratiot Ave., Detroit, MI 48205. Call (313)371-8600; FAX: (313)371-6002; *E-mail:* aarda@aol.com *Website*: http://www.aarda.org/

Immune Deficiency Foundation *Nat'l. Chapters in 21 states. Founded 1980.*
Provides support and education for families affected by primary immune
deficiency diseases. Newsletter, handbook, videotape and educational materials
for public and medical professionals. Scholarships and fellowship program.
Group development guidelines. Write: Immune Deficiency Fdn., 25 W.
Chesapeake Ave., #206, Towson, MD 21204. Call 800-296-4433; *Website*:
http://www.clark.net/pub/idf *E-mail:* idf@clark.net

(On-line) **SCID (Severe Combined Immunodeficiency) Mailing Group**
Founded 1997. Online self-help group for families afflicted with SCID or who
have lost a child to SCID (a very rare genetic disorder resulting in severe
infections). Provides opportunity for families to share information and resources
with one another. *E-mail:* scidemail@aol.com (administrator) *Website:*
http://patriot.net/ ~ callao/scid.html

IMPOTENCY

Impotents World Association (IA) and I-Anon *Nat'l. 100+ chapters.*
Founded 1981. Information and support for impotent men and partners of
impotent men. Uses an adaptation of the 12-step program of AA. Newsletter
included with affiliate membership ($25/yr). Physician reference list. Videotapes
and audio cassettes. Chapter development guidelines. For copy of "Knowledge
Is The Best Medicine," send written request with $3 postage/handling. Write:
Impotence World Assn., 10400 Little Patuxent Parkway, Suite 485, Columbia,
MD 21044-3502. Call 800-669-1603 or (301)565-2718; FAX: (410)715-9609.

INCONTINENCE

Continence Restored Inc. *Int'l. 8 affiliated groups. Founded 1984.* Forum
where persons with incontinence, their families and friends can express concerns
and receive assistance. Disseminates information on bladder control. Phone
support.' Assistance in starting groups. Write: Continence Restored, 407
Strawberry Hill Ave., Stamford, CT 06902. Call (203)348-0601.

Pull-Thru Network, The *Nat'l. 2 affiliated groups. Founded 1988.* Mutual
support for families with children born with anorectal malformations, who have,
or will have, a pull-thru type surgery. Also for families of children with a
permanent or temporary ostomy, or children with incontinence. Newsletter,
information and referral, phone support, support group meetings, pen pals, and
literature. Dues $31/full membership; $20/newsletter only. Write: The Pull-Thru
Network, 4 Woody Lane, Westport, CT 06880. Call (203)221-7530; *E-mail*:
pullthrunw@aol.com*Website*:http://members.aol.com/pullthrunw/pullthru.html

Simon Foundation for Continence *Nat'l. 500+ affiliated groups. Founded*
1983. Support and advocacy for people suffering from incontinence. Quarterly

newsletter, pen pals, books, videos, group development guidelines. Write: Simon Fdn. for Continence, P.O. Box 835, Wilmette, IL 60091. Call (847)864-3913 or 800-23-SIMON; FAX: (847)564-9758.

INCONTINENTIA PIGMENTI/ BLOCH-SIEMENS-SULZBERGER SYNDROME

National Incontinentia Pigmenti Foundation *Nat'l network. Founded 1995.* Dedicated to research, family support and physician awareness on incontinentia pigmenti. Maintains national database of patients. Write: Nat'l Incontinentia Pigmenti Fdn., 30 East 72nd St., 16th Fl., New York, NY 10021. Call (212)452-1231; FAX: (212)452-1406; *E-mail:* nipf@pipeline.com *Website:* http://medhelp.org/www.nipf.htm

INFERTILITY
(Also see Childlessness)

NINE (National Infertility Network Exchange) *Nat'l. Founded 1988.* Support for men and women with impaired fertility to understand, cope and reach a resolution. Monthly educational meetings, newsletter, talk line, library, advocacy, and professional referral. Dues $35/yr. Write: NINE, P.O. Box 204, East Meadow, NY 11554. Call (516)794-5772; FAX: (516)794-0008; *E-mail:* NINE204@aol.com

Organization of Parents Through Surrogacy *Nat'l. 3 regional groups. Founded 1988.* Support and advocacy organization for families built through surrogate parenting. Members work together to address legislative bills on surrogacy. Newsletter, information and referrals, phone support, conferences, literature, support group meetings. Dues $75/parents; $45/surrogates. Write: Org. of Parents Through Surrogacy, P.O. Box 213, Wheeling, IL 60090. Call (847)394-4116; FAX: (847) 394-4165; *E-mail:* opts@starnet.com *Website:* http://www.opts.com

Resolve *Nat'l. 55 chapters. Founded 1974.* Emotional support and medical referrals for infertile couples. Support groups, education for members and public. Quarterly newsletter, publications. Chapter development guidelines. Write: Resolve, 1310 Broadway, Somerville, MA 02144-1731. Call (617)623-0744; FAX: (617)623-0252; *Website:* http://www.resolve.org *E-mail:* resolveinc@aol.com

INTERSTITIAL CYSTITIS

Interstitial Cystitis Association *Nat'l. Coordinators in various states. 75 groups. Founded 1984.* Provides education, information and support for those with interstitial cystitis and their spouses and families. Quarterly newsletter

($40/yr). Write: Interstitial Cystitis Assn., P.O. Box 1553, Madison Square Station, New York, NY 10159. Call 800-HELPICA or (212)979-6057; FAX: (212)677-6139; *E-mail*: icinfo@aol.com *Website:* http://www.ichelp.com

INTESTINAL MULTIPLE POLYPOSIS

IMPACC (Intestinal Multiple Polyposis And Colorectal Cancer) *Nat'l network. Founded 1986.* Support network to help patients and families dealing with familial polyposis and hereditary colon cancer. Information and referrals, encourages research, and educates professionals and public. Phone support network, correspondence, and literature. Write: IMPACC, P.O. Box 11, Conyngham, PA 18219. Call Ann Fagan (717)788-1818 (day) or (717)788-3712 (eve); FAX: (717)788-4046; *E-mail*: impacc@epix.net

INVERTED DUPLICATION 15

IDEAS (Inverted Duplication Exchange, Advocacy and Support) *Nat'l network. Founded 1994.* Support and advocacy for people affected by inverted duplication 15. Information and referrals, phone support, literature, newsletter. Write: c/o Bennet, RD#1, Box 260B, Thomasville, PA 17364-9768. Call (717)225-5229 (day); *E-mail*: ideas@craftech.com

IRRITABLE BOWEL SYNDROME
(Also see Allergies, Gastrointestinal Disorders)

(Model) **Irritable Bowel Syndrome Self Help Group** *1 group in Toronto.* Mutual support for persons with irritable bowel syndrome, their families, and health care professionals. Literature, phone support, advocacy, assistance in starting similar groups. Write: Irritable Bowel Syndrome Self-Help Groups, 3332 Yonge St., P.O. Box 94074, Toronto, Ontario M4N 3R1 Canada. Call (416)932-3311; *Website*: http://www.ibsgroup.org *E-mail*: ibs@ibsgroup.org

IVEMARK SYNDROME/RIGHT ATRIUM ISOMERISM

Ivemark Syndrome Association *Nat'l network. Founded 1996.* Network of parents of children with Ivemark Syndrome, a congenital condition (aka Right Atrial Isomerism) that causes severe heart abnormalities, and affects the lungs, siting of internal organs, and absence of the spleen. Offers support and friendship to families. Write: Liz Fisher, 52 Keward Ave., Wells BA5 1TS, UK. Call 01749-672603.

JOSEPH DISEASE

International Joseph Diseases Foundation, Inc. *Int'l network. Founded 1977.* Support network for patients, families and health care professionals concerned

about Joseph Disease. Information, referrals to DNA marker test sites. Supports
and conducts research, helps patients find services. Newsletter, group
development guidelines. Write: Int'l Joseph Diseases Fdn., P.O. Box 2550,
Livermore, CA 94551-2550. Call (510)371-1287; FAX (510)371-1288.

JOUBERT SYNDROME

Joubert Syndrome Parents-In-Touch Network, Corp. *Int'l network. Founded
1992.* Mutual support and sharing of knowledge for parents of children with
Joubert Syndrome. Aims to educate physicians and support team. Information,
networking list, quarterly newsletter and bi-annual conference. Write: c/o Mary
J. VanDamme, 12348 Summer Meadow Rd., Rock, MI 49880. Call
(906)359-4707; *E-mail*: joubert@match.org

KAWASAKI DISEASE

Kawasaki Families' Network *Nat'l network. Founded 1996.* Provides
information and support for families affected by Kawasaki disease (an
inflammatory illness which primarily threatens the cardiovascular system).
Members can exchange messages online. Also, family page on website with brief
case histories. Newsletter, literature, pen pals. Write: Kawasaki Families'
Network, c/o Vickie Machado, 46-111 Nahewai Pl., Kaneohe, HI 96744. Call
(808)525-8053; FAX: (808)525-8055; *E-mail:* kawasaki@compuserve.com
Website: http://ourworld.compuserve.com/homepages/kawasaki *listserv:*
listproc@hawaii.edu

KIDNEY DISEASE

American Association of Kidney Patients (AAKP) *Nat'l. 24 chapters.
Founded 1969.* Provides information, education and mutual support for patients,
their families and friends. Consumer advocacy. Educational materials, quarterly
magazine, chapter development guidelines. Write: AAKP, 100 S. Ashley Dr.,
Suite 280, Tampa, FL 33602-5348. Call 800-749-2257 or (813)223-7099; FAX:
(813)223-0001; *E-mail*: aakpnat@aol.com *Website*: http://www.aakp.org

IgA Nephropathy Support Network *Nat'l network. Founded 1992.* Acts as
a clearinghouse of information for persons with IgA Nephropathy and a forum
in which patients can express their concerns. Promotes research into the causes
and cures. Information, phone support, confidential network of patients.
Newsletter. Write: c/o Dale Hellegers, President, 964 Brown Ave., Huntington
Valley, PA 19006. Call (215)663-0536.

Polycystic Kidney Research Foundation *Int'l. 47 affiliated groups. Founded
1982.* Funds research and provides emotional support and education for persons
with polycystic kidney disease and their families. Promotes public awareness.

Holds medical seminars and fundraisers. Conferences, phone support, newsletter, assistance in starting new groups. Write: PKR Fdn., 4901 Main St., Suite 200, Kansas City, MO 64112. Call 800-PKD-CURE (Mon-Fri, 8-5 CST); FAX: (816)931-8655; *E-mail*: pkdcure@pkrfoundation.org *Website*: http://ww.kumc.edu/pkrf/

KLINEFELTER SYNDROME

Klinefelter Syndrome and Associates *Nat'l network. 4 affiliated groups. Founded 1990.* An educational organization dedicated to increasing public awareness of Klinefelter Syndrome (and other male sex chromosome variations) and providing support and information to those dealing with the syndrome. Brochure on KS that describes basic symptoms, diagnoses and treatments. Newsletter ($25/USA; $28/Canada; $30/Int'l (US funds). Write: Klinefelter Syndrome and Assoc., P.O. Box 119, Roseville, CA 95678-0119. Call (916)773-1449; FAX: (916)773-1449; *Website*: http://www.genetic.org *E-mail:* ks47xxy@ix.netcom.com

Klinefelter's Syndrome Association of America *Nat'l network. Founded 1990.* Provides support and information for persons affected by Klinefelter's Syndrome. Provides current information on the syndrome, helps researchers get in touch with interested KS people, and makes referrals to contact names and support groups. Literature, newsletter, and phone support. Write: Klinefelter's Syndrome Assoc. of Amer., N5879 30th Rd., Pine River, CO 54965. Call Lynn Sallee (414)987-5782.

KLIPPEL-FEIL SYNDROME

The Klippel-Feil Syndrome Network *Int'l network. Founded 1996.* Provides information on Klippel-Feil Syndrome, a rare, congenital disorder primarily comprised of cervical-spine fusion, renal abnormalities and scoliosis. Networks families' together for emotional support. Support and information provided mainly on-line, but literature and pen pals are available. Write: KFS Network, 3405 Poolside Dr., Lake Worth, FL 33463; *E-mail*: kfsnet@gte.net *Website*: http://home1.gte.net/kfsnet/index.htm

KLIPPEL-TRENAUNAY
(Also see Sturge Weber)

Klippel-Trenaunay Support Group *Nat'l network. Founded 1986.* Provides mutual support and sharing of experiences among families of children with KT, and adults with KT. Newsletter, phone support, meetings every two years. Write: Klippel-Trenaunay Support Group, 4610 Wooddale Ave., Minneapolis, MN 55424. Call (612)925-2596; *Website*: http://www.tc.umn.edu/nlhome/m474/vesse001/k-t.html

LACTIC ACIDOSIS

Lactic Acidosis Support Group *Nat'l network. Founded 1988.* Mutual support for parents dealing with lactic acidosis. Provides information and referrals, phone support, pen pals, conferences. Newsletter. Write: Lactic Acidosis Support Group, 1620 Mable Ave., Denver, CO 80229-5056. Call (303) 287-4953.

LARYNGECTOMY

International Association of Laryngectomees *Int'l. 285 chapters. Founded 1952.* Acts as a bridge starting before laryngectomy surgery through rehabilitation, and for practical and emotional support. Newsletter. Chapter development guidelines. Write: Int'l Assn. of Laryngectomees, 7440 N. Shadeland Ave., #100, Indianapolis, IN 46250. Call (317)570-4568; FAX: (317)570-4570.

LATEX ALLERGY

ELASTIC (Education for Latex Allergy Support Team Information Coalition) *Nat'l. 47 chapters. Founded 1995.* Provides information and resource material for those living with, or and treating latex allergy. Phone support, conferences, literature. Affiliated newsletter "Latex Allergy News" ($40/yr). Dues $15/yr. Assistance in starting local groups. Regularly exchanges messages on America Online and Netcom. Write: ELASTIC, 196 Pheasant Run Rd., West Chester, PA 19380. Call (610)436-4801; FAX: (610)436-1198; *Website*: http://www.netcom.com/~nam1/latex_allergy.html or http://www.netcom.com/~ecbdmd/elastic.html *E-mail*: ecbdmd@a.ix.netcom.com

LAURENCE MOON BARDET BIEDL SYNDROME

Laurence Moon Bardet Biedl Syndrome *Nat'l network. Founded 1983.* Mutual support and networking for persons affected by Lawrence Moon Bardet Biedl Syndrome. Networks persons with each other through newsletter for support. Literature, information and referrals, phone support and conferences. Write: LMBBS Self-Help Network, c/o The Foundation Fighting Blindness, Executive Plaza, Suite 800, 11350 McCormick Rd., Hunt Valley, MD 21031-1014. Call 800-683-5555 or (410)785-1414; FAX: (410)771-9470; TDD: (410)785-9687; *Website*: http://www.blindness.org

LEAD POISONING

Parents Against Lead *Nat'l. 15 affiliated groups. Founded 1986.* Mutual support and assistance for parents whose children have lead paint poisoning.

Advocacy to reduce lead poisoning through legislative and educational changes. Monthly meetings, information and referrals, phone support. Write: Ruth Ann Norton or Anita Hampson, Parents Against Lead, 28 E. Ostend St., Baltimore, MD 21230. Call (410)727-4226 or 800-370-5323; FAX: (410)727-6775; *E-mail*: ranorton@ubmail.ubalt.edu.

LENNOX GASTAUT SYNDROME

(Online Support Group) **Lennox Gastaut Syndrome Support Group** *Founded 1997.* Provides support and information for parents of children with Lennox Gastaut Syndrome, a severe form of epilepsy. Information on symptoms, treatments, and coping skills. Opportunity for parents to read and post personal stories. *Website*: http://wssg@globalnet.co.uk   or http://members.aol.com/lennoxgast/supportal/htm

LEUKODYSTROPHY

United Leukodystrophy Foundation, Inc. *Nat'l network. Founded 1982.* Provides information and resources for leukodystrophy patients and their families. Communication network among families. Promotes research, public and professional awareness. Quarterly newsletter. National conference. Dues $25/family; $50/professional. Write: United Leukodystrophy Fdn., 2304 Highland Dr., Sycamore, IL 60178. Call (815)895-3211 or 800-728-5483; FAX: (815)895-2432; *E-mail:* ulf@ceet/niu.edu   *Website*: http://www.ceet.niu.edu/ulf.html

LIFE THREATENING / CHRONIC ILLNESS
(Also see specific disorder)

Center for Attitudinal Healing, The *Nat'l. 100+ affiliates. Founded 1975.* Support programs for children, adolescents and adults facing their own, or a family member's, life-threatening illness, loss and grief. All services free of charge. Quarterly newsletter. Write: Ctr. for Attitudinal Healing, 33 Buchanan, Sausalito, CA 94965. Call (415)331-6161; FAX: (415)331-4545; *Website*: http://www.healingcenter.org *E-mail*: home123@aol.com or cah@well.com

Make Today Count *Nat'l. Founded 1974.* Mutual support and discussion for persons facing a life-threatening illness. Open to relatives and friends. Chapter development guidelines. Write: c/o St. John's Regional Health Center, Mid-America Cancer Center, 1235 E. Cherokee St., Springfield, MO 65804-2263. Call Connie Zimmerman 800-432-2273 (Mid-America Cancer Center); FAX: (417)888-8761.

(Note) **Parents of Terminally Ill Children** is a concern for which we have received a significant number of inquiries. Aside from Candelighters and the

groups mentioned above, we are unaware of any national or model self-help support group that has yet been formed. If you learn of any existing group that you would recommend, or are interested in starting such a group, please call the Clearinghouse.

LIPOMYELOMENINGOCELE

Lipomyelomeningocele Family Support Network *Int'l network. Founded 1997.* Support network for parents of children with lipomyelomeningocele (aka tethered cord syndrome). Matches families for mutual support. Promotes awareness of the disorder. Information and referrals, phone support, newsletter ($10). On-line meetings. Write: LSFN, 321 Hopewell St., Birdsboro, PA 19508. Call (610)582-5937; *E-mail:* gmcafee@postoffice.ptd.net *Website:* http://develop.mainquad.com/web/chrismc/support.html

LIVER DISEASE
(Also see specific disorder)

American Liver Foundation *Nat'l. 21 chapters. Founded 1976.* Dedicated to fighting liver diseases, including hepatitis, through research, education and patient self-help groups. Also has information on gall bladder disorders. Members include patients, families, professionals and supporters. Chapters organized and operated by lay volunteers. Newsletter, chapter development guidelines. Write: American Liver Fdn., 1425 Pompton Ave., Cedar Grove, NJ 07009. Call (201)256-2550 or 800-223-0179; FAX: (201)256-3214; *Website*: http://www.liverfoundation.org *E-mail*: joe@liverfoundation.org

Children's Liver Alliance *Int'l network. Founded 1994.* Support for families of children with biliary atresia or any other pediatric liver disorder (pre- and post-liver transplant). Acts as a liaison between families and healthcare professionals. Newsletter, phone support, information and referrals, pen pals, advocacy. Bereavement support, library, Spanish Division. Internet Newsgroup (ListServ - TRNSPLNT). Write: Biliary Atresia and Liver Transplant Network, Inc. 3835 Richmond Ave., Box 190, Staten Island, NY 10312-0190. Call (718)987-6200 (Voice Mail/FAX); *E-mail*: livers4kids@earthlink.net *Website*: http://www.asf.org/balt.html

(Model) **CLASS (Children's Liver Assn. for Support Services)** *1 group in CA. Founded 1995.* All-volunteer statewide network dedicated to addressing the emotional, educational, and financial needs of families with children with liver disease or liver transplantation. Provides telephone hotline, newsletter, parent matching, literature and financial assistance. Supports research and educates public about organ donations. Write: CLASS, 26444 Dove Dr., Valencia, CA 91355. Call (805)255-0353. E-mail: supportsrv@aol.com

LOIN PAIN HEMATURIA SYNDROME

(Model) **Hearts and Hands** *1 group in NC. Founded 1993.* Emotional, spiritual and educational support for persons with either rare or undiagnosed illnesses, and their families. Also has a registry for Loin Pain Hematuria Syndrome. Write: c/o Winoka Plummer, 4115 Thomasville Rd., Winston-Salem, NC 27107. Call (910)788-1433.

LOWE SYNDROME

Lowe Syndrome Association *Int'l. Founded 1983.* Fosters communication among families with Lowe Syndrome. Provides medical and educational information. Supports medical research. Booklet, newsletter available. International conference. Dues $15 (can be waived if parents are in need). Write: Lowe Syndrome Assn., 222 Lincoln St., W. Lafayette, IN 47906. Call (317)743-3634; *E-mail:* kayeuulsa@aol.com

LUNG DISEASE
(Also see specific disorder)

American Lung Association *Nat'l.* Refers callers to regional resources for information on lung health, smoking and environment. Local chapters can refer to support groups for persons with chronic lung disorders (emphysema, chronic bronchitis, pulmonary problems, etc.) if available. These groups use names such as "Easy Breathers," or "Pulmonary Diseases Support Group." Call 800-586-4872.

LUPRON DRUG USE

National Lupron Victims Network *Nat'l.* Education and support for people who have taken Lupron who are now experiencing medical problems. Open to families and persons contemplating taking Lupron. Information, literature, advocacy, and phone support. Write: Nat'l Lupron Victims Network, P.O. Box 193, Collingswood, NJ 08108. Call Dr. Linda Abend (609)858-2131; FAX: (609)858-0550; *E-mail:* nlvn@voicenet.com *Website:* http://www.voicenet.com/~nlvn

LUPUS

Lupus Foundation of America, Inc., The *Nat'l. 95 chapters. Founded 1977.* Provides information and materials about lupus, referrals to services for people with lupus and their families. Conducts education and research programs. Membership and newsletter available through local chapters. Write: Lupus Fdn. of America, 1300 Piccard Dr., #200, Rockville, MD 20850-4303. Call

800-558-0121 or (301)670-9292; FAX (301)670-9486; *Website*: http://www.lupus.org/lupus *E-mail*: lupuslfa@mail.erols.com

LYME DISEASE

Lyme Disease Network *Nat'l network. Founded 1990.* Support, information, and referrals for victims of Lyme Disease and their families. Maintains computer information system. Patients can access information through gopher server, and communicate with each other through E-mail and share information through discussion groups. Write: Lyme Disease Network, 43 Winton Rd., E. Brunswick, NJ 08816. FAX: (732)238-8292; *E-mail:* carol_stolow@lymenet.org *Website*: http://www.lymenet.org

LYMPHANGIOLEIOMYOMATOSIS

LAM Foundation, The *Nat'l network. Founded 1995.* Provides support and hope for women and their families who have LAM (lymphangioleiomyomatosis), a rare lung disorder affecting young women, where smooth muscle tissues grow and cover the airways. Fund-raising activities to fund scientific research. Newsletter, patient directory, phone support. Write: The LAM Fdn., c/o Sue Byrnes, 10105 Beacon Hills Dr., Cincinnati, OH 45241. Call (513)777-6889 (Voice/FAX); *E-mail*: lamfoundtn@aol.com *Website*: http://www.kam.uc.edu

LYMPHEDEMA

National Lymphedema Network Inc. *Nat'l. Founded 1988.* Support groups and information re: primary and secondary lymphedema to patients and professionals. Newsletter, telephone hotline, conferences, pen pal program, referrals to treatment centers and physicians. Assistance in starting new groups. Dues $25. Write: Nat'l Lymphedema Network, 2211 Post St., #404, San Francisco, CA 94115. Call 800-541-3259. *Website*: http://www.hooked.net/~lymphnet *E-mail*: lymphnet@hooked.net

LYMPHOCYTOSIS, LARGE GRANULAR

(Interest in starting) **Large Granular Lymphocytosis** *No known network.* At time of printing, we had heard from one person interested in finding others to help start a support network for persons with large granular lymphocytosis. If interested, please contact the Clearinghouse for more information.

MALIGNANT HYPERTHERMIA

Malignant Hyperthermia Assn. of the U.S. (MHAUS) *Nat'l network. Founded 1981.* Education and support for malignant hyperthermia susceptible families. Information for health care professionals. Conducts limited research.

Newsletter, regional conferences. Write: MHAUS, 32 S. Main St., Box 1069, Sherburne, NY 13460. Call 800-98-MHAUS; FAX: (607)674-7910; *E-mail*: mhaus@norwich.net *Website*: http://www.mhaus.org

MAPLE SYRUP URINE DISEASE
(Also see Neurometabolic Disorders)

Maple Syrup Urine Disease Family Support Group *Nat'l network. Founded 1982.* Opportunity for support and personal contact for those with MSUD and their families. Information on MSUD. Strengthens the liaison between families and professionals. Encourages research and newborn screening for MSUD. Three newsletters, $10/yr. Write: c/o Dawn Marie Hahn, 1854 Agape Ct., East Earl, PA 17519. Call (717)445-5961; *Website*: http://www.msud-support.org/

MARFAN SYNDROME

National Marfan Foundation *Nat'l. 25 chapters and support groups. Founded 1981.* Provides information on Marfan Syndrome and related connective tissue disorders to patients, families and physicians. Provides a means for patients and relatives to share experiences and support one another. Supports and fosters research. Conference, newsletter, publications. Chapter development guidelines. Write: Nat'l Marfan Fdn., 382 Main St., Port Washington, NY 11050. Call 800-8-MARFAN or (516)883-8712; FAX: (516)883-8040; *E-mail*: staff@marfan.org *Website*: http://www.marfan.org

MASTOCYTOSIS

Mastocytosis Society *Nat'l network. Founded 1994.* Mutual support through a newsletter for persons with mastocytosis (a proliferation of mast cells) and their caregivers (family, health and mental health care workers). Pen pals, phone support. Write: Mastocytosis Soc., 4771 Waynes Trace Rd., Hamilton, OH 45011. Call (513)726-4602 or (410)479-1808 or (513)726-4642 (media); FAX: (513)726-4605; *Website*: http://www.gil.com.au/comm/mast/ *E-mail*: lbd001@aol.com or masto@dmu.com

McCUNE-ALBRIGHT SYNDROME

McCune-Albright Syndrome Division *Int'l network. Founded 1990.* Provides support for families of McCune-Albright Syndrome patients. Newsletters, updated medical information, phone support. Dues $20/yr. Write: MAGIC Foundation, 1327 North Harlen Ave., Oak Park, IL 60302. Call 800-3MAGIC3 (800-362-4423); FAX: (708)383-0899; *E-mail:* magic@nettap.com *Website*: http://www.nettap.com//~magic

MENKE'S DISEASE

Corporation for Menke's Disease *Nat'l. Founded 1984.* Parent and professional network that seeks to provide support and referrals for Menke's Disease families. National seminar. Networks physicians. Parent newsletter, sibling pen pal program, telephone support network. Write: Corp. for Menke's Disease, 5720 Buckfield Ct., Fort Wayne, IN 46804. Call (219)436-0137.

METABOLIC DISORDERS
(Also see specific disorder)

Research Trust for Metabolic Diseases in Children *Int'l network. 20 affiliated groups. Founded 1981.* Networks parents of children with any type of metabolic disorder for mutual support. Encourages research into the cures and pre-natal diagnosis of such disorders. Provides grants for treatment and cure. Information and referral to support groups, newsletter, phone support, pen pals. Write: Research Trust for Metabolic Diseases in Children, Golden Gates Lodge, Weston Rd., Crewe, Cheshire CW2 5XN, England. Call 01270-250221 (day); FAX: 01270-250244.

(Model) **Purine Research Society** *1 group in Bethesda, MD. Founded 1986.* Mutual support for patients with purine metabolic disorders and their families. Fundraising for research. Phone support, newsletter, information and referrals. Assistance in starting new support groups. Write: c/o Tahma Metz, 5424 Beech Ave., Bethesda, MD 20814. Call Tahma Metz (301)530-0354; FAX: 564-9597; *E-mail*: purine@erols.com *Website*: http://www2.dgsys.com/~purine/

METATROPIC DYSPLASIA DWARFISM

Metatropic Dysplasia Dwarf Registry *Nat'l network. Founded 1992.* Support and information for persons affected by metatropic dwarfism. Networks families and shares information. Phone support, information and referrals, limited literature. Write: Metatropic Dysplasia Dwarf Registry, 3393 Geneva Dr., Santa Clara, CA 95051. Call (408)244-6354; FAX: (408)296-6317; *E-mail*: figone@netgate.net

MILLER'S SYNDROME
(Also see Craniofacial Disfigurement, Amputation/Limb Deficiency)

Foundation for Nager and Miller Syndromes *Int'l. Founded 1989.* Networking for families that are affected by Nager or Miller Syndromes, or any cranio-facial disfigurement, limb anomalies or any rare condition. Provides referrals, library of information, phone support, newsletter, brochures, scholarships for Camp About Face. Write: FNMS, 1827 Grove St., #2,

Glenview, IL 60025-5104. Call 800-507-FNMS; FAX: (847)724-6449; *E-mail*: fnms@interaccess.com

MITOCHONDRIAL DISORDERS

Mitochondrial Disorders Foundation of America, The *Nat'l. 2 affiliated groups. Founded 1995.* Support and advocacy for patients, parents and caregivers affected by mitochondrial disorders. Information and referrals, fundraising, phone support, literature. Assistance in starting new groups. Write: Mitochondrial Disorders Fdn. of Amer., 5100-1B Clayton Rd., #187, Concord, CA 94521. Call (510)798-8798 (Voice/FAX); *E-mail*: 102125.1233@ compuserve.com *Website*: http://biochemgen.ucsd.edu/leighs/pals.htm

United Mitochondrial Disease Foundation *Int'l network. Founded 1996.* To promote research for cures and treatments for mitochondrial disorders. Provides support to affected families. Educates medical community about the complexity of these diseases. Newsletter, information and referrals, literature, conferences, phone support. Dues $25. Write: United Mitochondrial Disease Fdn., P.O. Box 1151, Monroeville, PA 15146-1151. Call (412)856-1297; FAX: (412)856-7072; *Website*: http://biochemgen.ucsd.edu/vmdf *E-mail*: 74743.2705@ compuserve.com

MOEBIUS SYNDROME

Moebius Syndrome Foundation *Nat'l. Founded 1994.* Communication and support network for persons with moebius syndrome (a paralysis of the 6th and 7th cranial nerves), and their families. Provides information, education, fundraising for research, newsletter, phone support, informal meetings, and national conference. Help in starting groups. Write: Moebius Syndrome Fdn., P.O. Box 993, Larchmont, NY 10538; call Kathryn Campbell (914)834-6008 (day); or write: Moebius Syndrome Fdn., P.O. Box 147, Pilot Grove, MO 65276; call Vicki McCarrell (816)834-3406 (eve); *Website*: http://www.ciaccess.com/moebius *E-Mail*: rcamp57@aol.com or vicki1@ix.netcom.com

MOYAMOYA DISEASE

Moyamoya Support Network *Nat'l network. Founded 1992.* Provides emotional support and information sharing for affected individuals and their families with this cerebrovascular disease. Information and literature. Write: Moyamoya Support Network, 4900 McGowan St., S.E., Cedar Rapids, IA 52403. Call 800-261-6692 or (319)364-6847.

MUCOLIPIDOSIS TYPE 4

ML4 Foundation *Nat'l network. Founded 1983.* Support network for families of children diagnosed with mucolipidosis type 4, a genetic disorder characterized by variable psychomotor retardation that primarily affects Ashkenazi Jews. Supports fund-raising for research. Information and referrals, phone support. Write: ML4 Fdn., 719 E. 17th St., Brooklyn, NY 11230. Call (718)434-5067; FAX: (718)859-7371; *Website*: http://www.ml4.org *E-mail*: ml4www@aol.com

MUCOPOLYSACCHARIDOSES

The MPS Society *Nat'l. 9 regional contacts. Founded 1974.* For families with mucopolysaccharidoses and related disorders. Support groups, public education, fund-raising for research, parent referral service for networking. Quarterly newsletter. Telephone support network. Write: Nat'l MPS Society, 17 Kraemer St., Hicksville, NY 11801. Call Marie Capobianco (516)931-6338; FAX: (516)822-2041; *E-mail*: CohenZEE@aol.com

MULTIPLE ENDOCRINE NEOPLASM TYPE I
WERNER SYNDROME

Canadian Multiple Endocrine Neoplasm Type I Society, Inc. *Nat'l network. Founded 1995.* Mutual support to persons afflicted with familial multiple endocrine neoplasia type 1 (aka Werner Syndrome), and their families. FMEN1 affects the endocrine glands. Literature, information and referrals, phone support and pen pals. Dues $10/yr. Write: Canadian Multiple Endocrine Neoplasm Type I Soc., Box 100, Meota, SK, Canada S0M 1X0. Call (306) 892-2080 (Voice/FAX).

MULTIPLE HEREDITARY EXOSTOSES /
HEREDITARY MULTIPLE OSTEOCHONDROMATA /
MULTIPLE CARTHAGINOUS EXOSTOSES

MHE Family Support Group *Int'l network. Founded 1993.* Support network for persons affected by multiple hereditary exostoses (aka hereditary multiple osteochondromata, or multiple carthaginous exostoses). Condition is characterized by benign bumps on bones which can vary in size, location and number. Provides current information, pen pals, phone support, conferences, information and referrals. Newsletter. Write: MHE Family Support Group, c/o Penny Flake, 1727 Ironwood Dr., Idaho Falls, ID 83402. Call (208)523-6459 (Voice/FAX).

"To understand any living thing, you must creep within and feel the beating of its heart."   *- W. Macneile Dixon*

MULTIPLE MYELOMA

(Model) **Bay Area Multiple Myeloma Support Group** *1 group in Oakland, CA. Founded 1990.* Sharing of information and support for persons with multiple myeloma. Exchange of current treatment and techniques. Provides information and referrals, phone support, hospital visits, assistance in starting local groups. Write: c/o Evelyn Hall, P.O. Box 16040, Oakland, CA 94610. Call (510)839-5554.

MULTIPLE SCLEROSIS
(Also see Disabilities General)

Multiple Sclerosis Association of America *Nat'l. 4 affiliated groups. Founded 1970.* Self-help organization where many staff and board members have M.S. Offers support group meetings, newsletter, information and referrals, phone support, conferences, pen pals and experienced, knowledgeable counseling. Independent living facilities available. Therapeutic equipment loan program. Assistance in starting local groups. Write: MS Assn. of Amer., 706 Haddonfield Rd., Cherry Hill, NJ 08002. Call 800-833-4MSA (day) or 800-LEARN MS; FAX: (609)661-9797; *Website*: http://www.msaa.com

National Multiple Sclerosis Society *Nat'l. 91 self-help groups. Founded 1946.* Funds research for multiple sclerosis, provides information and referrals, support groups for patients and families, Professional education. Newsletter. Write: Nat'l MS Soc., Information Resource Center, 733 Third Ave., New York, NY 10017-3288. Call 800-344-4867 or (212)986-3240; FAX: (212)986-7981; *Website*: http://www.nmss.org *E-mail*: nat@nmss.org

MULTIPLE SYMMETRICAL LIPOMATOSIS

MSL Help *Nat'l network. Founded 1996.* Support and networking for persons affected by multiple symmetrical lipomatosis (aka benign symmetric lipomatosis, Madelung's Disease, or Lanois-Bensaude Syndrome). MSL is a metabolic condition characterized by the growth of fatty masses symmetrically placed around the body. Provides encouragement, education and a sharing of resources for mutual support. Write: MSL Help, P.O. Box 2426, Stamford, CT 06906.

MUSCULAR DYSTROPHY
(Also see specific disorder)

Muscular Dystrophy Association *Nat'l. 152 chapters. Founded 1950.* Fights 40 neuromuscular diseases through worldwide research, nationwide network of clinics, and through professional and public education. Local chapters schedule support groups based upon interest and needs. Newsletter. Write: MDA, 3300

E. Sunrise Dr., Tucson, AZ 85718. Call (520)529-2000 (day); FAX: (520) 529-5300; *Website*: http://www.mdausa.org *E-mail*: 74431.2513@compuserve

S.M.D.I. Int'l (Society for Muscular Dystrophy Information) *Int'l network.* *Founded 1983.* Purpose is to share and encourage the exchange of non-technical, neuromuscular disorder and disability related information. Referrals to support groups, quarterly networking newsletter, pen pals, publication exchange. Dues $25-35. Write: SMDI, Int'l, P.O. Box 479, Bridgewater, NS Canada B4V 2X6. Call (902)685-3961; FAX: (902)685-3962 *E-mail*: smdi@auracom.com

MYALGIC ENCEPHALOMYELITIS

Myalgic Encephalomyelitis Association *Int'l. 100 groups. Founded 1976.* Support and information for all those are affected by myalgic encephalomyelitis. Information to medical professionals, care agencies and general public. Fund-raising for research. Quarterly newsletter, pen pals, information and referrals, conferences, assistance in starting groups. Write: Myalgic Encephalomyelitis Assn., Stanhope House, High St., Stanford-le-Hope, Essex SS17 OHA, United Kingdom. Call 0-1375-642466; FAX: 0-1375 360256.

MYASTHENIA GRAVIS

Myasthenia Gravis Foundation *Nat'l. 35 chapters. Founded 1952.* Promotes research and education into myasthenia gravis, a chronic neuromuscular disease. Provides supportive services for patients and families. Information and referral. Newsletter, support groups, annual and scientific meetings, patient registry. Write: Myasthenia Gravis Fdn., 222 S. Riverside Plaza, #1540, Chicago, IL 60606. Call (312)258-0522 or 800-541-5454; FAX: (312)258-0461; *E-mail*: MGFA@aol.com *Website*: http://www.med.unc.edu/mgfa/

MYELIN DISORDERS

Organization for Myelin Disorders Research and Support *Int'l network.* *Founded 1996.* A communication network among families affected by hypomyelination and myelin deficient disorders, and professionals. Aims to increase awareness, find causes and treatment, and fund research. Information and referrals, phone support, parent link, advocacy, newsletter. Write: Org. for Myelin Dis. Res. and Support, P.O. Box 54759, Cincinnati, OH 45254-0759. Call (513)752-6076 or (513)752-7877; FAX: (513)752-9106; *E-mail*: myelinrs@dot-net.net

"There are deep sorrows and killing cares in life, but the encouragement and love of friends were given to us to make all the difficulties bearable."
- John Oliver Hobbes

MYELOPROLIFERATIVE DISEASE

MPD Research Ctr., Inc. *Int'l. Umbrella organization. Founded 1989.* Patient support network enabling patients to share their experiences and problems. Supports research. Publishes materials pertaining to MPD. Professional involvement. Newsletter, phone support, conferences, information and referrals. Write: Harriet S. Gilbert, MD, MPD Research Ctr., 115 E. 72nd St., New York, NY 10021. Call 800-HELP-MPD or (212)535-8181; FAX: (212)535-7744; *Website:* http://www.acov.org/diseases/hematology.mpd

MYOSITIS

Myositis Association of America *Nat'l network. Founded 1993.* Dedicated to serving those with polymyositis, dermatomyositis, juvenile myositis, and inclusion body myositis. Education and support. Also serves as a clearinghouse between patients and scientists. Newsletter, research reviews, literature and telephone support. Area meetings available as well as annual conference. Dues: $30. Write: c/o Betty Curry, 1420 Huron Court, Harrisonburg, VA 22801. Call 800-821-7356 or (540)433-7686 (day); FAX: (540)432-0206; *E-mail:* maainfo@shentel.net *Website*: http://www.neuroguide.com/maa.html

MYOTUBULAR MYOPATHY

X-Linked Myotubular Myopathy Resource Group *Int'l network. Founded 1993.* Information for parents and doctors regarding myotubular myopathy, a rare disorder causing low muscle tone and diminished respiratory capacity in males. Exchanging of successes with other affected families. Phone support, information and referrals, newsletter, literature. Write: c/o Pam Scoggin, 2413 Quaker Dr., Texas City, TX 77590. Call (409)945-8569; · *Website*: http://www.members.aol.com/kmtm/homepage.htm *E-mail:* gscoggin@aol.com

NAGER SYNDROME

Foundation for Nager and Miller Syndromes *Int'l. Founded 1989.* Networking for families that are affected by Nager or Miller Syndromes, or any cranio-facial disfigurement, limb anomalies or any rare condition. Provides referrals, library of information, phone support, newsletter, brochures, and scholarships for Camp About Face. Write: FNMS, 1827 Grove St., #2, Glenview, IL 60025-5104. Call 800-507-FNMS; FAX: (847)724-6449; *E-mail*: fnms@interaccess.com

NAIL PATELLA SYNDROME

Nail Patella Syndrome Networking/Support Group *Int'l network. Founded 1996.* Support network for persons with nail patella syndrome to exchange information. Tries to provides a link to related research studies. Provides information and referrals, and literature. Communication network and pen pals via internet. Write: NPS Networking/Support Group, 67 Woodlake Dr., Holland, PA 18966; *Website:* http://www.members.aol.com/PACALI/index.html *E-mail:* PACALI@aol.com

NARCOLEPSY

Narcolepsy Network *Nat'l. 100 affiliated groups. Founded 1986.* Support and education for persons with narcolepsy and other sleep disorders, their families and interested others. Helps with coping skills, family and community problems. Provides advocacy and education, supports research. Newsletter, conferences, phone support and group development guidelines. Write: Narcolepsy Network, P.O. Box 42460, Cincinnati, OH 45242. Call (513)891-3522; FAX: (513)891-9936; *E-mail*: narnet@aol.com   *Website:* http://www.websciences.org/narnet

NECROTIZING FASCIITIS

National Necrotizing Fasciitis Foundation *Int'l network. 2 affiliated groups. Founded 1997.* Provides education and support for persons affected by necrotizing fasciitis (aka flesh-eating bacteria). Aim is to educate public and advocate for research. Provides literature, phone support, newsletter, pen pals, conferences, and information and referrals. Write: NNFF, c/o Jacqueline Roemmele, 18 Burnap Rd., Niantic, CT 06357. Call (860)739-3474 (Voice/FAX) or 800-347-7558; *Website*: http://www.nnff.com   *E-mail:* jroemmele@aol.com

NEMALINE MYOPATHY, CONGENITAL

Nemaline Myopathy Newsletter *Nat'l network. Founded 1991.* Newsletter networking families affected by pediatric/adolescent nemaline myopathy. Sharing of information on this rare disorder. Pen pals, literature, phone support, information and referrals. Write: Krystyn Orlicki, 6050 N. Jornada, Las Cruces, NM 88012. Call 800-593-6858 or (281)382-4506.

NEUROFIBROMATOSIS

National Neurofibromatosis Fdn., Inc. *Nat'l. 25 chapters. Founded 1978.* For patients with neurofibromatosis and their families. Promotes and supports research on the causes and cure of NF. Provides information, assistance and education. Dues $25/individual; $35/family. Quarterly newsletter. Professional grants awarded for research. Write: Nat'l Neurofibromatosis Fdn., 95 Pine St., 16th Fl., New York, NY 10005. Call 800-323-7938 or (212)344-6633; FAX: (212)747-0004; *E-mail*: nnff@aol.com *Website*: http://www.nf.org

Neurofibromatosis, Inc.   *Nat'l. 9 groups. Founded 1988.*   Dedicated to individuals and families affected by the neurofibromatoses (NF-1 and NF-2) through educational, support, clinical and research programs. Newsletter, networking, information and referrals, phone support. Assistance in starting groups. Write: Neurofibromatosis, Inc., 8855 Annapolis Rd., Suite 110, Lanham, MD 20706-2924. Call (301)577-8984 or 800-942-6825 (patient inquiries); FAX: (301)577-0016; TTY: (410)461-5213; *Website*: http://www.nfinc.com *E-mail*: nfinc1@aol.com

NEUROMETABOLIC DISORDERS
(Also see specific disorder)

Association for Neuro-Metabolic Disorders *Nat'l network. Founded 1981.* Education and support for families of children with neuro-metabolic disorders, such as PKU, MSUD and others. Parent support between families. Promotes research. Newsletter. Dues $5/yr. Telephone network, correspondence. Write: c/o Mrs. Cheryl Volk, 5223 Brookfield Lane, Sylvania, OH 43560-1809. Call (419)885-1497.

NEUTROPENIA
(Also see Shwachman)

Neutropenia Support Association, Inc. *Int'l. Founded 1989.* Information and support for patients, their families and the medical community on neutropenia. Aims to increase awareness, support research, and disseminate literature. Newsletter. Support group meetings. Write: Neutropenia Support Assoc., Inc., P.O. Box 243, Winnipeg, Manitoba R3M 3S7 Canada. Call (204)489-8454; in Canada 800-663-8876; *E-mail:* stevensl@neutropenia.ca

NEVOID BASAL CELL CARCINOMA

Nevoid Basal Cell Carcinoma Syndrome Support Network *Nat'l network. Founded 1994.* Emotional support for persons with nevoid basal cell carcinoma, a very rare condition. Support groups. Information and referrals, pen pals, conferences, phone support and a bi-monthly newsletter. Write: c/o Susan Charron, 162 Clover Hill St., Marlboro, MA 01752. Call (508)485-4873; *E-mail*: souldansur@aol.com

NEVUS, GIANT CONGENITAL

Nevus Network *Nat'l network. Founded 1983.*   To provide a network of support and information for people with a large birthmark called a giant congenital nevus and/or neurocutaneous melanosis. Write: Nevus Network, P.O. Box 1981, Woodbridge, VA 22193. Call (703)492-0253 or (405)377-3403; *Website*: http://www.geocities.com/hotsprings/3251/

(Model) **Giant Congenital Pigmented Nevis Support Group** *1 group in Waterbury, CT.* Mutual support for anyone affected by giant congenital pigmented nevi. Provides public education. Seeks to network with physicians treating this disease. Information and referrals, phone support, networking. Write: Brian Stockbridge, 60 Lockhart Ave., Waterbury, CT 06705. Call (203)754-4679.

NIEMANN PICK TYPE C

National Niemann-Pick Disease Foundation, Inc. *Int'l network. Founded 1991.* Support network for families affected by Niemann-Pick Disease. Provides education, funds research for treatment/cure. Encourages effective legislation concerning health care treatment of handicapped/chronically ill. Newsletter, information and referrals, literature, advocacy, phone support, group meetings, family conferences. Write: Nat'l Niemann-Pick Disease Fdn., 411 North Diane Court, Chandler, AZ 85226. Call (602)940-8164 (day).

NOONAN SYNDROME

Noonan Syndrome Support Group *Nat'l network. Founded 1996.* Provides information for persons with Noonan Syndrome, their families, and interested others. Networks individuals together for peer support. Information and referrals, speakers bureau, telephone helpline. Write: Noonan Syndrome Support Group, P.O. Box 145, Upperco, MD 21155. Call (410)239-6926; *Website*: http://www.paston.co.uk/users/maygurney/tnssg.html   *E-mail*: wanda@bellatlantic.net

OLLIER'S / MAFFUCCI'S DISEASE

Ollier's/Maffucci's Disease Self-Help Group *Nat'l network. Founded 1985.* Mutual support for parents of children with Ollier's or Maffucci's disease (rare conditions in which benign tumors form in the bones). Open to adults with these rare disorders. Provides a forum to discuss problems and collect current medical information. Quarterly newsletter, literature. Call (803)775-1757. Write: Bonnie Hatch, 1824 Millwood Rd., Sumpter, SC 29150. *E-mail*: olliers@aol.com *Website*: http://uhweb.edu/olliers/olliers.htm

OPITZ SYNDROME

Opitz Family Network *Int'l. Founded 1994.* Support, encouragement, education, and sharing of successes and ideas, for families affected by Opitz-G, Opitz-C and Opitz-FG Syndromes. Maintains database of members, literature, information, phone support, and newsletter. Referrals to other families. Write: Opitz Family Network, P.O. Box 516, Grand Lake, CO 80447. Call

(970)627-8935 (eve/weekends); *E-mail:* opitznet@rkymtnhi.com *Website*: http://rkymtnhi.com/opitz

OSTEOGENESIS IMPERFECTA

Osteogenesis Imperfecta Foundation *Nat'l. 4 chapters. Founded 1970.* Support for families dealing with O.I. Provides public education. Supports research. Literature, quarterly newsletter. Telephone support network. Write: Osteogenesis Imperfecta Fdn., 804 W. Diamond Ave., #210, Gaithersburg, MD 20878. Call 800-981-2663 or (301)947-0083; FAX: (301)947-0456.

OSTEOPOROSIS

National Osteoporosis Foundation *Nat'l. 12 affiliated groups. Founded 1986.* Provides public and professional education. Direct support for biomedical research into causes, prevention and treatment of osteoporosis. Advocates for increased federal research. Newsletter, information and referrals, conferences. Support group development guidelines and referral. Write: NOF, 515 North State St., Room 7450, Chicago, Il 60610. Call Liz Stone or Janet Hieschetter (312)464-4550; *Website*: http://www.osteo.org

OSTOMY

United Ostomy Association *Nat'l. 530 chapters. Founded 1962.* Dedicated to helping every person with an ostomy and related surgeries return to normal living. Also has support groups for parents of children with ostomies. Provides education, support to local chapters, and national identity. Chapter development help, visitation program, magazine. Write: United Ostomy Assn., 19772 MacArthur Blvd., #200, Irvine, CA 92612-2405. Call 800-826-0826 or (714)660-8624; FAX: (714)660-9262; *Website*: http://www.uoa.org *E-mail*: uoa@deltanet.com

OVERWEIGHT
(Also see Overeating)

NAAFA (National Association to Advance Fat Acceptance) *Nat'l. 56 chapters. Founded 1969.* Fights size discrimination and provides fat people with the tools for self-empowerment. Public education regarding obesity. Provides a forum for peer support and activism. Dues $40. Newsletter, educational materials, pen pals, and annual convention. Special Interest Groups include: men, women, diabetes, gays, sleep apnea, military, singles, mental health professionals, youth, and families. Write: NAAFA, P.O. Box 188620, Sacramento, CA 95818. Call 800-442-1214 (leave message); FAX: (916)558-6881; *Website*: naafa.org *E-mail*: 2azt04c@prodigy.com

T.O.P.S. (Take Off Pounds Sensibly) *Int'l. 11,500 chapters. Founded 1948.* Helps overweight persons attain and maintain their goal weights. Promotes a sensible approach to weight control. Chapters meet weekly for discussion and programs to provide support and motivation. Newsletter. Chapter development guidelines. Dues $20/USA; $25/Canada. Write: TOPS, P.O. Box 07630, 4575 S. 5th St., Milwaukee, WI 53207. Call 800-932-8677 (recording); *Website*: http://www.tops.org

(Model) **Gastroplasty Support Group** *1 group in New Jersey. Founded 1985.* Group of volunteer patients and professionals who educate and provide support for persons contemplating, or who have had silicone gastric banding. Deals with problems associated with weight loss. Monthly update letter, phone network, videotapes. Write: Joyce Dixon, Irvington General Hospital, 832 Chancellor Ave., Irvington, NJ 07111. Call Joyce Dixon (973)399-6080 or Dr. Lubomyr Kuzmak (973)374-1717 (Mon/Thurs/Fri).

OXALOSIS AND HYPEROXALURIA

Oxalosis and Hyperoxaluria Foundation *Nat'l network. Founded 1989.* Support and current information for patients, families, and medical professionals. Educates the public, supports research. Newsletter, information and referrals, phone support, pen pals, conferences. Dues $25/yr. Write: Oxalosis and Hyperoxaluria Fdn., 12 Pleasant St., Maynard, MA 01751. Call 888-721-2432 Pin# 5392 or (508)461-0614 (Voice/FAX); *E-mail*: exec-dir@ ohforg *Website*: http://www.ohf.org

PAGET'S DISEASE

(Model) **National Association for the Relief of Paget's Disease** *5 regional groups in UK. Founded 1973.* Offers support to persons with Paget's disease. Aims to raise awareness of this disorder through newsletter and publications. Sponsors research. Information and referrals, phone support, literature. Write: Nat'l Assn. for the Relief of Paget's Disease, 1, Church Rd., Eccles, Manchester, M30 0DL, UK. Call 0161-707-9225; FAX: 44 161-789-6755; *Website*: http://www.demon.co.uk/narpd *E-mail*: 106064.2032@ compuserve.com

PAIN, CHRONIC

American Chronic Pain Association, Inc. *Nat'l. 800 affiliated chapters. Founded 1980.* Help for people suffering from chronic pain. Support, understanding and sharing skills to maintain wellness. Workbooks for self-help recovery. Quarterly newsletter. Group development guidelines. Phone network. Outreach program to clinics. Write: American Chronic Pain Assn., P.O. Box

850, Rocklin, CA 95677. Call (916)632-0922; FAX: (916)632-3208; *E-mail*: ACPA@pacbell.net

National Chronic Pain Outreach Assoc., Inc. *Nat'l network. Founded 1980.* Clearinghouse for information about chronic pain and pain management. Aims to increase public awareness and decrease the stigma of chronic pain. Provides kit to develop local support groups, professional education, quarterly magazine and other materials. Dues $25/yr. Write: Nat'l Chronic Pain Outreach Assoc., P.O. Box 274, Millboro, VA 24460. Call (540)997-5004; FAX: (540)997-1305; *E-mail*: ncpoa1@aol.com *Website*: http://www.chronicpain.org

PAPILLOMATOSIS

American Laryngeal Papilloma Foundation *Nat'l network. Founded 1991.* Assists those afflicted with laryngeal papillomatosis. Sharing of experiences and information through networking. Seeks to provide financial aid to needy families and affected persons for vitamin supplement program. National registry. Newsletter, phone support, information and referral, conferences. Write: ALPF, P.O.Box 6108, Spring Hill, FL 34611-6018; phone: 800-649-4841 (patients only; code #17 after dialing) or (352)686-8583 (voice/FAX); or write: ALPF, 34 Washington Ave., Lake Hiawatha, NJ 07034; phone (973)299-7978; *Website*: http://www.alpf.org

Recurrent Respiratory Papillomatosis Foundation *Nat'l network. Founded 1992.* Networking for families affected by RRP (recurrent respiratory papillomatosis) and interested professionals. Newsletter, phone support. Write: RRPF, P.O. Box 6643, Lawrenceville, NJ 08648-0643. Call Bill Stern (609)530-1443; *Website*: http://members@aol.com/rrpf/rrpf.html *E-mail:* wfs@gfdl.gov

PARKINSON'S DISEASE

American Parkinson Disease Association, Inc. *Nat'l. 65 chapters. Founded 1961.* Network of 500 support groups for patients and families. Chapter development guidelines. Quarterly newsletter. Promotes research. 43 information and referral centers nationwide. Write: Amer. Parkinson Disease Assn., 1250 Hyland Blvd., Suite B4, Staten Island, NY 10305. Call (718)981-8001 or 800-223-2732; FAX: (718)981-4399; *Website*: http://www.apdaparkinson.com

Parkinson's Disease Foundation, Inc. *Int'l. Founded 1957.* Aims to provide Parkinson patients a better quality of life through funding of research, in the hopes of finding the cause and, ultimately, the cure. Provides referrals to support groups, newsletter, information and phone support. Assistance in developing new groups. Write: Parkinson's Disease Fdn., 710 W. 168th St.,

New York, NY 10032. Call (212)923-4700 or 800-457-6676 (day); FAX: (212)923-4778; *E-mail*: pdfcpmc@aol.com

Parkinson's Support Groups of America *Nat'l. 40 groups. Founded 1980.* Educates patients and families on necessity for full participation in normal life with Parkinson's. Encourages formation of support groups. Supports research and exchange of information. Speakers bureau. Chapter development guidelines. Write: c/o Ida Raitano, 11376 Cherry Hill Rd., #204, Beltsville, MD 20705. Call (301)937-1545.

PARRY-ROMBERG'S SYNDROME / PROGRESSIVE FACIAL HEMIATROPHY

(Online) **The Romberg's Connection** *Int'l network. Founded 1997.* Mutual support for persons affected by Parry-Romberg's Syndrome (aka progressive facial hemiatrophy or Romberg's Syndrome), a rare, genetic disorder, their families and friends. Aim is to locate affected persons and offer strength, hope, courage and friendship. Pen pals program online and via mail. Some face-to-face meetings. Phone support network in U.S. Future newsletter planned. *E-mail*: Rombergs@hotmail.com *Website*: http://www.geocities.com/HotSprings/1018/

PELVIC INFLAMMATORY DISEASE

(Model) **Canadian P.I.D. (Pelvic Inflammatory Disease) Society** *1 group in Vancouver. Founded 1986.* Information and referrals, counseling and resources for women with pelvic inflammatory disease, professionals and general public. Provides public education, coordination and distribution of information including booklets, brochures and videos. Telephone support network; research. Write; Canadian PID, P.O. Box 33804, Station D, Vancouver, B.C., Canada V6J 4L6. Call (604)684-5704 (Tue. and Fri., 1-5pm).

PERIPHERAL NERVE DISEASE
(Also see specific disorder)

Neuropathy Association *Int'l. 45 affiliated groups.* Founded 1995. Provides support, education and advocacy for persons with peripheral neuropathy. Promotes research into the cause and cure. Newsletter, literature, information and referrals, and phone support. Write: Neuropathy Assn., 60 E. 42nd St., Room 942, New York, NY 10165. Call 800-247-6968 or (212)962-0662; FAX: (212)692-0668; *Website*: http://www.neuropathy.org

Peripheral Neuropathy Group *Nat'l network. Founded 1994.* Self-help group for people with peripheral neuropathy (damaged nerves in the peripheral nervous system). There can be weakness and pain in the limbs, but not limited to these areas or symptoms. Some causes: diabetes, head/spine trauma, vitamin deficiency, etc. Newsletter ($12). Phone support, pen pals, information and referrals. For information, send self-addressed stamped envelope. Write: Peripheral Neuropathy Group Nat'l Network, 20076 State St., Corona, CA 91719. Call Lu (909)272-5877 or Linda (909)687-3026; FAX: (909)735-7870; *E-mail*: AmLuHu@aol.com or Lindalouh@juno.com

PETER'S ANOMALY

Peter's Partners *Int'l network. Founded 1997.* Support network for persons affected by Peter's Anomaly, their families, friends and interested professionals. Opportunity to exchange personal and medical information. Provides newsletter, pen pals, phone support and information and referrals. Write: Peter's Partners, 1201 Currey Rd., Nashville, TN 37217. Call (615)366-1890; FAX: (615)401-5086; *E-mail:* mccallk@ten-nash.ten.k12.tn.us

PHENYLKETONURIA
(Also see Neurometabolic Disorders)

Children's PKU Network *Nat'l network. Founded 1991.* Provides support and services to families with Phenylketonuria (PKU) and other metabolic disorders. Phone support, crisis intervention, information and referrals. Write: Children's PKU Network, 1520 State St., #240, San Diego, CA 92101. Call (619) 233-3202; FAX: (619)233-0838; *E-mail*: pkunetwork@aol.com

PINK DISEASE / MERCURY TOXICITY

Pink Disease Support Group *Int'l network.* Grassroots support organization for persons with, or parents of children with, Pink Disease (mercury toxicity in infants). Information and referrals, newsletter, local group meetings. Dues $10/year. Write: Pink Disease Support Group, P.O.Box 134, Gilgandra NSW 2827 Australia. Call Heather Thiele 0268 472 255 (after 7pm GMT) or from outside Australia 61 268 472 255; *E-mail:* nmanswer@powerup.com.au *Website:* http://www.powerup.com/au/ ~nmanswer

PITUITARY DISORDERS
(Also see specific disorder)

Cushing's Support and Research Foundation, Inc. *Int'l. 5 regional sites. Founded 1995.* Provides support for persons with Cushing's disease through information and referrals, advocacy, scientific research and education. Publishes newsletter. Regional get-togethers, conferences, pen pals and phone support. Assistance in starting local groups. Write: Cushing's Support and Research Fdn., 65 East India Row, 22B, Boston, MA 02110. Call (617)723-3674 (voice/FAX); *Website*: http://world.std.com/ ~csrf/

Pituitary Tumor Network Association *Int'l network. Founded 1992.* Mutual support for persons with all types of pituitary tumors (including acromegaly). Promotes early diagnosis, medical and public awareness, and continued research to find a cure. Newsletter, information and referrals, phone support, resource guide, support group meetings, conferences. Assistance in starting new groups. Write: PTNA, 16350 Ventura Blvd., #231, Encino, CA 91436. Call (805)499-9973; FAX: (805)499-1523; *Website*: http://www.pituitary.com

POLIO

International Polio Network *Nat'l network. Founded 1958.* Information on late effects of polio for survivors and physicians. Int'l conferences and proceedings. Quarterly newsletter, annual directory ($4). Guidelines and workshops for support groups. Membership $16. Handbook on late effects ($6.75). Write: Int'l Polio Network, 4207 Lindell Blvd., #110, St. Louis, MO 63108. Call (314)534-0475; FAX: (314)534-5070; *E-mail:* gini_intl@msn.com

PORPHYRIA

American Porphyria Foundation *Nat'l. 40 groups. Founded 1982.* Supports research, provides education and information to the public, patients and physicians, networks porphyria patients and support groups. Quarterly newsletter, pen pal program, telephone network. Annual donation $30. Write: Amer. Porphyria Fdn., P.O. Box 22712, Houston, TX 77227. Call (713)266-9617; *Website*: http://www.enterprise.net/apf/

POTTER SYNDROME

National Potter Syndrome Support Group *Nat'l network. Founded 1995.* Support group and information network for families that have babies affected by Potter Syndrome. Newsletter, information and referrals, phone support, parent match program. Write: c/o Evy Wright, 225 Louisiana Rd., Dyess AFB, TX 79607-1125. Call (915)692-0831; *E-mail:* oolwright@msn.com

PRADER-WILLI SYNDROME

Prader-Willi Syndrome Association *Nat'l. 38 chapters. Founded 1975.* Support and education for parents of, and professionals in contact with children with Prader-Willi Syndrome. Bi-monthly newsletter. Membership dues $30. Several publications. Chapter development kits available. Write: Prader-Willi Syndrome Assn., 2510 S. Brentwood Blvd., #220, St. Louis, MO 63144. Call 800-926-4797 or (314)962-7644; FAX: (314)962-7869; *Website:* http://www. athenet.net/~pwsa_index.html *E-mail:* pwsause@aol.com.

PRECOCIOUS PUBERTY

Precocious Puberty Support Network *Nat'l network. Founded 1989.* Network and exchange of information for children who are experiencing Precocious Puberty, and their families. Information and referrals, phone support, pen pals, conferences, literature. Newsletter ($20/year). Write: c/o MAGIC Foundation, 1327 N. Harlen, Oak Park, IL 60303. Call 800-3-MAGIC-3; *Website*: http://www.nettap.com/ ~ magic *E-mail:* magic@nettap.com

PREMATURE OVARIAN FAILURE

Premature Ovarian Failure Support Group *Nat'l network. 2 affiliated groups. Founded 1995.* Mutual support for women who have prematurely entered menopause. Information and referrals, phone support, literature. Assistance in starting groups. Write: c/o Catherine Corp., 110 S. Ingram St., Alexandria, VA 22304. Call (703)913-4787; *E-mail:* pof2@aol.com *Website:* http://mwmbers.aol.com/pof2/index.html

PRE-MENSTRUAL SYNDROME

(Note) **Pre-Menstrual Syndrome (PMS)** is a disorder for which we have received a significant number of inquiries. Regrettably, we are unaware of any support group or network that has yet been formed. If you learn of any existing group that you would recommend, or are interested in starting such a group, please call the Clearinghouse.

PROGRESSIVE OSSEOUS HETEROPLASIA

Progressive Osseous Heteroplasia Assn. *Nat'l network. Founded 1995.* Support network for patients and families affected by progressive osseous heteroplasia. Fundraising for research. Write: Progressive Osseous Heteroplasia Assn., 33 Stonehearth Square, Indian Head Park, IL 60525; phone: (708)246-9410. For complete detail of services available contact: Sandy Roth Wheeler, 275 Creek Rd., Frenchtown, NJ 08825; phone: (908)996-6046 or (908)996-4242.

PROGRESSIVE SUPRANUCLEAR PALSY

Society for Progressive Supranuclear Palsy, Inc. *Int'l network. Founded 1990.* Provides advocacy for, and support of, patients with progressive supranuclear palsy, their families and caregivers. Offers newsletter, information and referrals, phone support, conferences, pen pals, assistance in starting support groups. Dues $25. Write: SPSP, Inc., c/o Johns Hopkins Outpatient Ctr., #5065, 601 N. Caroline St., Baltimore, MD 21287. Call (410)955-2954 (M-Th,

HEALTHChapter 7

8am-4pm; Fri., 8am-10:30am) or 800-457-4777; FAX: (410)614-9260; *E-mail:* spsp@erols.com

PROSTATE PROBLEMS
(Also see Cancer)

Us Too, International *Int'l. 400+ affiliated groups. Founded 1990.* Mutual support, information and education for persons with prostate problems (including cancer), their families and friends. Newsletter, information and referrals, phone support. Assistance in starting groups. Write: Us Too Int'l, 930 N. York Rd., #50, Hinsdale, IL 60521-2993. Call 800-80-US-TOO (800-808-7866) or (630)323-1002; FAX: (630)323-1003; *Website*: http://www.ustoo.com *E-mail*: ustoo@ustoo.com

PROTEUS SYNDROME

Proteus Syndrome Foundation *Nat'l network. Founded 1996.* Provides education and support for families or children with proteus syndrome. Supports research into cause and cure of this disorder. Newsletter, pen pals, literature, and database of families. Fundraising. Write: Proteus Syndrome Fdn., 609 S.E. Mt. Vernon Dr., Blue Springs, MO 64014. Call Kim Hoag (816)229-9132 (day) or Barbara King (901)756-9375 (day).

PROZAC
(Also see Depression, specific disorder)

Prozac Survivors Support Group *Nat'l. 34 chapters. Founded 1990.* Mutual support and sharing of information for people who have been adversely affected by the antidepressant medication Prozac. Newsletter, group development guidelines. Write: c/o Bonnie Leitsch, 2212 Woodbourne Ave., Louisville, KY 40205. Call (502)459-2086.

PSEUDO-OBSTRUCTION / HIRSCHSPRUNG'S DISEASE
(Also see Gastrointestinal Motility Disorder)

American Pseudo-Obstruction and Hirschsprung's Disease Society *Int'l network. Founded 1988.* Answers the needs of families, patients and professionals dealing with gastrointestinal motility disorders in infants and children (including intestinal pseudo-obstruction, Hirschsprung's disease, and gastroesophageal reflux.) Promotes research. Publications, newsletter, video, annual educational symposiums. Adult patients welcomed. Dues vary. Write: APHS, 158 Pleasant St., North Andover, MA 01845. Call (508)685-4477; FAX: (508)685-4488; *Website*: http://www.tiac.net/users/aphs *E-mail*: aphs@mail/tiac.net/users.aphs

American Society of Adults with Pseudo-Obstruction, Inc. *Int'l network. Founded 1991.* Support and advocacy for patients of all ages affected with chronic intestinal pseudo-obstruction, their families and physicians. Information on other digestive motility disorders. ASAP Forum Journal, newsletter, group meetings, literature, information and referrals, phone support, conferences and correspondence between members. Dues $35/regular; $45/professional. Write: ASAP Int'l Corp. Hdqrts., 19 Carroll Rd., Woburn, MA 01801-6161. Call (617)935-9776; FAX: (617)933-4151; *E-mail:* asapgi@sprynet.com

PSEUDOTUMOR CEREBRI

Pseudotumor Cerebri Society *Nat'l network. 3 groups. Founded 1992.* Brings together individuals living with PTC to share common experiences. Education about the disease, treatment, research advances, and ways to a better life. Newsletter, monthly meeting, pen pals, information and referrals, literature, advocacy, conferences. Assistance in starting groups. Write: Pseudotumor Cerebri Soc., 1319 Butternut St., #3, Syracuse, NY 13208. Call (315)464-3937; *E-mail:* ingramp@vax.cs.hscsyr.edu

PSEUDOXANTHOMA ELASTICUM

National Association for Pseudoxanthoma Elasticum (NAPE) *Nat'l network. Founded 1988.* Support, education and advocacy for persons with PXE, and their families, interested others, and professionals. Newsletter, information and referrals, phone support. Annual donation $25. Write: Joyce Kohn, 1420 Ogden St., Denver, CO 80218. Call (303)832-5055; *E-mail:* derckd@ttuhsc.edu or pxenape@estreet.com *Website:* http://www.ttuhsc.edu/pages/nape/

PXE International, Inc. *Int'l. 25 affiliated groups. Founded 1995.* Support for persons affected by pseudoxanthoma elasticum (PXE), a calcification of connective tissue, their families and friends. Offers support groups, phone and mail contacts, literature, and quarterly newsletter. Maintains database of physicians, blood tissue registry, and blood and tissue bank. Supports, funds and directs research. Write: PXE Int'l, Inc., 23 Mountain St., Sharon, MA 02067. Call (617)784-3817 (voice/FAX); *E-mail:* pxe@tiac.net *Website:* http://www.med.harvard.edu/programs/PXE

PSORIASIS

National Psoriasis Foundation *Nat'l. Founded 1968.* Support and information for people who have psoriasis, their family and friends. Education to increase public awareness of the disorder. Fundraising for research. Bi-monthly newsletter. Pen pal program. Local psoriasis communication networks. Referrals to physicians. Group development guidelines. Write: Nat'l Psoriasis Fdn., 6600 SW 92nd Ave., #200, Portland, OR 97223. Call (503)244-7404 or

800-723-9166 (packet of information); FAX: (503)245-0626; *E-mail:* 76135.2746@compuserve.com *Website*: http://www.psoriasis.org

PULMONARY HYPERTENSION

Pulmonary Hypertension Association *Nat'l network. Founded 1990.* Support and information for patients with pulmonary hypertension (a cardio-vascular disease), their families and physicians. Encourages research, promotes awareness, provides resource references. Networking, phone help, pen pals, assistance in starting groups. Newsletter ($15). Write: Pulmonary Hypertension Assn., P.O. Box 24733, Speedway, IN 46224-0733. Call 800-748-7274; FAX: (215)542-5692; *E-mail:* maszep@aol.com *Website*: http://members.aol.com/maszep/index.html

RARE / UNDIAGNOSED DISORDERS
(Also see specific disorder)

NORD (National Organization for Rare Disorders) *Nat'l network.* Information and networking for persons with any type of rare disorder. Literature, information and referrals. Advocacy for orphan diseases. Networks persons or families with the same disorder for support. Write: NORD, P.O. Box 8923, New Fairfield, CT 06812-8923. Call 800-999-NORD (6673) or (203)746-6518; FAX: (203)746-6481; *E-mail:* nord@ix.net.com.com *Website*: http://www.nord-rdb.com/~orphan

(Model) **Hearts and Hands** *1 group in NC. Founded 1993.* Emotional, spiritual and educational support for persons with either rare or undiagnosed illnesses, and their families. Also has a registry for Loin Pain Hematuria Syndrome. Write: c/o Winoka Plummer, 4115 Thomasville Rd., Winston-Salem, NC 27107. Call (910)788-1433.

(Model) **One in a Million Kids Support Group** *1 group in California. Founded 1993.* Provides a local support network for parents and caregivers of children with either rare or undiagnosed disorders. Assistance in helping others to start similar groups. Meets bi-monthly. Write: One in a Million Kids Support Group, P.O. Box 156, Seal Beach, CA 90740. Call (310)588-2562; *E-mail*: ezrasam@aol.com

RAYNAUD'S DISEASE

(Model) **Raynaud's and Cold Sufferers Network** *1 group in New York. Founded 1992.* Mutual support to help sufferers cope with day-to-day activities to maintain or improve their quality of life. Aims to increase awareness of the disease among public and medical communities. Raises funds and supports research efforts. Newsletter, information and referrals, support group meetings,

literature, assistance in starting groups. Dues $5 (optional). Write: **Raynaud's and Cold Sufferers Network**, 94 Mercer Ave., Hartsdale, NY 10530. Call Lynn Wunderman (914)682-8341; *E-mail:* Lwunderman@aol.com

(Model) **Raynaud's Foundation** *20 groups in Chicago area. Founded 1992.* Provides support to persons with Raynaud's through information and referrals, literature, support group meetings and literature. Write: Raynaud's Fdn., P.O. Box 632, Park Ridge, IL 60068-9998. Call (732)622-9221; FAX: (732)622-9220 (if you leave a message, they will call back collect). *E-mail*: raynauds@aol.com *Website*: members.aol.com/raynauds

REFLEX ANOXIC SEIZURE DISORDER/ STEPHENSON'S SEIZURE/ WHITE BREATH HOLDING/PALLID ANOXIC SYNCOPE

Reflex Anoxic Seizure Information and Support Group *Int'l network. Founded 1993.* Network of parents and sufferers of Reflex Anoxic Seizure (characterized by temporary heart stoppage and a seizure-like response to any unexpected stimuli); also known as Stephenson's Seizure, White Breath Holding or Pallid Infantile Syncope. Information, education, video. Supports research. Dues $10. Write: T.C.A. Lobban, P.O. Box 175, Stratford-Upon-Avon, Warwickshire, CV37 84D, UK. Call 01789-450564 (United Kingdom); FAX: 01789-450564; *E-mail:* 106700.525@compuserve.com

REFLEX SYMPATHETIC DYSTROPHY

Reflex Sympathetic Dystrophy Syndrome Association *Nat'l. 100 independent groups. Founded 1984.* Aims to meet the practical and emotional needs of RSDS patients and their families. RSDS is a disabling disease involving nerve, skin, muscle, blood vessels and bones. The only common symptom in all patients is pain. Promotes research, educates public and professionals. Quarterly newsletter. Group development guidelines. Write: RSDS Assoc., 116 Haddon Ave., Haddonfield, NJ 08033-2306. Call (609)795-8845 (1:30-5pm); FAX: (609)795-8845; *Website*: http:cyboard.com/rsds

RESTLESS LEG SYNDROME

Restless Leg Syndrome Fdn., Inc. "The Night Walkers" *Nat'l network. Founded 1993.* Non-profit agency that provides information about restless leg syndrome, helps develop support groups, and supports research into cause and treatment of RLS. Quarterly newsletter which covers current research, treatment, and highlights human interest stories ($25). List of local support groups, and information bulletin available. Write: RLS Fdn., Dept. ASHC, P.O. Box 7050, Rochester, MN 55903-7050. Call (507)287-6465; FAX: (507)287-6312; *Website*: http://www.rls.org *E-mail:* rlsf@millcomm.com

RETT SYNDROME

International Rett Syndrome Association (IRSA) *Int'l. 18 affiliated groups. Founded 1985.* For parents, interested professionals and others concerned with Rett syndrome. Dues $35/Int'l, $30/family, $25/single. Provides information and referral, peer support among parents, and encourages research. Quarterly newsletter. Write: IRSA, 9121 Piscataway Rd., #2B, Clinton, MD 20735-2561. Call 800-818-RETT or (301)856-3334; FAX: (301)856-3336; *Website*: http://www2.paltech.com/irsa/irsa.htm; *E-mail*: Irsa@paltech.com

REYE'S SYNDROME

National Reye's Syndrome Foundation *Nat'l. Founded 1974.* Devoted to conquering Reye's Syndrome, primarily a children's disease affecting the liver and brain, but can affect all ages. Provides support, information and referrals. Encourages research. Local chapters usually formed by parents. $25 dues includes newsletter. Write: Nat'l Reye's Syndrome Fdn., P.O. Box 829, Bryan, OH 43506. Call 800-233-7393; FAX: (419)636-3366; *E-mail*: reyessyn@mail.bright.net *Website*: http://www.bright.net/~reyessyn

ROBINOW SYNDROME / FETAL FACE SYNDROME

Robinow Syndrome Foundation *Nat'l network. Founded 1991.* Aim is to locate, educate and support persons affected by Robinow Syndrome, (also known as Fetal Face Syndrome) a very rare syndrome. Write: Robinow Syndrome Fdn., 15955 Uplander St., NW, Andover, MN 55304-2501. Call Karla Kruger (612) 434-1152.

RUBINSTEIN-TAYBI SYNDROME

Rubinstein-Taybi Parent Group *Nat'l network. 312 member families. Founded 1984.* Mutual support, information and sharing for parents of children with Rubinstein-Taybi Syndrome. Newsletter, conferences, phone support, parent contact list. Write: Garry and Lorrie Baxter, P.O. Box 146, Smith Center, KS 66967. Call (785)697-2984; FAX: (785)697-2985.

RUSSELL-SILVER SYNDROME

Russell-Silver Syndrome Support Network *Nat'l network. Founded 1989.* Network and exchange of information for parents of children with Russell-Silver Syndrome. Information and referrals, phone support, pen pals, conferences, literature. Newsletter ($20/year). Write: c/o MAGIC Foundation, 1327 N. Harlen, Oak Park, IL 60303. Call 800-3-MAGIC-3; *E-mail:* magic@nettap.com *Website*: http://www.nettap.com/~magic

SARCOIDOSIS

National Sarcoidosis Resource Center *Int'l network. 2 affiliated groups. Founded 1992.* Mutual support for sarcoid patients and their families. Provides telephone support, networking, workshops and lectures, literature and education. Maintains national database, encourages research, provides support and physician referrals, resource guide. Dues $25/yr. Write: Nat'l Sarcoidosis Resource Ctr., P.O. Box 1593, Piscataway, NJ 08855-1593. Call (908)699-0733 (day/eve); FAX: (908)699-0882; *Website:* http://www.microfone.net/nsrc *E-mail:* nsrc@microfone.net

Sarcoidosis Foundation *Nat'l. 8 support groups. Founded 1982.* Support, information and referrals for families affected by sarcoidosis. Increases public awareness. Telephone network and group development guidelines. Write: c/o St. Michael's Medical Center, 268 Martin Luther King Blvd., Mail Drop 73B, Newark, NJ 07102. Call (973)624-4703.

SCLERODERMA

Scleroderma Federation, Inc. *Int'l. 12 groups. Founded 1982.* Promotes the welfare of persons with scleroderma and their families. Provides education, support groups, peer counseling, referrals, fundraising for research, newsletter, educational materials and group development guidelines. Write: Scleroderma Federation, Inc., Peabody Office Bldg., One Newbury St., Peabody, MA 01960. Call (508)535-6600 or 800-422-1113; FAX: (508)535-6696; *Website:* www.scleroderma.org *E-mail:* sclerofed@aol.com

United Scleroderma Foundation, Inc. *Int'l. 80 affiliated groups. Founded 1970.* Mutual support to help patients with scleroderma, and their families, cope with their illness. Funds research to find a cure. Distributes printed literature and medical reference lists, and provides assistance in starting groups and chapters. Conferences, newsletter, information and referrals. Dues $25. Write: United Scleroderma Fdn., P.O. Box 399, Watsonville, CA 95077-3399. Call 800-722-HOPE or (408)728-2202; FAX: (408)728-3328; *Website:* http://www.scleroderma.com *E-mail:* outreach@scleroderma.com

SCOLIOSIS

Scoliosis Association, Inc. *Nat'l. 28 chapters. Founded 1976.* Information and support network. Organization of scoliosis patients and parents of children with scoliosis. Establishes local patient and parent self-help groups. Encourages school screening programs. Supports research. Newsletter. Membership contribution $15. Guidelines for starting chapters. Write: c/o Stanley Sacks, Pres., P.O. Box 811705, Boca Raton, FL 33481-1705. Call 800-800-0669; FAX: (561)994-2455.

SELECTIVE MUTISM

Selective Mutism Foundation, Inc. *Nat'l network. Founded 1992.* Mutual support for parents of children with selective mutism, a psychiatric anxiety disorder in which children are unable to speak in social situations. Also open to adults who have, or outgrew, the disorder. Information, phone support, quarterly newsletter. Send self-addressed stamped envelope with 2 stamps to: Sue Newman, P.O. 450632, Sunrise, FL 33345-0632; call (954)748-7714 or Carolyn Miller, P.O. Box 13133, Sissonville, WV 25360; call (304)984-3971; *E-mail:* tbroadb594@aol.com *Website*: http://www.home.aol.com/tbroad.594

SHWACHMAN SYNDROME / JOHANSEN-BLIZZARD SYNDROME CARTILAGE-HAIR
(Also see Neutropenia)

Shwachman Syndrome Support *Int'l network. Founded 1994.* Mutual support and information for families affected by Shwachman Syndrome, which is characterized by pancreatic insufficiency, retarded bone growth and hematological abnormalities. Includes Johansen-Blizzard Syndrome, Cartilage-Hair and any unusual neutropenia. Advocates for research. Write: Shwachman Syn. Support Int'l, 4118 Quincy St., St. Louis, MO 63116. Call (316)352-1821; *Website*: http://www.xmission.com/ ~ 4sskids *E-mail:* 4sskids@mup.net

SHY-DRAGER SYNDROME

SDS Advocate *Int'l network. Founded 1993.* Provides information on Shy-Drager Syndrome and related disorders, to share coping strategies and caregiving ideas. Newsletter, information and referrals. Write: SDS Advocate, 9835 W. Lisbon Ave., Milwaukee, WI 53222. Call (414)628-1537 or (414)462-1365 or (502)647-3939.

SICKLE CELL DISEASE

Sickle Cell Disease Association of America, Inc. *Nat'l. 62 chapters. Founded 1971.* Education for the public and professionals about sickle cell disease. Support and information for persons affected by the disease. Support research. Quarterly newsletter, chapter development guidelines, phone network, videos. Write: Sickle Cell Disease Assn. of America, 200 Corporate Pointe, #495, Culver City, CA 90230-7633. Call (310)216-6363 or 800-421-8453; FAX: (310)215-3722.

"Nothing befalls a man except what is in his nature to endure."
- Marcus Aurelius

SILICONE IMPLANTS

AS-IS (American Silicone Implant Survivors, Inc.) *Nat'l. Founded 1991.* Education and support for women who have or had breast implants. Sharing of experiences, moral support and solutions for everyday problems that arise from silicone-related issues. Newsletter, information and referrals, seminars, meetings. Write: AS-IS, 1288 Cork Elm Dr., Kirkwood, MO 63122. Call (314)821-6250; FAX: (314)821-0199; *E-mail*: janetasis@aol.com

SJOGREN'S SYNDROME

National Sjogren's Syndrome Association *Int'l. 50 chapters. Founded 1990.* Provides emotional support to persons with Sjogren's Syndrome and their families. Educational information for patients and professionals. Encourages research. Support group meetings, conferences, phone support, newsletter, information and referrals. Assistance in starting groups. Meets on AOL. Write: Nat'l Sjogren's Syndrome Assn., 5815 N. Black Canyon Hwy., #103, AZ 85015-2200. Call (602)433-9844 or 800-395-NSSA; FAX: (602)433-9838.

Sjogren's Syndrome Foundation Inc. *Int'l. 25 groups/155 resource volunteers and overseas affiliates. Founded 1983.* Information and education for patients, families, health professionals and the public. Opportunities for patients to share ways of coping. Stimulates research for treatments and cures. Newsletter, chapter development guidelines, video tapes, annual symposium, Sjogren's handbook. Write: Sjogren's Syndrome Fdn., 333 N. Broadway, Jericho, NY 11753. Call (516)933-6365 or 800-4-SJOGRENS (for publications); FAX: (516)933-6368; *E-mail:* ssf@mail/idt.net *Website*: http://www.sjogrens.com

SMITH-LEMLI-OPITZ

Smith-Lemli-Opitz Advocacy and Exchange *Int'l. 2 affiliated groups. Founded 1988.* Network of families with SLO (RSH) children. Exchange of information, sharing of similar experiences, and correspondence between families. Provides education to medical community, new parents, and others. Phone support. Newsletter is planned. Dues $10/year. Write: Smith-Lemli-Opitz Advocacy and Exchange, 222 Valley Green Dr., Aston, PA 19014. Call (610)361-9663.

SMITH-MAGENIS SYNDROME

PRISMS (Parents and Researchers Interested in Smith-Magenis) *Int'l network. Founded 1992.* Parent-to-parent program offering support, advocacy and education for families affected by Smith-Magenis Syndrome. Information and referrals, literature, phone support, newsletter. Dues $20. Write: PRISMS, 11875 Fawn Ridge Lane, Reston, VA 20194. Call (703)709-0568; *E-mail:*

acmsmith@nhgrinih.gov *Website:* http://www.kumc.edu/gec/support/smith-ma-html

SOTOS SYNDROME

Sotos Syndrome Support Association *Int'l network. Founded 1984.* Provides information and mutual support for families of children with Sotos syndrome. Newsletter, information and referrals, phone support, pen pals, annual conferences. Write: Sotos Syndrome Support Assn., 2702 S. 49th St., Omaha, NE 68106. Call (402) 556-2445; *Website*: http://www.well.com/user/sssa *E-mail:* sss@well.com

SPASMODIC DYSPHONIA

National Spasmodic Dysphonia Association *Nat'l. 85+ affiliated support groups. Founded 1990.* Promotes the care and welfare of those with spasmodic dysphonia and their families. Aims to increase public awareness and education. Encourage formation of local support groups. Raises funds for research. Newsletter. Write: Nat'l Spasmodic Dysphonia Assn., 1 E. Wacker Dr., #2430, Chicago, IL 60601. Call 800-795-6732; FAX: (312)803-0138; *E-mail*: nsda@aol.com *Website*: http://www.ziplink.net/users/dystonia/spasdysp.html

(Model) Spasmodic Dysphonia Support Group of New York *1 group in New York. Founded 1987.* Provides members with the latest information regarding spasmodic dysphonia, emotional and practical support, workshops and discussions, encourages education for the public and physicians. Guest speakers, information and referrals. Write: A. Simons, 67-33 152 St., Flushing, NY 11367. Call (718)793-2442; *E-mail:* asimons@ibm.net

SPASMODIC TORTICOLLIS

National Spasmodic Torticollis Association *Nat'l. 50 Chapters. Founded 1983.* Support group for spasmodic torticollis victims and their families. Interest in research, public education and establishment of S.T. support groups throughout the U.S. Newsletter, list of neurologists, pen pals, telephone network, chapter development guidelines. Write: Nat'l Spasmodic Torticollis Assn., P.O. Box 424, Mukwonago, WI 53149-0424. Call 800-487-8385; FAX: (414)662-9887; *Website*: http://www.bluheronweb.com/nsta/nsta.htm

SPINA BIFIDA

Spina Bifida Association of America *Nat'l. 75 chapters. Founded 1972.* Encourages educational and vocational development of patients. Promotes public awareness, advocacy and research. Newsletter, chapter development guidelines, adoption referral program, scholarships, film/videotapes. Write: Spina Bifida

Assn. of Amer., 4590 MacArthur Blvd. NW, Suite 250, Washington, DC
20007. Call 800-621-3141 or (202)944-3285; FAX: (202)944-3295; *E-mail*:
spinabifda@aol.com *Website*: http://www.infohiway.com/spinabifida

SPINAL MUSCULAR ATROPHY /WERDNIG-HOFFMAN KUGELBERG-WELANDER DISEASE ARAN-DUCHENNE TYPE

Families of S.M.A. *Int'l. 8 chapters. Founded 1984.* Funding of research,
support and networking for families affected by spinal muscular atrophy
including Werdnig-Hoffman, Kugelberg-Welander Disease and Aran-Duchenne
Type. Provides educational resources, group development guidelines, quarterly
newsletter, pen pals, phone support and videotapes. Write: Families of SMA,
P.O. Box 196, Libertyville, IL 60048. Call 800-886-1762 or (847)367-7623
(voice/FAX); *Website*: http://www.abacus96.com/fsma/ *E-mail:*
sma@@interaccess.com

SPONDYLITIS

Spondylitis Association of America *Int'l. 10 affiliated groups. Founded 1983.*
Support and education for patients, their families, friends and health
professionals concerned with spondylitis. Links members geographically for
local support and programs. Publications, videotapes, newsletter and member
matching service. Write: Spondylitis Assn. of Amer., P.O. Box 5872, Sherman
Oaks, CA 91413. Call 800-777-8189 or (818)981-1616 (in CA); FAX:
(818)981-9826; *Website*: http://www.spondylitis.org *E-mail*: spondy@aol.com

STICKLER SYNDROME

Stickler Involved People (SIP) *Nat'l network. Founded 1995.* Network
offering support and education for persons affected by Stickler Syndrome. This
genetic disorder affects connective tissues, including the joints, eyes, palate,
heart and hearing. Phone support, information and referrals, literature, pen pals,
newsletter. Write: SIP, 15 Angelina, Augusta, KS 67010. Call (316)775-2993;
Website: http://members.aol.com/dhawley/stickler.html *E-mail:*
houch@southwnd.com

STREP, GROUP B

Group B Strep Association *Int'l network. Founded 1990.* Educates the public
about Group B Streptococcal infections during pregnancy. Information and
referrals, phone support, newsletter and assistance in developing state networks.
Write: Group B Strep Assn., P.O. Box 16515, Chapel Hill, NC 27516. Call
(919)932-5344; FAX: (919)932-5344; *Website*: http://www.groupbstrep.org

STROKE / APHASIA
(Also see Caregivers, Disabilities General)

National Aphasia Association *Nat'l umbrella organization. Founded 1987.* To educate the public about aphasia. Provides information to patients and their families. Referrals to local groups. young people's network for people (13-21) with acquired aphasia. Networking of parents to share information. Newsletter. Manual available for starting community groups. Write: Nat'l Aphasia Assn., 156 Fifth Ave., #707, New York, NY 10011. Call 800-922-4622; *Website*: http://www.aphasia.org *E-mail*: kein@aphasia.org

National Stroke Association *Nat'l. 7 chapters.Founded 1984.* Dedicated to reducing the incidence and impact of stroke through prevention, medical treatment, rehabilitation, family support and research. Research fellowships in cerebrovascular disease. Newsletter, professional publication, information and referrals. Guidance for starting stroke clubs and groups. Write: Nat'l Stroke Assn., 96 Inverness Dr., East, Suite 1, Englewood, CO 80112-5112. Call (303)649-9299 or 800-STROKES; FAX: (303)649-1328; TTY: (303)649-0122; *E-mail*: info@stroke.org *Website*: http://www.stroke.org

Stroke Clubs International *Int'l. 900+ Clubs. Founded 1968.* Organization of persons who have experienced strokes, their families and friends for the purpose of mutual support, education, social and recreational activities. Provides information and assistance to Stroke Clubs (which are usually sponsored by local organizations). Newsletter, group development guidelines. Write: Stroke Clubs, Int'l, 805 12th St., Galveston, TX 77550. Call (409)762-1022.

Stroke Connection of the American Heart Association *Nat'l.1200 groups. Founded 1979.* Maintains a listing of support groups for stroke survivors, their families, caregivers and interested professionals. Publishes Stroke Connection magazine, a forum for stroke survivors and their families to share information about coping with strokes. Provides information and referrals and carries stroke related books, videos and literature available for purchase. Write: Stroke Connection of the Amer. Heart Assn., 7272 Greenville Ave.,Dallas, TX 75231. Call 800-553-6321 (day); FAX: (214)987-4334; *Website*: http://www.amhrt.org *E-mail*: strokaha@amhrt.org

STURGE-WEBER / PORT WINE STAIN
(Also see Klippel-Trenauney, Vascular Malformations)

Sturge-Weber Foundation, The *Int'l network. Parent representatives in 23 states. Founded 1987.* Mutual support network for families affected by Sturge-Weber Syndrome, Port Wine Stain or Klippel-Trenauney Weber Syndrome. Disseminates information, funds and facilitates research. Quarterly newsletter, phone support, letter-writing among families. Group development guidelines. Write: Sturge-Weber Fdn., P.O. Box 418, Mt. Freedom, NJ 07970. Call (800)627-5482 or (973)895-4445; FAX: (973)895-4846: *E-mail:* crs0590@inforamp.net or SWF-Support@iname.com *Website:* http://www.inforamp.net/~crs0590/mission.html

SYRINGOMYELIA
(Also see CLOACA)

American Syringomyelia Alliance Project *Nat'l network. Founded 1988.* Support, networking, and information for people affected by syringomyelia and chiari. Newsletter, phone support, pen pals, conferences. Write: Amer. Syringomyelia Alliance Project, P.O. Box 1586, Longview, TX 75606-1586. Call (903)236-7079 or 800-272-7282; FAX: (903)757-7456; *E-mail:* 102563.3507@compuserve.com *Website:* http://www.syringe.org

TAKAYASU'S ARTERITIS

(Model) **Takayasu's Arteritis Association** *1 group in New Hampshire. Founded 1995.* Educates and supports Takayasu's Arteritis patients, their relatives, and medical community on Takayasu's Arteritis (an inflammation of the large elastic arteries and aorta). Pen pals, information and referrals, phone support, literature, newsletter, conferences. Write: Takayasu's Arteritis Assn., 31 Coburn Woods, Nashua, NH 03063. Call (603)881-8529. *E-mail:* dpatsos@jlc.net

TASTE / SMELL DISORDER

The Taste and Smell Dysfunction Foundation *Int'l. 2 chapters. Founded 1974.* To assist patients understand problems of taste and smell function (smell disorder, oral/nasal burning, oral malorder). Promotes research and disseminates information. Information and referrals, phone support, newsletter. Dues $25/yr. Write: Taste and Smell Dysfunction Fdn., 5125 MacArthur Blvd., NW, Washington, DC 20016. Call Dr. Robert Henkin (202)364-8921; FAX: (202)364-9727.

TAY-SACHS DISEASE

Late Onset Tay-Sachs Foundation *Nat'l network. Founded 1994.* Support and education for persons dealing with late onset Tay-Sachs. Aims to educate medical and community at large. Advocacy, newsletter, information and referrals, phone support, conferences, and literature. Write: Late Onset Tay-Sachs Fdn., 1303 Paper Mill Rd., Erdenheim, PA 19038. Call 800-672-2022 (day); FAX: (215)836-5438; *E-mail:* mpf@bellatlantic.net or 72624.3502@compuserve.com *Website:* http://www.webknx.com/LOTSF or http://neuro-www2.mgh.harvard.edu/LOTS/main.html

National Tay-Sachs and Allied Diseases Association *Nat'l. 6 affiliated groups. Founded 1957.* Devoted to the detection, prevention and cure of Tay-Sachs and other fatal degenerative disorders through programs of research, education and support services. Families of affected children are assisted by the availability of a parent peer network, a repository of specialized knowledge. Write: Nat'l Tay-Sachs and Allied Diseases Assn., 2001 Beacon St., Brookline, MA 02146. Call 800-906-8723 or (617)277-4463; FAX: (617)277-0134; *E-mail:* ntsad-boston@worldnet.att.net *Website:* http://mcrcr4.med.nyu.edu/~murphp01/taysachs.htm

TEMPOROMANDIBULAR JOINT DYSFUNCTION (TMJ)

TMJ Association *Int'l network. 14 affiliated groups. Founded 1986.* Education and support for persons with temporomandibular joint dysfunction. Newsletter, information and referrals, phone support, literature and legislative action. Assistance in starting groups. Write: TMJ Assn., P.O. Box 26770, Milwaukee, WI 53226-0770. Call (414)259-3223; FAX: (414)259-8112.

THROMBOCYTOPENIA ABSENT RADIUS

TARSA (Thrombocytopenia Absent Radius Syndrome Association) *Int'l network. Founded 1981.* Information, networking and support for families children with T.A.R. Syndrome (a shortening of the arms), and for affected adults. (Does not include ITP). Newsletter, pen pal program, phone network. Write: TARSA, 212 Sherwood Dr., Egg Harbor Twp., NJ 08234-7658. Call (609)927-0418; FAX: (609)653-8639; *E-mail:* edwardp2@aol.com or purinton@earthlink.net

THROMBOTIC THROMBOCYTOPONIC PURPURA

TTP Support Group *Int'l network. Founded 1993.* Mutual support, information and advocacy for persons affected by thrombotic thrombocytopenic purpura, a blood disorder dealing with platelets. Physician referrals. Newsletter, information and referrals, literature, support group meetings. Write: TTP Support Group, P.O. Box 10259, Baltimore, MD 21234.

THYROID PROBLEMS

Thyroid Foundation of America *Nat'l. 10 affiliated groups. Founded 1985.* Information and support for persons concerned with any type of thyroid problem, including hypothyroidism, hyperthyroidism, goiter, thyroid lumps or nodules, postpartum thyroiditis and cancer. Information, referrals to local support groups and physicians, literature. Dues $25 (which includes a newsletter). Assistance in starting groups. Write: TFA, Ruth Sleeper Hall, Room 350, 40 Parkman St., Boston, MA 02114-2698. Call 800-832-8321;

FAX: (617)726-4136; *Website*: http://www.tfaweb.org/pub/tfa   *E-mail*: tfa@clark.net

TOURETTE SYNDROME

Tourette Syndrome Association *Nat'l. 48 chapters. Founded 1972.* Education for patients, professionals and public. Promotes research into the causes, treatments and cures. Provides services to families and professionals to enable patients to achieve optimum development. Chapter development guidelines, newsletter. Dues $45. Write: Tourette Syndrome Assn., 42-40 Bell Blvd., #205, Bayside, NY 11361-2820. Call (718)224-2999 or (800)237-0717 or 888-4-TOURETT; FAX (718)279-9596; *Website*: http://tsa.ngh.harvard.edu/ *E-mail*: tourette@ix.netcom.com

TRACHEO ESOPHAGEAL FISTULA

TEF/VATER Support Network *Int'l. Founded 1992.* Offers support and encouragement for parents of children with tracheo esophageal fistula, esophageal atresia and VATER. Aims to bring current information to parents and the medical community. Newsletter, information and referrals, phone support. Write: c/o Greg and Terri Burke, 15301 Grey Fox Rd., Upper Marlboro, MD 20772. Call (301)952-6837.

TRACHEOSTOMY

(Note) **Tracheostomy** is a condition for which we have received a significant number of inquiries. Regrettable, we are unaware of any support group or network that has yet been formed. If you learn of any existing group that you would recommend, or are interested in starting such a group, please call the Clearinghouse.

TRANSPLANT RECIPIENT, ORGAN
(Also see Heart, specific disorder)

Second Wind Lung Transplant Association *Nat'l.* Developed by transplant patients. Opportunity for persons who have undergone, or who will undergo, lung transplants to share their stories on a web page. Newsletter available. Write: Second Wind Lung Transplant Assn., 9030 W. Lakeview Court, Crystal River, FL 34438. Call (352)563-0135; FAX: (352)563-0728; *Website*: http://www.web-site.com/2ndwind/index.htm or http://www.arthouse.com/secondwind *E-mail:* secondwind@xtalwind.net

TRIO (Transplant Recipients International Organization) *Int'l. 43 chapters. Founded 1983.* Works to improve the quality of life of transplant candidates, recipients, donors, and their families. TRIO serves its members in the areas of:

donor awareness, support, education, and advocacy. Annual international meeting, bi-monthly newsletter, monthly membership update, support network, chapter development assistance. Write: TRIO, 1000 16th St., NW, #602, Washington, DC 20036-5705. Call 800-TRIO-386 or (202)293-0980 FAX: (202)293-0973. *E-mail*: trio@primenet.com *Website*: http://www.primenet.com/trio

TRANSVERSE MYELITIS

Transverse Myelitis Association *Nat'l network. Founded 1994.* Mutual support and networking for families affected by transverse myelitis. Acts as a clearinghouse for information. Literature, pen pals, advocacy, group meetings, phone support. Write: Deanne Gilmur, 3548 Tahoma Pl. W., University Place, WA 98466-2141. Call (253)565-8156 (eve); *E-mail:* srulyosef@aol.com

TREACHER COLLINS SYNDROME

Treacher Collins Foundation *Nat'l network. Founded 1988.* Support for families, individuals and professionals re: Treacher Collins Syndrome and related disorders. Provides networking, educational materials, newsletter, information and referrals, phone support, resource list, bibliography and central library, videos and booklets. Write: Treacher Collins Fdn., P.O. Box 683, Norwich, VT 05055. Call (802)649-3050 or 800-TCF-2055.

TRIGEMINAL NEURALGIA/TIC DOULOUREUX

Trigeminal Neuralgia Assn. *Nat'l. 24 groups. Founded 1990.* Provides information, mutual support and encouragement to patients and their families to reduce isolation of those affected. Aims to increase public/professional awareness, and promote research into cause and cure. Quarterly newsletter. Phone support, pen pal program. Local groups being formed in several states. Write: Claire Patterson, P.O. Box 340, Barnegat Light, NJ 08006. Call (609)361-1014.

TRISOMY
(Also see Chromosome Disorders)

9-TIPS (Trisomy International Parent Support) *Int'l network. Founded 1992.* Support for families of children with Trisomy 9. Provides parental network system. Updates on available medical resources. Annual newsletter. Write: c/o Joan Conard, Children's Hospital of Michigan, 3901 Beaubien Blvd., Detroit, MI 48201-2196. Call (313)745-4513 (day); or Alice Todd (909)862-4470 (Voice/FAX) for parents; FAX: (313)745-4827

S.O.F.T. (Support Organization For Trisomy) *Nat'l. 45 chapters. Founded 1979.* Support and education for families of children with trisomy 18 and 13 and related genetic disorders. Education and awareness for professionals. Quarterly newsletter. Pen pal program, phone network. Regional gatherings. Annual international conference, booklets. Dues $20. Write: SOFT, c/o Barbara Van Herreweghe, 2982 S. Union St., Rochester, NY 14624. Call Barbara Van Herreweghe (716)594-4621.

Trisomy 12P Parent Support Organization *Nat'l network. Founded 1997.* Mutual support, sharing of experiences and coping skills for parents of children with trisomy 12P. Information and encouragement for parents of newly diagnosed children. Newsletter. Listing of other trisomy 12P families. Write: Trisomy 12P Parent Support Organization, 105 Mill Pond Rd., Roswell, GA 30076. Call Cindy Smith (770)993-4796.

TUBE-FEEDING

Oley Foundation, Inc. *Nat'l. 60 affiliated groups. Founded 1983.* Promotes optimal care for those requiring long-term specialized nutritional therapy. The focus is to enrich and enhance the lives of those requiring nutrition support. Supports research. Newsletter. Outreach system of patient volunteers, and annual conference. Home pen family network for families. Write: Oley Fdn., 214 HUN Memorial, Albany Medical Center A-23, Albany, NY 12208. Call 800-776-6539 (day) or (518)262-5079; FAX: (518)262-5528; *Website*: http://www.wizvax.net/oleyfdn

TUBEROUS SCLEROSIS

National Tuberous Sclerosis Association *Nat'l. Area Representatives. Founded 1974.* Encourages research, support and education among families with tuberous sclerosis. Quarterly newsletter, pen pal program, parent-to-parent contact program, support group meetings, audio and video tapes available. Write: Nat'l Tuberous Sclerosis Assn., 8181 Professional Pl., Suite 110, Landover, MD 20785. Call (301)459-9888 or 800-225-NTSA; FAX: (301)459-0394; *Website*: www.ntsa.org *E-mail:* NTSA@ntsa.org

TURNER'S SYNDROME

Turner's Syndrome Society *11 chapters in Canada. Founded 1981.* Provides support and education to Turner's Syndrome persons and families. Tapes, publications, referral to U.S. and Canada groups. Quarterly newsletter. Pen pal program, chapter development guidelines, annual conference. Write: Sandi Hofbauer, Exec. Dir., Turner's Syndrome Soc., 814 Gelncairn Ave., Toronto, Ontario M6B 2A3 Canada. Call 800-465-6744 or (416)781-2086; FAX: (416)781-7245.

Turner Syndrome Society of the U.S. *Nat'l. 32 chapters. Founded 1988.*
Self-help organization for women, girls, and their families affected by Turner's
syndrome. Increases public awareness about the disorder. Quarterly newsletter,
chapter development assistance, annual conference. Write: c/o Lynn Tesch, 1313
SE Fifth St., #327, Minneapolis. MN 55414. Call (612)379-3607; FAX:
(612)379-3619; *E-mail:* tesch005@tc.umn.edu *Website:*
http://www.turner-syndrome-us.org

Turner Syndrome Support Network *Nat'l network. Founded 1989.* Network
and exchange of information for parents of children with Turner's Syndrome.
Information and referrals, phone support, pen pals, conferences, literature.
Newsletter ($20/year). Write: c/o MAGIC Foundation, 1327 N. Harlen, Oak
Park, IL 60303. Call 800-3-MAGIC-3; *E-mail:* magic@nettap.com *Website:*
http://www.nettap.com/ ~ magic

TWIN TO TWIN TRANSFUSION SYNDROME

Twin to Twin Transfusion Syndrome Foundation *Nat'l. 6 chapters. Founded
1992.* Emotional, educational and financial support for persons affected by
Twin to Twin Transfusion Syndrome. TTTS affects identical multiple
pregnancies when blood passes disproportionately between the shared placenta
and can cause death or disabilities. Pen pals, newsletter, literature, phone
support, visitation, conferences. Guidelines for professionals on multiple birth
loss during pregnancy. Help in starting new chapters. International registry.
Write: TTTS, 411 Longbeach Parkway, Bay Village, OH 44140. Call (216)
899-8887; FAX: (216)899-1184; *Website:* http://www.tttsfoundation.com
E-mail: tttsfound@aol.com

TYPE ONE FIBER HYPOTROPHY

(Interest in starting) **Type One Fiber Hypotrophy** *No known support network.*
At time of printing, we have heard from one person who is interested in starting
a support network for parents of children with type one fiber hypotrophy, a
muscle fiber disorder. If interested in helping to start this network, please
contact the Clearinghouse for more information.

UREA CYCLE DISORDERS

National Urea Cycle Disorders Foundation *Nat'l network. Founded 1990.*
Links families, friends and professionals who are dedicated to the identification,
treatment and cure of urea cycle disorders, a genetic disorder causing an enzyme
deficiency in the urea cycle. Networks families together for support, educates
professionals and public, and supports research. Phone support, literature,
newsletter. Dues $25. Write: Nat'l Urea Cycle Disorders Fdn., P.O. Box 32,

Sayreville, NJ 08872. Call 800-38-NUCDF (800-386-8233); *Website*: http://www.execpc.com/ ~ fenders/nucdf/html

VACCINE INJURY

National Vaccine Information Center (Dissatisfied Parents Together) *Nat'l. Reps in all states. Founded 1982.* NVIC/DPT is a support, information and advocacy group for parents whose children were adversely affected by vaccines. Advocates for safety reforms in the mass vaccination system and safer vaccines. Promotes education for parents and professionals. Various literature ($5-13); newsletter ($18). Dues $25/yr. Write: NVIC, 512 W. Maple Ave., #206, Vienna, VA 22180. Call (703)938-DPT3 or 800-909-SHOT; FAX: (703)938-5768; *Website*: http://www.909shot.com *E-mail:* kwnvic@aol.com

VASCULAR MALFORMATIONS
(Also see specific disorder)

National Vascular Malformation Foundation *Nat'l network. Founded 1990.* Support and information for persons affected by vascular malformations (tumors or flat lesions made up of abnormally sized blood vessels). Information packets, referrals to physicians, annual conference, pen pals. Interactive newsletter. Write: NVMF, 8320 Nightingale, Dearborn Heights, MI 48127. Call (313) 264-1243; FAX: (313)274-1393.

VENTILATOR-ASSISTED, -USERS

International Ventilator Users Network *Int'l network. Founded 1987.* Information sharing by ventilator users and health care professionals experienced in home mechanical ventilation. Newsletter. Membership: USA $17; Overseas Surface $15; Overseas Air $17. Handbook on ventilators and muscular dystrophy $6. Write: Int'l Ventilator Users Network, 4207 Lindell Blvd., #110, St. Louis, MO 63108. Call (314)534-0475; FAX: (314)534-5070; *E-mail*: gini_intl@msn.com

VESTIBULAR DISORDERS

Vestibular Disorders Association *Int'l. 100 independent groups. Founded 1983.* Information, referrals and support for people affected by disorders caused by inner ear problems. Public education, group development assistance, quarterly newsletter, library of resources, phone support network. Write: Vestibular Disorders Assn., P.O. Box 4467, Portland, OR 97208-4467. Call 800-837-8428 or (503)229-7705; FAX: (503)229-8064; *Website*: http://www.teleport.com/ ~ veda *E-mail:* veda@teleport.com

247

VITILIGO

National Vitiligo Foundation *Nat'l. 14 affiliated groups. Founded 1985.* Mutual help and education for persons with vitiligo, a skin disorder affecting pigmentation. Fund-raising for research. Semi-annual newsletter. Telephone network. Write: Nat'l Vitiligo Fdn., P.O. Box 6337, Tyler, TX 75711. Call (903)531-0074; FAX: (903)531-9767; *E-mail:* 73071.33@compuserve.com *Website*: http://pegasus.uthct.edu/vitiligo/index.html

VOMITING, CYCLIC

Cyclic Vomiting Syndrome Assn. *Int'l. 12 affiliated groups. Founded 1993.* Mutual support and information for families and professionals dealing with cyclic vomiting Syndrome. Networking, phone support, educational materials, and research support. Newsletter. Write: CVSA, c/o Kathleen Adams; 13180 Caroline Court, Elm Grove, WI 53122. Call (414)784-6842; FAX: (414)821-5494; *E-mail:* kadams@post.its.mcw.edu *Website*: http://ezinfo.ucs.indiana.edu/~jdbickel/cvs.html

VON HIPPEL LINDAU

VHL Family Alliance *Int'l network. 31 groups. Founded 1993.* Opportunity for families affected by VHL to share their knowledge and experiences with each other and the medical community. Goal is to improve diagnosis, treatment and quality of life for VHL families. Newsletter, phone support and education. Help in starting groups. Write: VHL Family Alliance, 171 Clinton Rd., Brookline, MA 02146. Call 800-767-4845 or (617)232-5946; FAX: (617)232-5946. *E-mail*: vhl@pipeline.com *Website*: http://www.vhl.org

VULVAR DISORDERS

The Vulvar Pain Foundation *Int'l. 110 networks/30 support groups. Founded 1992.* Provides research, treatment, information and emotional support to women experiencing vulvar pain. Identifies interested health care professionals. Participates in research. Newsletter, phone support, pen pals, videos, seminars, low oxalate cookbook. Dues vary ($40-$70). Assistance in starting new groups. For information send $2 with self-addressed stamped envelope. Write: The VP Fdn., P.O. Drawer 177, Graham, NC 27253. Call (910)226-0704 (Tues and Thurs, 8:30-4:30); FAX: (910)226-8518.

WEAVER SYNDROME

Support for Families with Weaver Syndrome *Nat'l network. Founded 1995.* Grassroots group of parents interested in networking with other families affected by Weaver Syndrome to combine efforts and resources, and to look at long-term expectations for this condition. To be proactive regarding medical needs. Phone support, pen pals. Write: Support for Families with Weaver Syndrome, c/o Patty Mer, 4357 153rd Ave. SE, Bellevue, WA 98006. Call (425)747-5382 or (425)235-1665.

WEGENER'S GRANULOMATOSIS

Wegeners Foundation, Inc. *Nat'l network. Founded 1990.* Provides support and education for persons with Wegeners granulomatosis. Encourages research into the causes and treatment of this rare disabling disease. Provides information and referrals, phone support, newsletter. Write: Wegeners Fdn., 9000 Rockville Pike Bldg. 31A B1W30, Bethesda, MD 20892. Call Linda Baltrusch (703)931-5852 (Voice/FAX); *E-mail:* 1baltrusch@aol.com

Wegeners Granulomatosis Support Group *Int'l. 3 affiliated groups. Founded 1986.* Non-profit health organization for patients with life-threatening uncommon Wegener's granulomatosis and related vascular illnesses. Provides information to patients and physicians about this disorder and educates families, friends and general public about the devastating effects of Wegener's, it's symptoms and treatment. Dues $10/US; $20/Int'l (which includes bimonthly newsletter). Write: Wegener's Granulomatosis Support Group, P.O. Box 28660, Kansas City, MO 64188-8660. Call 800-277-9474; FAX: (816)436-8211; *E-mail:* wgjimiva@uit.net *Website:* http://www.wgsg.org/wgsg

WILLIAM'S SYNDROME

Williams Syndrome Association *Nat'l network. 11 chapters. Founded 1983.* To encourage research related to Williams syndrome, find and support families with Williams syndrome, and share information among parents and professionals re: educational, medical and behavioral experiences. Newsletter. Write: Williams Syndrome Assn., P.O. Box 297, Clawson, MI 48017-0297. Call (810) 541-3630; FAX: (248)541-3631; *E-mail:* T.Monkaba@aol.com *Website:* http://www.williams-syndrome.org

WILSON'S DISEASE

Wilson's Disease Association *Nat'l network. 5 affiliated groups. Founded 1979.* Provides information about Wilson's disease, a genetic disorder that causes excessive amounts of copper accumulation in the body, affecting the liver and brain. Provides mutual support and aid for those affected by the disease and their families. Promotes research into treatment and cure. Quarterly newsletter. Telephone support network. Write: Wilson's Disease Assn., 4 Navaho Dr., Brookfield, CT 06804. Call 800-399-0266; FAX: (203)743-6196; *Website:* http://www.medhelp.org/wda/wil.htm

WOLF-HIRSCHHORN SYNDROME

4P- Parent Contact Group *Nat'l network. 1 group in England. Founded 1984.* Provides support and information to families only of children with Wolf-Hirschhorn Syndrome. Offers phone support, biographies on other children with this syndrome. Newsletter. Write: 4P- Parent Contact Group, 2048 S. 182 Circle, Omaha, NE 68130. Call (402)330-7135; *E-mail*: TomBecR@aol.com *Website:* http://members.aol/com/lbent503/whs

WOMEN'S HEALTH
(Also see specific disorder)

Nat'l Black Women's Health Project/Self-Help Division *Int'l. 150 groups; 16 chapters. Founded 1981.* Only organization dedicated solely to improving Black women's health status. Provides wellness education programs, self-help group development, empowerment training. Newsletter, fact sheets, policy briefs, and national conferences. Dues vary. Write: NBWHP, 1211 Connecticut Ave. NW Suite 310, Washington, DC 20036. Call (202)835-0117; FAX: (202)833-8790; *E-mail*: nbwhpdc@aol.com

Nat'l Latina Health Organization *Nat'l network. Founded 1986.* Works toward bilingual access to quality health care through self-empowerment, educational programs, health advocacy, outreach and developing public policy specifically aimed at Latinas. Information and referrals, phone support, literature. Self-help facilitator training, maintains the Latina Health Resource library, conducts school-based youth programs and mentorship program. Write: Nat'l Latina Health Org., P.O. Box 7567, Oakland, CA 94601. Call (510)534-1362; FAX: (510)534-1364.

XERODERMA PIGMENTOSUM

Xeroderma Pigmentosum Society *Int'l network. Founded 1995.* Provides sharing of support, information and coping skills for families affected by xeroderma pigmentosum (hypersensitivity to light). Quarterly "information" newsletter. Promotes research into finding a cure. Information and referrals, phone support, conferences, pen pals, literature, advocacy in community, education and protection. Summer Sundown Camp for patients of all ages and their families. Write: XP Soc., Box 4759, Poughkeepsie, NY 12603. Call (914)473-4735; *E-mail*: caren@xps.orgmhv.net *Website:* http://www.xps.org

MENTAL HEALTH

"The first principle of achievement is mental attitude.
Man begins to achieve when he begins to believe."
- Elbert Hubbard

ANXIETY / PHOBIAS /
AGORAPHOBIA / PANIC ATTACKS
(Also see Mental Health General, Speech/Stuttering)

ABIL (Agoraphobics Building Independent Lives), Inc. *Nat'l. 28 groups. Founded 1986.* Mutual support, encouragement, goal setting, hope and education for persons with agoraphobia, anxiety or panic-related disorders, their families and friends. Information and referrals, phone support, newsletter, assistance in starting groups. Write: ABIL, Inc., 3805 Cutshaw Ave., Suite 415, Richmond, VA 23230. Call (804)353-3964; FAX: (804)353-3687; *E-mail:* abil1996@aol.com

AIM (Agoraphobics In Motion) *Nat'l. 13 groups. Founded 1983.* Self-help group that uses specific behavioral and cognitive techniques to help people recover from agoraphobia, anxiety, and panic attacks. Includes relaxation techniques, small group discussions, and field trips. Newsletter, pen pals. Group development guidelines ($27). Write: AIM, 1719 Crooks, Royal Oak, MI 48067-1306. Call (248)547-0400.

Anxiety Disorders Association of America *Nat'l network. Founded 1980.* Promotes the welfare of people with phobias and related anxiety disorders. An organization for consumers, health care professionals and other concerned individuals. Publishes national membership directory, self-help group directory, ADAA Reporter, and newsletter. Write: ADAA, 11900 Parklawn Dr., #100, Rockville, MD 20852-2624. Call (301)231-9350; FAX: (301)231-7392; *E-mail:* AnxDis@aol.com *Website:* http://www.adaa.org

Fear of Success Anonymous *Nat'l. 6 affiliated groups. Founded 1989.* Gathering of men and women who are committed to obtaining and enjoying the benefits of success, as we individually define it, in all areas of our lives. Follows the 12-steps to overcome fears, avoid self-sabotaging behavior and take action. Group meetings, newsletter, phone lists, workshops, and assistance in starting groups. Write: Fear of Success Anonymous, 16161 Ventura Blvd., #727, Encino, CA 91436. Call (818)907-3953. *Website:* http://fosa.home.ml.org

GROW, Inc. *Int'l. 143 groups in IL, NJ, DE and RI. Founded 1957.* 12-step mutual help program to provide the know-how for avoiding and recovering from depression, anxiety and other mental health problems. Offers a caring and sharing community to attain emotional maturity, personal responsibility, and recovery from mental illness. Leadership training and consultation to develop new groups available. Write: GROW, Inc., 2403 W. Springfield Ave., Box 3667, Champaign, IL 61826. Call (217)352-6989; FAX: (217)352-8530.

(Model) **Council on Anxiety Disorders** *2 affiliated groups in Georgia. Founded 1988.* Education, support and encouragement for people with anxiety disorders. Packets available nationwide that include personal stories, resources for information about treatment of panic disorder, phobias, obsessive-compulsive disorder, post-traumatic stress, separation anxiety, and general anxiety. Cassette tapes, quarterly newsletter and group development guidelines available. Write: Council on Anxiety Disorders, Route 1, Box 1364, Clarkesville, GA 30523. Call (706)947-3854; FAX: (706)947-1265; *E-mail:* slvau@stc.net

CONSUMERS OF MENTAL HEALTH / PSYCHIATRIC SURVIVORS
(Also see Mental Health General, Disabilities General, specific disorder)

Dual Disorders Anonymous *Nat'l. 28 groups in IL; 20 in other states. Founded 1982.* Fellowship of men and women who come together to help those members who still suffer from both mental disorder and alcoholism and/or drug addiction. Uses the 12-step program of A.A. Group development guidelines. Write: Dual Disorders Anonymous, P.O. Box 681264, Schaumberg, IL 60168-1264. Call (847)956-1660.

GROW, Inc. *Int'l. 143 groups in IL, NJ, DE and RI. Founded in 1957.* 12-step mutual help program to provide know-how for avoiding and recovering from depression, anxiety and other mental health problems. Offers a caring and sharing community to attain emotional maturity, personal responsibility, and recovery from mental illness. Leadership training and consultation to develop new groups available. Write: GROW, Inc., 2403 W. Springfield Ave., Box 3667, Champaign, IL 61826. Call (217)352-6989; FAX: (217)352-8530.

Heartway Projects *Nat'l. Founded 1992.* Dedicated to supporting the rights of mentally ill people to create a higher quality of life. Creates consumer-generated and run self-help groups and projects to empower individuals. Education, literature, information and referrals, phone support, advocacy, and support group meetings. Write: Heartway Projects, P.O. Box 46, Malo, WA 99150-0046. Call (509)779-4756; *E-mail:* ajiles@tincn.tincan.org

Reclamation, Inc. *Nat'l network. Founded 1974.* Alliance of mentally restored people helping to reclaim the human dignity destroyed by the stigma of mental illness. Directs ex-patients in worthwhile, positively visible projects to improve image. Publishes quarterly newsletter. Staffed and funded by ex-patients. Write: Don H. Culwell, Director, 2502 Waterford Dr., San Antonio, TX 78217. Call (210)822-3569.

NADD: An Association for Persons with Developmental Disabilities and Mental Health Needs *Nat'l. 4 affiliated groups. Founded 1983.* Promotes the development of resources for person with mental retardation and mental illness through education, advocacy, research and exchange of information. Conferences, audio tapes and books, and directory of members available. Write: NADD, 132 Fair St., Kingston, NY 12401. Call (914)331-4336; FAX: (914)331-4569; *E-mail:* nadd@mhv.net

Schizophrenics Anonymous *Int'l. 70+ chapters. Founded 1985.* Organized and run by people with schizophrenia-related disorders. Offers fellowship, support and information. Focuses on recovery, using a 6-step program, along with medication and professional help. Weekly meetings, guest speakers, phone network, newsletter, and help in starting groups. Write: Schizophrenics Anonymous, c/o MHA in Michigan, 15920 W. Twelve Mile, Southfield, MI 48076. Call (248)557-6777; FAX: (248)557-5995; *E-Mail:* mha-mi@juno.com

(Model) **FAIR (Family And Individual Reliance)** *5 groups in Texas. Founded 1981.* Statewide mutual support groups for persons with present or past mental or emotional illness. Separate groups for family and friends. Bi-annual retreat, "how-to" manual ($12), facilitators training manual ($5), and quarterly newsletter. Write: FAIR, c/o Mary Dees, MHA in Texas, 8401 Shoal Creek Blvd., Austin, TX 78757. Call (512)454-3706; FAX: (512)454-3725.

(Model) **On Our Own, Inc.** *1 group in Baltimore, MD. Founded 1981.* Mutual support and advocacy for mental health consumers. Drop-in center provides educational, social and recreational activities. Provides assistance in starting similar drop-in centers. Write: On Our Own, P.O. Box 18899, Baltimore, MD 21206. Call 800-553-9899 (in MD) or (410)488-4480; FAX: (410)488-4482; *E-mail:* onourown@aol.com

(Model) **Well Mind Association of Greater Washington** *Founded 1967.* Provides education about mental illness as principally a metabolic disorder. Explores the connection between mental illness and environmental, biological and physiological factors. Newsletter, phone support, information, referrals to practitioners, literature, books and tapes. Assistance in starting new groups. Write: Well Mind Assn. of Greater Washington, P.O. Box 201, Kensington, MD 20895-0201. Call (301)774-6617; FAX: (301)946-1402.

(Resource) **National Empowerment Center** *Founded 1992.* Consumer-run center that provides information on various self-help resources of interest to mental health consumers. Provides networking, conference calls, information on upcoming conferences and workshops. Write: National Empowerment Center, 20 Ballard Rd., Lawrence, MA 01843. Call (508)685-1518 or 800-POWER-2-U; FAX: (508)681-6426; TTY: 800-889-7693; *Website:* http://www.concentric.net/~power2U

(Resource) **National Mental Health Consumers Self-Help Clearinghouse** Consumer self-help resource organization geared towards meeting the individual and group needs of mental health consumers. Assistance in advocacy, listings of publications, on-site consultations, information and referrals, training, educational events. Funded by Center of Mental Health Services. Write: Nat'l MH Consumers Self-Help Clearinghouse, 1211 Chestnut St., #1000, Philadelphia, PA 19107-4103. Call 800-553-4-KEY, FAX: (215)636-6310; *Website:* http://www.libertynet.org/~mha/cl_house.html

DEPRESSION / MANIC-DEPRESSION / POST-PARTUM DEPRESSION
(Also see Mental Health General, Consumers of Mental Health)

GROW, Inc. *Int'l. 143 groups in IL, NJ, DE and RI. Founded 1957.* 12-step mutual help program to provide know-how for avoiding and recovering from depression, anxiety and other mental health problems. Offers a caring and sharing community to attain emotional maturity, personal responsibility, and recovery from mental illness. Leadership training and consultation to develop new groups. Write: GROW, Inc., 2403 W. Springfield Ave., Box 3667, Champaign, IL 61826. Call (217)352-6989; FAX: (217)352-8530.

Depressed Anonymous *Int'l. 30+ affiliated groups. Founded 1985.* 12-step program to help depressed persons believe and hope they can feel better. Newsletter, phone support, information and referrals, workshops, conferences and seminars. Information packet ($5). Write: Depressed Anonymous, P.O. Box 17471, Louisville, KY 40217. Call Hugh S. (502)569-1989; *Website:* http://www.depressionselfhelp.com *E-mail:* depanon@ka.net

DAD (Depression After Delivery) *Nat'l. 100 affiliated groups. Founded 1985.* Support and information for women who have suffered from post-partum depression. Telephone support in most states. Newsletter ($30/yr), group development guidelines, pen pals, conferences. Write: DAD, P.O. Box 1282, Morrisville, PA 19067. Call (215)295-3994 or 800-944-4773 (leave message); *Website:* http://www.behavenet.com/dadinc

DRADA (Depression and Related Affective Disorders Assn) *Int'l. 60 affiliated groups. Founded 1986.* Aims to alleviate the suffering arising from depression and manic-depression by assisting self-help groups, providing education and information, and supporting research. Newsletter, literature, phone support, assistance in starting new groups, and young people's outreach project. Write: DRADA, Meyer 3-181 600 N. Wolfe St., Baltimore, MD 21287-7381. Call (410)955-4647 (Baltimore, MD) or (202)955-5800 (Washington, DC); FAX: (410)614-3241; *E-mail:* drada@welchlink.welch.jhu.edu

National Depressive and Manic-Depressive Association *Nat'l. 275 chapters. Founded 1986.* Mutual support and information for persons with depressive and manic-depressive illness, and their families. Provides public education on the nature of depressive illnesses. Annual conferences, chapter development guidelines, and quarterly newsletter. Bookstore, catalog, and mail orders. Write: NDMDA, 730 N. Franklin, #501, Chicago, IL 60610. Call 800-826-3632 or (312)642-0049; FAX: (312)642-7243; *Website:* http://www.ndmda.org/

NOSAD (National Organization for Seasonal Affective Disorder) *Nat'l. Founded 1988.* Disseminates information and provides education about the causes, nature and treatment of seasonal affective disorder (SAD). Promotes development of services for patients and their families. Encourages research into the cause and cure of SAD. Newsletter. Write: NOSAD, P.O. Box 40190, Washington, DC 20016.

Postpartum Support International *Int'l. 250 affiliated groups. Founded 1987.* To increase the awareness of the emotional changes women can experience during pregnancy and after the birth of a baby. Information on diagnosis and treatment of postpartum depression. Education, advocacy, annual conference. Encourages formation of support groups, and helps strengthen existing groups. Phone support, referrals, literature, newsletter. Write: Postpartum Support Int'l, 927 N. Kellogg Ave., Santa Barbara, CA 93111. Call (805)967-7636 (day); FAX: (805)967-0608; *E-mail:* thonikman@compuserve.com

(Model) **MDSG-NY (Mood Disorders Support Group, Inc.)** *3 affiliated groups in New York City area. Founded 1981.* Support and education for people with manic-depression or depression, their families and friends. Guest lectures, newsletter, rap groups, assistance in starting groups. Write: MDSG, Inc., P.O. Box 1747, Madison Sq. Station, New York, NY 10159. Call (212)533-MDSG; FAX: (212)475-5109; *Website:* http://www.psycom.net/mdsg.html

FAMILIES OF MENTALLY ILL
(Also see Mental Health General, and specific disorder)

Attachment Disorder Parents Network *Nat'l. 5 affiliated groups. Founded 1988.* Support and information for parents and professionals dealing with children with attachment disorder. Newsletter, phone support, information and referrals. Write: Attachment Disorder Parents Network, P.O. Box 18475, Boulder, CO 80308. Call (303)443-1446.

Federation of Families for Children's Mental Health *Nat'l. 122 affiliated groups. Founded 1989.* Parent-run organization that focuses on the needs of children and youth with emotional, behavioral or mental disorders and their families. Provides information, advocacy, newsletter, and conferences. Write: Federation of Families for Children's Mental Health, 1021 Prince St.,

Alexandria, VA 22314-2971. Call Barbara Huff (703)684-7710; FAX: (703)836-1040 *Website:* http://www.ffcmh.org *E-mail:* ffcmh@crosslink.net

National Alliance for the Mentally Ill (NAMI) *Nat'l. 1187 affiliates. Founded 1979.* Network of self-help groups that provide emotional and educational support for relatives and individuals affected by mental illness. Bi-monthly newsletter, affiliate development guidelines. Conducts anti-discrimination campaign. Write: NAMI, 200 N. Glebe Rd., #1015, Arlington, VA 22203-3754. Call 800-950-6264 (group referrals) or (703)524-7600; FAX: (703)524-9094; *Website:* http://www.nami.org *E-mail:* namioffc@nami.com

Relatives Project, The *Nat'l. 12 groups. Founded 1994.* Self-help group for families and friends of those with mental or emotional problems. Helps caregivers or those dealing with a troublesome relationship. Members learn coping skills and techniques to manage their own stress, create a peaceful domestic environment. Assistance in starting new groups. Write: Relatives Project, c/o Phyllis Berning, Abraham A. Low Institute, 550 Frontage Rd. #2797, Northfield, IL 60093. Call (847)441-0445; FAX: (847)441-0446.

Schizophrenia Society of Canada *Nat'l. 10 provincial chapters. Founded 1979.* Information, support and advocacy for families and friends of persons with schizophrenia. Conducts public awareness campaigns, advocacy events and fund-raising. Newsletter, guidelines and assistance for starting self-help groups, information and referrals, phone help, conferences, brochures, handbooks, and videos. Dues $5/yr. Write: Schizophrenia Soc. of Canada, 75 The Donway W. #814, Don Mills, Ontario Canada M3C 2E9. Call (416) 445-8204; FAX: (416)445-2270; *Website:* http://www.schizophrenia.ca

Spouse and Partners Council *Nat'l. 11 affiliated groups. Founded 1994.* Mutual support to help well spouses deal with their partner's mental illness through support groups and phone support. Provides advocacy, conferences, workshops. Assistance in starting groups available. Various dues. Sponsored by Nat'l Assn. for the Mentally Ill. Write: Spouses and Partners Council, P.O. Box 222, Augusta, Maine 04332. Call (207)622-5767 (voice/FAX). *E-mail:* jrdd@samtel.com

(Model) **FAIR (Family And Individual Reliance)** *5 groups in Texas. Founded 1981.* Offers mutual support groups statewide for family and friends of persons with present or past mental or emotional illness, with separate groups for persons with mental illness. Bi-annual retreat. Publishes "how-to" manual ($12). facilitators training manual ($5), and quarterly newsletter. Write: FAIR, c/o Mary Dees, MHA in Texas, 8401 Shoal Creek Blvd., Austin, TX 78757. Call (512)454-3706 or (512)454-3725.

(Model) **Parents Involved Network** *1 group in Philadelphia, PA. Founded 1984.* Parent-run, self-help/advocacy, information and referral for families of

children/adolescents who have emotional or behavioral disorders. Provides support, telephone information and referral, and linkage with other parents and parent organizations. Newsletter. Write: Parents Involved Network, 1211 Chestnut St., 11th fl., Philadelphia, PA 19107. Call 800-688-4226 or (215)751-1800; FAX: (215)636-6300; *E-mail:* fine@libertynet.org

(Model) **REACH ("Reassurance to Each")** *20 groups in Minnesota. Founded 1977.* Offers groups for families and friends of persons with mental illness, for education and information. Groups are free, confidential and open to new participants at any time. Information and technical assistance available for starting REACH Groups. Write: REACH, c/o MHA of MN, 205 W. 2nd St., #412, Duluth, MN 55802. Call (218)726-0793; 800-315-5375 (in MN); FAX: (218)727-1468.

MENTAL HEALTH (GENERAL)
(Also see Disabilities General, specific disorder)

16 Steps of Empowerment *Nat'l. 100+ groups. Founded 1992.* Offers support for a wide variety of quality of life issues, such as addiction, codependency, abuse, empowerment, etc. The 16 steps focus on a positive approach to help members celebrate personal strengths, have choices, stand up for themselves, heal physically, express love, and see themselves as part of the entire community, not just the recovery community. Write: 16 Steps of Empowerment, 362 N. Cleveland Ave., Suite 1, St. Paul, MN 55104. Call (612)645-5782; *Website:* http://members.aol.com/empower16/steps.htm *E-mail:* empower16@aol.com

C.U.S.A. (Catholics United for Spiritual Action) *Nat'l. 120 correspondence groups. Founded 1947.* Correspondence support groups for persons of all faiths with any type of handicap or chronic illness. Catholic in founding, but open to all. Emphasis on spiritual values and mutual support. Through group letters members find close relationships, understanding and courage. Dues $10/yr. (can be waived). Write: C.U.S.A., 176 W. 8th St., Bayonne, NJ 07002. Call Ann Marie (201)437-0412 (day); *E-mail:* ams4@juno.com

Disabled Artists' Network *Nat'l network. Founded 1985.* Mutual support and exchanging of information for professional visual artists with physical or mental disabilities. Provides information and referrals, pen pal program and reports to active members only. Write: Disabled Artists' Network, P.O. Box 20781, New York, NY 10025. Include self-addressed stamped envelope.

Emotional Health Anonymous *Nat'l. 50 chapters. Founded 1970.* Fellowship of people who meet to share experiences, strengths and hopes with each other so they may solve common problems of mental health. Patterned after the 12-step program of Alcoholics Anonymous. Group development guidelines and newsletter. Write: Emotional Health Anonymous, P.O. Box 429, Glendale, CA 91209-0429. Call (310)679-2671.

Emotions Anonymous *Int'l. 1300 chapters. Founded 1971.* Fellowship for people experiencing emotional difficulties. Uses the 12-step program sharing experience, strength and hopes in order to improve emotional health. Chapter development guideline, and catalog. Write: E.A., P.O. Box 4245, St. Paul, MN 55104-0245. Call (612)647-9712; *Website:* http://www.mtn.org/EA *E-mail:* eaisc@mtn.org

Friends' Health Connection *Nat'l network.* A communication support network that connects people of all ages with any disorder, illness or handicap. Also networks caretakers, families and friends. Members are networked with each other based on health problem, symptoms, hobbies, lifestyle, interests, occupation, location and other criteria, and communicate via letters, phone, tapes, e-mail, and face-to-face. It is intended for emotional support, not for romantic purposes. Fee $20 (optional). Write: Friend's Health Connection, P.O. Box 114, New Brunswick, NJ 08903. Call 800-483-7436; FAX: (908)249-9897; *E-mail:* fhc@pilot.njn.net *Website:* http://www.48friend.com

International Association for Clear Thinking (IACT) *Int'l. 100 chapters. Founded 1970.* For people interested in living their lives more effectively and satisfactorily. Uses principles of clear thinking and self-counseling. Newsletter, group handbook. chapter development kit, audio tapes, facilitator leadership training, and self-help materials available. Write: IACT, P.O. Box 1011, Appleton, WI 54912. Call (920)739-8311; FAX: (920)582-9783.

Recoveries Anonymous *Int'l. 20 groups. Founded 1983.* A solution-focused 12-step fellowship, designed especially for those who have yet to be successful in their search for recovery. For those who know the 12-steps work and want to learn how to use them. Open to anyone, including friends and family. Newcomer guide ($2); Group start-up kit ($25). Write: Recoveries Anonymous, P.O. Box 1212, Hewitt Sq. Stn., E. Northport, NY 11731. Call (516)261-1212.

Recovery, Inc. *Int'l. 700+ groups. Founded 1937.* A community mental health organization that offers a self-help method of will training; a system of techniques for controlling temperamental behavior and changing attitudes toward nervous symptoms, anxiety, depression, anger and fears. Publications for members. Information on starting groups and leadership training. Write: Recovery, Inc., 802 N. Dearborn St., Chicago, IL 60610. Call (312)337-5661; FAX: (312)337-5756; *E-mail:* spot@recovery-inc.com *Website:* http://www.recovery-inc.com

TARA (Total Aspects of Recovery Anonymous) *Int'l. 17 affiliated groups. Founded 1989.* 12-step recovery program to provide a loving and safe environment where members are free to address the entire spectrum of addictive and dysfunctional behaviors. Guidelines for developing groups. Write: TARA, 3799 Montclair, Cameron Park, CA 95682. Call (916)676-3366.

(Model) **CAIR (Changing Attitudes In Recovery)** *30 groups in California. Founded 1990.* A self-help "family" sharing a common commitment to gain healthy esteem. Includes persons with relationship problems, addictions, mental illness, etc. Offers new techniques and tools that lead to better self-esteem. Assistance in starting groups. Handbook ($9.95), audio tapes, and leader's manual. Write: Psych. Assoc. Press, 706 13th St., Modesto, CA 95354. Call (209)577-1667 (day); FAX: (209)577-3805.

(Model) **Enthusyattituditiks (En-thooz-e-at-ah-two-da-tiks)** *1 group in No. Carolina. Founded 1992.* Members support one another to live life with more enthusiasm, joy and laughter to share with less fortunate folks. Ideal for folks who have dealt with, and want to let go of their old struggles. Newsletter, phone support, group meetings, information and referrals. Dues $10. Provides help in starting groups. Handbook ($5). Send self-addressed envelope with inquiries. Write: Enthusyattituditiks, P.O. Box 907, Fletcher, NC 28732. Call Joyce Rue-Potter (704)687-3845.

(How-To Guide) **All Together: A Guide for Dissociative Identity Disorder Self-Help Groups.** Since there is no current national group for multiple personality/dissociative disorder, we are providing information on this 53-page how-to guide which was edited by Jody Szczech, and is available for $10 postpaid from: Clearinghouse For Self-Help Groups, 339 East Ave., Suite 201, Rochester, NY 14604; phone: (716)325-3145 ext. 14.

(Note) **Anger Control** is a concern for which we have received a significant number of inquiries. Regrettably, we are unaware of any national or model self-help support group that has yet been formed. If you learn of any existing groups that you would recommend, or are interested in starting such a group, please call the Clearinghouse.

(Note) **Compulsive Lying** is a concern for which we have received a significant number of inquiries. Regrettably, we are unaware of any national or model self-help support group that has yet been formed. If you learn of any existing groups that you would recommend, or are interested in starting such a group, please call the Clearinghouse.

"The deepest need of man is the need to overcome his separateness, to leave the prison of his aloneness."

- Erich Fromm

OBSESSIVE-COMPULSIVE DISORDER / TRICHOTILLOMANIA
(Also see Mental Health General)

Obsessive-Compulsive Anonymous *Nat'l. 50 affiliated groups. Founded 1988.* 12-step self-help group for people with obsessive-compulsive disorders. Assistance available for starting groups. Write: OCA, P.O. Box 215, New Hyde Park, NY 11040. Call (516)741-4901.

O.C. Foundation, Inc. *Nat'l. 8 chapters. Founded 1986.* Dedicated to early intervention in controlling and finding a cure for obsessive compulsive disorders and improving the welfare of people with OCD and other related OCD spectrum disorders. Provides education, research, mutual support, bi-monthly newsletter, and group development guidelines. Exchanges messages on Prodigy Medical BBS: Depression/Anxiety/OCD. Write: O.C. Fdn., P.O. Box 70, Milford, CT 06460-0070. Call (203)878-5669 (day); (203)874-3843 (recorded message); FAX: (203)874-2826; *Website:* http://pages.prodigy.com/alwillen.ocf.html *E-mail:* JPHS28A@prodigy.com

Trichotillomania Learning Center *Int'l. 61 affiliated groups. Founded 1991.* Information and support to patients, families and professionals about trichotillomania (compulsive hair pulling). Newsletter, information and referrals, phone support, pen pals, and literature. Provides assistance in starting similar groups. Write: TLC, 1215 Mission St., Suite 2, Santa Cruz, CA 95060. Call (408)457-1004; FAX: (408)426-4383.

(Model) **Council on Anxiety Disorders** *2 local groups in Georgia. Founded 1988.* Meetings provide education, support and encouragement for people with anxiety disorders. Packets are mailed nationwide that include personal stories, resource list of places to contact and information about treatment of panic disorder, phobias, obsessive-compulsive disorder, post-traumatic stress, separation anxiety, and general anxiety. Cassette tapes, quarterly newsletter, and group development guidelines. Write: Council on Anxiety Disorders, Route 1, Box 1364, Clarkesville, GA 30523. Call (706)947-3854; FAX: (706)947-1265; *E-mail:* slvau@stc.net

"Everything can be taken from a man but one thing; the last of the human freedoms--to choose one's attitude in any given set of circumstances, to choose one's own way. "

- Viktor Frankl

MISCELLANEOUS

"The man who needs no help is a lonely man indeed."
- Dagobert D. Runes

ACCIDENT / TRAUMA VICTIMS
(Also see Bereavement, Disabilities, Near Death)

Wings of Light, Inc. *Nat'l. 3 support networks. Founded 1995.* Support and information network for individuals whose lives have been touched by aircraft accidents. Separate networks for: airplane accident survivors; families and friends of persons killed in airplane accidents; and persons involved in rescue, recovery and investigation of crashes. Information and referrals, and phone support. Write: Wings of Light, 16845 N. 29th Ave., Suite 1-448, Phoenix, AZ 85023. Call 800-613-8531 or (602)516-1115; FAX: (602) 572-2511; *Website:* http://www.flightdata.com/wol *E-mail:* awaasings@aol.com

(Model) **Trauma Recovery, Inc.** *2 groups in Maryland. Founded 1979.* Mutual support for people recovering from serious injuries, and their family members. Offers emotional support, friendship and practical help with day-to-day problems. Write: Trauma Recovery, c/o Linda Wolfe, 1992 Gooseneck Rd., Pasadena, MD 21122. Call Linda Wolfe (410)255-3074.

(On-line Resource) **Car Accident Web Site** While not an online support group, rather a book promotion site, some stories of victims are shared here and web resources provided. (If you are a veteran of a traumatic car accident, and you are seriously interested in joining with others to start a support network to help new survivors, the American Self-Help Clearinghouse can help you.) Also available from us is a discounted copy of Jack Smith's book, "Car Accident: A Practical Recovery Manual" ($10 postpaid). *Website:* http://www.stresspress.com/car

(Note) **Post Traumatic Stress Disorder** is a concern for which we have received a significant number of inquiries. Regrettably, we are unaware of any national or model self-help support group that has yet been formed. If you learn of any existing groups that you would recommend, or are interested in starting such a group, please call the Clearinghouse.

AGING / OLDER PERSONS
(Also see Caregivers, Widowhood, Women, Toll-Free Numbers)

AARP (American Association of Retired Persons) *Nat'l. 4000 chapters. Founded 1958.* Non-profit membership organization dedicated to addressing the needs and interests of persons 50 and older. Seeks through education, advocacy and service to enhance the quality of life for all by promoting independence, dignity and purpose. Write: AARP, 601 E St., NW, Washington, DC 20049. Call (202)434-2277.

Gray Panthers *Nat'l. 62 chapters. Founded 1970.*   Multi-generational education and advocacy movement/organization that works to bring about fundamental social changes including a national health care system, elimination of all forms of discrimination, and economic justice. Newsletter, newspaper, chapter development guidelines. Dues $20/US; $35/Org; $40/Int'l. Write: Gray Panthers, 2025 Pennsylvania Ave., NW, #821, Washington, DC 20006. Call (202)466-3132; FAX (202)466-3133.

Older Women's League (OWL) *Nat'l. 80 chapters. Founded 1980.* Membership organization that advocates on behalf of various economic and social issues for midlife and older women (social security, pension rights, health insurance, employment, caregiver support, elder abuse, etc.). Newsletter, and chapter development guidelines. Dues $25/yr. Write: OWL, 666 11th St., NW, Washington, DC 20001. Call (202)783-6686 or 800-825-3695; FAX: (202) 638-2356.

Phenix Society *Int'l. 15 affiliated chapters. Founded 1973.*   Holistic and spiritually-oriented fellowship seeking to explore meaning, wisdom and potential of later years of life. Phenix Clubs aim to develop spiritually and improve quality of life through reading, weekly meetings and discussions. "Mind Expander" newsletter ($6). Club handbook, annual national meetings, and group development guidelines. Write: Phenix Soc., Box 351, Cheshire, CT 06410. Call (203)387-6913.

ARTISTIC CREATIVITY

ARTS Anonymous (Artists Recovering Through the Twelve Steps) *Int'l. 150 meetings throughout U.S. Founded 1984.*   A spiritual program based on the 12-steps and 12-traditions of A.A. The only requirement for membership is a desire to fulfill your creative potential. Retreats, literature, and meeting start-up guidelines. For meeting information, send self-addressed stamped envelope to: ARTS Anonymous, P.O. Box 175 Ansonia Station, NY, NY 10023-0175. (Outside NY, NJ, CT area include $2 and names of nearby cities or towns). With touch tone phone call (212)873-7075 (they will call back collect); *Website:* http://www.pagehost.com/ARTS *E-mail:* jaymark@brigadoon.com

CAREGIVERS
(Also see Aging, and specific health disorder)

CAPS (Children of Aging Parents) *Nat'l. 26 groups. Founded 1977.* Non-profit membership organization dedicated to the needs of caregivers of the elderly. National support network offers information, referral and counseling.

Bi-monthly newsletter-capsule and low-cost materials. Assistance in starting groups. Write: CAPS, 1609 Woodbourne Rd., Suite 302A, Levittown, PA 19057. Call 800-227-7294 or (215)945-6900; FAX: (215)945-8720.

National Family Caregivers Association   *Nat'l network. Founded 1992.* Dedicated to improving the quality of life for family caregivers. Networks members together for support. Provides information and referrals, resources, literature, and phone support. Dues $18/yr. Write: Nat'l Family Caregivers Assn., 9621 E. Bexhill Dr., Kensington, MD 20895-3014. Call (301)942-6430 or 800-896-3650; FAX: (301)942-2302; *Website:* http://www.nfcacares.org *E-mail:* info@nfcacares.org

Well Spouse Foundation   *Int'l. 90 support groups. Founded 1988.* Provides support and information to the well spouses of the chronically ill, educators, human service professionals and the public about the needs of spousal caregivers. Bi-monthly newsletter, round-robins, and guidelines and assistance for starting new groups. Write: Well Spouse Fdn., 610 Lexington Ave., #814, New York, NY 10022-6005. Call 800-838-0879 or (212)644-1241; FAX: (212)644-1338; *E-mail:* wellspouse@aol.com

(Model) **Advocacy Center for Long-Term Care**   *Statewide (Minnesota). Founded 1972.* Provides services to Minnesota-based consumer councils and their members through technical assistance to residents, families and staff in starting or improving councils. Provides workshops and training. Variety of printed resource materials on long-term care topics, how-to on starting Nursing Home Family Councils and Resident Councils, and catalog. Write: Advocacy Center for Long-Term Care, 2626 E. 82nd St., Suite 220, Bloomington, MN 55425. Call (612)854-7304; FAX: (612)854-8535.

(Model) **DEBUT (Daughters of Elderly Bridging the Unknown Together)** *1 group in Indiana. Founded 1981.* Support group designed by, and for, women struggling with the responsibilities, emotions, and decisions involved in the care of aging parents. Phone network, and weekly meetings. Write: DEBUT, Area 10 Agency on Aging, 7500 Reeves Rd., Bloomington, IN 47404-9688. Call Pat Meier (812)876-5319.

CAMPUS GROUPS

(Model) **Campus Support Groups Program** *Founded 1988.* Approximately 25 groups, on University of Illinois at Urbana-Champaign campus, address academic, health, cultural, women's and other issues. The program is sponsored by the Counseling Center and provides leadership training, logistical support, newsletter, and ongoing consultation. Training packet available. Some groups meet via computer, several with anonymous access. Offers a credit course in "Issues in Support Group Leadership" through the EdPsych Department. Write: Campus Support Groups Program, 232 Student Services Building, 610 E. John

St., Champaign, IL 61820. Call (217)244-0454 or (217)333-3704; FAX: (217) 244-9645; *E-mail:* cspg@uiuc.edu   *Website:* http://www.udos.uiuc.edu/ Counseling_center/csgp/csgphome.htm

CLUTTER / MESSINESS

Clutterers Anonymous *Nat'l. 15 affiliated groups. Founded 1989.* Mutual support to help people who have problems with clutter, compulsive saving, poor organization and procrastination, to help bring order into their lives and have more control over the state of their possessions. Also for concerned families and friends. Assistance in starting groups. Send self-addressed stamped business size envelope to: Clutterers Anonymous, P.O. Box 25884, Santa Ana, CA 92799-5884.

Messies Anonymous *Nat'l. 25 groups. Founded 1981.* 12-step group that aims to improve the quality of life of disorganized homemakers by providing motivation and a program for change to help members improve self-image as control of house and life is obtained. Optional dues. Quarterly newsletter ($16/2 years). Send a self addressed stamped envelope to: Messies Anonymous, 5025 SW 114th Ave., Miami, FL 33165. Call (305)271-8404; *E-mail:* SRFMA@aol.com

CODEPENDENCY

Co-Dependents Anonymous *Int'l. 3900+ groups worldwide. Founded 1986.* Twelve-step self-help program of recovery from co-dependency, where members share experience, strength, and hope in the effort to find freedom and peace in relationships with themselves and others. Newsletter ($8/yr). Library of literature and audio tapes. For group information in the United States call (602)277-7991; for international group information call (706)647-7736; FAX: (706)647-1755. For international information write: World Services of CoDA, P.O. Box 7051, Thomaston, GA 30286; *E-mail:* wscoda@alltel.net *Website:* http://www.ourcoda.org

Love-N-Addiction *Int'l. 73 chapters. Founded 1986.* Explores how loving can become an addiction. Builds a healthy support system to aid in recovery from addictive love into healthy love. Uses ideas from book "Women Who Love Too Much" by Robin Norwood. Chapter development guidelines ($15). Write: Love-N-Addiction, P.O. Box 759, Willimantic, CT 06226. Call Carolyn Meister (860)423-2344 (will return call collect or leave mailing address).

(Model) **CAIR (Changing Attitudes in Recovery)** *30 groups in CA. Founded 1990.* Self-help "family" sharing a common commitment to gain healthy esteem. Includes persons with relationship problems, addictions, mental illness, etc. Offers new techniques and tools that lead to better self-esteem: Assistance in

starting groups, handbook ($9.95), audio tapes, and leader's manual available. Write: Psych. Assoc. Press, 706 13th St., Modesto, CA 95354. Call (209)577-1667 (day); FAX: (209)577-3805.

CRIME VICTIMS / OFFENDERS
(Also see Bereavement General)

MADD (Mothers Against Drunk Driving) *Nat'l. 600+ chapters. Founded 1980.* The mission of MADD is to stop drunk driving and support victims of this violent crime. Newsletter, and chapter development guidelines. Write: MADD, 511 E. John Carpenter Freeway, #700, Irving, TX 75062-8187. Call (214)744-6233; FAX: (972)869-2206; victim hotline: 800-GET-MADD; *Website:* http://www.madd.org

National Organization for Victim Assistance *Nat'l. 3000 organizations and members. Founded 1975.* Support and advocacy for victims and survivors of violent crimes and disasters. Newsletter, information and referrals, phone help, conferences, and group development guidelines. Dues $30/ind; $100/org. Write: NOVA, 1757 Park Rd., NW, Washington, DC 20010. Call (202)232-6682; FAX: (202)462-2255; *E-mail:* nova@access.digex.net *Website:* http://www.access.digex.net/nova

National Victim Center *Nat'l. Founded 1985.* Provides crime victims with information, resources, and referrals to existing support groups. Quarterly newsletter, conferences, information and referrals. Write: Nat'l Victim Ctr., 2111 Wilson Blvd., #300, Arlington, VA 22201. Call 800-394-2255 (information and referrals) or (703)276-2880; FAX: (703)276-2889; *E-mail:* nvc@mail.nvc.org *Website:* http://www.nvc.org

Parents of Murdered Children *Nat'l. 300 chapters and contact persons throughout US and Australia. Founded 1978.* Provides self-help groups to support persons who survive the violent death of someone close, as they seek to recover. Publishes newsletter. Court accompaniment also provided in many areas. Write: POMC, 100 E. 8th St., B-41, Cincinnati, OH 45202. Call (513)721-5683 (office); FAX: (513)345-4489; *E-mail:* NatlPOMC@aol.com *Website:* http://www.metroguide.com/pomc

RID (Remove Intoxicated Drivers) *Nat'l. 152 chapters in 41 states. Founded 1978.* Citizens' project organized to advocate against drunk driving, educate the public, reform legislation and aid victims of drunk driving. Newsletter and chapter information kit ($20). For descriptive pamphlet send self-addressed stamped envelope. Write: RID, c/o Doris Aiken, P.O. Box 520, Schenectady, NY 12301. Call (518)372-0034 or (518)393-HELP; FAX: (518)370-4917.

S.O.S. (Survivors Of Stalking), Inc. *Nat'l network. Founded 1995.* Purpose is to assist persons affected by the crime of stalking and promote social change through education and public awareness. Newsletter, literature, information and referrals, advocacy, telephone support network. Write: S.O.S., P.O. Box 20762, Tampa, FL 33622-0762.   Call (813)889-0767 (Voice/FAX); *Website:* http://www.soshelp.org *E-mail:* soshelp@soshelp.orggate.net

(Model) **CASA (Cleptomaniacs And Shoplifters Anonymous)** *1 group in Michigan. Founded 1992.* Secular, non-12 step group for recovering shoplifters, kleptomaniacs and other persons suffering from dishonesty related to fraud, stealing or cheating. Pen pals, information and referrals, phone support and assistance in starting similar groups provided. Write: Terry S., 1955 Pine Ridge Lane, Bloomfield Hills, MI 48302. Call (810)855-8632 (eve); *E-mail:* shulmann@umich.edu *Website:* http://www.casa.com

(Model) **Fortune Society** *1 group in New York City. Founded 1967.* Support and education for ex-offenders. Provides substance abuse treatment, tutoring, employment assistance, AIDS/HIV education and services, counseling and court advocacy for parolees and probationers. Most of the counselors are ex-offenders and/or in recovery from drug addiction. Assistance for starting similar groups. Write: Fortune Soc., 39 W. 19th St., 7th fl., New York, NY 10011. Call (212)206-7070; FAX: (212)366-6323.

(Model) **Ontario Seventh Step Organization** *13 groups in Ontario. Founded 1978.* Sponsors groups in correctional facilities for inmates and street groups for "at risk" individuals. Uses a process of reconciliation for young and adult offenders who are, or may be in conflict with the law. Uses "hot seat" where people are questioned and confronted by their peers about their behavior and its repercussions. Members help each other talk out their resentments and modify their thinking. Honesty with self, thinking realistically and using personal strengths to reach goals are emphasized. Each group uses volunteers including non-con and ex-cons who have proven themselves by staying away from trouble. Write: Ontario Seventh Step Org., 1081 Bloor St. W., Toronto, Ontario M6H 1M5 Canada. Call (416)530-4311 (voice/FAX).

(Model) **Shoplifters Anonymous** *3 local groups in Minnesota. Founded 1980.* 12-step fellowship for those wishing to stop their compulsive stealing or shoplifting. Offers support and advice. Packet of information ($5). Write: S.A., P.O. Box 24515, Minneapolis, MN 55424. Call (612)925-4860; *E-mail:* mplssla@aol.com

(Model) **SOSAD (Save Our Sons And Daughters)** *1 group in Detroit, MI. Founded 1987.* Crisis intervention and violence prevention program that provides support and advocacy for survivors of homicide or other traumatic loss. Weekly bereavement groups, professional grief counseling and training, education on peace movement to youth, advocacy, and public education. Monthly newsletter, conferences, rallies and assistance in starting groups

provided. Write: SOSAD, 2441 W. Grand Blvd., Detroit, MI 48208-1210. Call (313)361-5200.

CULTS

(Resource) **reFOCUS (recovering FOrmer CUltists Support)** *Nat'l network. 20 independent groups. Founded 1984.* Support for former members of closed, high demand groups, relationships or cults. Referrals to independent support groups, other former cult members by group or area, therapists, services, and literature. Newsletter, workshops, conferences. Write: reFOCUS, P.O. Box 2180, Flagler Beach, FL 32136. Call (904)439-7541; FAX: (904)439-7537; *E-mail:* carol2180@aol.com   *Website:* http://members.aol.com/carol2180/refocus.htm or http://www.nwrain.net/ ~ refocus

DONORS' OFFSPRING (ARTIFICIAL INSEMINATION)
(Also see Infertility, Marriage)

Donors' Offspring, Inc. *Int'l. Founded 1981.* Information, support and reunion registry forms for sperm donors and offspring. Newsletter ($20 for 2 years), monthly national phone conference. Assistance in starting new groups. Write: Donor's Offspring, P.O. Box 37, Sarcoxie, MO 64862. Call (417)673-1906 (voice/FAX); *E-mail:* candace1@usa.net

DREAMSHARING

Community Dreamsharing Network   *Nat'l network. Founded 1987.* Information on dream-related activities. Helps community dream groups to recruit members and network. Participants in dream-sharing groups are often people seeking creative inspiration, warm friendship, social interaction, and internal self-guidance in their passage through a difficult life transition. Dream-sharing is not presented as psychotherapy. Professionals participate on same level as other group members. Quarterly networking newsletter ($10). Send $2 and self-addressed stamped envelope for sample to: Community Dreamsharing Network, P.O. Box 8032, Hicksville, NY 11802-8032. Call (516)735-1969; FAX: (516)731-2395.

EMPLOYMENT

9 to 5, National Association of Working Women *Nat'l. 26 chapters. Founded 1973.* Support, advocacy and legislative assistance on issues that affect women who work. Dues $25/yr. Phone support, conferences, newsletters. Hotline organizers can advise women on how to make changes on their jobs. Group development guidelines. Write: 9 to 5, 1430 W. Peachtree St., #610, Atlanta, GA 30309. Call Job Problem Hotline 800-522-0925 (day); FAX: (404)876-1649.

40 Plus of New York *Nat'l. 22 clubs. Founded 1939.* Mutual aid for unemployed managers, executives and professionals. Members must have earned at least $40,000 yearly. Career counseling, resume preparation, interviewing skills and mentoring provides. $100 application fee; $200 dues first 6 mos.; afterwards $100/per month (for office expenses). Also groups in 12 other states (CA, CO, HI, IL, MN, OH, OR, PA, TX, UT, WA, Wash. DC, and Canada) Write: 40 Plus of NY, 15 Park Row, New York, NY 10038. Call (212)233-6086; FAX: (212)227-2974; *E-mail:* 40+ny@quicklink.com

Business and Professional Women/USA *Nat'l. 2800 chapters. Founded 1919.* Organization comprised of working women, to promote workplace equity and provide networking opportunities. Lobbying efforts, tri-annual magazine, periodic publications, resource center, and grassroots community action projects. National convention held annually. Membership dues $31. Write: Business and Professional Women, 2012 Massachusetts Ave., NW, Washington, DC 20036. Call (202)293-1100; FAX: (202)861-0298; *Website:* http://www.bpwusa.org

(Model) **Employment Support Center** *7 groups in Washington, DC area. Founded 1984.* Provides technical assistance for self-help groups for the unemployed, underemployed, and those in job transition. Trains leadership for groups. Maintains extensive network of group leaders, employment professionals, job seekers. Job bank, consultations, network meetings and programs, small business seminars, newsletter, self-help and job search sessions. "Self-Help Bridge to Employment" manual ($25 prepaid). Write: ESC, 711 8th St., NW, Washington, DC 20001. Call (202)628-2919; FAX: (202)628-2920; *E-mail:* jobseekers@hotmail.com

(Model) **Job Transition Support Group** *1 group in Minnesota. Founded 1976.* Support and encouragement for people laid off from their jobs, or seeking a change. Weekly meetings include speakers' presentations and small group discussions. Facilitated by volunteers who have experienced job termination or transition. Group development guidelines ($5). Write: Job Transition Support Group, c/o Colonial Church of Edina, 6200 Colonial Way, Edina, MN 55436. Call (612)925-2711 (Church); FAX: (612)925-1591.

(Model) **MATCH (Mother's Access To Careers at Home)** *2 affiliated groups in Virginia and Maryland. Founded 1990.* Provides networking, business and emotional support and advocacy for mothers who have, or wish to pursue, careers from home. Newsletter, information and referrals, phone support, special interest groups, and assistance in starting new groups. Write: Caroline Hull, MATCH, 11913 Millpond Ct., Manassas, VA 20112-3285. Call (703)205-9664.

(Model) **Philadelphia Unemployment Project** *1 group in Philadelphia, PA. Founded 1975.* Membership organization comprised of unemployed workers. Provides information, support and advocacy, assistance with mortgages, food vouchers and job clubs with possible leads to jobs. Helps uninsured people find

health care; works for better health access overall. Provides assistance in starting similar groups. Write: Philadelphia Unemployment Project, 116 South Seventh St., #610, Philadelphia, PA 19106. Call (215)592-0933; FAX: (215)592-7537; *E-mail:* pupuic@libertynet.org

(Model) **Shoulder to Shoulder** *1 group in Connecticut. Founded 1991.* Support for female partners of the unemployed or underemployed persons. Provides emotional support, networking, phone pals, and referrals to local services. Deals with stress and coping skills. Assistance in starting similar groups. Write: c/o Donna Montelle, River Rd., Killingworth, CT 06419; phone: (203)421-5799; or Maryann Grimaldi, P.O. Box 304, Madison, CT 06443; phone: (203)245-3920; FAX: (203)245-3926.

(Model) **Women Employed** *1 group in Chicago, IL. Founded 1973.* Promotes economic advancement for women through service, education and advocacy. Provides career development services, job bank, career counseling, networking, conferences to link women, quarterly newsletter, and publications list. Dues $35-$45. Write: Women Employed, 22 W. Monroe St., #1400, Chicago, IL 60603-2505. Call (312)782-3902; FAX: (312)782-5249.

FOOD CO-OPS

World SHARE (Self-Help And Resource Exchange) *Int'l. 26 U.S. affiliates. Founded 1983.* Builds healthy communities by creating opportunities and incentives, through self-help activities, for people to participate together in solving community problems. Provides access to affordable food and supplies volunteer services to communities. By donating just two hours a month to a community activity, participants can save 50% on a monthly food package. Group development guidelines. Write: World SHARE, 6950 Friars Rd., San Diego, CA 92108. Call (619)686-5818; FAX: (619)686-5815; *E-mail:* info@wshare.com

HAZARDOUS WASTE
(Also see Toll-Free Specialty Numbers)

CCHW Center for Health, Environment and Justice *(formerly Citizen's Clearinghouse for Hazardous Wastes) Nat'l. 7,000 groups. Founded 1981.* Grassroots environmental crisis center, providing information and networking for people affected by toxic waste. Assists in organizing self-help groups; provides them with scientific and technical backup. Holds conferences, and provides information and referrals. Newsletters. Write: CCHW, P.O. Box 6806, Falls Church, VA 22040. Call (703)237-2249; *E-mail:* cchw@essential.org *Website:* http://www.essential.org/cchw

LIGHTNING / SHOCK
(Also see Accident/Trauma, Bereavement, Disabilities)

Lightning Strike and Electric Shock Survivors Int'l, Inc. *Int'l network. Founded 1989.* Mutual support for survivors of lightning or electric shock, their families and family members of non-survivors. Studies the long-term after effects. Information and referrals, phone support, annual conferences, help in starting support groups. Newsletter. Write: LS&ESSI Inc., 214 Canterbury Rd., Jacksonville, NC 28540-5307. Call Steve Marshburn, Sr. (910)346-4708 (voice/FAX); *E-mail:* Lighting@internet.net *Website:* http://www.mindspring.com/~lightingstrike

MALPRACTICE

(Model) **Litigation Stress Support Group** *1 group in New Jersey. Founded 1986.* Peer support and networking for doctors, dentists and their families going through malpractice suits. Telephone support network. Assistance in starting similar groups. Write: Litigation Stress Support Group, 2 Princess Rd., Lawrenceville, NJ 08648. Call (609)896-1766 (day); FAX: (609)896-1884.

MEN
(Also see Separation/Divorce, Parenting)

Bald-Headed Men of America *Nat'l. 6 affiliated groups. Founded 1973.* Self-help group that instills pride in being bald. Exchanging feelings and experiences through group discussions have led to acceptance of being bald. "We believe the best cure for baldness is to promote a positive mental attitude...with humor." Annual conference held 2nd weekend in Sept. Newsletter. Write: Bald-Headed of America, 102 Bald Dr., Morehead City, NC 28557. Call (919)726-1855; FAX: (919)726-6061; *E-mail:* jcapps410v@aol.com

National Men's Resource Center *Nat'l network. Founded 1982.* Resource center that focuses on men's issues, organizations, publications, research, conferences, and special events for men. Maintains events calendar on website. Write: Nat'l Men's Resource Ctr., P.O. Box 800-SW, San Anselmo, CA 94979-0800; *Website:* http://www.menstuff.org *E-mail:* menstuff@aol.com

National Organization for Men *Nat'l. 50 chapters. Founded 1983.* Seeks equal rights for men, uniform national divorce, custody, property and visitation law. Lawyer referral. Conducts educational seminars. Quarterly newsletter. Write: Nat'l Org. for Men, 11 Park Place, New York, NY 10007. Call (212)686-MALE or (212)766-4030; *Website:* http://www.tnom.com

NOHARMM (National Organization to Halt the Abuse and Routine Mutilation of Males) *Nat'l. 30 affiliated groups. Founded 1992.* Advocacy and education for men concerned about circumcision. Empowers men to speak out for the rights of children to have body ownership. Discussion groups for affected men, and for men undergoing restoration. Provides information and referrals, newsletter, literature, and help in starting groups. Write: NOHARMM, P.O. Box 460795, San Francisco, CA 94146. Call (415)826-9351; FAX: (415)642-3700.

NORM (National Organization of Restoring Men) *(formerly RECAP) Int'l. 13+ affiliated groups. Founded 1989.* (Meetings for MEN ONLY; information for all) Provides a safe environment in which men can, without fear of being ridiculed, share their concerns about circumcision/restoration and for a desire to be intact and whole again. Confidential discussions of goals and methods of restoration, information and referrals, phone support, and assistance in starting new groups. Write: NORM, c/o R. Wayne Griffiths, 3205 Northwood Dr. #209, Concord, CA 94520-4506. Call (510)827-4077 (eve); FAX: (510)827-4119; *E-mail:* waynerobb@aol.com

(How-To Guide) **Men's Friends: How to Organize and Run Your Own Men's Support Group.** Since, to our knowledge, there are few national associations of men's self-help groups, we are providing information on this helpful how-to guide. Written by Bill Kauth, the manual has 27 chapters. (You need only read the first five to start the group.) Copies are available for $17.50 postpaid from: Men's Awareness, 8120 S. 68th St., Franklin, WI 53132.

NEAR DEATH EXPERIENCE
(Also see Accident/Trauma)

IANDS (International Association for Near-Death Studies) *Int'l. 35 affiliated groups. Founded 1981.* Support group for anyone who has had a near-death experience, their families and professionals working with them. Information and education for interested public. Promotes research. Newsletter, referrals, and group development guidelines. Write: IANDS, P.O. Box 502, E. Windsor Hill, CT 06028-0502. Call (860)528-5144; FAX (860)528-9169; *Website:* http://www.iands.org/iands

NEIGHBORHOOD / HOUSING

(Resource) **ACORN** is a non-profit network of neighborhood development and housing organizations across the country run by and for low and moderate income people. Write: ACORN, 739 8th St., SE, Washington, DC 20003. Call (202)547-9292; *Website:* http://www.acorn.com

(Resource) **Community Information Exchange** provides help to neighborhood groups in the form of housing and community development technical assistance and information. Newsletter, computer bulletin board. Membership $50 for

community organization. Write: Comm. Info. Exchange, 1029 Vermont Ave., N.W., Washington, DC 20005. Call (202)628-2981; FAX: (202)783-1485.

PATIENTS RIGHTS

(Model) **New England Patients' Rights Group** *1 group in Massachusetts. Founded 1993.* Mutual support for healthcare consumers, many of whom are suffering because of deficiencies or negligence in the system. Advocates for consumer empowerment, quality, accurate information, informed consent, insurance needs, patients' rights and protection. Newsletter. Write: New England Patients Rights Group, P.O. Box 141, Norwood, MA 02062. Call (617)769-5720; FAX: (617)769-0882.

PEOPLE OF COLOR

(Model) **BEBASHI (Blacks Educating Blacks About Sexual Health Issues)** *1 group in Philadelphia. Founded 1985.* Information and education among the African American and Latino communities about sexual health issues, especially HIV/AIDS. Peer-counseling, guest speakers, workshops, phone help, testing, social services, support groups. Write: BEBASHI, 1233 Locust St., Suite #401, Philadelphia, PA 19107-5414. Call (215)546-4140; FAX: (215)546-6107.

POLICE OFFICERS

Spouses of Police Officers *Int'l. 20 affiliated groups. Founded 1996.* Safe and supportive network where spouses of police officers can share their issues and concerns. Information and referrals provided to various services for law enforcement families. Phone support, parenting skills education, literature, seminars, conferences, and newsletter ($12), and assistance in starting similar groups. Referrals to support groups nationwide. Write: Spouses of Police Officers, c/o Sue Woods, 4715 Strack Rd., Suite 213, Houston, TX 77069. Call (281) 895-0088; FAX: (281)895-0099; *Website:* http://www.murlin.com/~webfx/sopo.

PREJUDICE

(Model) **Racism and Bigotry Anonymous** *2 groups in California. Founded 1990.* 12-step program designed to heal the hurt/pain experienced as a result of racism and bigotry. Provides context for anyone willing to come out of denial of how they have been hurt/shamed by the painful effects of racism/bigotry. Phone support, information and referrals, and assistance in starting groups. Write: Racism and Bigotry Anonymous, P.O. Box 23091-0091, Oakland, CA 94623. Call Maurice B. 800-587-4207; FAX: (415)929-9386.

PROSTITUTION / SEX INDUSTRY

(Model) **PRIDE (from PRostitution to Independence, Dignity and Equality)** *1 group in Minnesota. Founded 1978.* Provides PRIDE support groups and other services to assist women and children in escaping the sex industry (including prostitution, pornography and stripping). Write: PRIDE, c/o Family and Children Service, 3125 E. Lake St., Minneapolis, MN 55406. Call Kristin (612)728-2064 or (612)728-2062 (24 hr. crisis line; collect calls accepted); FAX: (612)729-2616.

SEXUAL ORIENTATION / GAY & LESBIAN

COLAGE (Children Of Lesbians And Gays Everywhere) *Nat'l. 35 affiliated groups. Founded 1990.* Support and advocacy run by and for daughters and sons of lesbian and gay parents. Helps with custody cases. Information and referrals, phone support, conferences, pen pals, literature, and newsletter. Dues $10. Assistance in starting new groups provided. Write: COLAGE, 2300 Market St., #165, San Francisco, CA 94114. Call (415)861-KIDS; FAX: (415)255-8345; *E-mail:* colage@colage.org *Website:* http://www.colage.org

COURAGE *Int'l. 56 groups. Founded 1980.* Provides spiritual support and fellowship for men and women with homosexual tendencies who are striving to live chaste lives in accordance with the Roman Catholic Church's teachings. The companion group, EnCourage, is for families and friends. Newsletter, phone help, conferences, assistance in starting groups. Write: COURAGE, c/o St. Michael's Rectory, 424 W. 34th St., NY, NY 10001. Call (212)421-0426; FAX: (212)268-7150; *E-mail:* NYCourage@aol.com *Website:* http://www.allencol.edu/pastoral/courage.htm/

Dignity/USA *Nat'l. 88 chapters. Founded 1969.* Organization of lesbian, bisexual and gay Catholics, their families and friends. Concerned with spiritual development, feminism, education and advocacy. Newsletter, and chapter development guidelines. Write: Dignity/USA, 1500 Massachusetts Ave., NW #11, Washington, DC 20005. Call 800-877-8797; FAX: (202)429-9808; *E-mail:* dignity@aol.com

Gay and Lesbian Parents Coalition Int'l *Int'l. 103 affiliated groups. Founded 1979.* Support, education and advocacy for gay and lesbian parents and prospective parents, and their families. Support group meetings, information and referrals, phone support, conferences, pen pals, literature, newsletter, and assistance in starting groups. Dues $10-25. Write: Gay and Lesbian Parents Coalition Int'l, Box 50360, Washington, DC 20091. Call (202)583-8029 (24 hrs); FAX: (301)907-4737; *E-mail:* glpcinat@ix.netcom.com *Website:* http://www.glpci.org

Homosexuals Anonymous *Nat'l. 55 chapters. Founded 1980.* An Anti-homosexual Christian fellowship of men and women who have chosen to help each other to live free from homosexuality. Group support through weekly meetings provided. Newsletter, and chapter manual. Write: Homosexuals Anonymous, P.O. Box 7881, Reading, PA 19603. Call (610)376-1146 or 800-288-HAFS.

International Foundation for Gender Education *Int'l. 264 affiliates. Founded 1987.* Mutual support for cross-dressers and transsexuals and their families, through education, information and cooperative action. Telephone crisis line, research library, information and referrals, peer counseling, conferences, newsletter, magazine and literature. Write: Int'l Fdn. for Gender Education, P.O. Box 229, Waltham, MA 02254-0229. Call (617)899-2212 or (617)894-8340; FAX: (617)899-5703; *E-mail:* ifge@world.std.com *Website:* http://www.transgender.org/tg/ifge/index.html (information and referrals) or http://www.tiac.net/users/dba/ifge/ifge.htm (bookstore)

Intersex Society of North America *Int'l. 2 affiliated chapters. Founded 1993.* Provides peer support for intersexuals to overcome the stigma of the condition and education for parents and professionals to provide better care. Newsletter, information and referrals, phone support, literature, advocacy, support group meetings. Internet mailing list to network members. Write: Intersex Soc. of N. Amer., P.O. Box 31791, San Francisco, CA 94131. Call (415)436-0585; *Website:* http://www.isna.org *E-mail:* info@isna.org

National Gay and Lesbian Task Force *Nat'l. Founded 1973.* Advocacy and lobbying for the rights of gays, lesbians, bisexuals and transgendered persons. Technical assistance for state and local gay groups. Information and referral to organizations nationwide. Education to raise public awareness. Newsletter. Write: Nat'l Gay and Lesbian Task Force, 2320 17th St., NW, Washington, DC 20009-2702. Call (202)332-6483; FAX: (202)332-0207; TTY: (202)332-6910. *Website:* http://www.ngltf.org *E-mail:* ngltf@ngltf.org

P-FLAG (Parents, Families and Friends of Lesbians and Gays) *Int'l. 420 chapters worldwide. Founded 1981.* Helps families understand and accept gay family members. Help in strengthening families, support groups for families and friends, educational outreach, newsletter, chapter development guidelines, family AIDS groups, grassroots advocacy, information and referrals. Dues $30. Write: P-FLAG, 1101 14th St., NW, Suite 1030, Washington, DC 20005. Call (202)638-4200; FAX: (202)638-0243; *E-mail:* info@pflag.org *Website:* http://www.pflag.org

Renaissance Education Association, Inc. *Nat'l. 4 chapters; 12 affiliated groups. Founded 1987.* Mutual support group for both transvestites and transsexuals. Networks with other support groups. Information and referrals, phone support, pen pals, newsletter ($24/yr), and assistance in starting new groups. Write: Renaissance Education Assn., 987 Old Eagle School Rd., Suite 719, Wayne, PA 19087. Call (610)975-9119 (day/eve); FAX: (610)971-0144; *Website:* http://www.ren.org *E-mail:* bensalem@bbs.cpcn.com

Society for the Second Self *Nat'l. 31 chapters. Founded 1976.* Organization offering support and companionship for heterosexual crossdressers and their wives and girlfriends. Emphasizes privacy and confidentiality of membership. Pen pal program, newsletter, chapter development guidelines, and membership directory. Conducts annual convention for crossdressers and their wives. Write: Soc. for Second Self, Box 194, Tulare, CA 93275. Call (209)688-9246 (eve); *E-mail:* mb@genie.geis.com

Straight Spouse Support Network (SSSN) *Int'l network. 33 groups and 50 state/country contacts. Founded 1991.* Confidential support network of heterosexual women and men, formerly or currently married to gay, lesbian, bisexual or transgender partners. Helps spouses cope with the coming-out crisis, and assists in building bridges of understanding for mixed-orientation couples and their children. Information and referrals, and newsletter. Write: SSSN, 8215 Terrace Dr., El Cerrito, CA 94530-3058. Call (510)525-0200; *E-mail:* khgt90A@prodigy.com *Website:* http://www.glpci.org/ ~ sssn

(Model) **Your Turf** *1 group in Connecticut. Founded 1979.* Rap group for teenage gays, lesbians and bisexuals. Provides a safe area for teens to deal with same-sex orientation. Peer-counseling, social activities, and group development guidelines. Write: Your Turf, c/o Hartford Gay and Lesbian Health Collective, 1841 Broad St., Hartford, CT 06114. Call (860)278-4163; FAX: (860)724-3443; TTY: (860)278-4163; *E-mail:* THC@Hartnet.org

SHORT / TALL
(Also see specific disorder)

Growth Hormone Deficiency Support Network *Nat'l network. Founded 1989.* Network and exchange of information for families of children with growth hormone deficiency disorders. Information and referrals, phone support, pen pals, conferences, literature, newsletter ($20/yr). Write: c/o MAGIC Foundation, 1327 N. Harlen, Oak Park, IL 60303. Call 800-3-MAGIC-3; *Website:* http://www.nettap.com/ ~ magic *E-mail:* magic@nettap.com

Human Growth Foundation *Nat'l. 48 chapters. Founded 1965.* Local chapters provide members the opportunity to meet other parents of children with growth related disorders. Mutual sharing of problems, research and public education. Monthly and quarterly newsletter, and chapter development guidelines. Write: Human Growth Fdn., 7777 Leesburg Pike, Falls Church, VA 22043. Call (703)883-1773 or 800-451-6434; FAX: (703)883-1776; *E-mail:* hgfound@erols.com

Little People of America *Nat'l. 40 chapters. Founded 1957.* Dedicated to helping people of short stature. Provides fellowship, moral support, and information for people whose height is 4 feet 10 inches or under. Teenagers program, parent support groups, newsletter. Write: Little People of America, P.O. Box 9897, Washington, DC 20016. Call 888-LPA-2001.

MAGIC Foundation for Children's Growth, The *Nat'l network. Founded 1989.* Provides public education and networking for families of children with growth-related disorders. Provides information and referrals, phone support, pen pals, and conferences. Write: The MAGIC Foundation, 1327 N. Harlen, Oak Park, IL 60303. Call 800-3-MAGIC-3; *Website:* http://www.nettap.com ~ magic *E-mail:* magic@nettap.com

Tall Clubs International *Int'l. 61 groups. Founded 1938.* Social support for tall persons, men at least 6'2", women at least 5'10". Also advocacy for clothing and other special needs of tall people. Sky riders program for persons under 21. Group development guidelines, information and referrals, conferences, and newsletters. Write: Tall Clubs Int'l, P.O. Box 1964, Bloomfield, NJ 07003-1964. Call 888-468-2552; *Website:* http://tall. org or http://www.bluplanet.com/tallweb/

SPEECH / STUTTERING
(Also see Anxiety/Phobias, and specific disorder)

International Foundation for Stutterers, Inc. *Int'l. 6 chapters. Founded 1980.* Aims to eliminate stuttering through speech therapy in conjunction with self-help groups. Provides education for public and professionals about stuttering and self-help. Newsletter, speakers, phone help system, guidelines on forming self-help groups. Write: Int'l Fdn. for Stutterers, P.O. Box 462, Belle Mead, NJ 08502. Call Elliot Dennis (609)275-3806 (eve).

National Stuttering Project *Nat'l. 79 groups. Founded 1977.* Provides information about stuttering. Self-help chapter meetings provide supportive environment where people who stutter can learn to communicate more effectively. Networking of groups. Referrals, advocacy, monthly newsletter, and group development guidelines. Dues $35/20 senior/student/low income. Write: Nat'l Stuttering Project, 5100 E. LaPalma, Suite 208, Anaheim Hills, CA 92807. Call 800-364-1677; FAX: (714)693-7554; *E-mail:* NSPMAIL@aol.com *Website:* http://members.aol.com/nsphome

Selective Mutism Foundation, Inc. *Nat'l network. Founded 1992.* Mutual support for parents of children with selective mutism, a psychiatric anxiety disorder in which children are unable to speak in social situations. Also open to adults who have, or outgrew, the disorder. Information, phone support, quarterly newsletter. Send self-addressed stamped envelope with 2 stamps to: Sue Newman, P.O. 450632, Sunrise, FL 33345-0632; call (954)748-7714 or

Carolyn Miller, P.O. Box 13133, Sissonville, WV 25360; call (304)984-3971; *E-mail:* tbroadb594@aol.com *Website*: http://www.home.aol.com/tbroad.594

Speak Easy International Foundation, Inc. *Int'l. 8 chapters. Founded 1981.* Self-help group for adult and adolescent stutterers. Must have speech dysfunction or phobia. Phone network, peer counseling, newsletter. Conducts annual national symposium. Dues $60/yr. Write: Antoinette and Bob Gathman, 233 Concord Dr., Paramus, NJ 07652. Call Antoinette or Bob (201)262-0895.

TALK (Taking Action Against Language Disorders for Kids) *Int'l network. Founded 1992.* Resource network for parents of children with speech and language impairments (e.g. Asperger, autism, Landau-Kleffner, apraxia, etc.) Advocacy, networking of parents, newsletter, phone support, sibling support, information and resources. Dues $10/year. Write: TALK, 22980 Donna Lane, Bend, OR 97701. Call (541)389-0004.

Toastmasters International *Int'l. 8000 chapters. Founded 1924.* Mutual help for people to improve speaking skills, express themselves more effectively and to gain confidence. For those who are hesitant to speak before an audience. Leadership training and monthly magazine. Various membership fees. Write: Toastmasters Int'l, P.O. Box 9052, Mission Viejo, CA 92690-7052. Call (714)858-8255; FAX: (714)858-1207; *Website:* http://www.toastmasters.org

VETERANS / MILITARY

Blinded Veterans Association *Nat'l. 50 regional groups. Founded 1945.* Offers information, support and outreach to blinded veterans. Provides help in finding jobs, information on benefits and rehabilitation programs. Bi-monthly newsletter, and chapter development guidelines. Regional meetings held. Write: BVA, 477 H St., NW, Washington, DC 20001. Call (202)371-8880 or 800-669-7079; FAX: (202)371-8258; *E-mail:* bva@bva.org

Disabled American Veterans *Nat'l. 2221 chapters. Founded 1920.* Assists veterans in gaining benefits earned in military service. Sponsors self-help groups for all disabled veterans and their families. Supports legislation benefiting disabled vets. Bi-monthly magazine and guidelines for developing groups. Write: Disabled American Veterans, P.O. Box 14301, Cincinnati, OH 45250-0301. Call (606)441-7300; FAX: (606)442-2090; TDD: (202)554-3501; *E-mail:* ahdav@one.net *Website:* http://www.dav.org

Friends of the Vietnam Veterans Memorial *Nat'l network. Founded 1986.* Locator and networking services for families, friends and fellow veterans of those who died in Vietnam. Program to honor those whose names are not on Memorial, but died as a result of their experience in Vietnam. Provides newsletter, name rubbings from Vietnam Memorial, and referrals. Write: FVVM, 2030 Clarendon Blvd. #412, Arlington, VA 22201. Call

(703)525-1107; *Website:* http://www.sersoft.com/vietwall or http://www .vietwall.org *E-mail:* vietwall@aol.com

National Gulf War Resource Center, Inc. *Int'l. 22 affiliated groups. Founded 1995.* Supports the efforts of grassroot organizations that assist veterans affected by the Persian Gulf War. Conducts research into the causes of Gulf War Syndrome. Information and referrals, advocacy, phone support, and literature provided. Write: Nat'l Gulf War Resource Ctr., P.O. Box 823, Decatur, GA 30031; phone: (404)373-5507; FAX: (404)373-5527, or 1224 M St., NW, Washington, DC 20005. Call (202)628-2700 ext. 162; FAX: (202)628-6997; *Website:* http://www.gulfweb.org

Society of Military Widows *Nat'l. 27 chapters. Founded 1968.* Support and assistance for widows/widowers of members of all U.S. uniformed services. Helps in coping with adjustment to life on their own. Promotes public awareness. Newsletter and chapter development guidelines. Dues $12. Write: Soc. of Military Widows, 5535 Hempstead Way, Springfield, VA 22151. Call (703)750-1342; *Website:* http://www.penfed.org/naus/home.htm

Vietnam Veterans of America, Inc. *Nat'l. 600 chapters. Founded 1978.* Devoted to the needs and concerns of Vietnam era veterans and their families. Leadership and advocacy in all areas that have an impact on veterans, with an emphasis on Agent Orange related problems and post traumatic stress disorder. Monthly newspaper, and group development guidelines. Write: Vietnam Veterans of America, 1224 M St., NW, Washington, DC 20005-5183. Call (202)628-2700; *Website:* http://www.vva.org *E-mail:* 71154.702@ compuserve.com

WOMEN
(Also see Employment)

National Organization for Women *Nat'l. 600+ chapters. Founded 1966.* Organization of women and men committed to equal rights. Provides advocacy, educational meetings, national newsletter, and chapter development guidelines. Write: NOW, 1000 16th St., N.W. #700, Washington, DC 20036. Call (202)331-0066: FAX: (202)785-8576; TDD: (202)331-9002; *E-mail:* now@now.org *Website:* http://www.now.org

(Model) **SOWN (The Supportive Older Women's Network)** *50 groups in Philadelphia area. Founded 1982.* Helps women (60+) cope with their specialized aging concerns through support groups, leadership training, consultation, outreach and networking. Newsletter. Write: SOWN, 2805 N. 47th St., Philadelphia, PA 19131. Call (215)477-6000; FAX: (215)477-6555; *E-mail:* sown@erols.com

YOUTH / STUDENTS
(Also see Addictions, Toll-Free Specialty Numbers)

International Youth Council *Int'l. 30 chapters. Founded 1972.* Brings teens from single parent homes together to share ideas and problems, develop leadership skills, and plan fun activities. Networking and guidelines for starting groups. Sponsored by local chapters of Parents Without Partners. Write: Int'l Youth Council, c/o PWP, 401 N. Michigan Ave., Chicago, IL 60611-4267. Call 800-637-7974 (Parents Without Partners).

Just Say No International *Int'l. 13,000 clubs. Founded 1985.* Through its youth power empowerment and leadership model, provides youth with skills necessary to form teams that identify problems, assess, plan and implement service activities in their schools and communities. "Just Say No" provides training, materials, on-going consultation and membership. Supports youth to lead healthy, productive, drug-free lives. Write: Just Say No, 2000 Franklin St., #400, Oakland, CA 94612. Call 800-258-2766; FAX: (510)451-9360; *E-mail:* youth@justsayno.org

MAD DADS, Inc. (Men Against Destruction Defending Against Drugs and Social-disorder) *Nat'l. 49 affiliated groups. Founded 1989.* Grass-roots organization of fathers aimed at fighting gang- and drug-related violence. Provides family activities, community education, speaking engagements, and "surrogate fathers" who listen to and care about street teens. Assistance in starting groups. Also groups for kids, mothers, grandparents. Write: MAD DADS, c/o Eddie Staton, 3030 Sprague St., Omaha, NE 68111. Call (402)451-3500; FAX: (402)451-3477; *Website:* http://maddadsnational.com *E-mail:* maddadsnational@infinity.com

SADD (Students Against Destructive Decisions) *Nat'l. 25,000 groups. Founded 1982.* To help eliminate drunk driving, end underage drinking and drug abuse, alert students to dangers of alcohol use and its resulting consequences, and to organize peer counseling programs for students concerned about alcohol and drugs. Newsletter, and group development guidelines. Special programs include "Student Athletes Detest Drugs." Write: SADD, P.O. Box 800, Marlboro, MA 01752. Call (508)481-3568; FAX: (508)481-5759.

"The sea rises, the light fails, lovers cling to each other, and children cling to us. The moment we cease to hold each other, the moment we break faith with one another, the sea engulfs us and the light goes out."
- James Baldwin

LAST MINUTE ENTRIES

AGING

Consumers United for Assisted Living   *Nat'l. Chapters in development. Founded 1997.* Emotional support, information and education for frail elderly residents in assisted living facilities, and their families. Newsletter, materials and referrals. Write: CUAL, 10300 Eaton Place, Suite 310, Fairfax, VA 22030. Call (703)691-9278; FAX: (703)691-8592.

ALCOHOL

Recovered Alcoholic Clergy Association   *Nat'l network. Founded 1965.* Network of Episcopal clergy supporting one another in recovery from alcoholism. Networking, semi-annual national meetings, local networking groups. Newsletter. Call 800-944-2979; *E-mail*: racatown@willowtree.com *Website*: http://www.geocities.com/HotSprings/88721

LANDMINE SURVIVORS

Landmind Survivors Network   *Int'l network. Founded 1997.* Network of landmine survivors providing help to one another. Maintains a database of medical facilities, prosthetic clinics and rehabilitation projects available to help victims. Write: Landmine Survivors Network, 1701 K St., NW, Suite 805, Washington, DC 20006. *Website*: http://www.landminesurvivors.org

NYSTAGMUS

(Online) **American Nystagmus Network** Online mailing list for persons with nystagmus (an involuntary rapid movement of the eyeball), affected families and interested professionals. Informal communication via listserv.   *Website:* http://www.fas.harvard.edu/~jbeall

POST-INSTITUTIONALIZED CHILDREN

Parent Network for the Post-Institutionalized Child   *Int'l network. Founded 1993.* Support and information for families who have children from hospitals, orphanages, and other institutions for the irrecuperable children of economically deprived countries, and who are now exhibiting emotional and behavioral problems resulting from such deprivation. Newsletter. Write: P.O. Box 613, Meadow Lands, PA 15347. Call (412)222-1766 (area code will be 745 in 4/98); FAX: (770)979-3140; *E-mail:* PNPIC@aol.com

Chapter 8

SPECIALTY TOLL-FREE NUMBERS

The following toll-free numbers may be a helpful, cost-free resource for persons seeking additional information about a particular subject. Many of these non-profit agencies provide information and referrals, literature and other services regarding specific topics.

Please note: TTY/TDD refers to telecommunication devices for the deaf and should not be accessed by a regular phone. Also, both "800" and "888" numbers are toll-free. Don't forget to dial a "1" beforehand.

ADOPTION / FOSTER CARE

National Adoption Center 800-862-3678; FAX: (215)735-9410 (Mon-Fri, 9am-5pm ET) •Information on adoption agencies and support groups. Networks parents and children with special needs. *Website:* http://www.adopt.org/adopt

AGING / SENIOR CITIZENS

Eldercare Locator 800-677-1116 (Mon-Fri, 9am-11pm ET) • Information for families and friends of the elderly. Referrals to various types of services available (insurance, medicaid, taxes, respite care, etc).

National Council on Aging 800-424-9046; FAX: (202)479-0735 • Information and referrals for elderly persons, their families and professionals. *Website:* http://www.ncoa.org

National Institute on Aging 800-222-2225; FAX: (301)589-3014 (Mon-Fri, 8:30am-5pm ET) •Publications on the health needs of elderly persons. Referrals to agencies. *E-mail:* niainfo@access.digex.net *Website:* http://www.gov.nia

AIDS

Access Project 800-734-7104 • Treatment counseling and referrals to services for persons with HIV.

AIDS Clinical Trials Information Services *(Bi-lingual)* 800-874-2572; TDD: 800-243-7012; FAX: (301)519-6616 (Mon-Fri, 9am-7pm ET) • Information on clinical trials and drugs for HIV infections and AIDS. Referrals to testing sites. Offers free materials. *E-mail:* actis@cdcnac.org *Website:* http://www.actis.org

CDC National AIDS Clearinghouse 800-458-5231; FAX: (301)519-6616 (Mon-Fri, 9am-7pm ET) • Information on resources, support groups, educational materials, financial assistance, services, clinical trials, etc. *E-mail*: aidsinfo@cdcnac.org *Website:* http://www.cdcnac.org

HIV/AIDS Treatment Information Service 800-448-0440; TDD: 800-243-7012; FAX: (301)738-6616 • Information on federally-approved treatments for HIV infection and AIDS.

National AIDS Hotline *(Bi-lingual)* 800-342-AIDS; Spanish: 800-344-7432 (Mon-Fri, 8am-2am ET); TDD: 800-AID-7889 (Mon-Fri, 10am-10pm ET) Teen line: 800-234-TEEN (Mon-Fri) or 800-440-TEEN (weekends) • Answers basic questions about AIDS/HIV (prevention, transmission, testing, health care). Referrals. Free literature. Sponsored by American Social Health Association.

Project Inform 800-822-7422 (Mon-Fri, 9am-5pm; Sat, 10am-4pm PT) • Information about experimental drugs, treatment of AIDS, mail service, quarterly newsletter, and journal. *Website:* http://www.prosinforg

ALCOHOL

Alcohol Rehabilitation for Elderly 800-354-7089 • Information and referrals for chemically dependent persons over 55.

American Council on Alcoholism 800-527-5344; (410)889-0100 (in MD); FAX: (410)889-0297 (Mon-Fri, 9am-5pm ET) • Makes referrals to treatment centers and DWI classes.

C-SAT National Drug Hotline *(Bi-lingual)* 800-662-4357; Spanish: 800-662-9832 (Mon-Fri, 9am-3am ET) • Information on substance abuse. Referrals to local drug treatment and counseling centers. Sponsored by Ctr. for Substance Abuse Treatment, Drug Information Trtmt, and Referral Hotline.

National Clearinghouse for Alcohol and Drug Information 800-788-2800 (touch tone) or 800-729-6686 (rotary); FAX: (301)468-6433 (Mon-Fri, 8am-7pm ET) • Information on alcohol, tobacco and drug abuse and prevention. Referrals to treatment centers, research, support groups, and community programs. *Website:* http://www.health.org *E-mail:* info@heath.org

National Council on Alcohol and Drugs 800-475-HOPE (24 hrs) • Recorded information on local treatment centers. Sends written information.

National Council on Alcoholism and Drug Dependence 800-622-2255 • Information on counseling services for alcohol or drug abuse.

Teen Helpline 800-637-0701 (Mon-Fri, 9am-5pm MT) • Refers parents to teen programs and drug and alcohol treatment centers. Helps parents find financial assistance for these programs. *Website:* http://www.vpp.com/teenhelp/

ALZHEIMER'S DISEASE

Alzheimer's Disease Education and Referral Center 800-438-4380; FAX: (301)495-3334 (Mon-Fri, 8:30am-5pm ET) • Information on Alzheimer's disease. Publications, information on clinical trials. Sponsored by Nat'l Inst. on Aging. *Website:* http://www.alzheimers.org/adear

ASTHMA / ALLERGY

Asthma and Allergy Network - Mothers of Asthmatics 800-878-4403; FAX: (703)352-4354 • Emotional support and patient education resources for persons with asthma and allergies. Newsletter. *E-mail:* aanma@aol.com   *Website:* http://www.podi.com/health/aanma/

Asthma and Allergy Referral Line 800-822-2762 (24 hrs) or (414)272-6071 • Pamphlets on asthma and allergies, and referrals to doctors.

Asthma Control Program 800-843-2474 • Education about asthma to better understand, treat and manage asthma. Leave name and they will send you information. Sponsored by Glayo-Wellcome.

National Jewish Lung Line 800-222-LUNG (Mon-Fri, 8am-5pm MT) • Information and referrals. Registered nurses answer questions on lung diseases (asthma, allergies) or immune disorders (lupus). Referrals to doctors. Literature.

ATTORNEY REFERRAL

Attorney Referral Network 800-624-8846 (24 hrs) • Computerized legal service recommends attorneys in callers' area. Does not make referrals to pro-bono or legal aid attorneys.

BLIND / VISUALLY IMPAIRED

American Foundation for the Blind 800-232-5463; TDD: (212)502-7662 (Mon-Fri, 10am-4pm ET) • Information and referral for agencies, and catalog of publications.

Blind Children's Center 800-222-3566; 800-222-3567 (in CA); FAX: (213)665-3828; (Mon-Fri, 7am-5pm PT) • Information and referral for parents of visually impaired children. Educational correspondence program. Several booklets and newsletter. Referrals to support groups (in Los Angeles area). *Website*: http://www.blindcntr.org/bcc *E-mail:* info@blindcntr.org

DB-Link 800-438-9376 (Voice); TTY: 800-854-7013 • Information and referrals to education, health, employment, technology, communication, recreation activities, etc. for children who are deaf-blind. Newsletter. *CompuServe*: 73324,2140 *Specialnet TRD;* leslieg@fstr.wosc.ossme.edu

Guide Dog Foundation 800-548-4337; FAX: (516)361-5192 • Provides seeing eye dogs to the blind free of charge. *Website:* http://www.guidedog.org *E-mail:* guidedog.org

Job Opportunities for the Blind 800-638-7518 (Mon-Fri, 12:30am-5pm ET) • Free services for blind persons who are looking for work. Literature. *E-mail:* nfbcaccess.digex.net

Prevent Blindness America 800-331-2020 or 800-221-3004; FAX: (847)843-8458 • Fights vision loss through research, education and direct services. Literature on vision, eye health, and safety. *E-mail:* 7477.100@compuserve.com *Website:* http://www.preventblindness.org

Recording For The Blind and Dyslexic 800-221-4792; FAX: (609)987-8116; (Mon-Fri, 8:30am-4:30pm ET) • Information on free cassettes, recorded textbooks and publications to eligible handicapped persons. Information on volunteer programs for recording tapes. *Website:* http://www.rfbd.org

Vision World Wide 800-431-1739 or (317)254-1332 • Information, referrals, and publications for persons with low vision. *Website:* http://www.netdirect.net/vision-enhancement

BONE MARROW TRANSPLANTS

BMT LINK 800-LINK BMT • Information and referral for bone marrow transplants. Referrals to support groups. Peer-support, one-on-one counseling, Information on becoming a donor.

National Bone Marrow Transplant Link 800-627-7692, 800-654-1247 or 800-526-7809 (Mon-Fri, 8am-6pm CT) • Information on becoming a marrow donor. Maintains computerized data bank of donors nationwide.

BUSINESS

U.S. Small Business Administration 800-827-5722 • Offers information on starting and financing businesses for minorities and vets. Counseling, training, video tapes and publications. *Website:* http://www.sba.gov

CANCER

Alliance for Lung Cancer Advocacy, Support and Education 800-298-2436 • Operates a national "phone buddies" program, in addition to other services. *E-mail:* info@alease.org *Website:* http://www.telepoer.com/~alease

AMC Cancer Information and Counseling Line 800-525-3777 (Mon-Fri, 8:30am-5pm MT) • Information and counseling for cancer issues.

American Cancer Society *(Bi-lingual)* 800-227-2345 (Mon-Thur, 9am-8pm; Fri., 9am-4pm) • Information and referrals on various issues related to cancer (treatment, services, literature, transportation, equipment, and support).

American Institute for Cancer Research 800-843-8114 • Information on diet and nutrition and their link to cancer. Networks patients and families for support. Brochures, seminars, and funding. *Website:* http://www.aicr.org

Anderson Network 800-345-6324 • Acts as a comprehensive cancer center that matches cancer patients with others with exact diagnoses for support. *Website:* http://www.mdacc.tmc.edu:80/~andnet/

Cancer Care, Inc. 800-813-HOPE • Free counseling for cancer patients and their families. Financial assistance, information and referrals, community and professional education, on-going telephone and in-person support groups. *E-mail:* cancarenj@aol.com *Website:* http://www.cancercareinc.org

Cancer Information Service *(Bi-lingual)* 800-422-6237; TTY: 800-332-8615 • Trained professionals answer questions about causes of cancer, symptoms and treatment. Information and referrals. Sponsored by National Cancer Institute.

Dana Farber Cancer Institute Family Studies Cancer Risk Line 800-828-6622 • Information re: familial cancers.

Gynecologic Cancer Foundation 800-444-4441 • Makes referrals to physicians who specialize in the treatment of gynecological cancer.

Gilda Radner Familial Ovarian Cancer Registry 800-682-7426 (Mon-Fri, 8:30am-4pm ET) • Information on the warning signs of cancer, diagnostic tests and family history. Sponsored by Roswell Park Cancer Inst.

International Myeloma Foundation 800-452-2873 • Information, seminars, grants and newsletter on myeloma.

Mathews Foundation for Prostate Cancer Research 800-234-6284 • Current information on prostate cancer. *E-mail:* mathews@sna.com

National Cancer Hotline 800-433-0464 • Networks persons with cancer with home volunteers with same type of cancer. Free books about cancer.

National Children's Cancer Society 800-5-FAMILY • Aims to improve the quality of life for children with cancer through financial assistance, advocacy and education. *Website:* http://www.cybergate.org *E-mail:* nccs@cybergate.org

S. Koman Breast Cancer Foundation 800-462-9273 (Mon-Fri, 9am-4pm CT) • Information on breast cancer and breast health.

CAREERS

National Job Corps Information Line *(Bi-lingual)* 800-733-5627 (Mon-Fri, 8:30am-6:30pm ET) • Referrals to job corps training programs for persons 16-24. Helps persons to earn H.S. equivalency diplomas.

Women Work 800-235-2732 • Directs women to employment opportunities in their areas. Referrals to local support groups.

CHILD ABUSE

Child Help USA Hotline 800-422-4453 (24 hrs) • General information on child abuse and related issues. Referrals to local agencies for child abuse reporting. Crisis counseling.

National Family Violence Hotline 800-222-2000; FAX: (202)467-4924 • Provides taped message with information only. Sponsored by National Council on Child Abuse and Family Violence. *E-mail:* nccafv@compuserve.com

CHOLESTEROL

Cholesterol 800-231-3438 (Mon-Fri, 8am-4:30pm CT) • Distributes information on nutrition and related topics (weight loss and cholesterol). Sponsored by Nutrition Info. Svcs.

NIH National Heart, Lung & Blood Institute Helpline 800-575-WELL • Information on the prevention and treatment of high blood pressure and high blood cholesterol.

CONSUMERS

FDA National Hotline 800-532-4440 or (301)443-3170 • Information on any FDA-regulated product, including information on breast implants. Consumer package available.

People's Medical Society 800-624-8773 (Mon-Fri, 9am-5pm ET) • Helps medical consumers become aware of their medical rights. Literature available for a fee. *E-mail:* peoplesmed@compuserve.com

U.S. Consumer Product Safety Commission *(Bi-lingual)* 800-638-2772 (need push button phone) • Recorded information on product safety. Free literature.

CRANIOFACIAL DISFIGUREMENT

Children's Craniofacial Association 800-535-3643 (24 hrs) or (214)994-9902 • Information and referrals on craniofacial disorders in children, doctor referrals, and educational material. Leave name, address and diagnosis.

CREDIT COUNSELING

Consumer Credit Counseling Services 800-388-2227 • With touch-tone phone, callers can find out about credit counseling services in their local areas. Sponsored by the Nat'l Foundation for Consumer Credit.

CRIME VICTIMS

Juvenile Justice Clearinghouse 800-638-8736 (Mon-Fri, 8:30am-7pm) • Information and referrals on juvenile justice programs and department of justices.

We Tip Hotlines 800-78-CRIME (general); 800-87-FRAUD (felony) • Takes reports on crimes or felonies.

CYSTIC FIBROSIS

Cystic Fibrosis Foundation 800-344-4823; Pharmacy: 800-541-4959 (Mon-Fri, 8:30am-5:30pm ET) • Information, brochures, pharmaceutical services, and updates on research. *Website:* http://www.cff.org

DEAF / HEARING IMPAIRED

ASHA Hearing and Speech Helpline 800-638-8255 (Voice/TDD) (Serves Continental US, PR, Mexico) (Mon-Fri, 9:30am-4:30pm ET) • Information on speech, hearing and language disabilities. Referrals to clinics, maintains listing of listening devices, and has special packets of information for military families and other populations. Sponsored by Amer. Speech Language and Hearing Assn.

Captioned Films/Videos 800-237-6213 (Voice--ordering); 800-538-5636 (Voice/TDD), 800-237-6819 (TTY--ordering) (Mon-Fri, 8:30am-5pm ET) • Information on educational and other films for the deaf or hearing impaired. *E-mail:* info@cfv.org

DB-Link 800-438-9376 (Voice); 800-854-7013 (TTY) • Information and referral on education, health, employment, technology, communication, recreation, etc. for children who are deaf-blind. Newsletter. *CompuServe:* 73324.2140 *Specialnet:* TRD; leslieg@Fstr.wosc.ossme.edu

Deafness Research Foundation 800-525-3323 • General information on deafness. Awards grants to doctors working with deaf population.

Ear Well 800-327-9355; FAX: (703)750-9302 (Mon-Fri, 9am-5pm ET) • Information and literature on any hearing-related issue. Lists doctors, audiologists, and hearing aid dispensers. Sponsored by Better Hearing Institute. *Website* http://www.betterhearing.org *E-mail:* betterhearing@juno.com

HEAR Now 800-648-4327; FAX: (303)695-7789 (Mon-Fri, 8am-5pm MT) • Helps financially needy individuals obtain hearing aids or cochlear implants. Newsletter, information and referrals. Maintains national hearing aid bank. *E-mail:* 127737.1272@compuserve.com

Hearing Aid 800-521-5247 (Mon-Fri, 10am-4pm ET) • Provides general literature on hearing aids and hearing loss. Sponsored by Int'l Hearing Society.

Lead Line House Ear Institute 800-352-8888; 800-287-4763 (in CA) (Mon-Thur, 8am-6pm PT) • Answers questions on deafness. Information on technology, support groups, and specific medical conditions. Ask for Barbara Lincoln. Sponsored by Tripod.

National Institute on Deafness and Other Communication Disorders 800-241-1044 or 800-411-1222 (referrals) • Information on hearing, speech, language, smell and taste, voice and balance disorders, and clinical trials.

DEPRESSION

Depression Awareness, Recognition and Treatment Helpline 800-421-4211 • Provides brochures on depression. Sponsored by Nat'l Inst. of Mental Health.

National Foundation for Depressive Illness 800-248-4344 • Recorded message has information on the signs of depression and manic-depression.

DIABETES

American Dietetic Association 800-366-1655 (Mon-Fri, 10am-5pm ET) • Provides information on diet. Brochures on non-insulin diabetes, infant feeding, and child nutrition. Sponsored by Nat'l Center for Nutrition and Dietetics.

NIH National Diabetes Outreach Program Helpline 800-438-5383 • Educational information on diabetes. Publishes "Do Your Level Best" kit and diabetes kit to public and health care professionals. Sponsored by National Inst. of Diabetics, Digestive & Kidney Diseases.

DISABILITY

Ability Access, Inc. 800-858-5116 • Networking for persons with disabilities, has an interactive computer information system and bulletin board, and provides information on products, travel, employment, etc.

Childcare Plus 800-235-4122 • Information and referrals to families of children (birth to 5) with disabilities, and inclusion training for professionals.

HEATH Resource Center 800-544-3284 (Voice/TDD); FAX: (202)833-4760 • Information and referrals on post-secondary education and adult training

programs for people with disabilities. Sponsored by U.S. Dept. of Education.
E-mail: heath@ace.nche.edu *gopher:* //bobcat.ace.nche.edu

Job Accommodation Network 800-526-7234 (Voice/TDD), 800-ADA-WORK;
FAX: (304)293-5407 (Mon-Thur, 8am-8pm; Fri, 8am-7pm ET) • Information
on accommodations for people with any job-related disability. Sponsored by
Pres. Comm on Employment of People with Disabilities. *E-mail:*
jan@jan.icdi.wvu.edu *Website:* janweb.iedi.wvu.edu

National Accessible Apartment Clearinghouse 800-421-1221 • Helps people
with disabilities find accessible apartments. Owners and managers may also use
this service to register their accessible units.

National Easter Seal Society 800-221-6827 (Mon-Fri, 8:30am-5pm ET) •
Publications for persons with disabilities. *Website:* http://www.seals.com

National Respite Locator 800-773-5433 • Information on temporary care for
those caring for a child with a disability or chronic illness. *Website:*
http://chtop.com/locator.htm

NICHCY 800-695-0285; FAX: (202)884-8441 (Mon-Fri, 10am-5pm ET) •
Information on education rights for persons with disabilities from birth to age
22. Sponsored by Dept. of Education. *E-mail:* nichcy@aed.org *Website:*
http://www.aed.org/nichey

Northeast Disability and Business Technical Assistance Center 800-949-4232
(Voice/TDD); FAX: (609)392-3505 • Information and technical assistance to
employers, individuals with disabilities, and others in the implementation of the
Americans with Disabilities Act. *E-mail:* ada@njdhs.uu.holonet.net

Paws With a Cause 800-253-PAWS or (616)877-PAWS • Trains dogs for
disabled persons.

Rural Institute on Disabilities 800-732-0323; FAX: (406)243-4370 (Mon-Fri,
8am-4:30pm MT) • Assistance for persons with disabilities in rural areas.
Technological services, early intervention, children of Vietnam Veterans, and
services for the elderly. *E-mail:* ruralinstitute.umt.edu

Tele-Consumer Hotline 800-332-1124 (Voice/TTY) • Information, referrals
and publications about equipment and phone services specially designed to aid
consumers with speech, vision, hearing or mobility impairments. *Website:*
http://teleconsumer.org/hotline

Through the Looking Glass 800-644-2666 or (510)848-1112; FAX: (510)
848-4445 • Information and referrals for disabled parents. Newsletter, phone
support. *Website:* http://www.lookingglass.org *E-mail:* tlg@lookingglass.org

U.S. Equal Employment Opportunity Commission 800-669-3362 (publications) or 800-669-4000 (technical assistance) • Information, speakers, technical assistance, training and referrals re: enforcing ADA and prohibiting discrimination in employment of disabled persons. *Website:* http://www.eeoc.gov

DISCRIMINATION

Office on Civil Rights 800-368-1019; (202)863-0100 in DC (Mon-Fri, 9am-5pm ET) • Refers people who feel they have been discriminated against by a federally-funded facility.

DOMESTIC VIOLENCE

National Domestic Violence Hotline 800-799-7233; TDD: 800-787-3224 • Information and referrals for victims of domestic violence. *Website:* http://www.inetport.com/~ndvh

DOWN SYNDROME

Down Syndrome Hotline 800-221-4602 or (212)460-9330; FAX: (212) 979-2873 (Mon-Fri, 9am-5pm ET) • Free packets to new parents. Provides information on education, support groups, medical research, newsletter, phone support, information on conferences. Sponsored by National Down Syndrome Society. *Website:* http://www.ndbs.org

DRUG ABUSE

800-COCAINE 800-262-2463 (24 hrs); FAX: (212)496-6035 • Information and referral service for drug and alcohol addiction, treatment, and support groups. Sponsored by National Medical Enterprises.

888-MARIJUANA 888-627-4582 (24 hrs) • Confidential information on substance abuse and referrals to treatment programs, self-help groups, other hotlines and crisis centers nationwide.

Alcohol Rehabilitation for Elderly 800-354-7089 • Information and referrals for chemically dependent persons over 55.

American Council for Drug Education 800-488-3784 (24 hrs) • Literature, counseling, and referrals to support groups for all types of drug-abuse concerns. Guide to talking with children about drugs. Affiliated with Phoenix House.

C-SAT National Drug Hotline *(Bi-lingual)* 800-662-4357; Spanish: 800-662-9832 (Mon-Fri, 9am-3am ET) • Confidential information on drug or alcohol abuse and related issues. Referrals to local drug treatment centers and counseling centers. Sponsored by Ctr. for Substance Abuse Treatment, Drug Information Trtmt, and Referral Hotline.

National Clearinghouse for Alcohol and Drug Information 800-729-6686 (touch tone) or 800-729-6686 (rotary); FAX: (301)468-6433 (Mon-Fri, 8am-7pm ET) • Information on alcohol, tobacco and other drug abuse, and prevention. Referrals to treatment centers, research, support groups, and community programs. *Website:* http://www.health.org *E-mail:* info@heath.org

National Council on Alcohol and Drug Dependency 800-622-2255 • With touch tone phone, refers callers to counseling and treatment centers for alcohol and drug abuse.

National Council on Alcohol and Drugs 800-475-HOPE (24 hrs) • Information on local treatment centers. Sends written information.

National Substance Abuse Hotline 800-DRUG-HELP or 800-HELP-111 (24 hrs) • Confidential helplines that provide information on substance abuse and referrals to treatment programs, self-help groups, other hotline numbers, and crisis centers nationwide.

Residents Initiatives 800-955-2232 (Mon-Fri, 9am-6pm ET); FAX: (301)519-6655 • Information and assistance to the public and assisted housing community on drug-related crime control. Sponsored by HUD.

Teen Help Adolescent Resources 800-637-0701 (Mon-Fri, 9am-5pm MT) • Refers parents to teen drug/alcohol treatment programs. Helps parents find financial aid for these programs. *Website:* http://www.vpp.com/teenhelp/

DWARFISM

Little People's Research Foundation 800-232-5773 or (410)494-0055 (Mon-Fri, 9am-5pm ET) • Referrals (primarily research) and literature on dwarfism. Networks parents for support.

DYSLEXIA

Orton Dyslexia Society 800-ABCD-123; (410)296-0232 in MD (Mon-Fri, 8:30am-4:30pm ET) • Information and referrals for persons with dyslexia.

Recording For The Blind 800-221-4792; FAX: (609)987-8116 (Mon-Fri, 8am-4:30pm ET) • Information on free cassettes and recorded textbooks and consumer publications to eligible handicapped persons worldwide. Information on volunteer programs for recording tapes. *Website:* http://www.rfbd.org

EDUCATION

Clearinghouse for Immigrant Education 800-441-7192 (Mon-Fri, 9am-5pm ET) • Resource center to facilitate access to materials, organizations and people involved with the effective education of immigrant students.

291

ERIC Clearinghouse on Disabled and Gifted Education   800-328-0272 (Mon-Fri, 9am-5pm ET) • Information on special/gifted education. Free packets of information addressing a variety of issues, including attention deficit disorder, gifted children, behavior disorders, inclusion, etc. Customized searches. *E-mail:* ericec@cec.sped.org *Website:* http://www.cec.sped.org/ericec.htm

Federal Student Aid Information Center 800-433-3243 (Mon-Fri, 8am-8pm ET) • Information on federal student aid. Sponsored by U.S. Dept. of Education. *Website:* http://www.ed.gov/prog_info/sfa/studentguide

National Association for the Education of Young Children   800-424-2460 (Mon-Fri, 9am-5pm ET) • Information and referrals re: early childhood education. *Website:* http://www.naeyc.org.naeyc

National Job Corps Information Line *(Bi-lingual)* 800-733-5627 (Mon-Fri, 8:30am-6:30pm ET) • Referrals to job corps training for persons 16-24. Helps persons to earn H.S. equivalency diplomas.

ENERGY / UTILITIES

Energy Efficiency and Renewable Energy Clearinghouse   800-363-3732 Mon-Fri, 9am-7pm) •Information on energy efficiency and renewable energy. Answers technical questions. Referrals. Sponsored by Dept. of Energy. *Website:* http://www.eren.doc.gov (general) or http://www.eren.doc.gov/erec/factsheets /erec.html (publications)

ENVIRONMENTAL

American Public Information on Environment   800-320-2743 (Mon-Fri, 8:30am-5pm ET) • Information, education and aid to families with environmental concerns. *Website:* http://www.american.pie.org *E-mail:* apie800@aol.com

Environmental Protection Agency   800-426-4791 (safe drinking water); 800-535-0202 (hazardous waste cleanup) • Information and policy regulations on a variety of environmental concerns.

Indoor Air Quality Information Clearinghouse 800-438-4318; FAX: (202)484-1510 • Information and referral on indoor air quality. Sponsored by the EPA. *E-mail:* iaqinfo@aol.com

NIH Environmental Health Helpline 800-643-4794 (Mon-Fri, 8am-8pm ET) • Information on health risks from electric magnetic fields. *E-mail:* envirohealth@infoventures.com *Website*: http://www.infoventures.com/e-hlth/

EPILEPSY

Epilepsy Information Service 800-642-0500 • Answers general questions on epilepsy.

EYE CARE

National Eye Care Program 800-222-3937 (Mon-Fri, 8am-4pm PT) • Assists financially disadvantaged persons (65+) with medical eye care. Sponsored by Amer. Academy of Ophthalmology. *Website:* http://www.eyenet.org

FACIAL DISFIGUREMENT

FACES: The National Association for the Craniofacially Handicapped 800-332-2373; FAX: (423)267-3124 • Assists children and adults with craniofacial disorders resulting from disease, accident or birth defect. Financial assistance, referrals to support groups, newsletter, information and referrals to services and medical professionals.

FITNESS / AEROBICS

Aerobics and Fitness Association of America 800-445-5950 (Mon-Fri, 8am-5pm PT) • Information on non-medical aspects of fitness programs. Information on injuries, low-impact aerobics and video guide referrals. *Website:* http://www.efaa.com

American Running and Fitness Association 800-776-2732 (Mon-Fri, 9am-5pm) • Provides information on aerobic sports. Makes referrals to sports medicine clinics, podiatrists and orthopedists. *E-mail:* arfarun@aol.com *Website:* http://www.arfa.org

FOOD HANDLING

Food Safety Helpline 800-535-4555 (24 hr) • Disseminates information on food handling. Helps persons understand labels on meat and chicken. Sponsored by U.S. Dept of Agriculture.

FOOT CARE

Foot Care Information Center 800-366-8227 • Information on foot care and podiatric medicine. Literature and brochures. Sponsored by American Podiatric Medical Association.

GAMBLING

National Council on Compulsive Gambling 800-522-4700 • Information, referrals to support groups, and counseling to compulsive gamblers.

GASTROINTESTINAL DISORDERS

International Foundation for Functional Gastrointestinal Disorders 888-964-2001 • Education, assistance and support re: any gastrointestinal disorder

(including irritable bowel disease, fecal incontinence, lactose intolerance, dyspepsia, etc.)

GAY & LESBIAN

Gay and Lesbian National Hotline 888-843-454 (Mon-Fri, 6pm-11pm) • Peer-counseling, information and referrals for gays and lesbians.

HEALTH

American Board of Medical Specialties 800-776-2378 (Mon-Fri, 9am-6pm ET) • Will tell you if your physician is board certified. *Website:* http://www.certifieddoctor.org

Agency for Health Care Policy/Research Publications 800-358-9295 • Develops and disseminates research-based information to increase the scientific knowledge to enhance consumer and clinical decision-making, improve health care quality, and promote efficiency in the organization of public and private systems of health care delivery. Free pamphlets. *Website:* http://www.ahcpr.gov

Friend's Health Connection 800-483-7436 • A communication support network that connects persons of all ages with any disorder, illness or handicap for emotional support. *Website:* http://www.48friend.com *E-mail:* fnc@pilot.njin.net

Medic Alert Foundation International 800-432-5378 • Provides medic alert bracelets and necklaces engraved with information on an individual's medical condition, allergies, etc.

Medicare 800-638-6833 (Mon-Fri, 8am-8pm ET) • Information on Medicare. Sends out publications. Answers general information on Medicare and fraud.

NIH Clinical Center Patient Referrals 800-411-1222 (Mon-Fri, 8am-4:30pm ET) • Information on current clinical trials. Determines eligibility of persons for participation in these free clinical trials. *Website:* http://www.hih.gov

NIH Office of Alternative Medicine 888-NIH-OCAM • Information on current research projects being conducted on alternative medicine.

National Health Information Center 800-336-4797, (301)565-4167 in MD; FAX: (301)984-4256 (Mon-Fri, 9am-5pm ET) • Information and referrals to support groups, professional societies, government agencies and publications relating to health issues. Literature and brochures. *E-mail:* whicinfo@health.org *Website*: http://www.gov/healthfinder.gov

National Immunizations Information Hotline *(Bi-lingual)* 800-232-2522; Spanish: 800-232-0233 • Information and referrals on immunizations for infants, adults and health care professionals.

National Institute for Occupational Safety and Health 800-356-4674 • Information on all aspects of occupational health and safety. *Website:* http://www.cdc.gov//siosh//homepage.html

Occupational Therapy Consumer Line *(Bi-lingual)* 800-668-8255 (Mon-Fri, 9am-4pm ET) • Offers practical information on dealing with various health problems that interfere with daily living. Literature.

Office of Rare Diseases 800-411-1222 • Information on rare diseases. Links patients with research investigators and research projects. Sponsored by NIH. *Website:* http://www.rarediseases.info.nih.gov.ord

Visiting Nurse Preferred Care 800-426-2547; FAX: (303)753-0218 • Referrals to local Visiting Nurse Associations.

HEART

American Heart Association 800-242-8721 • Information on heart health. *Website:* http://www.amhrt.org

Heart Information Service 800-292-2221 • Answers questions on cardiovascular disease via phone or mail. Literature on aneurisms, heart transplants, women and heart disease. Referrals to support groups. Sponsored by Texas Heart Institute. *Website:* http://www.tmc.edu/thi1   *E-mail:* his@biost1.thi.tmc.edu

National Heart, Lung and Blood InfoLine 800-575-9355 • Information on heart, lung and blood issues.

HOSPICE

Children's Hospice International 800-242-4453 or (703)684-0330 (volunteer information) (Mon-Fri, 9am-5pm ET) • Refers patients to hospices and specialists in their areas. Bibliography, manuals.

National Hospice Helpline 800-658-8898 (day) • Information on hospice care for terminally ill persons. Referrals to hospice programs nationwide.

HOSPITAL

Hill Burton Hotline 800-638-0742; 800-492-0359 in MD (Mon-Fri, 9:30am-5:30pm ET) • Information about free hospital care for low income persons. Directory of U.S. medical centers that are part of Hill Burton program.

Shriner's Hospital 800-237-5055 (Mon-Fri, 8am-5pm ET) • Information on free hospital care available to children under the age of 18 needing orthopedic care or burn treatment.

HOUSING

Housing and Urban Development (HUD) 800-245-2691 • Information on government housing.

IMPOTENCY

Impotence Information Center 800-843-4315 • Free information about the causes and treatments of impotence, including brochures and doctor referrals. Answers "Information Center."
Impotency Information 800-867-7042 or 800-253-8600 ext. 3600 (information services) • Free information kit on impotency. Sponsored by Upjohn.

INCONTINENCE

Incontinence Information Center 800-543-9632 • Free information about the causes and treatments of incontinence. Brochures and doctor referrals. Answers "Information Center."

National Association for Continence 800-252-3337 or (864)579-7900 (Mon-Fri, 8am-5pm ET) • Information on incontinence. Referrals to physicians.

INSURANCE

National Insurance Consumer Helpline 800-942-4242 (Mon-Fri, 8am-8pm ET) • General information on life, health, home, business and auto insurance.

KIDNEY DISEASE

American Kidney Fund 800-638-8299 (Mon-Fri, 8am-5pm ET) • Information and referrals, and financial assistance to kidney patients.

National Kidney Fund 800-622-9010 or (212)889-2210 (Mon-Fri, 8:30am-5:30pm ET) • Education and research information on kidney disease. Referrals to local affiliates.

LEGISLATION

Project Vote Smart 800-622-7627 • Information about all elected officials and candidates for Federal and gubernatorial offices.

U.S. Government Federal Information Center 800-688-9889 (Voice), 800-326-2996 (TDD) •Information about federal government programs and agencies including patents, taxes, government jobs, social security, rules and regulations, passports, visas, state departments and veteran affairs.

LEPROSY

American Leprosy Mission   800-LEPROSY or 800-543-3131 (Mon-Fri, 8am-5pm ET) • Information on programs that fight leprosy in 23 countries.

LIFE-THREATENING ILLNESS

Children's Wish Foundation International   800-323-9474 • Grants wishes to terminally ill children up to age of 18.

Choice in Dying, Inc.   800-989-WILL • Dedicated to serving the needs of dying persons and their families. Counseling. Answers questions on living wills and medical power of attorneys.

Dream Factory   800-456-7556 • Grants dreams for chronically ill children.

Grant-A-Wish Foundation   800-933-5470 • Programs and services for children with life threatening illnesses.

Make-A-Wish Foundation   800-722-9474 • Grant wishes to children with serious illnesses.

Medical Escrow Society   800-422-1314 (24 hrs) • Information on obtaining advance cash from life insurance policies for those persons with a life threatening illness.

Special Wish Foundation   800-486-9474 (Mon-Fri, 9am-4pm ET) • Grants wishes to children with terminal illnesses.

Sunshine Foundation   800-767-1976 • Grants the dreams and wishes of chronically and terminally ill children ages 3 to 21.

LITERACY

National Literacy Hotline   800-228-8813 (24 hrs) • Information and referrals to local literacy programs. Referrals for both volunteers and people needing literacy services. Sponsored by Coalition of Literacy.

LYME DISEASE

National Lyme Disease Foundation 800-886-LYME (24 hrs) • Information and referrals for Lyme disease. Education, literature, advocacy.

MENTAL HEALTH

National Clearinghouse Family Support/Children's Mental Health 800-628-1696 (24 hrs) • Leave message and you will receive either a return call or written information. Sponsored by Portland State Univ.

National Mental Health Association 800-969-6642 (Mon-Fri, 9am-5pm ET) • Brochures on various mental health topics including manic-depression, bereavement, post-traumatic stress disorder, and warning signs of mental illness.

MENTAL RETARDATION

American Association on Mental Retardation 800-424-3688 (Mon-Fri, 9am-5pm ET) • Provides general information on mental retardation.

METABOLIC DISORDER

World Life Foundation 800-289-5433 • Support, research, information and referrals for persons interested in rare metabolic disorders. Assists in ground/air transportation needs to treatment centers.

MILITARY / VETERANS

VA Persian Gulf Helpline 800-749-8387 • Insures that veterans with medical problems get prompt and thorough attention.

MISSING CHILDREN

Child Find Hotline 800-I-AM-LOST (Mon-Fri, 9am-5pm ET) • Helps parents to locate children. Also helps lost children who need assistance.

Missing Children Help Center 800-872-5437 • Assists parents locate missing children for free.

National Center for Missing and Exploited Children 800-843-5678 • Information re: missing and exploited youth. Helps parents locate missing children.

Vanished Children Alliance 800-VANISHED (24 hrs); (408)296-1113 (business 8:30am-4pm PT) • Help for parents of missing children (conducts investigations, etc). Educational training and materials, listening, counselors, speakers bureau, parents support group, and in-house legal assistance.

MULTIPLE SCLEROSIS

Multiple Sclerosis Foundation 800-441-7055 (Mon-Fri, 9am-5pm ET) • Support services for those diagnosed with MS. Awards grants for research.

Information and referrals on traditional and alternative treatments, newsletter, and phone support.

NARCOLEPSY

Narcolepsy and Sleep Disorders 800-829-1933 • Counseling for persons with narcolepsy and other sleep disorders. Fund-raising, literature.

NEUROLOGICAL IMPAIRMENT

National Institute of Neurological Disorders 800-352-9424 • Information on neurological disorders. Sponsored by NIH.

NUTRITION / DIET

NIH Weight Control Information 800-WIN-8098 • Automated messages re: weight control and obesity for diabetes and digestive diseases.

Nutrition Information Hotline 800-231-DIET (Mon-Fri, 8am-4pm CT) • Information on nutrition via mail. Leave message and they will mail you packet.

ORGAN DONATION

Barbara Ann DeBoer Foundation Helpline 800-895-8478; (847)981-0130 (in Chicago area) • Help for people in need of organ transplants or other life saving procedures. Helps find funding resources, assists with community fund-raisers. *E-mail:* prbadf@aol.com

Children's Organ Transplant Association 800-366-2682 (Mon-Fri, 8am-5pm ET) • Public education on organ transplants. Assists families in fund-raising for transplant and transplant-related expenses. Assistance for both children and adults who are U.S. citizens in need of an organ transplant.

Minority Organ Tissue Transplant Education Program 800-393-2839 • Educational information re: organ transplants. Makes referrals to physicians.

Organ Donor Hotline 800-24-DONOR (24 hrs) • Distributes donor cards, and answers questions on organ donation and transplants. Sponsored by Dept. of Health and Services.

Organ Transplant Fund 800-489-3863 (Mon-Fri, 8:30am-4:30pm CT) • Support services, financial assistance and advocacy to organ transplant candidates. Fund-raising. Medication and emergency grant programs.

OSTEOPOROSIS

NIH Osteoporosis and Related Bone Disorders Helpline 800-624-BONE • educational materials re: osteoporosis and other bone disorders. Referrals to support groups. *E-mail:* drbdnrc@nof.org *Website:* http://www.osteo.org

PAGET'S DISEASE

Paget's Foundation 800-237-2438 • Information, brochures, patient's guide, doctor referrals, professional packets and newsletter on Paget's disease, as well as primary hyperparathyroidism.

PAIN

Back Pain Hotline 800-247-2225 • Answers questions on back pain.   ·

PARKINSON'S DISEASE

National Parkinson's Foundation 800-327-4545; 800-433-7022 in FL; (305) 547-6666 in Miami; FAX: (305)243-4403 (Mon-Fri, 8am-5pm ET) • Professional will answer any question on Parkinson disease. *Website:* http://www.parkinson.org *E-mail:* mailbox@npf.med.miami.edu

PESTICIDES

National Pesticide Telecommunication Network 800-858-7378 (Mon-Fri, 6:30am-4:30pm CT) • Information on most aspects of pesticides. Sponsored by EPA. *Website:* http://www.orst.edu/info/npth *E-mail:* nptn@ace.orst.edu

PREGNANCY

National Abortion Federation 800-772-9100 • Information and referrals regarding abortions. Financial aid.

Planned Parenthood 800-230-7526 (referrals); 800-829-7732 (administration) (Mon-Fri, 8:30am-5pm) • Referrals to neighborhood planned parenthood clinics nationwide.

Pregnancy Hotline 800-238-4269 (24 hrs) • Information and counseling to pregnant women. Referrals to free pregnancy test facilities, foster and adoption centers. Sponsored by Bethany Christian Services.

PRESCRIPTIONS, LOW COST

Pharmaceutical Manufacturers Association 800-762-4636 • Directory of various pharmaceutical assistance programs for persons who cannot afford prescriptions on their own.

PRIMARY IMMUNE DEFICIENCY

Jeffrey Modell Foundation 800-JEFF-844 (24 hrs) • Information on specific primary immune deficiency diseases. Referrals to major medical centers and psychiatric and social support services. Information on insurance reimbursement.

PROSTATE

Prostate Information Center 800-543-9632 • Distributes free general information about prostate disease including brochures and doctor referrals. Answers "Information Center."

RARE DISORDERS

NORD (National Organization for Rare Disorders) 800-999-6673; (203)746-6518 (in CT) (Mon-Fri, 9am-5pm ET) • Information, networking and literature for persons with rare disorders. *Website:* http://www.nord-rdb.com/~orphan

REHABILITATION

Center for Rehabilitation Technologies 800-726-9119 (day); FAX: (301)495-5626 • Information on products, technology, resources and services relating to the needs of people with disabilities. *E-mail:* zena.rubin@arch.gatech.edu *Website:* http://www.naric/naric

National Rehabilitation Information Center 800-346-2742; (301)588-9284 in MD (Mon-Fri, 8am-6pm ET) • International resource and research center for the rehabilitation of disabilities.

ROSACEA

National Rosacea Society 888-NO-BLUSH • Information and educational materials on rosacea, a chronic, acne-like condition of the facial skin. *E-mail:* rosacea@aol.com

RUNAWAYS

National Runaway Hotline 800-231-6946 (24 hrs) • Information and referrals. Message relay service to parents.

National Runaway Switchboard 800-621-4000 (24 hrs) • Information and referrals for runaways re: shelter, counseling, food pantries, transportation. Suicide and crisis counseling.

NineLine 800-999-9999 (24 hrs) • Crisis/suicide hotline. Referrals for youth or parents re: drugs, domestic violence, homelessness, runaways, etc. Provides message relays. Takes reports of abuse. Helps parents with problems with their kids. If all counselors are busy, stay on line and one will be with you as soon as possible. Sponsored by Nine Line/Covenant House.

Youth Crisis Hotline 800-HIT-HOME (24 hrs) • Crisis hotline and information and referral for runaways or youth with other problems and their parents. Sponsored by Youth Development Int'l. *Website:* http://www.ydi.org

RURAL ISSUES

Rural Information Center 800-633-7701 • Information on rural issues. Provides brief database searches for free. *Website:* http://www.nal.usda.gov/ric

SELF ABUSE HOTLINE

SAFE (Self-Abuse Finally Ends) 800-DONT-CUT • Referrals to . local programs dealing with self-abuse and self-mutilation. Information on treatment options.

SEXUALLY TRANSMITTED DISEASE

National STD Hotline 800-227-8922 (Mon-Fri, 8am-11pm ET) • Education, research and public policy about sexually transmitted diseases. Information on minor and major STD infections (including yeast, chancroid, herpes, genital warts, syphilis and gonorrhea). Referrals, information on prevention, free pamphlets. *Website:* http://www.sunsite.unc.edu/ASHA

SOCIAL SECURITY

Social Security 800-772-1213 • Information on all aspects of social security. Can speak with a person or use touch-tone phone to hear messages.

SPINAL CORD INJURY

American Paralysis Association 800-225-0292 • Information and referrals on research. *Website:* http://www.apacure.com

National Spinal Cord Injury Hotline 800-526-3456 (Mon-Fri, 9am-5pm ET; 24 hrs. for new injuries) • Information, referral and peer support for spinal cord injured persons and their families.

Paralyzed Vets of America 800-424-8200 (Mon-Fri, 8:30am-5pm ET) • Provides information, referral and advocacy for disabilities, paralyzed vets.

American Paralysis Associations 800-225-0292 • Provides information and referrals on research. *Website:* http://www.apacure.com

STUTTERING

Stuttering Foundation of America 800-992-9392 (24 hrs) • Information and referrals for stutterers and those who treat stutterers. Phone support, conferences. Nationwide referral list of speech pathologist who specialize in stuttering. *Website:* http://www.stuttersfa.org *E-mail:* stuttersfa@aol.com

SUDDEN INFANT DEATH

American SIDS Institute 800-232-SIDS; 800-847-7437 in GA (Mon-Fri, 8am-5pm ET) • Dedicated to the prevention of SIDS. Promotes infant health through research, clinical services, and education and support for families. *Website:* http://www.sids.org *E-mail:* prevent@sids.org

SIDS Alliance 800-638-7437; (410)653-8226 in MD (24 hrs) • Information on medical research, referrals to community services, education.

SURGERY

American Society of Plastic and Reconstructive Surgeons 800-635-0635 • Referrals to plastic surgeons, information on particular plastic surgeons as to qualifications. *Website:* http://www.plasticsurgery.org

SYRINGOMYELIA

Syringomyelia Hotline 800-ASAP-282 • Leave a message and they will send information on syringomyelia by mail.

TAX INFORMATION

IRS Federal Tax Information 800-829-1040 (Mon-Fri, 8:15am- 5:15pm ET) • Information regarding federal tax questions and problems (30 day waiting period for written requests.) *Website:* http://www.irs.ustreas.gov

TRANSPORTATION

National Patient Air Transport Hotline 800-296-1217 • Information and referral for persons who need cost effective transportation for specialized treatment after an illness or accident.

World Life Foundation 800-289-5433 • Provides air transportation for persons who need non-emergency treatment.

TRAUMA

American Trauma Society 800-556-7890; (301)420-4189 in MD (Mon-Fri, 8:30am-4:30pm ET) • Information, referrals and educational materials on the

303

prevention of physical traumas. *Website:* http://www.amtrauma.org   *E-mail:* atstrauma@aol.com

UROLOGIC DISEASE

American Foundation for Urologic Disease   800-828-7866; 800-242-2383 (booklets) (Mon-Fri; 8:30am-5pm ET) • Educational information for patients and others interested about urological diseases.

YOUTH

Boy's Town National Hotline   800-448-3000 (24 hours) • Free, confidential short-term crisis intervention, information and referrals for general population. Works with children and families.

KID SAVE   800-543-7283 (24 hrs) • Information and referrals to public and private services for children and adolescents in crisis. Referrals to: shelters, mental health services, sexual abuse treatment, substance abuse, family counseling, residential care, adoption/foster care, etc.

NineLine   800-999-9999 (24 hrs) • Nationwide crisis/suicide hotline. Referrals for youth or parents re: drugs, domestic violence, homelessness, runaways, etc. Provides message relays, reports of abuse. Helps parents with problems with their kids. If all counselors are busy, stay on line and one will be with you as soon as possible. Sponsored by Nine Line/Covenant House.

Safe Sitter   800-255-4089 • Trains adolescents 11-13 on how to be effective baby sitters.

Teen Help Adolescent Resources   800-637-0701 (Mon-Fri, 9am-5pm MT) • Refers parents to teen programs and drug and alcohol treatment centers. Helps parents locate financial aid for these programs. *Website:* http://www.vpp.com/teenhelp/

Youth Crisis Hotline   800-HIT-HOME (24 hrs) • Crisis hotline and information and referral for runaways or youth with other problems and their parents. Sponsored by Youth Development Int'l.

ADDENDUM

STATE ABBREVIATIONS

AL	Alabama		MT	Montana
AK	Alaska		NE	Nebraska
AZ	Arizona		NV	Nevada
AR	Arkansas		NH	New Hampshire
CA	California		NJ	New Jersey
CO	Colorado		NM	New Mexico
CT	Connecticut		NY	New York
DE	Delaware		NC	North Carolina
DC	District of Columbia		ND	North Dakota
FL	Florida		OH	Ohio
GA	Georgia		OK	Oklahoma
HI	Hawaii		OR	Oregon
ID	Idaho		PA	Pennsylvania
IL	Illinois		RI	Rhode Island
IN	Indiana		SC	South Carolina
IA	Iowa		SD	South Dakota
KS	Kansas		TN	Tennessee
KY	Kentucky		TX	Texas
LA	Louisiana		UT	Utah
ME	Maine		VT	Vermont
MD	Maryland		VI	Virgin Islands
MA	Massachusetts		WA	Washington
MI	Michigan		WV	West Virginia
MN	Minnesota		WI	Wisconsin
MS	Mississippi		WY	Wyoming
MO	Missouri			

CANADIAN ABBREVIATIONS

AB	Alberta		NS	Nova Scotia
BC	British Columbia		ON	Ontario
MB	Manitoba		PE	Prince Edward Island
NB	New Brunswick		PQ	Quebec
NF	Newfoundland		SK	Saskatchewan
NT	NW Territory		YT	Yukon Territory

CURRENT AND FUTURE AREA CODE CHANGES

Below is a proposed list of new area codes in United States.

Old	New	Region and State	Effective Date	Grace Period
407	561	Central Florida	05/13/96	04/13/97
214	972	Dallas, Texas	09/14/96	05/03/97
513	937	Cincinnati, Ohio	09/28/96	06/14/97
713	281	Houston, Texas	11/02/96	05/03/97
310	562	Los Angeles, California	01/25/97	07/25/97
317	765	Central Indiana	02/01/97	06/27/97
619	760	San Diego, California	03/22/97	09/27/97
501	870	East Arkansas	04/14/97	10/06/97
206	425	Everett-Kent, Washington	04/27/97	11/16/97
206	253	Auburn-Tacoma, Washington	04/27/97	11/16/97
412	724	Pittsburgh, Pennsylvania	06/01/97	Overlay
810	248	Oakland County, Michigan	04/10/97	09/13/97
817	940	North Central Texas	05/25/97	08/24/97
817	254	South Central Texas	04/25/97	08/24/97
714	949	Southern California	05/31/97	06/30/98
904	850	North Florida	06/30/97	06/30/98
904	N/A	North Florida	06/30/97	06/30/98
201	973	North New Jersey	06/01/97	12/06/97
908	732	Central New Jersey	06/01/97	12/06/97
301	240	West Maryland	06/01/97	Overlay
410	443	East Maryland	01/06/97	Overlay
818	626	North Los Angeles basin, California	06/14/97	02/21/98
801	435	Utah	06/22/97	02/01/98
216	440	Cleveland, Ohio	06/28/97	01/01/98
210	830	North of San Antonio, Texas	07/07/97	11/06/97
210	956	Laredo-Brownsville-McAllen, Texas	07/07/97	11/06/98
913	785	North & West of Kansas City, Kansas	07/20/97	10/01/98
414	920	East & North of Milwaukee, Wisconsin	07/26/97	10/25/98
415	650	San Francisco, California	08/02/97	02/01/98
916	530	Northeast California	11/01/97	05/01/98
313	734	Ann Arbor-Wayne-Ypsilanti, Michigan	12/13/97	N/A
617	781	Suburbs of Boston, Massachusetts	06/21/98	N/A
508	978	Northeast Massachusetts	06/21/98	N/A
803	843	Florence and coastal South Carolina	04/01/98	09/01/98
510	925	I-680 corridor of SF Bay, California	03/01/98	N/A
408	831	Central Valley, California	07/11/98	N/A
615	931	South Central Tennessee	1998	N/A
303	570	North and West of Denver, Colorado	1998	N/A
805	N/A	Central California	1999	N/A
213	323	Los Angeles, California	1999	N/A

For update, e-mail request to *info@ssisamples.com*

GROUP NAMES

16 Steps of Empowerment, 108
40 Plus of New York, 268
49XXXXY, 155
4P- Parent Contact Group, 250
5P- Society, 179
8P Duplication Support Group, 154
9-TIPS, 244
9 to 5, Nat'l Assn. of Working Women, 267
A.L.S. Assn., 160
AARP (Amer. Assn. of Retired Persons), 261
Aarskog Syndrome Family Support Unit, 155
ABCD, Inc., 172
Ability OnLine Support Network, 134
Abortion Survivors Anonymous, 123
AboutFace, 186
Abused Parents of America, 144
Academics Recovering Together, 108
ACC Network, 156
ACES, 150
ACHE Support Group, 193
Achromatopsia Network, 126
Acid Maltase Def. Assn., 155
Acorn, 271
Acoustic Neuroma Assn., 167
ADD Anonymous, 134
Addison News, 156
Adoptees In Search, 138
Adoptees' Liberty Movement Assn., 138
Adoptive Families of America, Inc., 138
Adult Children of Alcoholics, 113
Advocacy Center for Long-Term Care, 263
Advocates for Ind w/High Func Autism, 126
African Amer. Breast Cancer Alliance, 170
Agoraphobics Building Ind. Lives, 251
Agoraphobics In Motion, 251
Aicardi Syndrome Newsletter, Inc., 157
Al-Anon Family Groups, 113
Alagille Syndrome Alliance, 158
Alateen, 114
Alcoholics Anonymous World Services, 113
Alcoholics Victorious, 114
Alive Alone, Inc., 121
Alliance of Genetic Support Groups, 191
Alpha 1 Nat'l Assn., 159
Alzheimer's Disease & Rel. Disorders , 160
AMEND, 121
Amer Pseudo-Obstr/Hirschsprung Dis., 190
Amer. Amputee Fdn., Inc., 125
Amer. Assn of Kidney Patients, 206
Amer. Assn. of Suicidology, 123
Amer. Autoimmune Rel Diseases Assn., 202
Amer. Behcet's Assn., 165
Amer. Brain Tumor Assn., 167
Amer. Celiac Society, 190
Amer. Chronic Pain Assn., Inc., 224

Amer. Council of The Blind , 126
Amer. Council on Adoptable Children, 139
Amer. Diabetes Assn., 182
Amer. Fdn. for Suicide Prevention, 123
Amer. Hyperlexia Assn., 200
Amer. Laryngeal Papilloma Fdn., 225
Amer. Liver Fdn., 210
Amer. Lung Assn., 212
Amer. Parkinson Disease Assn., Inc., 225
Amer. Porphyria Fdn., 228
Amer. Silicone Implant Survivors, 237
Amer. Sleep Apnea Assn., 162
Amer. Soc of Adults w/Pseudo-Obst, 231
Amer. Soc. of Handicapped Physicians, 131
Amer. Society for Deaf Children, 129
Amer. Syringomyelia Alliance Project, 241
Amer. Tinnitus Assn., 129
Amputee Coalition of America, 125
Androgen Insensitivity Synd Sprt Grp, 160
Anencephaly Support Fdn., 161
Anesthetists in Recovery, 108
Angelman Syndrome Fdn., Inc., 161
Anorchidism Support Group - USA, 162
Anxiety Disorders Assn. of America, 251
Apert Support and Information Network, 162
Apert Syndrome Pen Pals, 162
Aplastic Anemia Fdn. of America, 161
Arachnoiditis Info & Support Network, 163
Arc, The, 136
Arthritis Fdn., 163
ARTS Anonymous, 262
Asbestos Victims of America, 164
Asperger Syndrome Support Group, 126
ASPO/Lamaze, 148
Assn. for Chldrn for Enforce. of Sprt, 150
Assn. For Glycogen Storage Disease, 192
Assn. for Macular Diseases, Inc., 126
Assn. for Neuro-Metabolic Disorders, 221
Assn. for Repetitive Motion Syndromes, 172
Assn. for the Care of Children's Health, 145
Assn. of Birth Defect Children, 145
Assn. of Couples for Marriage Enrich., 141
Assn. of Late-Deafened Adults, 131
Asthma and Allergy Fdn. of America, 164
Attachment Disorder Parents Network, 255
Attention Deficit Info Network, 135
Augustine Fellowship (SLAA), 118
Autism Network Int'l, 124
Autism Society of America, 124
Avenues (Arthrogryposis), 163
Bald-Headed Men of America. 270
Barn Builders Peer Support Group, 131
Batten Disease Support & Res. Assn., 165
Batterers Anonymous, 107
Bay Area Multiple Myeloma Sprt Group, 171

BEBASHI, 272
Because I Love You, 145
Beckwith-Wiedemann Support Network, 165
Beginning Experience, The, 124
Bell's Palsy Research Fdn., 166
Benign Essen Blepharospasm Res Fdn., 166
Benzodiazepine Anonymous, 117
Bereaved Parents of the USA, 121
Blacks Ed Blacks about Sexual Hlth, 272
Blinded Veterans Assn., 126
Blood & Marrow Transplant Newsletter, 167
Body Positive of New York, 157
BPES Family Network, 166
Brain Injury Assn., Inc., 134
Brain Tumor Society, The, 167
Burns United Support Group, 129
Business and Professional Women/USA, 268
C.M.T. Int'l, 173
CAIR (Changing Attitudes In Recovery), 259
Calix Society, 114
CALM, 179
Campus Support Groups Program, 263
Canadian Mult Endocrine Neoplasm T-1, 216
Canadian P.I.D., 226
Candlelighters Childhood Cancer Fdn., 168
CAPS (Children of Aging Parents), 262
Car Accident Web Site, 261
Catholics United for Spiritual Action, 132
CCHS Family Support Network, 178
CCHW Ctr for Health, Env. & Justice, 269
CDGS Parent to Parent Forum, 171
Celiac Sprue Assn. USA, Inc., 172
Center for Attitudinal Healing, The, 209
Cesarean Support Education & Concern, 148
CFC Support Network, 172
CFIDS Assn., Inc., 175
CFS Survival Assn., 175
CHADD, 135
Changing Attitudes in Recovery, 112
Chapter Nine Group of Hollywood, 112
Charcot Marie Tooth Assn., 173
CHARGE Syndrome Fdn., Inc., 174
CHASER, 193
Chemically Dependent Anonymous, 108
CHERUBS Assn., 197
Child Abuse Prevention Services, 103
Childfree Network, The, 139
Children of Divorce & Separation, 150
Children Of Lesbians/Gays Everywhere, 273
Children's Brain Tumor Fdn., Inc., 168
Children's Liver Alliance, 210
Children's Liver Assn. for Support Svcs, 210
Children's PKU Network, 228
Children's Rights Council, 150
Chromosome 18 Registry & Research, 155

Chromosome 3 Disorders, 175
Chromosome Deletion Outreach, 178
Chronic Granulomatous Disease Assn., 192
CHUCK, 121
Cleft Palate Fdn., 176
Cleptomaniacs & Shoplifters Anon, 266
Clergy Serving Clergy, 112
CLIMB, Inc., 122
Cloaca Syndrome Support Network, 176
Clutterers Anonymous, 264
Co-Anon Family Groups, 115
Co-Dependents Anonymous, 264
Coalition for Disabled Musicians, Inc., 132
Cobalamin Network, 176
Cocaine Anonymous, 115
Cochlear Implant Club Int'l, Inc., 130
Coffin-Lowry Syndrome Fdn., 177
Cogan's Contact Network, 177
Cohen Syndrome Support Group, 177
COLAGE, 273
Coma Recovery Assn., 134
Comm to Halt Useless College Killings, 121
Committee for Mother & Child Rights, 150
Community Dreamsharing Network, 267
Community Information Exchange, 271
Compassionate Friends, The, 122
Concerned United Birthparents, 138
Confinement Line, The, 149
Congenital Adrenal Hyperplasia, 178
Congenital Hypothyroidism Sprt Ntwrk, 201
Conjoined Twins Int'l, 178
Continence Restored Inc., 203
Cooley's Anemia Fdn., 161
COPS (Concerns of Police Survivors), 120
Cornelia de Lange Syndrome Fdn., Inc., 178
Coronary Club, Inc., 193
Corporation for Menke's Disease, 214
COSA (Codependents of Sex Addicts), 118
Council for Equal Rights in Adoption, 138
Council of Citizens w/Low Vision, 127
Council on Anxiety Disorders, 252
COURAGE, 273
Creative Grandparenting, 140
Crohn's and Colitis Fdn. of America, 179
CROHNS, 179
CUB, 138
Cushing's Support & Research Fdn., 227
Cyclic Vomiting Syndrome Assn., 248
Cystinosis Fdn., 180
Cystinuria Support Network, 180
DAD (Depression After Delivery), 254
DAD-to-DAD, 142
Dancing Eye Syndrome, 180
Dandy-Walker Syndrome Network, 181
DeBarsy Syndrome Nat'l Network, 181

Nat'l Sjogren's Syndrome Assn., 237
Nat'l Soc for MVP and Dysautonomia, 194
Nat'l Spasmodic Dysphonia Assn., 238
Nat'l Spasmodic Torticollis Assn., 238
Nat'l Spinal Cord Injury Assn., 137
Nat'l Stroke Assn., 240
Nat'l Stuttering Project, 276
Nat'l Tay-Sachs & Allied Diseases, 242
Nat'l Tuberous Sclerosis Assn., 245
Nat'l Urea Cycle Disorders Fdn., 246
Nat'l Vaccine Information Center/DPT, 247
Nat'l Vascular Malformation Fdn., 247
Nat'l Victim Center, 265
Nat'l Vitiligo Fdn., 248
NATHHAN, 146
Natl Assn for Native Amer Cldrn of Alc, 114
Nat'l Assn. For Parents of Vis Imp, 127
Nemaline Myopathy Newsletter, 220
Neurofibromatosis, Inc., 221
Neuropathy Assn., 226
Neutropenia Support Assn., Inc., 221
Nevoid Basal Cell Carcinoma Syn Sprt, 169
Nevus Network, 221
New Beginnings, Inc., 152
New England Patients' Rights Group, 272
Nicotine Anonymous World Services, 119
No Kidding!, 140
No. Amer Cncl of Sep/Div Catholics, 151
NOHARMM, 270
Noonan Syndrome Support Group, 222
NORD, 232
NORM (Nat'l Org. of Restoring Men), 271
O-Anon, 118
O.C. Fdn., Inc., 260
Obsessive-Compulsive Anonymous, 260
Older Women's League (OWL), 262
Oley Fdn., Inc., 245
Ollier's/Maffucci's Disease SH Group, 222
On Our Own, Inc., 253
One in a Million Kids Support Group, 232
Ontario Seventh Step Organization, 266
Open ARMS (Abortion Rel Ministries), 122
Opitz Family Network, 222
Opsoclonus-Myoclonus Parent Talk, 180
Org for Myelin Disorders Res/Support, 218
Org of Parents Through Surrogacy, 204
Organic Acidemia Assn., Inc., 156
Osteogenesis Imperfecta Fdn., 223
Overcomers In Christ, 110
Overcomers Outreach, Inc., 110
Overeaters Anonymous, 118
Oxalosis and Hyperoxaluria Fdn., 224
P-FLAG, 274
PAGER, 190
Paralyzed Veterans of America, 137

Parents Against Lead, 208
Parents Anonymous, 103
Parents Friends Lesbians & Gays, 274
Parents Helping Parents, 147
Parents Involved Network, 256
Parents of Murdered Children, 122
Parents Section, AG Bell Assn. for Deaf, 130
Parents United Int'l, Inc., 104
Parents Without Partners (PWP), 152
Parkinson's Disease Fdn., Inc., 225
Parkinson's Support Groups of America, 226
Partners/Friends of Incest Surv Anon, 106
Patient Adv for Advanced Cancer Trmt, 170
People First, 133
People Living Through Cancer, 171
Peripheral Neuropathy Group, 226
Perspectives Network, The, 134
Peter's Partners, 227
Phenix Society, 262
Philadelphia Unemployment Project, 268
Phoenix Society for Burn Survivors, 129
Pill Addicts Anonymous, 117
Pills Anonymous, 117
Pilot Parents Program, 147
Pink Disease Support Group, 227
Pituitary Tumor Network Assn., 227
Polycystic Kidney Research Fdn., 206
Post Partum Education for Parents, 144
Postpartum Support Int'l, 149
Prader-Willi Syndrome Assn., 228
Precocious Puberty Support Network, 229
Premature Ovarian Failure Sprt Group, 229
Prescription Parents, Inc., 176
PRIDE, 273
PRISMS, 237
Progressive Osseous Heteroplasia Assn., 229
Project on Women and Disability, 133
Proteus Syndrome Fdn., 230
Prozac Survivors Support Group, 230
Pseudotumor Cerebri Society, 231
Psychologists Helping Psychologists, 110
Pull-Thru Network, The, 203
Pulmonary Hypertension Assn., 232
Purine Research Society, 214
PXE Int'l, Inc., 231
Racism and Bigotry Anonymous, 272
Rainbow Alliance of the Deaf, 131
RAINBOWS, 120
Rational Recovery Systems, 110
Ray of Hope, Inc., 123
Raynaud's and Cold Sufferers Network, 232
Raynaud's Fdn., 233
REACH ("Reassurance to Each"), 257
Reach to Recovery Discussion Groups, 170
Realtors Concerned for Realtors, 112

We welcome your suggestions, comments, and additions to the Self-Help Sourcebook. Please send any comments to us at the address below.

We hope to update and print a seventh edition in the spring of 2000. To receive an order form, please send a self-addressed stamped envelope to:

American Self-Help Clearinghouse
Attn: Sourcebook
Northwest Covenant Medical Center
25 Pocono Road
Denville, NJ 07834-2995

Behcet's Syndrome, 165
Bell's Palsy, 166
benign essential blepharospasm, 166
benign symmetric lipomatosis, 217
benzodiazepine addiction, 117
bereavement (general), 120-124
bereavement, abortion, 122-123
bereavement, children who lost a parent, 120
bereavement, children who lost a sibling, 120, 122,
bereavement, families of slain police officers, 120
bereavement, families of organ donors, 120
bereavement, loss from drunk drivers, 265
bereavement, loss from hazing/college group, 121
bereavement, loss from heart defect (online), 60
bereavement, loss from homicide, 265-266
bereavement, loss from plane accident, 120, 161
bereavement, loss from suicide, 123
bereavement, loss of all/only child(ren), 121
bereavement, loss of child, 121-123
bereavement, loss of child(ren) in multiple birth, 122
bereavement, loss of infant/fetus, 121-123
bereavement, loss of police officer, survivors, 124
bereavement, loss of spouse, 124
bereavement, loss of twin, 120
bereavement, loss of Vietnam veteran, 277
bereavement, miscarriage, stillbirth, infant loss, 121-123
bereavement, parents of a twinless twin, 120
bereavement, parents who lost child to heart defects (online), 60
bereavement, pet, 121
bereavement, post-abortion, 122-123
bereavement, widow/widower, 124
bigotry, 272
bile duct injury, 166
biliary atresia, 210
bipolar disorders, 254-255
biracial families/persons, 142
birth defects, parents of children with, 145
birth of a child, 143, 148-149
birth parents of adopted children, 138-139
birthfathers, 139
birthmark, 221-222
bisexuality, 273-275
Black women's health, 250
bladder control problems, 203
bleeding disorder, 196
blended families, 153
blepharophimosis, ptosis, epicanthus inversus, 166
blind / visually impaired, 126-128
blind helplines, 283-284
blind-deaf (Ushers Syndrome, 128
blinded veterans, 277

- D -

- G -

- H -

lung cancer helpline, 285
lung disorders, 211
lung transplant, 243
Lupron drug use, 211
lupus, 211
lyme disease, 212
lymphangioleiomyomatosis, 212
lymphangioma, 179
lymphedema,212
lymphocytosis, large granular, 212
lymphoma, 168

- M -

macular disease, 126-127
Madelung's Disease, 217
Maffucci's disease, 222
male pattern baldness, 270
male sex chromosome variations, 207
malignant hyperthermia, 212
malpractice victims, 270
manic-depression, 254-255
maple syrup urine disease, 213, 221
Marfan syndrome, 213
marijuana addiction, 116
marital problems (dentists with), 112
marriage, 141-142
marriage, affected by infidelity, 142
marriage, interracial, 142
marriage, wives of older men, 142
marrow transplant, 167
mastocytosis, 213
MCAD, 187
McCune-Albright Syndrome, 213
medic alert helpline, 295
medical rights, 272
medical rights helpline, 287
Medicare helpline, 295
men, equal rights in divorce, 150-151, 270
men, who abuse women, 107
men's issues, 270-271
Meniere's disease, 130
meningoencephalitis, 185
Menke's Disease, 214
menopause, premature, 229
mental disabilities (general), 131-134
mental health, 251-260
mental health consumers, 252-254
mental health general, 257-259
mental illness and mental retardation, 253

multiple carthaginous exostoses, 216
multiple endocrine neoplasia type 1, 216
multiple hereditary exostoses, 216
multiple myeloma, 168, 171, 217
multiple personality disorder, 107
multiple sclerosis, 217; (online), 59
multiple symmetrical lipomatosis, 217
multiples, parents of, 147
murdered persons, families of, 122
muscular dystrophy, 217-218
musicians, disabled, 131
mutism, 236
MVP, 194
myalgic encephalomyelitis, 218
myasthenia gravis, 218
myelin disorders, 218
myelodysplastic syndrome (aplastic), 161
myeloma, multiple, 217
myeloma helpline, 285
myeloproliferative disease, 219
myoclonic encephalopathy of infants, 180
myositis, 219
myotubular myopathy, 219

- N -

Nager Syndrome, 219
nail patella syndrome, 219
narcolepsy, 220
nasal burning, 241
native American children of alcoholics, 114
near death experience, 271
neck and oral and head cancer, 171
necrotizing fasciitis, 220
neighborhood development, 271
nemaline myopathy, 220
neonatal death, 121-123
nephropathy, IgA, 206
nephrogenic diabetes insipidus, 182
nervous problems, 251-252, 257-259,
network, parents of children with rare disorders, 146
networking for disabled/ill, 132
neurocutaneous melanosis, 221-222
neurofibromatosis, 220-221
neurogenic diabetes insipidus, 182

- R -

racism, 272
ranchers, disabled, 131
rape victims, 107
rare disorders, 232
rare disorders, undiagnosed, 232
rational-emotive behavior therapy (addictions), 111
Raynaud's 232-233
realtors, addicted, 112
recovered repressed memories (sex abuse), 104
recovering couples, 111-112
recruitment, 199
rectal cancer, 168
recurrent respiratory papillomatous, 225
reflex anoxic seizure disorder, 233
reflex sympathetic dystrophy, 233
relationship addiction, 264
relationship problems, 112, 259
rehabilitation helpline, 302
relationships, marriage enrichment, 141
relationships, recovering couples, 111-112
religious leaders, sexually abused by, 104-105
remarriage, 151
Rendu-Olser-Weber Syndrome, 197
repetitive motion injury, 172
repressed memories (sexual abuse), 104
rescue personal, plane accident, 161
residential care facility residents, 280
respiratory illness, 211
restless leg syndrome, 233
resume writing, 268-269
retinal degeneration, 127
retinitis pigmentosa, 127
retired persons, 261-262
Rett Syndrome, 234
Reye's Syndrome, 234
rheumatoid arthritis, 163
right atrium isomerism, 205
ritual abuse survivors, 107
RLS, 233
RN's, addicted, 109
Robinow Syndrome, 234
rod monochromacy disorder, 155
Romberg's Syndrome, 225

success, fear of, 251
sudden infant death syndrome, 122
suicide survivors, 123
surgery helpline, 304
surrogate parenting, 204
survivors of abuse (16 Steps), 108
survivors of electrical shocks, 270
survivors of lightening, 270
survivors of mind control, 107
survivors of landmines, 280
survivors of near death, 271
survivors of physical/emotional abuse, 103
survivors of plane accidents, 161
survivors of satanic/ritual abuse, 107
survivors of sexual abuse, 104-107
survivors of suicide, 123
syringomyelia, 176, 241

- T -

Takayasu arteritis, 241
tall persons, 276
TAR Syndrome, 242
taste disorder, 241
Tay-Sachs, 241-242
tax information helpline, 304
teachers, addicted, 108
teachers, parents of children molested by, 105
teen parents, 143, 153
teens, 279
teens bereaving loss of loved one, 120, 122
teens, chemical abuse prevention for, 109, 111, 116
teens experiencing divorce of parents, 150, 152
teens from alcoholic families, 114
teens from single parent homes, 152, 279
teens from stressful homes, 103
teens, gay, lesbian, bisexual, 275
teens, overeating, 117-118
teens physically/emotionally abused, 103
teens sexually abused, 104-107
teens with chronic/life-threatening illness, 209
TEF, 243
temporomandibular joint dysfunction, 242
terminal illness, 209
tethered cord syndrome, 210
thalassemia, 161
therapists, addicted, 112
therapists, sexually abused by, 105-106

unemployment, 268-269
unfaithful spouses, 142
unwed parents, 152-153
urea cycle disorders, 246
urologic disease helpline, 304
Ushers Syndrome, 128

- V -

vaccine injury, 247
vaginal delivery after cesarean birth, 148
Valium addiction, 117
vascular malformations, 247
VATER, 176, 243
ventilator-assisted users, 247
vestibular disorders, 247
veterans, 277-278
veterans, blinded, 126
veterans, paralyzed, 137
victims of car accidents, 161
victims of child abuse laws, 103
victims of crime, 265-266
victims of drunk drivers, 265
victims of electrical shocks, 270
victims of false memory (sexual abuse), 104
victims of incest, 103-107
victims of lightening strikes, 270
victims of malpractice suits, 270
victims of mind control, 107
victims of plane accidents, 161
victims of prejudice, 272
victims of rape, 107
victims of satanic/ritual abuse, 107
victims of sexual abuse, 103-107
victims of stalkers, 265
Vietnam veterans, 277
violent crime, victims of, 265-266
vision loss, 126-128
visitation rights (men), 270
visitation problems, 150-151
visitation rights, grandparents, 140-141
visiting nurse helpline, 296
visual agnosia, 157
visually impaired, 126-128
vitiligo, 248
vomiting, cyclic, 248
Von Hippel Lindau, 248
vulvar disorders, 248

- W -

water on the brain, 199
Weaver Syndrome, 248
Wegener's Granulomatosis, 249
weight control, 224
well spouses, 262-263
Werdnig-Hoffman Syndrome, 239
Werner Syndrome, 216
white breath holding, 233
white lung disease, 164
widows/widowers, 124, 151
widows/widowers, of military personal, 278
Williams's Syndrome, 249
Wilson's Disease,249
wives (also see spouses)
wives of older men, 142
wives of unemployed, 269
Wolf-Hirschhorn Syndrome, 250
woman, battered, 107
Women, 278
women who love too much, 264
women's health, 250
work issues, 267-269
workaholics, 119

- X -

Xanax addiction, 117
xeroderma pigmentosum (XP), 250
X-linked myotubular myopathy, 219

- Y -

youth, 279
youth, campus groups, 263
youth crisis line, 305
youth, drug/substance abuse prevention for, 109, 111, 116
youth, from alcoholic families, 114
youth, from single families, 152, 279
youth, gay, lesbian, bisexual, 275
youth leaders, sexually abused by, 105
youth, overeaters, 117-118
youth, parents, 143, 153
youth, sexually abused, 104-107
youth with life-threatening illness, 209